The Ten Woke Commandments
(You Must *Not* Obey)

By Simon Hankinson

The Ten Woke Commandments
(You Must *Not* Obey)

By Simon Hankinson

Academica Press
Washington

Library of Congress Cataloging-in-Publication Data
Names: Hankinson, Simon (author)
Title: The ten woke commandments you must not obey | Hankinson, Simon
Description: Washington : Academica Press, 2025. | Includes references.
Identifiers: LCCN 2025942480 |
ISBN 9781680533613 (hardcover) | 9781680533637 (paperback) |
9781680533620 (e-book)
Copyright 2025 Simon Hankinson

Contents

Publisher's Foreword

Paul du Quenoy, Ph.D., FRSA

"Be of good cheer – and keep fighting," is Simon Hankinson's eleventh commandment and the subject of the final chapter in his *tour-de-force* review of major issues addressed by the "woke" trend that has recently breezed through American society. Five years ago, an observer of Hankinson's acumen might – as other observers reasonably did – have sought to identify and define the "woke" phenomenon for those who were only starting to become aware of it, perhaps addressing a mixture of derision or outrage to publics too reticent, too polite, or simply too surprised to resist.

It is unusual today for a publisher to pen a foreword for one of his own company's books, but at Simon's invitation I was delighted to do so.

I came to own and operate Academica Press unexpectedly in 2017, toward the end of a successful but trying academic career in which I had some woke-induced tangles that left me with no appetite to continue – at least for as long as woke conditions prevailed in our colleges and universities. Not long after, I found myself publishing a "cancelled" book – the late James Flynn's *A Book Too Risky To Publish: Free Speech and Universities* (Academica Press, 2019), as we retitled it to account for its cancellation. Jim's original publisher in the United Kingdom had contracted, edited, marketed, printed, and, I believe, even packed the book for shipment when it abruptly sent a lawyer's letter canceling the project due to purported concerns about quoted material. The lawyers were not worried about Jim's original prose or ideas, but about primary sources he had merely reproduced and cited, which they feared could rise under UK law to prohibited speech inciting racism.

A scholar of the left best known for his social theories of intelligence, Jim had twice been fired from U.S. institutions in the early 1960s for exercising academic free speech and subsequently built a life and career in New Zealand, where he became a celebrated university professor, world famous public intellectual, and, as a citizen of that country, sometime candidate for political office.

Jim recounted the sad initial story of his book in *Quillette*, prompting an immediate e-mail from me asking if it needed a new home. After some discussion, he happily agreed. Jim's moving commitment to principle – and to free speech – motivated me to take a great personal and professional interest in what wokeism was doing to our national and international institutional life, and to lead Academica into what was then a culture of dissent against a dominant narrative controlled by the illiberal left in our country and elsewhere. Indeed, within weeks of publishing Jim's book, I was speaking out on a National Association of Scholars event panel alongside Charles Murray and Amy Wax, intellectual giants in their fields who had both suffered cancel culture episodes long before George Floyd and Black Lives Matter thrust the entire Anglosphere into the depths of DEI. I have not stopped speaking, writing, and publishing since.

Alongside Academica's standard mission of publishing high-quality scholarly and popular non-fiction, we have sought out and been approached by the cancelled, the proscribed, and the concerned. We have published, and will continue to publish, authors who are otherwise controversial and outcast, who deal with subjects that other publishers find "problematic," and who share stories and data that mainstream media companies all too often ignore, if not disparage.

Choosing that direction was, if I may say, a bold move given the currents of the time, one that very few other publishers were willing to take, fearing media hostility, internal resistance, potential legal trouble, the disappearance of those all-important cocktail party invitations, and, of course, losses to the bottom line. I chose to take those risks and lean in. After my academic experiences, and with a young son who I believe will benefit far more from a principled example than cowardly "go along to get along" cynicism, I would have found it hypocritical not to stand up for freedom of speech, thought, and expression, principles that Academica proudly champions and from which it will not detour while I remain at its helm.

Years later, Academica's business is strong while institutions that adopted wokeism are losing prestige, profits, and people; across the board, they are "getting woke and going broke." With Simon Hankinson's book, I am confident that Academica has helped turned the page from the apprehensive dissent we embraced not that long ago to a new narrative of resurgence and resilience. As a trained historian, I have never believed that history has "sides," but if it does all indicators suggest we are on the "right side" of it. Readers of the pages that follow will find trenchant analyses of issues to which the woke have staked moral claims and pretended to a monopoly of virtue. With the skill of a diplomat, a career Simon pursued with distinction for more than two decades in the U.S. Department of State, he not only lays out the contours of the problem but offers deft counterarguments, solid solutions, and inspiring guides that will enable future generations to protect and defend liberties that only a few years ago seemed haphazard. Books like his remind us that the price of liberty is eternal vigilance. Simon Hankinson stands tall and proud as one of its sentinels.

Saint-Jean-Cap-Ferrat, July 2025

Acknowledgements

This book was always a mission, never a grind. That it grew from notes and nuggets to a finished product I ascribe to Providence. I give my sincere thanks to Brian, for invaluable drafts, edits, and improvements; to Lora and Jim, for taking a chance on a retired FSO; to Victoria, for support and top cover; to Derrick and Kevin, for inspiration and leadership; to polymath Paul for the green light; to Karina of the eagle eye; to Megyn and Matt (and the SBG) for shows I never miss; to the two of three Johns who put friendship before politics; to my many friends at State, Heritage, and elsewhere for their open minds, kind words, and stout hearts; to my BFFs; to Mike and Jay for their wise counsel; to Rick, Al, Liz, and Hen for always having my back; to Andreea for a perfect cover; to Lucky for always listening, never criticizing; and last and most, to the woodland creatures without whom nothing is possible.

Introduction

Why did I write this book? In a word: truth. The motto of my high school is *Whatsoever Things Are True*. It made little sense to me at the time. Now, it is the center of my work. Objective truth is always on the run under communism and dictatorship, but in the past few years, it has been under assault in the free world, too—even in the United States. Science is meant to be the process of testing theories against evidence and adjusting accordingly, in a never-ending empirical pursuit of truth. Today, people increasingly speak of "my truth," instead of *the* truth. Instead of experience, they speak of "lived experience," as if the act of experiencing events could change their reality, resulting in different facts for different people.

The colleges and universities that educate journalists, teachers, and other professionals have, over the past few generations, become entrenched bastions of leftwing ideology and teaching. Unsurprisingly, as colleges have injected more and more ideology into their courses, graduates have become activists. The results are now evident in all our institutions, from academia to government to industry—and nowhere more so than in the media.

Why is it necessary to define the Ten Woke Commandments? Because the leftist and far-leftist political agitators that I refer to as the "woke" throughout this book do not speak in the language of ideals or "shoulds." They speak and act in the language of mandates and "shalls." The political commandments of the woke allow no wiggle room or space for discussion. You *must* accept that "trans women" (biological men) are women. You *must* believe all women (except when they are conservative). You *must* support defunding the police. You *must* accept the absurd directives of government bureaucrats who curtail your God-given and constitutionally protected rights and force you to act, speak, and accept falsehoods against your will. If you don't follow their compulsory and fickle commandments, you will be cancelled, doxed, personally attacked, or even "swatted."

The commandments described in this book are a summary of ten aspects of social and political life wherein the woke have taken it upon themselves to carve out a set of policy dictates. To them, these commandments are unassailable and must be imposed on and accepted by the general public despite any religious, moral, scientific, or other conscientious objections any individual may have. This introduction provides a brief preview of the many places where woke ideology and practice have attempted to conquer Americans' social space and take away our right to freedom of thought and expression.

The expression "red pilled" comes from the movie *The Matrix*. The idea is that "[t]he pills represent a choice between remaining in a state of blissful ignorance (blue) or accepting a painful reality (red)."[1] For me, the spare time I had to read during the COVID-19 pandemic was the catalyst for a coalescing of several parallel phenomena that I had observed. I started gathering notes and articles and began to write. Four years later, this book is the result.

Not everyone reads, writes, and talks for a living. Some Americans have to get a job right after high school instead of getting to spend four years at college doing "studies" degrees, often on someone else's dime. Many have full-time jobs, or kids to care for, and little time to read. Others are, like *The Daily Wire*'s Matt Walsh, autodidacts with insatiable curiosity. What all these Americans have in common is a strong sense of what's right. They hear a lot of nonsense at work, school, and even church, but they don't always have the facts at their fingertips to challenge it. I hope that this book gives readers some ideas and facts to use the next time they are confronted with a woke fallacy. Here's a preview of the themes in the ten chapters ahead.

The Media

Traditional, or "legacy," media, as in network and cable television, print media, and national radio, has lost much of its credibility as an objective source of information over the past few decades. The reasons why are hard to pin down. One is that journalists come from a different class than in previous generations, and they consider their role to be more activist than before. As Batya Ungar-Sargon writes in her book *Bad News*, "journalism has become a profession of astonishing privilege over the past century, metamorphosing from a blue-collar trade into one of the occupations with the most highly educated workforces in the United States."[2]

Reporters are no longer rough-hewn, high-school-educated, working-class muckrakers whose chief goal is to dig up the truth, reveal scandal, and hold the powerful accountable. Today, they are more likely to be second-generation college-educated "progressives" from the professional middle classes. Less Chevy Chase from *Fletch*, more Jeffrey Goldberg of *The Atlantic*. As Ungar-Sargon writes, "today American journalism comforts the comfortable, speaks power to truth, and insists on an orthodoxy that protects the interests of the elites..."[3]

The legacy media's final meltdown occurred after three crucial moments: the election of Donald Trump in 2016, followed in March 2020 by COVID-19, and then the May 2020 death of George Floyd and ensuing civil unrest. The legacy media's handling of these three events was professional suicide. The major networks and national newspapers covered President Trump and his Administration with demonstrable bias.[4] They lied about George Floyd and pushed the false narratives of mass incarceration and disproportionate police violence against black men.[5] They made no attempt to discover the true origins of the coronavirus, instead incuriously and obsequiously deferring to the state-sanctioned propaganda they were fed. They pretended that Joe Biden was the honest, eloquent, savior of democracy instead of a dissembling third-rate career politician with no consistent values or policies. In the face of his obvious senescence, they did the White House's dirty work of hiding him, covering for his gaffes, and nearly enabling him to run for a second term.

Wilfred Reilly, professor at Kentucky State and author of the book *Hate Crime Hoax*, summed up the state of the national media by 2024, commenting on Twitter (now X):

> Almost literally every major left-wing hype story is a lie. Recall this, the Hunter Biden laptop, Jessie Smollett, "Black genocide" overall, Sarah Braasch and Amy Cooper, "W-on-B inter-racial crime" overall,

"hands up: don't shoot," Russiagate, the sharp-as-a-tack Joe Biden, "trans genocide," "Palestinian genocide" overall, the Very Fine People hoax, the efficacy of masks, the Canadian Mass Graves hoax...etc...every time liberal sparring partners bring up "right-wing misinformation."[6]

Throughout this book, I critique the mainstream media's degradation into a mouthpiece for the Left and their role in pushing the woke agenda. In Chapter 7, I explore in greater detail how the mainstream media work diligently to convince the public not to believe their own eyes and ears, but rather to swallow hook, line, and sinker a long list of blatantly biased notions, non sequiturs, and falsehoods that would make George Orwell blush.

Education

At school, America's children are being taught spurious notions, and when young people enter the workforce—including in the federal, state, and local governments—they are forced to accept and propagate those lies to keep their jobs or advance their careers. American schools teach that the United States is a white supremacist country in which "people of color"— a term which includes selected minorities only—cannot succeed without state-sanctioned discrimination in their favor. Children are taught that sex is a "construct," which means that one can "identify" as the opposite sex to one's biological reality. They are taught that those who don't accept self-identified "gender" as reality are bigots and transphobes, and that challenging gender ideology is "hate speech" that must be suppressed.

Over the past few years, I spoke to several groups of eighth-grade students from an expensive private school. Thirty years ago, I taught eighth-grade history at a private school, so I have some solid ground on which to make a comparison of these students to students of a previous generation. The eighth-graders I see today are as racially diverse as can be imagined. And they are the same awkward, smart, curious kids I recall from the 1990s. But compared to the kids I taught, the eighth-graders I meet today have been wholly indoctrinated into a depressing world of social Marxism in which invisible forces perpetually either oppress them or make them feel guilty for unknowingly oppressing others. One girl asked me what I thought of "affinity spaces." I responded: "Why do you segregate yourselves by color at school?" The word "segregate" seemed to shock the kids, as that's something they associate with bad practices. But that is exactly what they are doing. Colleges now segregate dorms, cafeterias, clubs, and even graduations by skin color—in the name of fighting racism—apparently without the slightest sense of irony.

In another group, a girl rushed from the room in tears because of a discussion—calm and reasonable—that several students and I were having about affirmative action. Earlier, her teacher had interrupted her, not letting her respond to my question "are you oppressed?" Instead, the young female teacher rather angrily gave her own answer, one which came straight from the teacher's college or liberal arts school courses she had taken, in something probably called "critical pedagogy." In this framework, children, women, and people of color are oppressed, making this young black girl doomed to fail. The teacher said that she, too, was oppressed, as a woman, though she also apologized for her "privilege" of being white. In fact, neither of these two women is oppressed. The teacher spouts the ideology (and wears the tattoos and nose ring) that have become tribal markers of the elite circles of her profession. Both she and the eighth-grade girl hold all the cards for success in American society, with or without a deck stacked in their favor. They've just been led to believe otherwise.

Meeting these kids was a practical lesson in the theory I read about all day. They live in a free country with boundless educational and economic opportunities. Their generation of non-white students has a better chance at getting into competitive college and then graduate school, with lower test scores, than any other U.S. demographic, even if those other applicants come from rich families. But I didn't seem to reach them; the indoctrination went too deep. They had been taught "the narrative of America as a white-supremacist state,"[7] with no exposure to alternate perspectives and a highly selective exposure to facts.

The eighth-graders seemed unaware that there are legions of black and other non-white thinkers out there who do not subscribe to this reductionist, miserable worldview. These middle schoolers, whose own parents are successful professionals of non-European origin, still do not know about black entrepreneurs like Larry Elder, ethnically Indian lawyers like Harmeet Dhillon and black judges like Clarence Thomas, or black politicians like Virginia Lieutenant Governor Winsome Earle-Sears and U.S. Representative Byron Donalds from Florida. They had apparently never heard of exceptional black academics and writers like Thomas Sowell, Carol Swain, or Glenn Loury.

Gender ideology

Perhaps the most incredible intellectual affliction of the past decade has been gender ideology, which holds that a person's innate feeling or sense of "gender" is more real, and should trump, one's biological sex. "Gender" for these ideologues is sometimes a synonym for sex and sometimes not, depending on the purpose. Proponents of gender ideology, the most vigorous—and sometimes violent—of whom are men, brook no opposition. They have, in a short time, brainwashed, bullied, or cowed individuals, academia, professional bodies, and governments into accepting a wide range of radical and often contradictory ideas.

Wokeness, and gender ideology in particular, has spread almost simultaneously throughout the Anglosphere, where, without the benefit of the U.S. Constitution and its First Amendment allowing free speech, other countries have fared even worse than the United States. In Australia, a person calling himself "Roxy Tickle," who insists he is a woman, successfully sued a female-only meeting website called Giggle to force his way in.[8] In the United Kingdom, an official organ of Britain's National Health Service says that men can breastfeed.[9] What this means is that men who take domperidone, a gastrointestinal drug, off-label, produce some kind of bodily fluid which they then give to babies, despite the drug being "known to cause heart arrhythmias and cardiac arrest." Also in England, a school chaplain told students: "You should no more be told you have to accept LGBT ideology than you should be told you must be in favour of Brexit, or must be Muslim."[10] For this modern heresy, he was fired by his school, blacklisted by his Church of England Diocese as a "risk to children," and reported to Prevent, an organization established by the British government to "stop people becoming terrorists or supporting terrorism."[11]

In Canada, a serial litigant who identifies as a woman has successfully sued spas to wax "her" genitals and evades criminal liability at every turn.[12] Another trans-identifying Canadian man—an academic, no less—identifies as a teenage girl and had been able to use the female changing room with minor girls at a public pool thanks to Ontario's policy of accepting gender self-declared identification without question.[13]

In the United States, men and boys participate in girls' and women's sports, causing injuries and taking titles. Men convicted of sex offenses have been placed in women's prisons. During the Biden Administration, the United States pushed these policies, under the umbrella of protecting "gender identity," in U.S. foreign policy and supported them through the United Nations system.

I analyze and break down the woke commandments related to gender ideology throughout the book, giving particular emphasis to it in Chapter 4, "You Shall Not Know 'What Is a Man,'" and Chapter 5, "You Shall Not Know 'What Is a Woman.'"

Nations, Borders, and Immigration

Today's woke activists have adopted a belief that national borders are meaningless. They believe that all foreigners, including the destitute, criminals, terrorists, and enemies of the state, have a fundamental right to enter and remain in any country they want. This runs fully counter to all existing laws and customs. Yet, the woke insist that if you dispute their destructive ideas about immigration, you are an unredeemable racist or fascist. That is because, they assume, the only reason you wouldn't want hordes of foreigners in your country is because you don't like "oppressed" people of other races and cultures. Leftists have adopted a fully globalist perspective, which is associated with their belief that nation-states themselves are wrong or unnecessary.

Colonization and immigration were the original the sources of America's population. A continued inflow of selected immigrants who can enrich our nation is a good thing. But unrestricted admission of the unvetted, unskilled, or those unwilling to assimilate is not. Because the woke have been successful in pushing their perspective on immigration, the United States now has many millions of inhabitants who do not speak

English, have little intention of adapting to our way of life, and take more from the fiscal pot than they contribute. And yet, because of liberal politicians and their promotion of "sanctuary cities" and other pro-illegal-migrant policies, many of them receive full welfare benefits and can even vote.

Developed, "first world," countries today all face the same problem: they are desirable places to live yet have declining birth rates. Meanwhile, the "third world" has high birth rates, low living standards, political instability, and violence. The question of our era is whether sovereign nations can enforce the immigration laws passed by their elected legislators, or if the masses of the "global majority" get to choose, without challenge, where they want to live. Former President Joe Biden chose the latter. Through a combination of executive overreach (using immigration parole for entire countries), ignoring laws (releasing instead of detaining aliens caught on the border), and creating incentives (funding leftist NGOs to promote and facilitate illegal immigration), President Biden opened this country's borders to untold millions from around the world. His Administration saw records set for the highest daily, monthly, and yearly numbers of illegal alien encounters in U.S. history.

The re-election of Donald Trump in November 2024 was a firm rebuke of open-borders globalism, but the country is divided like never before on this issue. Globalism vs. nationalism is the fight of this century. I explore issues related to the woke perspectives on nations, borders and immigration in greater detail in Chapter 1, "You Shall Have No Borders," and Chapter 8, "You Shall Have No Nation."

History Calls Us to Action

Those of us who read history know that there is nothing new under the sun. Empires rise and fall. Nothing lasts forever. But we also know that individuals can sometimes make history; that individual agency and courage can change its course, and that everyone must do his part to build and defend his civilization. Not every generation is called to heroic action. The Greatest Generation that won World War II, defeated fascism, and set the country up to beat communism, was great because its members heard the call of destiny and rose to the occasion. Their children, of the baby boom, spent their inheritance unwisely. I am part of Generation X, and I refuse to give up on my children and grandchildren.[14] It seems the Millennials, particularly young women, have been the most affected and weakened by what Canadian professor Gaad Saad calls the "woke mind virus." But in Generation Z, we see some hope of a revival of the values and traditions that made this country great.

This book is meant to describe the challenge, and the way forward. It is meant to inspire, not to depress. I mean to encourage action through hope, in the best tradition of the American people. To help you to take action, I end each chapter with three suggestions—of a person to follow, a book to read, and a group to support. For every one of these, there are many more out there.

Chapter 1

The First Commandment:
You Shall Have No Borders

Our world is continually becoming more closely linked through easier travel and instant communications. Yet despite increasing global integration, politics remains local, and local politics is bounded by political borders. Whether a nation is empire-sized like China and the United States, or tiny like Lichtenstein and Tonga, its politics focuses mostly inwards, to solve problems and establish legal frameworks *inside* its own boundaries. Just like strong families are the basis of a stable society, strong nations are the basis of a stable world. And strong nations need strong borders.

In Latin, *limes* means a boundary—it's where we get the word "limit." Life without limits would be chaos, as would a world without borders. From the earliest human civilizations, we have accepted borders to demark one person or tribe's land from another, and limits on how individuals may act toward one another. The most radical Western leftists want to eradicate as many limits as possible—from distinctions between the ages and sexes, to borders between peoples and nations. As professor Eric Kaufman writes, "[t]he cultural left envisioned a grand narrative of progress whose next phase would move from individual rights to group rights, citizen rights to rights across borders, and gay rights to trans rights."[1] The "progress" that leftists want is towards globalism, without nation-states, and a government that consists of a centralized, technocratic, "enlightened" global elite.

Ultra "progressive" politicians, academics, and activists at the vanguard of woke politics believe that international borders should be eliminated, either *de jure* (through law) or *de facto* (through creating facts on the ground).[2] Their argument is based on a family of theories that we can call "woke" for short. I'll discuss some of these manifestations and iterations of "woke" ideology later in the book, like critical race theory (CRT), gender ideology, and "diversity, equity and inclusion" (DEI). Proponents of woke ideology like to "deconstruct" everything—history, culture, sex, art—to supposedly remove artificial barriers. They believe much of what conservatives, and many average Americans, hold dear and want to preserve—family, country, religion—are patriarchal and "white" systems that oppress the masses.

As it pertains to nations, woke theorists believe that borders are mere constructs: fictional ideas that exist exclusively for the economic benefit of capitalists and elites who desire to maintain their status through the exclusion of undesirable "others" who can threaten their privileged positions.[3] Only by tearing down borders, they argue, can humanity free the global proletariat who struggles to achieve the promised land of "equity."[4] It's strange that leftist activists and politicians view physical country borders as *impeding* freedom, since historically, the creation of meaningful borders that defined a sovereign state was viewed as an *expansion* of freedom, not the opposite. This is because before the idea of territorial sovereignty became the norm, borders were fluid and constantly changing due to the ebb and flow of aristocratic loyalties, wars, and alliances. Prior to the 1700s, for example, ordinary people in feudal Europe had no inalienable rights, but were formally the property (as serfs, peasants, vassals, or slaves) of various lords and kings. The king—not the "state" or the people—was the sovereign. As Louis XIV famously said, *L'état, c'est moi*—I am the state.

Most people were the subjects of fiefdoms, estates, and empires, and they had few legal rights. Territory was conquered, reconquered, and split up on a regular basis, as lords, princes, and kings changed. The establishment of physically bounded, territorially sovereign states with borders was seen as a positive evolution for ordinary people. It meant that all the people inside a state were sovereign in their relations with outsiders, and outsiders had no right to interfere with their internal national affairs. Ordinary people began to develop *national* identity separate from their identity as the vassals of a certain local landowner or lord. This ultimately led to notions of citizenship rights, the redress of grievances, and other basic foundations of freedom that Westerners take for granted today.

The globalists hate borders because they separate successful nations from unsuccessful ones.

The Left relies on various arguments to defend its call for open borders and the dissolution of nation-states. Let's take a look at these arguments, and the myths and fallacies that underlie open-borders ideology.

Myth 1: Walls Don't Work

"At times, marriages, like nations and churches, survive by policing their borders," wrote English novelist and poet George Eliot.[5] Walls are a physical manifestation of personal and national borders as old as mankind. Almost as soon as our primitive ancestors came down from trees to the plains and slept in the open, they sought out natural caves and safe places they could defend from animals and other humans. They sought out high ground and began building earthworks around it. As soon as he could build with more than dirt, man built houses—and walls—to separate his kin from outsiders. Houses grew into castles, for feudal leaders, protected by walls and moats. As feudal lords conquered larger and larger territories, they became kings and emperors. From Offa's Dike in England to the Kumbhalgarh Fort in India, rulers built walls to separate their people from hostile or competing peoples. The Great Wall of China was built two centuries before Christ to keep northern barbarians out. So was Hadrian's Wall 300 years later.

Open borders activists like to say: "show me a 10-foot wall, and I'll show you an 11-foot ladder." That argument boils down to: "if a wall doesn't keep everyone out, it is useless." But unlike drinking vessels, border walls are not designed for perfection. A wine glass is designed to hold all the wine in it. If even a small amount leaks, that's a complete failure. The same with natural gas supply pipes, nuclear power plants, and the Wuhan Institute of Virology—the downside of even a small leak can be catastrophic and renders the vessel not fit for its purpose. Border walls, on the other hand, are not about 100 percent integrity but about creating effective deterrence. They are designed to make it much harder for people to cross into foreign territory without authorization. They can't make it impossible. But, have you ever cleaned out your gutters at the top of a 12-foot ladder? It's not something everyone can do, let alone the average border jumper. By going high, walls raise the physical bar to climb them, and limit how many will try. By going deep into the ground, walls make it harder to tunnel under them. And by being strong, they make it harder to flatten, breach, or force your way in. Walls are about percentages, not totals. A border wall that keeps 95 percent of aspiring illegal crossers from trying to scale it and channels them to official ports of entry or areas of border vulnerability due to landscape allows Border Patrol to concentrate on these key spots instead of having to patrol the entire border.[6]

Myth 2: There Is a Universal Right to Migrate

The woke belief in free migration and open borders runs fully counter to the laws of virtually every country on Earth. Each nation governs who gets in, who stays, and on what terms. American law, for example, sets out the rules on who may enter the country, as well as when, where, and how. Our main law is the Immigration and Nationality Act (INA), which has been amended many times since it passed in 1952. The INA divides people into U.S. citizens and non-citizens, or "aliens." Aliens can be legal, if they entered and remain using a valid visa or other lawful method; or they can be illegal.

Each non-U.S. citizen who wishes to enter the United States may or may not do so depending on whether he follows the correct procedures and meets eligibility requirements. He must have a valid visa issued by a U.S. embassy or consulate overseas, which lets him come to an airport or land port of entry on the border and ask to be let in. Customs and Border Protection makes that final decision and allows him into the country subject to time limits and other conditions. There is also a U.S. Refugee Admissions Program, which allows a limited number of foreigners to enter based on their proving that they are being persecuted by their own governments because of one of five allowable categories—race, religion, nationality, membership in a particular social group, or political opinion.

If an alien is a "resident alien," also called a "legal permanent resident" or "green card" holder, he has a permanent to enter at will. There is also a Visa Waiver Program (VWP) for select countries, whose nationals can usually visit for up to 90 days without a visa by filling out an application online. If that is approved, VWP nationals can then drive to the border or fly into a U.S. airport and present a valid passport at an official port of entry. If an alien's Visa Waiver application is denied for any reason, he must apply for a visa. Except for these, and a few other exceptional categories, any other foreigner who intends to visit, work, or settle in the United States must have a visa.

To get a visa, a foreign national must pay a fee, fill out forms proving who he is, provide fingerprints and a photo, and persuade a U.S. consular officer in his country during a personal interview that he is coming to the U.S. for lawful purposes and doesn't intend to work illegally or remain beyond the allowed period. For that reason, visas are much harder to get in poor, undeveloped countries than in richer, more politically stable ones. The law does not allow unauthorized entry, such as walking across an open, unmarked borderland, under almost any circumstance. Non-citizens must cross at an official U.S. border port of entry. If they try to enter between ports of entry, they are supposed to be detained until the conclusion of whatever immigration process applies in their case.

Congress writes the laws and the president signs them. Congress gets to decide how many people can come to the United States, how long they can stay, and on which terms. Every country has its own rules—I am not aware of any country that has no immigration restrictions whatsoever and lets anyone come in, anytime, from anywhere. To adopt such a policy would be to cede national sovereignty entirely. Maybe that's the idea, because woke activists insist that there is a human right to migrate and live anywhere you want.[7] Open-borders advocates believe that any policy that restricts people's movement (especially when they are poor) into another country (especially when it is rich) is "repression" or a display of "hegemonic elitism."[8] This belief is rooted in a fanatical obsession with racism, real or imagined. Woke activists view all Western societies as imbued with what they call "structural" or "systemic" racism. Structural or systemic racism is the idea that racism is fundamentally incorporated into the very nature of Western societies. It's baked in, and you can't avoid it. Anyone who claims not to be a racist is in denial. The woke see racism in literally everything: Your house is racist.[9] Your car is racist.[10] Your hair is racist.[11] And *you* are most certainly racist.[12] I'll talk more about that later in the book, especially Chapter 6.

The woke claim that any society that has been built primarily by Europeans is racist to its core. To overcome the imagined structural racism, they think, all boundaries—physical, mental, and otherwise—must be eliminated and rebuilt in an "anti-racist" way. In the eyes of the woke, the elimination of meaningful national borders, and allowing millions of aliens to freely enter Western countries is anti-racist, so it's one step in the direction of eliminating white supremacy and structural racism. When conservatives secure our borders and enforce the immigration laws by arresting and deporting illegal aliens, woke activists inevitably accuse them of not following the rule of law.[13] But when it comes to mass parole, catch-and-release at the border, asylum, Temporary Protected Status, and other policies that support an imagined international right to migrate, the Left ignores the rule of law entirely.

Myth 3: Borders and Nation-States Are Immoral

The woke believe that nation-states with secure borders are morally wrong.[14] In their view, borders serve the economic and political desires of wealthy elites. The woke don't seem to get how closely their political philosophy is rooted in communist ideology.[15] When American and other Western politicians advocate integrating the world to conform with their progressive, globalist agenda, they are borrowing from the Marxist idea of a global state. This vision was explicitly stated in the propaganda of the Third Communist International, known as the Comintern, a group of socialists in countries around the world run, and often funded, by the Soviet Union between the world wars. The stated goal of communist power is "the struggle by all available means, including armed force, for the overthrow of the international bourgeoisie and the creation of the international Soviet republic as a transition stage to the complete abolition of the state."[16]

Woke politicians and activists intentionally, or perhaps sometimes inadvertently, promote the communist agenda of eliminating the state and its supposedly artificial borders.[17] Domestically, they see society through a simplistic victim–perpetrator framework, where every social and economic relationship between individuals is reduced to one party as victim and the other as the perpetrator of violence, theft, injustice, or other forms of domination. Internationally, they see the same power dynamic in relations between countries. Leftists see poor countries as innocent victims of global capitalist exploitation, regardless of these countries' governments, corruption, or internal politics. They see all migrants—conflating illegal migrants with legal immigrants—as deserving of protection, accommodation, and benefits wherever they choose to go, regardless of whether they qualify as refugees under international law or qualify for entry under each nation's own laws. They refuse to acknowledge that some migrants have nefarious intentions and engage in criminal activity, or that admitting migrants with no verification of their identity and previous criminal past poses a risk.[18] Everyone understands that, sadly, political and criminal exploitation, corruption, human trafficking and other human rights abuses are found in the migrants' homelands all over the world. However, poor living conditions aren't enough for a person to qualify for asylum. Economic need, or the desire to improve your personal situation is understandable, but it doesn't give you a right to move into your neighbor's basement or take his car. Similarly, it doesn't give you the right to travel halfway round the world and automatically gain entry to someone else's country. Just like your neighbor gets to decide whether to invite you to his house, countries get to decide whether to invite you in.

The 1951 Geneva Refugee Convention is the basis for international refugee and asylum law for the U.S.. The convention was created after World War II, with the recent persecution of Jews and the ongoing persecution of dissidents from communism in mind. It defined "refugee" as any person who

> [a]s a result of events occurring before 1 January 1951 and owing to well-founded fear of being persecuted for reasons of race, religion, nationality, membership of a particular social group or political opinion, is outside the country of his nationality and is unable or, owing to such fear, is unwilling to avail himself of the protection of that country; or who, not having a nationality and being outside the country of his former habitual residence as a result of such events, is unable or, owing to such fear, is unwilling to return to it.[19]

America's INA of 1952 added refugee or asylum protections in 1965 for aliens who demonstrated persecution on account of race, religion, or political opinion, and those who had fled a communist or communist-dominated country or any country in the Middle East. The U.S. enacted the 1951 convention and its 1967 protocol into law in the Refugee Act of 1980.[20]

Neither the Refugee Act nor the U.S. law that implemented it were ever intended as a screening mechanism for mass economic migration in perpetuity—which is what we face today. Our asylum and refugee laws are being used as vehicles for unlimited mass migration. First, the sheer number of cases has overwhelmed the system. In general, "any alien who is physically present in the United States or who arrives in the United States...may apply for asylum."[21] The secretary of Homeland Security may grant asylum if that alien meets the statutory definition of "refugee" – see above. In general, the Department of Justice's immigration courts handle "defensive" asylum claims made by aliens whom the government is trying to deport. U.S. Citizenship and Immigration Services (USCIS) handles "affirmative" asylum claims from aliens who are already in the country, in whatever immigration status. Both of these systems were already clogged before President Biden took office, but the millions who were allowed in under his Administration delivered a crushing new workload that will take years or decades to work through, even if no new cases were added.[22]

There is fraud by applicants for asylum of each of the five categories noted above, but the category of "membership of a particular social group" (PSG) has been particularly abused. The origins of the term are murky, but U.S. courts have ruled that the claimed persecution necessary to qualify for refugee status must be at the hands of the applicant's government, not private actors. Later, administrative judges widened that principle to include "death squads" and other non-governmental actors, when the government in question was unable or unwilling to control them. Today, the PSG category has been blown so wide open that almost anyone can qualify. The official guidance given to USCIS adjudicating officers on what the term encompasses is voluminous, and the possible categories encompassed under PSG are extremely wide.[23] As now-Supreme Court Justice Samuel Alito wrote in 1993, "'virtually any set including more than one person could be described as a 'particular social group.'"[24]

One infamous case from 2025 illustrates the PSG problem. In March, the federal government deported "Maryland man" Kilmar Armando Abrego Garcia. He became a poster child for anti-enforcement, pro-illegal immigrant activists and politicians. Senator Chris Van Hollen of Maryland went to visit him in CECOT, the high security prison El Salvador's President Nayib Bukele had built to house the gang members he took off his country's streets. In 2019, a U.S. immigration judge had found Abrego Garcia to be a member of the El Salvadoran gang MS-13. He had come to the U.S. illegally as a teenager and didn't apply for asylum within a year as required. So, when he did years later, he was denied. But the judge did grant him "withholding of removal" to one country—his native El Salvador. On what grounds? That he could be harmed due to being a member of a particular social group – his immediate family. Because his mother reportedly ran a pupusa business at home, and the family claimed that a gang was extorting and threatening them, the whole family somehow became a PSG for the judge's purposes.

Everyone has a family. With a definition of PSG that wide, there's not much of a filter on asylum claims. There is no fee to apply, and no penalty for lying. And, if an applicant is denied, with more than 20 million illegal aliens here, and more than 1.3 million already holding removal orders against them, deportation isn't likely. America's refugee and asylum system is clogged with unfounded cases, to the detriment of the minority of meritorious cases. Exploiting asylum and refugee protections is a major tool for woke activists across the Western world to remove borders and gradually replace independent nation states with a multicultural, globalist population easier to mold into world socialism.

Contemporary globalism was initiated by politicians and business leaders who appear to have genuinely believed that the social well-being of people around the world would be improved by integrating economies via free trade and free currency exchange.[25] The idea was that successful trading partners have incentives to avoid conflict, and expansion of trade and development into the third world would "lift all boats" by providing work and other opportunities in the least-developed countries while lowering costs for businesses and consumers in the most-developed countries.[26] But in the 21st century, the globalist agenda has been coopted by leaders like former U.S. President Barack Obama, French President Emmanuel Macron, former Canadian Prime Minister Justin Trudeau, and Brazilian President Luiz Inácio Lula da Silva, who push for enhancing "global governance" while diminishing the power of the United States.[27] Naturally, these leftist leaders are seldom critical of communist China, the rising communist one-party state.

Myth 4: There Is No Difference Between Legal and Illegal Residents

Globalist leftists try to remove any formal distinction between legal and illegal residents. Until recently, American politicians and the media made a very clear distinction between U.S. citizens (those who were born in the United States, as well as naturalized citizens) and illegal aliens (those who either entered the country illegally or overstayed a visa). The woke no longer accept this distinction as meaningful, because, as their favorite lawn sign says, "No human being is illegal."[28]

For woke activists, the fact that illegal aliens are in violation of the law, and so could be at least eligible for deportation, and at worst criminally liable, doesn't matter. From their point of view, anyone who attempts to arrest or otherwise process illegal migrants for deportation is not only cruel, but racist. Racism is the lens through which they see every human interaction, including immigration relationships between individuals and nations.

From the woke perspective, "no human being is illegal" – which means in practice that they believe there should be no privileges and rights that American citizens have that aliens here illegally should not also have. Woke activists believe that illegal residents should have the right to drive, the right to free public education, access to all social welfare programs, the same right to work as ordinary citizens—and even the right to vote.[29] This attitude aligns perfectly with their support of a one-world socialist government. More about this in Chapter 8.

Myth 5: Global Human Rights Trump National Political and Civic Rights

Conservatives view rights and benefits as stemming from citizenship in a particular state and loyalty to a particular nation, and that these rights and benefits require civic duties in exchange, such as following the law and paying taxes. The woke, in contrast, are obsessed with (ever-expanding) human rights, civil rights, and the ability of people they view as disenfranchised or marginalized to obtain government and societal benefits without having any associated obligations. This comes from their Marxist focus on economic exploitation of the poor by the rich, or the powerless by the powerful. Communism, which is in its nature authoritarian and anti-democratic, is supposed to ensure that all working proletarians are provided with a basic standard of living. To achieve this, they seize control of all forms of production and the markets for all goods and services. They strip individuals of their rights to privacy and private property, as well as their control over their own time and energy. Most important, communists strip individuals of their allegiance to family, nation, and God.

Leftists don't distinguish between citizens and non-citizens, believing that everyone present in the United States should receive the same benefits—housing, education, food, shelter, health care, unemployment benefits—regardless of immigration status.[30] As they also believe that we have no right to keep foreigners out of the country, that essentially means that they want anyone on Earth to be able to enter whatever country he wants and immediately receive full rights there. This is global citizenship, and it is the antithesis of America, where Americans have built a uniquely free, strong, and prosperous society. Diluting the value of our citizenship is the surest way to destroy what we have created.

The U.S. Constitution and the American system of government are based on the idea of basic, God-given rights, plus a government by consensus built on the social contract theory. The social contract replaces the state of nature, in which life was "solitary, poor, nasty, brutish, and short," in the words of Thomas Hobbes.[31] In the social contract, citizens agree to give up certain freedoms in exchange for defined benefits and general social order. For example, we give the government a monopoly on violence in exchange for the government preventing and punishing crime. The woke leftist fails to understand that the social contract is between a citizen and his nation, not any person and the world. An illegal migrant has violated the law by entering a sovereign country without following the laws of that nation.[32] By violating the law of the country he or she enters, the illegal migrant does not give up his or her basic universal human rights, as agreed between nations under international treaties. But he does not get a free ride into the American social contract without our say-so. An illegal migrant is not entitled to the same legal protections afforded to citizens of the country he entered illegally. Woke activists do not accept this distinction between citizen and alien, which is why they use the euphemism "undocumented immigrant" or "undocumented noncitizen" instead of illegal alien.

Myth 6: Protecting the Integrity of the Voting System Is Racist

Democracy requires regular free, fair elections; without them, governments cannot implement the will of the people. All democratic societies have criteria for determining who is eligible to vote. In ancient Greece, citizenship was granted to all free, adult males who were residents of the city-state. All citizens were required to vote, and there were penalties for anyone who either chose not to vote or simply missed the election. Modern democracies mostly see voting as a right, not an obligation. Australia requires registered voters to vote and fines them if they don't, and 22 other countries have mandatory voting, but most democracies don't punish eligible voters who do not vote.

The U.S. Constitution of 1788 did not specify who should have the right to vote and left most election details to the states. Later, a series of amendments clarified federal election procedure and expanded the franchise for national elections. By 1971, all citizens over 18 were eligible, excepting convicted felons in some states. In early America, legal voters were almost exclusively property-owning or tax-paying adult males. Usually this meant white men, but not in all cases. In some states, women and African Americans and others were entitled to vote, as long as they owned property and paid taxes.[33]

The Naturalization Act of 1790 was our first real immigration law. It said that any free white person of "good character," living in the U.S. for two years, could apply for citizenship. It was pretty easy to immigrate to the U.S. in the 19th century, although the Chinese Exclusion Act of 1882 barred most Chinese. The Immigration Act of 1891 created a federal office for immigration and a professional corps of immigration inspectors at ports of entry. Immigrants were allowed to settle, but they did not achieve the right to vote until they became property owners. Gradually, in the 19th and 20th centuries, the franchise expanded, adding men with no property, black men, women, and finally all adults over 18. All adult American citizens now have the right to vote, except convicted felons in some states. Immigration law has changed over time, but non-citizen immigrants have never had the right to vote in federal elections.

The battle between the Left and the Right in most modern democracies involves political parties convincing voters that their interests will be promoted. At the federal level in America today, Democrats and Republicans fight for control of the Congress, the courts, and the presidency. Numerically, most data show that nationally there are more Democratic or Democrat-leaning voters, but they are concentrated in certain cities and certain states on the East and West Coasts. Because of the nature of the U.S. laws on representation, the result is often that Democrats control the House of Representatives while the Republicans control the Senate. The presidency vacillates between Democrat and Republican because even though there are numerically more Democratic voters, Republicans can achieve success in the Electoral College where small states have a statistically greater impact. Based on who wins the presidency, over time the federal courts may lean either left or right depending on who was in office when retirements and replacements occur.

Many conservatives believe that Democrats have been subtly trying to create a one-party socialist state through laws and policies that allow millions of illegal migrants to enter the United States with the assumption that they will vote Democrat. They argue that leftists have allowed millions of illegal immigrants to flood into certain American states, primarily along the southern border, so that those states will "flip blue," meaning that the Republican majority in those states will disappear. In this way, Democrats would be able to control Congress.[34] It would also result in fewer "red states" voting for Republicans in the Electoral College for president, which in turn would effect judicial appointments.

It is illegal for non-citizens to vote in federal elections, but there is ample evidence that it happens. The Left claims there is no conclusive evidence that illegal immigrants have swayed federal elections, and scoffs at attempts to ensure election integrity. But there have been initiatives at the state and local levels to allow anyone to vote without showing valid identification or verifying citizenship.[35] Many states already don't require ID to vote. Some of these initiatives began during the coronavirus pandemic when Democratic politicians supported mail-in voting, purportedly to avoid physical contact during the lockdowns. Mail-in voting and absentee voting, which used to be allowed only in rare exceptional circumstances, are now approved extensively across the United States.[36]

Whether illegal immigrants voting will affect federal elections in the future remains to be seen, but it is certain that leftists and a great majority of "anti-Trumpers" view any limitations on voting by migrants as racist. Leftists want as many migrants and foreigners in the United States as possible in their endless pursuit of "diversity," and also because under current rules, the census counts everyone, including aliens who are illegally present. As the census determines how congressional seats are apportioned, mass illegal migration tends to boost congressional representations in states with high numbers of illegal residents. The Left regard any policy restricting the right to vote, even for people illegally present in the country, as reminiscent of bygone eras when blacks, native Americans, women, and others were not allowed to vote.

Conclusion

For most of U.S. history, Republicans and Democrats argued about immigration policy, but they agreed on the need to have secure borders and to enforce the law. President Bill Clinton signed the 1996 Illegal Immigration Reform and Immigrant Responsibility Act, which attempted to put some teeth into immigration law enforcement.[37] Even Barack Obama admitted that he didn't have a magic wand he could wave to change immigration policy without Congress passing new laws, although he did arrogate legislative power through his Deferred Action for Childhood Arrivals program.[38] But in the past decade, the Democratic

Party, led by its most leftwing faction, has come to support *de facto* open borders, with very limited enforcement—and hardly ever deportation—for those who violate immigration laws. Hard-core leftist politicians, academics, and activists do not believe America is better than other countries. They are not proud of our history and traditions, nor do they value our citizenship above other loyalties. In their ideal world, America goes away, to be replaced by a socialist, progressive global utopia. But their utopian, rose-tinted view of the world gives no credence to history. The Left's vision of a stateless, free-migration paradise fails to credit the genius of the American system in delivering unparalleled prosperity, freedom, and security; or to account for the utter failure of every communist or socialist country to deliver the same.

A person to follow: Bill Melugin, Los Angeles–based correspondent, Fox News. @BillMelugin_on X.

A book to read: *Overrun: How Joe Biden Unleashed the Greatest Border Crisis in U.S. History*, by Todd Bensman, 2023.

A group to support: Border Security and Immigration Center, the Heritage Foundation, www.heritage.org/border-security

Chapter 2

The Second Commandment:
You Shall Put Your Trust in Institutions

Tearing it all down is the core of the leftist belief system; leftists want the institutions, schools, government, corporations, and associations that formed the skeletal strength of our nation for two centuries to be destroyed and rebuilt. This theme is evident on campus posters and slogans like "Defund the Police," "Hey hey, ho ho, Western civ has got to go,"[1] and "By any means necessary." Over the past half century or so, that's what the "progress" in progressive means in practice: progress towards destroying Western civilization through revolution and replacing it with a socialist utopia.

A fine summary of this ethos comes from the student group Columbia University Apartheid Divest (CUAD), the campus "coalition of student organizations" which led sometimes-violent protests and demonstrations after the Hamas attacks against Israelis on October 7, 2023. Though its immediate goal is to "challenge the settler-colonial violence that Israel perpetrates" and "the Zionist project" itself (meaning Israel's very existence), CUAD describes itself as a continuation of the student movement against the Vietnam War, apartheid in South Africa, and the generic "revolutionary" movement. Its mission statement says that "collective safety will arise when everyone has access to clean air, clean water, food, housing, education, healthcare, freedom of movement, and dignity."[2] In other words, when we have a global, socialist utopia.

Western history, democracy, capitalism, tolerance—it is ironic that woke leftists hate the very civilization in which they themselves thrive. They ignore the reality that the history of Western societies was no more violent than that of their prized third-world cultures. They are willfully blind to the fact that in American society, they are free to criticize the government, be as LGBTQ+ as they want, and live off other taxpayers, whereas in most of the world these things are either illegal or impossible. Like a man sawing at the very branch on which he sits, high above the alligators below, CUAD and its ilk tell themselves that America is a white supremacist, evil patriarchy. As leftist radicals profit from a privilege unimaginable to their ancestors, they criticize even their woke universities for not being left enough, and even leftwing politicians like Joe Biden for supporting Israel's right to exist. Living in this paradox brings to mind a Soviet-era saying, sometimes ascribed to Alexander Solzhenitsyn: "They lie to us, we know they're lying, they know we know they're lying, but they keep lying to us, and we keep pretending to believe them."

This chapter isn't intended to provide an exhaustive list of the American institutions that have been corrupted by "diversity, equity, and inclusion" (DEI), gender ideology, critical race theory, and leftism. It provides a mere sampling to give readers an idea of how far the rot has spread, and how much work is to be done if society is to recover. First, behind the walls of schools and universities, a woke takeover has been going on unchecked for years. For K–12 schools, the veil was partially lifted by the virtual schooling, via Zoom videos, that took place during the COVID-19 crisis.

1. K–12 Schools

From one-room schoolhouses of the growing West to teeming urban elementary, middle, and high schools, education has been the engine of American integration and assimilation. Public school was the one place where children of all religions met as equals, learned a shared history and values in a shared language, and learned to embrace and tolerate those different from them. Thanks to our mix of private, religious, and public schools, U.S. literacy was around 80 percent in the late 19th century, while in the rest of the world it was around 20 percent.[3] Sadly, the U.S. has ceased making progress. The reasons include broken families, unaccountable teachers, low expectations, poor discipline, and a tendency to ignore those real causes and blame all of the above on the usual suspects like "systems" and "structural racism." It all starts with kindergarten through grade 12, which for several generations, most American children have attended.

If at First You Don't Succeed, Lower the Bar

The National Assessment of Educational Progress (NAEP), known for being the organization that publishes the "nation's report card," has tracked the performance of the nation's public school students since 1992. In 2025, the NAEP results revealed that no real progress had been made since it began tracking performance some 30 years ago. Student scores in most subjects had dropped to historic lows in 2022, with COVID-19 being blamed. But by 2025, they had dropped even further, "despite an unprecedented infusion of federal funding that flowed into schools, fueling tutoring and other interventions aimed at addressing learning loss."[4] With test scores falling year by year, even as school districts spend more and more, teachers' unions and politicians have run out of excuses for low student performance. School failure is a political problem. The raw material—children—is no better or worse than a century ago.

Because of opposition from the Left, the obvious solutions to K–12 failure—no phones in the classroom, better discipline, higher standards, longer hours, more homework, parental responsibility—are politically off the table. So, instead, politicians, administrators, and teachers' unions often just lower the bar. In New York City, the four Regents Examinations—in English, math, science, and social studies—are supposed to be a measure of high school achievement. In 2022, one teacher found that a student could pass the multiple-choice algebra exam by guessing "C" on every question, as the pass rate was 19.8 percent and there are only five answers to each question.[5] Private schools put little stock in the exam, but public schools are stuck with it.

With a collapse in K-12 education, it's not surprising that the effects are felt upstream. In 2020, the California state supreme court ordered that the qualifying score for the state bar exam be lowered from 1440 to 1390, out of a maximum 2000 points, in 2020. Belying the ostensible reason—a response to pandemic-related learning loss that year—the court made the change permanent.[6]

"Equitable" Grading

Admitting that they are lowering the bar for passing grades would not sell well, so the Left comes up with euphemisms. One is "equitable" grading. Parents Defending Education break down the jargon on their website, but what this boils down is that students are not held accountable for missing class, not turning in assignments, and failing tests. The only metric is a vague idea of "mastery" at the end, which a teacher given to this dogma is highly likely to find so that all the students can pass the course and validate the method.[7]

"Equity" grading is championed by Joe Feldman, who makes a good living training and consulting off the method. He recommends "no penalties for late work and no grades for homework. No points for good behavior, classroom participation or perfect attendance, either."[8] Including these metrics, Feldman says, brings "implicit bias into the grade because not all students learn in that particular way."[9] Equitable grading naturally found a receptive audience in big, failing school systems in Boston, Los Angeles, New York City, San Diego, and Las Vegas, as well as the Democrat-run states Maine, Minnesota and Oregon.[10]

In California, San Francisco's public schools announced a new "Grading for Equity" rubric in May 2025 where homework and weekly tests don't count and a student's final grade comes down to one final exam which can be "retaken multiple times—even if students skip assignments or fail to attend class."[11] A score of 80% equals an "A" grade, a 41% still merits a "C," and the lowest level to pass is 21%. As journalist Derek Thompson wrote of the change, "It's hard to see the difference between this policy and what you'd get if a bunch of 10-year-olds locked the teachers in a closet and rewrote the rules."[12]

But so-called "equitable grading" runs counter to both recent research by Roland Fryer of Harvard and the practical success of schools like Katherine Birbalsingh's Michaela School in London, England about how to motivate and get the best from under-privileged kids in poor learning environments. We'll discuss this later in the book.

In addition to lowering standards, politicians and schools have added significant elements based on DEI, social-emotional learning, and other non-knowledge to the already light teaching curriculum, taking time from

English, history, math, and other useful subjects. In both administration and teaching, woke ideologues have placed considerations of race above learning—to the detriment of all students.

How can society turn things around? Harvard economists Will Dobbie and Roland Fryer's research into charter schools draws conclusions that seem obvious. They found

> that traditionally collected input measures—class size, per pupil expenditure, the fraction of teachers with no certification, and the fraction of teachers with an advanced degree—are not correlated with school effectiveness. In stark contrast, we show that an index of five policies suggested by over forty years of qualitative research—frequent teacher feedback, the use of data to guide instruction, high-dosage tutoring, increased instructional time, and high expectations—explains approximately 45 percent of the variation in school effectiveness.[13]

By showing that the reason why poor and non-white children were not succeeding in school was not due to racism but to other factors, some of which were social, Dobbie and Fryer touched a third rail in academia. (A look at what happened to Fryer for this and other sins against leftist orthodoxy, later.)

Replacing Subject Matter with Ideology

Though critical race theory (CRT) is taught—some would say, as the dominant philosophy—in American teachers' colleges, public school administrators have long denied that it is taught in K–12 classes. The truth of that denial depends on how one defines CRT. There are euphemisms galore for the concepts underlying CRT, namely the division of all humans into oppressor or oppressed categories based on one's "intersectional" identity, and the constant stress on immutable characteristics like race, sex, and "gender identity." The group Parents Defending Education has shown examples from across the country, but especially progressive states like California. Using concepts like "emotional and social learning" (ESL), schools can insert CRT into their curricula. Using concepts such as "ethnic studies"[14] or "multicultural awareness," they can smuggle in political bias, for instance against Israel and for Palestinian activism.[15]

According to a an article by nine Ethnic Studies practitioners in *Convergence* magazine, "[t]he 1968 Third World Liberation Front and Black Student Union strike at San Francisco State led to the country's first Ethnic Studies program," and in 2022, "[t]eachers have formed the Coalition for Liberated Ethnic Studies to defend and spread education that centers BIPOC[16] knowledge, experiences and narratives in service of collective liberation."[17] The California legislature passed a law in 2021 mandating one semester of "ethnic studies" for every high school student before they can graduate, starting with the 2025 freshman class.[18] This opened the door to a cast of grifters and vendors to sell curriculums of doubtful academic use or integrity. Parents and taxpayers who oppose mandatory Ethnic Studies do so not just because it adds an unfunded mandate to a state school system that already fails adequately to educate for the workforce, but because the materials in the curriculum are often anti-Western, anti-capitalist, and antisemitic.

"Ethnic studies" has various definitions, but they all fit into the general woke worldview of DEI, CRT, and the Marxist oppressor-oppressed framework in which Europeans are oppressive colonialists and all other ethnic groups are oppressed. Oppression among and between ethnic groups is given little attention, though it is a feature of all human history, throughout the world.

According to "Ethnic Studies leader" Brian Lozenski:

> Ethnic Studies centers the heritage knowledges and lived experiences of those who have borne the brunt of colonial devastation, including global Indigenous communities, women and genderqueer people, neurodivergent and the dis-abled, and those living in poverty [and] de-centers those of European descent and, for instance, inquires about the relationships between Black and Indigenous peoples. . . . Ethnic Studies explores the colonial roots of the dispossession of Palestinian land and the creation of Zionism.[19]

California's own Ethnic Studies Model Curriculum "is based on African American, Chicana/o/x and Latina/o/x, Native American, and Asian American and Pacific Islander studies" and seeks to "address institutionalized systems of advantage and address the causes of racism and other forms of bigotry including, but not limited to, anti-Blackness, anti-Indigeneity, xenophobia, antisemitism, and Islamophobia within our culture and governmental policies," writes Kayla Bartsch in the *Federalist*.[20]

On the other side of the country, Pennsylvania's "Culturally-Relevant and Sustaining Education Program Framework Guidelines" required that teachers "[b]elieve and acknowledge that microaggressions are real," "[d]isrupt harmful institutional practices, policies, and norms by advocating and engaging in efforts to rewrite policies, change practices, and raise awareness," and "deepen their awareness of their own conscious/unconscious biases."[21] As Neetu Arnold of the *City Journal* reported, in May 2025, the school district of Southern York, PA removed these state guidelines from their teacher-training programs, realizing their basis in critical theory, with its divisive concepts of "systemic oppression," and putting kids into categories of "marginalized and oppressed, based on their race or other identity groupings"[22] But as Arnold notes, in school board elections, only 5-10 percent of locals bother to vote, which allows a small number of ideologues to wield disproportional power. Conservatives must consider school board elections as among the most important, not the least of parental and civic responsibilities.[23]

Race-Based School Closure

Facing lower student numbers and a budget crisis in 2024, the San Francisco Unified School District needed to close some schools. The plan it devised for choosing which ones to close was put together by Stanford University professor Francis Pearman, with "equity" counting for half the points on his scale.[24] Under this plan, Sutro Elementary School would close, but Dr. George Washington Carver Elementary School would stay open. Sutro's feeder population is 75 percent Asian, and the kids do too well in tests. Meanwhile, Carver has failed to meet state standards but is 45 percent black and 22 percent Hispanic.[25] According to *The Washington Free Beacon*, "elementary schools with similar demographics as Carver—predominantly black or Hispanic—typically scored highest on Pearman's formula, saving them from closure. The majority of schools on the chopping block had predominantly white or Asian populations."[26]

Race-Based Teacher Hiring and Firing

In 2022, the Minneapolis Public School District agreed in contract negotiations with the state of Minnesota's teachers' union that in the event of layoffs, it would fire teachers in order of least seniority—but only if they were white. Teachers from an "underrepresented population" would be exempted from layoffs, according to the contract terms. The school district argued that this measure was to "remedy the effects of past discrimination."[27] In an email to *The Washington Times*, the Minneapolis Public School District said that it had agreed to this term with the Minneapolis Federation of Teachers (MFT) "to support the recruitment and retention of teachers from underrepresented groups as compared to the labor market and to the community served by the school district."[28] This was blatantly racist. James Dickey of the Upper Midwest Law Center said that "[t]he object of this provision is clearly to lay off white teachers first, regardless of merit, based on the color of their skin, and that is a big problem under the Constitution and the 14th Amendment."[29] Jonathan Butcher of The Heritage Foundation said that the contract between the Minneapolis Public School District and the MFT "violates the Civil Rights Act and the Equal Protection Clause of the US Constitution."[30]

Teachers' Unions

In America's biggest Democrat-run cities and states, teachers' unions have a symbiotic relationship with politicians like Chicago Mayor Brandon Johnson and New York Mayor Eric Adams. The unions get these Democrats elected, and in turn, the politicians agree to raise pay and benefits, ease working conditions, and de-link teacher performance from student outcomes. In addition to lowering the bar for students so they all pass, teachers' unions also want to reduce qualitative assessments of teachers themselves. In New York City, teachers successfully sued to remove the requirement that they should pass a basic literacy exam, claiming the test was racist since a higher proportion of white takers passed it than blacks or Latinos.[31] The New Jersey Education Association, a state teachers' union, called for ending the "edTPA," a basic skills test for teachers. They argued that this would allow for more people to enter the profession – but if they were not smart enough to pass a basic test, what could they impart to struggling students?

On the national level, Heritage Foundation education expert Jonathan Butcher explains how the American Federation of Teachers (AFT), now led by president Randi Weingarten, has dominated the Department of Education ever since it was created, placing union demands over student outcomes.[32] According to critics, Weingarten, who is estimated to earn half a million dollars a year in salary and benefits,[33] vociferously argued for closing schools during the coronavirus pandemic and keeping them closed as long as possible.[34] In a 2023 congressional hearing, however, she implausibly claimed that "opening schools safely—even as the pandemic surged—guided the AFT's every action."[35]

The AFT is one of the two big national teachers' unions, along with the National Education Association (NEA). "The NEA gave its first presidential endorsement ever in 1976, when Walter Mondale promised them [sic], at an NEA annual meeting, that the Carter administration would form an education department," explained Anthony Fisher in *Reason* magazine.[36] This led to the creation of the federal Department of Education (DoE) in 1980, which President Donald Trump severely reduced in early 2025 with a view to dismantling it entirely.

As Butcher writes, since 1980, national spending per public school student has consistently risen—while student performance has not. Over the past 50 years, administrators and other "non-instructional" staff increased by 700 percent in public K–12 schools, while teacher numbers increased by only 243 percent.[37] Despite—or because of—all that extra staff, reading proficiency nationwide is now the lowest since the NAEP began keeping score in 1992. In 2024, only 67 percent of eighth graders met or exceeded the basic level.[38]

Public schools are funded by state and local taxes, with only around 8 percent of their budgets coming from the federal government. But public schools received massive federal injections—nearly $190 billion—of extra money to help during the COVID-19 shutdowns. As Butcher writes, rather than invest in programs that improve student performance, "many administrators used the cash for pay increases and signing bonuses for teachers who swapped schools."[39] The AFT receives federal grants for continuing education and training for teachers, amounting to more than $2 billion in 2020 alone. Butcher found no evidence that these training programs and other social justice, anti-racist, DEI programs have any positive impact on student performance.[40]

When President Trump began reducing staff and shutting down the DoE in 2025, the NEA was, not surprisingly, one of the parties that sued to stop him. The NEA, along with the National Association for Advancement of Colored People (NAACP)[41] and public workers' union American Federation of State, County, and Municipal Employees (AFSCME)[42] sued to prevent the DoE's closure.[43] The NEA claimed that closing the DoE would increase class sizes, cut job training, stop student loans, end civil rights protection, and reduce programs for students with special needs or disabilities. The DoE countered that "sunsetting the Department of Education will be done in partnership with Congress and national and state leaders" and that the DoE would continue "vigilantly enforcing federal civil rights laws in schools and ensuring students with special needs and disabilities have access to critical resources."[44] Conservatives point out that the core functions of the DoE can easily be carried out by other federal agencies; for example, the Department of Justice can handle civil rights complaints, and the Treasury can take the student loans. Grants for special education can be made directly to states, which pay for 92 percent of school funding anyway, to spend without the middleman of the DoE.

2. Universities and Colleges

With a few exceptions, American academia is overwhelmingly leftist. A poll by Inside Higher Ed taken before the November 2024 election found that of 1,000 college professors surveyed, 78 percent supported Kamala Harris and Tim Walz, while only 8 percent backed Donald Trump and JD Vance.[45] Given the politics on most campuses today, the few conservative professors are wise to fear being outed by their students—according to the College Fix, "a 2023 survey found 74 percent of college students would report their professor for saying something offensive [to them]."[46] A 2022 survey by the William F. Buckley, Jr. Program at Yale "found that 67% of college students support requiring professors and administrators to sign diversity statements as a condition of employment...65% believe private companies should do the same for new hires, and 50.8% believe universities should 'require that students, professors, and faculty state their preferred gender pronouns when introducing themselves.'"[47] Only 45 percent were opposed to speech codes on campus – meaning fewer than half of Yale students surveyed supported real free speech.

Leftwing indoctrination is baked into every aspect of higher education. Santi Tafarella, an English professor at a community college in Los Angeles County, described how his college president wanted to adopt a "Diversity, Equity, Inclusion and Accessibility Glossary of Terms" published by the California Community Colleges system.[48] The definitions support his contention that the glossary is "a manifesto" for "hiring, faculty evaluations and even course outlines" that "commits them to a radical, racially charged ideology." "Merit" is defined by the glossary as "a concept that...is embedded in the ideology of Whiteness," which "protects White privilege under the guise of standards." Tafarella says that not only is critique of the DEI agenda fiercely attacked by his college leadership, but that administrators are making active involvement and propagation of the ideology necessary to get hired and promoted.

A study by the National Association of Scholars (NAS) showed that DEI-related language in scientific publications rose by 42 times from 2010 to 2021.[49] The study found the greatest DEI infestation in published websites at Ivy League universities. The two main sources of funding for scientific research are the National Institutes of Health and the National Science Foundation, both of which were ideologically aligned with the Biden Administration.[50]

Students for Fair Admissions

In 1979, the Supreme Court decided in the *Bakke* case that race could be one factor taken into consideration in college admissions. In the 2003 *Grutter v. Bollinger* decision, the Court continued to kick the *Bakke* can down the road, allowing race to be considered as a factor in college admissions but opining that "governmental use of race must have a logical end point," which Justice Sandra Day O'Connor thought would be in a few decades.

The affirmative action status quo from *Bakke* and *Grolinger* was challenged by a group called Students for Fair Admissions (SFFA), which sued Harvard University and the University of North Carolina at Chapel Hill in 2014.[51] The two cases were combined and after some initial losses, decided by the Supreme Court in 2023.[52]

SFFA claimed that the colleges admissions policies were racially discriminatory. Opponents, which included the colleges but also the American Council on Education and 40 higher-education groups, argued that if colleges couldn't take race into account in deciding to admit, it would infringe on their academic freedom and on their First Amendment rights, by prohibiting applicants from sharing "life experiences" that the colleges could otherwise take into account as part of a "holistic" admission process. This process was intended to raise the number of black and Latino students, who on average score lower on standardized tests like the SAT, LSAT, and MCAT than white and Asian applicants. The "holistic" approach penalizes Asian applicants most of all, rating them lower on nebulous factors like leadership, confidence, and likability to compensate for their higher test scores. By using the holistic approach, which does not rely on objective criteria, medical schools are able to rig the race proportions of incoming classes by essentially setting a lower bar for MCAT scores for black applicants than whites or Asians, as this chart (used with permission) from the American Enterprise Institute shows.[53]

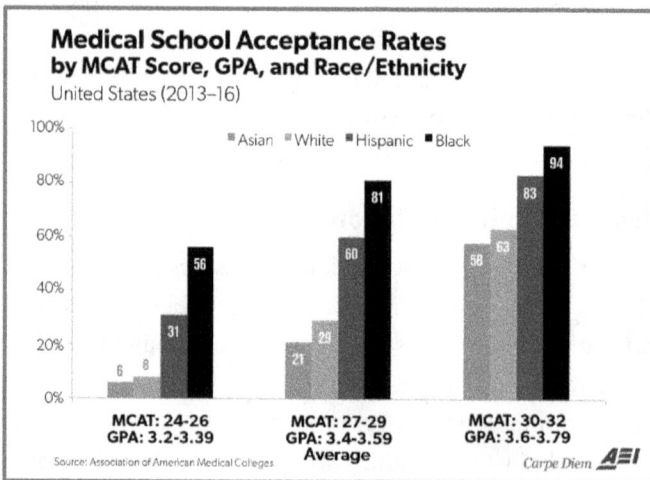

Medical School Acceptance Rates
by MCAT Score, GPA, and Race/Ethnicity
United States (2013–16)

Asian   White   Hispanic   Black

MCAT: 24-26 / GPA: 3.2-3.39 — 6, 8, 31, 56
MCAT: 27-29 / GPA: 3.4-3.59 — 21, 29, 60, 81
MCAT: 30-32 / GPA: 3.6-3.79 — 58, 63, 83, 94

Average

Source: Association of American Medical Colleges   Carpe Diem AEI

In its landmark SFFA decision, the Supreme Court finally jumped off the fence it had been straddling since *Bakke* and ruled that race-based discrimination was against the law.

SFFA argued that the time for race-based favoritism is over and that merit alone, as defined by objective measurements, should determine entrance requirements. In classic "affirmative action," all things being equal, a black student is more likely to be admitted to a competitive school with lower test scores than a white or (especially) Asian student.

But it was clear long before the case was decided that Ivy League and other competitive institutions were so committed to race-based admissions that they would find ways around the decision and the law. Classic affirmative action would be renamed or redesigned to accomplish the same goal while evading the Supreme Court's clear decision.

During the SFFA hearings before the decision was rendered, The *Washington Post*'s Eugene Robinson made the case for continued racial preferences.[54] Robinson argued that legacy admissions, where the children of alumni are given preference, are a kind of affirmative action, as is reserving spots for children of donors, and athletes in sports such as squash or rowing that are not common in "high schools most minority students attend."

Robinson says that "[a]ffirmative action will no longer be necessary when the larger conditions that make it necessary have been done away with." This, he proposes, will be "when the racial wealth gap is closed" or "when the mean SAT scores for Black, Hispanic and American Indian/Alaska Native high school students consistently are on par with those of White and Asian students." Robinson is saying that we can only treat people equally when the outcome for all races is equal. This is the argument of Ibram Kendi: if there is any disparity in outcomes between racial groups, there is racism. Theirs is an impossible bar to meet.

After the SFFA case, while accepting that classic affirmative action is dead, Harvard economist Roland Fryer made the case for using "sophisticated analytics" to predict student success based on a range of factors.[55] He argues not for eliminating "affirmative action," but using a "machine-learning model" that "would be fed historical admissions data, including candidates' family background and academic achievement, and noncognitive skills such as grit and resilience, along with outcomes of past admission decisions." This could better predict, he argues, applicants' performance and "sidestep other thorny issues in college admissions" like the validity of standardized tests.

Fryer explains that 71 percent of black and Hispanic students at Harvard come from wealthy backgrounds, and that only a "tiny fraction attended underperforming public high schools."[56] He confirms that first-generation and second-generation immigrants from Africa make up about 41 percent of all black students in the Ivy League, though they are only 10 percent of the overall African American population. Cameroonians, Ghanaians, and Nigerians are immigrant groups that all earn more than the total U.S. national average.[57]

Grade Inflation

In 2024, Tunku Varadarajan of *The Wall Street Journal* interviewed Harvard professor Harvey Mansfield, who retired at 92 after teaching at the university for 50 years. Mansfield said that when he went to Harvard in 1949, a third of professors were Republicans, and he now leaves behind a department without a single professor "who isn't a liberal or progressive."[58] Mansfield also rails against grade inflation; at Harvard today, the median grade is an "A minus."[59] Grade inflation, Mansfield tells Varadarajan, not only fails to provide potential employers with information they need to distinguish the best recruits, but is bad for democracy "because it makes society attempt something—or satisfy itself that it's done something—that is impossible, which is to do away with human inequalities."[60]

Activist Professors

Traditional college professors are supposed to teach their students to think for themselves, and to weigh alternate theories and points of view. But an increasing number of academics consider themselves more activists than teachers. One example is Dan-el Padilla Peralta of Princeton. He is a "classics" professor who calls his own field "equal parts vampire and cannibal." Peralta believes that classics is the foundation of white supremacy, and according to a colleague, "he's not sure the discipline deserves a future."[61] When anti-Israel student protests followed Israel's reaction to the Hamas massacre and kidnappings on October 7, 2023, Peralta was among faculty who signed a letter supporting Princeton students and boycotting Columbia University.

Peralta came from the Dominican Republic as a child, and his family overstayed their visas and became illegal immigrants. Leftist academics such as Peralta do not like nations or borders any more than they like classical antiquity. In his book *Undocumented*, Peralta wrote, "Demography is a b**ch. Holla at me if you want me to break it down for you." By this, Peralta implies that without immigration enforcement, the "global majority"—defined as everyone but Europeans and their descendants—will be able to dominate every country.[62]

Academia was a logical choice for someone who combined open borders and globalist entitlement with values antithetical to the American founders. Peralta eventually worked his way up to associate professor of classics at Princeton. In 2021, he spoke to incoming students about free speech: "I envision a free speech and an intellectual discourse that is flexed to one specific aim, and that aim is the promotion of social justice, and an anti-racist social justice at that." In their mentoring of students, he went on, Princeton faculty should teach them about

> the institutional peculiarities of Princeton and Princeton culture—but not with a view to habituating them into a practice of assimilation or indoctrinating them in the belief that somehow this is the best damn place of all, but in order to supply them with the tools with which they can tear down this place and make it a better one.[63]

These fragile, angry, sanctimonious young people will find that the first part—tearing down—is easy, with the connivance of cowards and sycophants in university administrations. The second—building a new Princeton—will be impossible without any values, loyalty, courage, or conscience to hold their new creation together.

DEI Hiring Doom-Loop

The way faculty become increasingly of one ideological bent (leftist) is through hiring practices that punish diverse viewpoints and reward DEI orthodoxy. The National Association of Scholars regularly reports on how colleges insert DEI litmus tests into job applications and grant proposals.

For example, the University of Oregon requires departments to take a job applicant's commitment to DEI into account in hiring, with the implication that an applicant's race should also be considered.[64] The university's commitment to "strong, diverse applicant pools" clearly means finding applicants who are not males of European origin, not those with diverse backgrounds and opinions. Oregon's job applicants are required to submit DEI statements, which are judged using a rubric created by the University of California, Berkely, that "penalizes faculty who say that they plan to 'treat everyone the same' or who criticize so-called 'affinity groups.'"[65]

"Positionality" Statements

One of the bizarre rituals of woke American institutions is the "land acknowledgements" made before meetings or speeches, where speakers identify one of the many previous occupants of the land they are standing on. This is performance art, not history. The so-called native tribes, too, displaced the animals who were there before them, and, in most cases, the other tribes that they subjected or conquered. America, just like in Europe, is a palimpsest of human layers created by migration and violent subjugation.

Similar to land acknowledgements are "positionality statements," in which academics self-flagellate and confess their original sins at the top of what should be a scholarly paper. This exercise comes out of "standpoint theory," which holds that there are no essential truths, but only relative ones shaped by where we all stand. Colin Wright of *Reality's Last Stand* cites a cringe-worthy example: The authors begin their paper by saying they "are cis-gender menstruating individuals who identify as intersectional feminists. Some are part of the LGBTQIA+ community and others are allies."[66] It's hard to think of anything more opposite of empirical science than this disclaimer, which prompts one not to take anything that follows seriously.

Plagiarism: Plentiful But Shoddy Publication

Making it easier for leftist academics to push DEI and other woke ideology is the rot undermining teaching, scholarship, and the mechanisms meant to protect their integrity. In a March 2025 report for The Heritage Foundation, college professor Jay Greene explains that in addition to being predominantly leftist, "[a]cademia has slowly become a racket in which professors do not work very hard and focus too often on unproductive and low-quality research."[67] Greene points to an astonishing 35,000 academic journals, and, as of 2022, more than 5 million published academic articles a year.[68] Given that output, it's not shocking that, as Lokman Meho explained, "as many as 50% of papers are never read by anyone other than their authors, referees and journal editors," and 90 percent of published academic papers are never cited at all.[69]

For many supposedly scientific studies, other researchers cannot reproduce the same results using the same inputs. In addition, researchers use techniques like "p-hacking"—manipulating data to produce results that support their desired goal.[70] Some studies supporting gender ideology and transgender medical intervention are good examples of this type of inductive reasoning, seen in Chapters 4 and 5. Jay Greene recommends raising teaching loads for both tenured and tenure-track professors, which would have the side effect of reducing incentives to produce bulk, low-quality research.[71]

Academia is also rife with plagiarism, and it often goes unpunished. As Christopher Rufo of the Manhattan Institute wrote in 2024, he was one of "a handful of reporters, including Christopher Brunet, Aaron Sibarium, and Luke Rosiak, who flipped the rock in academia and discovered widespread fraud, plagiarism, and dishonesty" that had been largely ignored hitherto.[72] A few examples will suffice to illustrate:

Jerlando Jackson, Michigan State University's (MSU's) dean of the College of Education was accused of serial plagiarism, with clear supporting evidence[73] showing that he lifted extensive sections word for word from the work of other authors. *The Washington Free Beacon* said that Jackson "plagiarized extensively over the course of his career," citing "nearly 40 examples of plagiarism that span nine of Jackson's papers, including his Ph.D. thesis, and range from single sentences to full pages."[74] Yet after a "preliminary assessment" of the case, "it was determined that there was not sufficient credible evidence to support further review of the Allegation," according to MSU, and the university administration dismissed all charges. MSU further claimed that that Jackson was "the target of racist, vile, and despicable attacks" and that the plagiarism claim was made by opponents of DEI.[75] But the motives of whoever complained are irrelevant to whether Jackson plagiarized other scholars and writers, which is the cardinal sin in higher education. The decision to let academics like Jackson off without penalty, while accusing those who found his plagiarism of racist motives, undermines the most basic integrity of the institution and sends a terrible message to students.

Before the November 2024 presidential election, Rufo demonstrated clear evidence that Kamala Harris had plagiarized several sources.[76] Rufo writes that as California's attorney general, Harris and co-author Joan O'C. Hamilton wrote the book *Smart on Crime: A Career Prosecutor's Plan to Make Us Safer*. Citing Austrian "plagiarism hunter" Stefan Weber, Rufo says that Harris "without proper attribution, reproduced extensive sections from a John Jay College of Criminal Justice press release," "stole long passages directly from Wikipedia," and "lifted promotional language from an Urban Institute report, and failed to cite her source."[77]

As with Jackson, Harris's defenders dismissed the accusations because of the source—a conservative intellectual—not on the substance of the claim. Jonathan Turley explained in *The Hill* that "[t]he seriousness of the allegation often depends on how sympathetic the media is toward the author."[78] Snopes (a website that supposedly debunks online falsehood) quotes plagiarism expert Jonathan Bailey as saying of those who find plagiarism that "[t]heir intention is to find plagiarism that they can then use to attack the relevant person or institution."[79] This may be true, but it does not address the facts alleged—either the author stole other people's work and words by copying them without attribution, or he did not. Plagiarism is either present or it is not; the motivations of those finding it or accusing authors of it are entirely irrelevant.

Leftist Faculty

In the *Independent Review*, Phillip Magness and David Waugh write that "sixty percent of faculty now identify as 'liberal' or 'far left.' This left-leaning supermajority is responsible for rampant discrimination against non-left job seekers, both conservatives and moderates."[80]

Starting around 2000, say the authors, "faculty opinion took a hard left turn such that professors on the political left are now approaching a supermajority in the academy." They point out that the death of viewpoint diversity among academics is not echoed in society at large, leading to a mismatch between the parents and taxpayers who fund higher education and the profession that provides the service.

The science, technology, engineering, and math (STEM) fields are slightly better, but in "some fields such as English and history…conservatives are practically nonexistent."[81] According to survey data the authors cite, "liberal and far-left faculty members grew from 44.8 percent in 1998 to 59.8 percent in 2016–17," and faculty members who identify as far left have grown from 4.2 percent in 1992 to "11.5 percent of all university faculty."[82] Magness and Waugh note that in addition, or because of, this leftward trend, "faculty and university administrators have increasingly prioritized overt political activism as a primary emphasis of classroom instruction." On top of which, unfortunately, the feedback loop of leftist faculty hiring people who agree with them threatens to harden the current balance in perpetuity.

Antisemitism in Higher Education:
An Ivy League Reckoning Before Congress

For universities, chinks in the armor protecting the rot in academia from public attention began appearing once the national protests, riots, and general insanity inspired by the May 2020 death of George Floyd had burned out and people took stock. But just how far-Left most of our campuses had become wasn't really revealed until after October 7, 2023. The horrific terror attacks by Hamas on Israel produced a reaction from college students and faculty that was completely predictable to those who had been following the ball, but came as a shock to many Americans—particularly parents of students, major donors, and secular Jews.

On December 5, 2023, the leaders of four elite universities testified before Congress.[83] The appearance of the presidents of Harvard (Claudine Gay), Penn (Liz Magill), American University (Pamela Nadell), and MIT (Sally Kornbluth) before the House Committee on Education and the Workforce was one of the most watched hearings in history, and for good reason. At the hearing, the questioning by Congresswoman Elise Stefanik of Claudine Gay starkly highlighted the inconsistency of her stance on free speech.

Gay failed to explain her college's position on antisemitism in her congressional testimony, and which limits Harvard had on student behavior. A few days later Chris Rufo and other researchers revealed evidence that Gay had plagiarized from other academics, including from (fellow black woman) scholar Carol Swain, PhD.[84] Gay had plagiarized chunks of not only her doctoral thesis, but half the (rather few) academic articles she had written. Swain, to whose research Gay helped herself liberally, said that Harvard's "board of trustees needs to apply the same standards to her as they would apply to a white person under the same circumstances." Which are, in Swain's opinion, that "a white male would probably already be gone."[85]

Did Harvard's board take this tough but fair position, to preserve institutional integrity and send the message to students and faculty about what is acceptable? Of course not. The Harvard Corporation (Harvard's governing board) supported Gay, called her plagiarism "a few instances of inadequate citation," found "no violation of Harvard's standards for research misconduct," and gave her the chance to correct her work years after the fact and "insert citations and quotation marks that were omitted from the original publications."[86] Many expelled students and fired teachers might like to have this option. Gay later resigned and has become a case study of how DEI can corrupt higher education. Gay had been chosen as president of Harvard despite a thin academic record including no authored books and only a dozen papers.[87] According to Swain,

> Ms. Gay's work wouldn't normally have earned tenure in the Ivy League. Tenure at a top-tier institution normally demands ground-breaking originality; her work displays none. In a world where the privilege of diversity is king, Ms. Gay was able to parlay mediocre research into tenure and administrative advancement at what was once considered a world-class university.[88]

Harvard University

In March 2022, Harvard's Shorenstein Center on Media, Politics, and Public Policy hosted[89] a workshop called "Systemic Racism at Harvard: Self-Assessment and Personal Growth," which "addressed the issue of systemic racism at Harvard" and "engaged in self-reflection, mindfulness, and open-ended prompts that invited participants to consider how we can grow in anti-racist knowledge and practices related to our work at Harvard." Note that it is simply assumed that systemic racism exists at Harvard University.

Bill Ackman, a Harvard graduate incensed by the university's stance on Hamas and Israel, made it his mission to reveal the intolerance and leftist bias at Harvard, led by President Gay. He alleges, based on inside sources, that Gay herself was a "diversity hire" chosen for her race and sex and not because she was the best candidate. Under her leadership, Harvard has used DEI as a screen to ensure the hiring of leftwing professors, such that now only 3 percent of Harvard's academic staff openly identify as conservative.

In 2006, then-President Larry Summers resigned because he had raised the question of why women were less prevalent in the sciences than men. Summers had tried to ride out the criticism, but he was shivved by faculty in a no-confidence vote. Gay, meanwhile, was supported by the majority of Harvard's faculty. As *The Wall Street Journal* explained, Gay has doggedly rooted out *wrong think* during her tenure.[90] In 2019, she helped to remove a black law professor, Ronald Sullivan, because he had been working on the legal defense of film mogul Harvey Weinstein.

Gay was instrumental in the hounding out of another black Harvard professor, Roland Fryer, after he published research that also didn't fit the progressive world view (his work is discussed below and in Chapters 9 and 10).[91]

When Charles Murray was invited to Harvard to speak in 2020, Gay criticized the professor who had invited Murray, and that professor was later let go. Murray is a brilliant academic who publishes accurate research. His crime is that the conclusions don't fit the progressive narrative.

In 2023, Harvard came in dead last—with a score of zero—in an annual free speech rating by the Foundation for Individual Rights and Expression (FIRE).[92] Andrew Sullivan, journalist and by no means a staunch conservative, writing about the college Hamas hearings, ended with this recommendation: "End DEI in its entirety. Fire all the administrators whose only job is to enforce its toxic orthodoxy. Admit students on academic merit alone. Save standardized testing—which in fact helps minorities."[93]

In a May 2025 interview with the Manhattan Institute's Christopher F. Rufo, Harvard researcher Omar Sultan Haque called the college corrupted beyond repair. He said he "stopped teaching at Harvard last year primarily because of its anti-truth-seeking culture, radical left-wing bias, racial and gender discrimination, and prevailing anti-intellectualism." Harvard's "culture and practices prioritize ideological conformity over open inquiry and debate, suppressing dissenting viewpoints and compromising academic freedom," Haque said. He points out one easy way colleges like Harvard get around the Supreme Court's ban on race preferences in *Students for Fair Admissions v. Harvard*: asking essay questions or interview questions that allow students or faculty applicants to show-case their intersectional cards. For example, questions about "life experiences" are designed not to look for military service or scouting badges, but stories of racial oppression and grievance based on identity.[94]

Princeton University

In April 2024, two Princeton graduate students were arrested for trespassing after they and a larger group occupied a campus building and tried to erect a "tentifada" encampment. In response to the arrests, some Princeton professors and students wrote letters that "condemned the university, accused it of racism, and defended the pro-Palestinian demonstrators who occupied a building" according to *National Review*. Dan-el Padilla Peralta (see above) was among four professors who signed the letter supporting the student protesters.[95] The student letter was signed by Princeton's Black Student Union, Pride Alliance, Sri Lankans of Princeton, and the Latinx Graduate Student Association Leadership Committee.

Princeton faculty has grown ever leftward not by accident, but due to policy and practice. President Trump took on the Ivy League universities in 2025 by withholding federal funding, beginning a battle that will be waged for years. Columbia University agreed, in theory, to the federal demands to rein in antisemitism on campus and stop unlawful discrimination in academic courses, hiring, and admissions. Harvard refused and sued the government for taking its money.

Princeton, under President Christopher L. Eisgruber, followed the Harvard line. Eisgruber told students in 2020 that Princeton was guilty of "systemic racism" and that racism was embedded in the very "structures of the university itself." His response was to increase the DEI offices and staff, set up arguably illegal hiring programs, and allow racially segregated graduations. The DoE under President Trump's first term took Eisgruber at his word, and sent a letter "raising concerns that the university has been making false assurances to the public and to the Education Department that it does not discriminate based on race," and warning of penalties and sanctions.[96] This effort came at the tail end of the Trump Administration, and the effort to call Princeton's bluff ended under the Biden DoE.

In April 2024, Christopher Rufo reported on what he calls Princeton's "entrenched a system of racial discrimination and segregation" against whites, Jews, and men under Eisgruber's leadership.[97] Rufo found a massive DEI bureaucracy at Princeton committed to promoting "demographic evolution," a euphemism for hiring via racial quotas that would be necessary to reach Eisgruber's goal of "increasing by 50 percent the number of tenured or tenure-track faculty members from underrepresented groups over the next five years."

Some legal experts believe that Princeton has violated state and federal Civil Rights Acts through biased contracting with suppliers and discriminatory hiring. Despite public blustering, Princeton administrators may know they are in trouble: Rufo reports that "the university has been quietly scrubbing its website of DEI materials."[98]

Professor Joshua Katz

Summing up the totalitarian state's attitude to those who stray from dogma, Stalin's chief of secret police Lavrentiy Beria said "show me the man and I'll show you the crime." In a state without freedom of speech and the rule of law, a pretext can be easily found to get rid of anyone with inconvenient views. This is the academic climate that led to Princeton's firing of professor Joshua Katz. His 25 years at the Ivy League university in New Jersey were, according to most reports, extraordinary not just for his intellectual power and range but for his skill and care in teaching, which is not always the hallmark of star professors. What brought Katz down was ostensibly the resurrected case of an affair he had with a then-

21-year-old graduate student around 2006, for which he had already been disciplined in 2017 by, inter alia, losing a year's pay. He had committed no crime in having a relationship with a grown woman, but it was a breach of the professional rules he had agreed to. The real reason Princeton wanted him gone was Katz's refusal to toe the leftist party line on race after George Floyd's death in May 2020.

Katz wrote an article in *Quillette*, an online publication that encourages heterodox thought. One thing he objected to was the overt racism of "anti-racism" in advocating perquisites and pay for faculty "of color" that was not available to white (or presumably Asian, since they don't seem to count as "of color" in this context) faculty. Katz also dared to criticize a short-lived, radical campus group called the Black Justice League. One could debate the merits of his arguments while acknowledging that as a tenured professor he should be able to say what he likes, short of breaking the law or advocating the commission of a crime. But as Katz said later, "In the summer of George Floyd, certain opinions about the state of America that would have been considered normal only a few months earlier suddenly became anathema."[99]

A few minutes on YouTube watching some Princeton students critical of Katz tells all you need to know about their views. Their understanding of history is sophomoric, their expectations of the world are as arrogant as they are puerile, and their inability to comprehend the enormity of their good fortune to be living in our present age, let alone attending Princeton, is breathtaking. When Katz dared to challenge the Maoist student mob to consider another viewpoint, Princeton's president Eisgruber and most of the faculty turned on him in lockstep. The student with whom he'd had an affair 15 years earlier insisted for no apparent reason that Princeton look into her case, for which Katz had already been disciplined, again. An investigation (double jeopardy applying only in criminal law, not in campus kangaroo court) was resurrected, and Katz was eventually found by Princeton to have "not been fully honest and cooperative with an investigation into his sexual relationship with an undergraduate student" back in 2006 and 2007.[100] In the words of Professor Brian Caplan of George Mason University, "Princeton claimed to find new details that put the affair in a far worse light, justifying the revocation of Katz's tenure," and then fired him.[101] A professor who knew and taught ancient and obscure languages, and whose talent as a lecturer and teacher were celebrated, was sacrificed by a university to the woke gods.

Lest you be tempted to take Princeton seriously as the top national university it once was, know that it has recently decided that, in order to attract more minority students to its classics program, it will no longer require classics students to learn to read or write Greek or Latin.

In August 2020, after the rabid reaction to his *Quillette* piece but before the resurrected accusation concerning his 2006 and 2007 affair, Katz said at a seminar that "free speech is a bedrock principle. If we cannot agree on this, then we are lost as a nation." Katz is not alone. Peter Boghosian of Portland State, Kathleen Stock of Sussex University, Dorian Abbot of the University Chicago, and many other academics have been driven out of their institutions by craven administrators in fear of their ill-informed and intolerant student masters.

Professor Roland Fryer

Roland Fryer is an economics professor at Harvard who, according to Brown University economist Glenn Loury, is "not [just] the most gifted *black* economist of his generation, [but] the most gifted *economist* of his generation."[102] Fryer poked the woke bear by defying the dogma, popularized by lower-wattage academic Ibram X. Kendi, that all achievement gaps between races must be due to racism to the exclusion of all other factors. Fryer, who grew up poor and overcame many challenges himself, dared to ask hard questions of the "anti-racist" grifter establishment and, worse, crunch some numbers. As discussed, his research found that little of the efforts so far—pouring more money into school infrastructure and equipment, paying teachers more, or adopting woke curricula to pander to supposed cultural values—did much good in closing the enduring black–white–Asian achievement gap in school test scores.

What worked, not shockingly, was to set high expectations for poor and disadvantaged students and help them to meet them through longer hours working at school and home, rigorous academics, orderly classrooms, and student discipline. Fryer dares to ask questions and research taboos, like whether black students in some schools equate academic success, and the habits that bring it, with "acting white" and, thus, with race betrayal. His goal is to help struggling students to do better. Kendi and his ilk would rather throw in the towel and lower the bar for what is considered success, damning yet another generation of young blacks to the "soft bigotry of low expectations."[103]

Like Katz, Fryer was brought down by a sex scandal, in his case, vague accusations of sexual harassment that appear to boil down to coarse language used too freely among easily offended colleagues. A documentary by Rob Montz told the story.[104] Despite its best efforts, Harvard's internal Star Chamber faculty discipline process could only manage to get Fryer recommended for additional sensitivity training, but that didn't stop the chamber's members from using the accusations and the investigation itself as an excuse to curtail his teaching, research, and campus profile. As Loury says, "Those at Harvard responsible for this state of affairs should be utterly ashamed of themselves... I can't help but suspect that they have effectively buried vital research not because it was poorly done but because they found the results to be politically inconvenient."[105]

University of New Hampshire

The Ivies are bad, but less-elite schools have also put DEI in an almost sacred space in their priorities. In February 2024, the University of New Hampshire had to cut $14 million from its budget. To balance the books, the university elected to close its art museum and fire 75 staff, but chose to keep the DEI office open. The museum reportedly had the same budget as the college spends on DEI staff: about a million dollars a year.[106]

University of Michigan

Few American schools have invested more in DEI through money, staff, and reputation, than the University of Michigan, the Ivy League–adjacent academic powerhouse of the Midwest.

In November 2024, the university's controlling Board of Regents was reported to be considering defunding its massive DEI office.[107] According to an X post by Mark Perry, a former professor of economics at Michigan and now a scholar at the American Enterprise Institute (AEI), the Michigan DEI office employs at least 241 paid staff members whose main duties are to provide DEI programming and services as either their exclusive or primary job responsibility. In addition, 76 faculty or staff members work part-time as "DEI Unit Leads" advancing diversity efforts... [The AEI scholars] believe that the actual number of DEI staff at UM is actually significantly higher than 317, and likely exceeds 500 employees.[108]

Michigan has spent about $250 million on DEI programs in the past few years, but despite that huge investment, a late 2024 *New York Times* article alleged that instead of achieving its goals, DEI at Michigan had, in fact, created less unity and inclusion on campus.[109]

Michigan's programs, from engineering to the art museum, are suffused with DEI cant. In addition to indoctrinating both faculty and students with "anti-racism" and anti-bias training, Michigan uses "diversity statements" in staff hiring and promotion to weed out those applicants or candidates who do not sufficiently espouse the dogma. One hiring program called Collegiate Fellows is run by the National Center for Institutional Diversity, the university's in-house DEI advocacy center. It appears to have been designed explicitly to hire by race. Aspiring Collegiate Fellows are asked to submit diversity statements "addressing how they would advance D.E.I. goals" in specific ways. Not surprisingly, at least 80 percent of those hired through the program were "people of color."[110]

The state of Michigan's black population is about 14 percent, about the same as that of the United States as a whole. In the 1990s, with "affirmative action" programs allowing preferential treatment of applicants according to race, Michigan's black enrollment reached a peak of 9 percent. In 2006, Michigan voters passed a ballot initiative which banned all racial preferences in public education and employment. The University of Michigan launched a massive DEI plan in response to try to boost black enrollment by means other than direct racial preferences. The school created a central Office of Diversity, Equity, and Inclusion, and each of the university's schools had its own plan and staff. The university's main campus in Ann Arbor employed "nearly 16,000 nonfaculty employees," according to Nicholas Confessore, a ratio of administrators to teaching staff of two to one. The policing of professors' lessons and student speech, complaints against staff and students, and internal dissent rose to a totalitarian scale. The nadir was perhaps reached in 2022, when the school newspaper published an article about alleged "microaggressions" by a professor of cartoons.[111]

Despite all the DEI staff, money, and programming, the percentage of blacks enrolled as undergraduates at the University of Michigan is only about 5 percent today, and Confessore cites a 2022 campus survey in which "students and faculty members reported a less positive campus climate than at the program's start and less of a sense of belonging," and "were less likely to interact with people of a different race or religion or with different politics."[112] After two decades of saturation DEI, Confessore writes that "the most common attitude I encountered about D.E.I. during my visits to Ann Arbor was a kind of wary disdain."[113] As its model of including DEI in the hiring process to weed out non-believers has been adopted by other colleges, the fate of Michigan's DEI program has wider implications.

Can DEI Be Rooted Out from Higher Education?

In early 2023, the University of North Carolina (UNC) intended to set up a new School of Civic Life and Leadership to end "political constraints on what can be taught in university classes." The school planned to hire 20 professors from outside the existing UNC staff. The College Fix reported that the ratio of Democratic to Republican professors at UNC was 16 to one, but that at Ohio State it was "only" seven to one and at the University of Nebraska at Omaha it was five to one. *The Wall Street Journal* rightly applauds UNC's initiative, writing that "if change can happen there, maybe it can happen anywhere."[114] More recently, John Sailer of the National Association of Scholars reported that "the UNC Board of Governor's [sic] Committee on University Governance just passed a motion preventing compelled speech in admission and hiring... This policy will considerably limit or even prohibit diversity statements."[115]

In 2024, both the Massachusetts Institute of Technology (MIT) and Harvard's Faculty of Arts and Sciences said they would no longer require job candidates to submit diversity statements; such "compelled statements," MIT President Sally Kornbluth said, "constituted a form of compelled speech that do not work."[116] Nina Zipser, Harvard's dean for Faculty Affairs and Planning, said the university dropped the statements due to feedback from faculty who thought that they were "too narrow in the information they attempted to gather and relied on terms that, for many, especially international candidates, were difficult to interpret."[117]

In 2025, the Trump Administration was using federal research funding, civil rights laws, student visa approvals, and every other available leverage to fight woke colleges. The Administration wants universities to unwind their DEI offices, end racial discrimination in hiring and admissions, restore protection to women's sports and spaces, and stop tolerance of antisemitism among staff and students. As of early 2025, some schools, such as Columbia University, had agreed to the federal terms, while others, such as Harvard, were digging in for a long fight. However it ends, conservatives have at long last begun to put up a fight.

3. Professional Associations

Not surprisingly, the national associations that govern accreditation and professional standards are as woke as the colleges that indoctrinate their membership. Let's look at a few.

Bar Associations

At the national level, the American Bar Association (ABA) has 400,000 members and calls itself "the largest voluntary professional association in the world."[118] The ABA accredits most U.S. law schools and sets standards for the profession. In 2022, it adopted a new standard requiring law students to learn about "bias, cross-cultural competency, and racism."[119]

At the state level, as Aaron Withe writes in the *Federalist*, "many state bars file court briefs supporting progressive causes, sponsor programs pushing social justice agendas, publish magazines filled with left-leaning political content, and lobby for legislation straight from the progressive wish list."[120] As of May 2024, 31 states require lawyers to be members of the state's bar association. That month, the Freedom Foundation filed an amicus brief with the U.S. Supreme Court in *Crowe v. Oregon State Bar*, a case "challenging forced membership in state bar associations as violation of freedom of association."[121]

Constitutional lawyer Ilya Shapiro had a brief career as a law professor at Georgetown University. An awkward tweet he sent criticizing President Joe Biden's decision to nominate a black woman to the Supreme Court, rather than the best-qualified person, caused a backlash from the Left that eventually forced him to leave. He joined the Manhattan Institute as a scholar. In his book 2025 book *Lawless: The Miseducation of America's Elites*, Shapiro describes his experience at Georgetown and looks at American legal training in general.[122] He predicts that "[l]aw students who police their professors' microaggressions and demand the 'deplatforming' of 'harmful' speakers will eventually be on the federal bench."[123] Shapiro explains the concept of "movement lawyering," which the ABA supports because, it says, "support is needed as people take to the streets and hold spaces to collectively heal and as we work over the long haul to dismantle systems of oppression, including white supremacy, cis-heteropatriarchy, and capitalism in our country."[124] Movement lawyering, according to the Movement Law Lab, a group working to bring "the power of lawyers to social justice movements," seeks social change which "involves more than tinkering in the margins of systems, mitigating immediate harms or even changing laws. It requires redesigning the underlying systems and structures of society, shifting norms and culture, and most importantly changing who has economic and political power."[125]

Medical Associations

The American Medical Association (AMA) and the Association of American Medical Colleges (AAMC) are empowered to certify all U.S. medical schools. *The Federalist* reported that the AMA earned $300 million in 2023 from licensing fees from the Current Procedural Terminology (CPT) codes that doctors use to bill insurers. Those fees are paid for by companies for their employees, or by the federal government through Medicare and Medicaid. U.S. laws require the use of the CPT codes for federal programs, ensuring a monopoly for the AMA. Meanwhile, the AMA pays its CEO nearly $3 million a year and spends $25 million on lobbying Congress, advocating, among other things, "gender affirming care," which it calls "medically necessary."[126]

Meanwhile in 2022, the AAMC issued guidelines for faculty and students which state that U.S. has always had "systemic health and health care inequities grounded in racism, sexism, homophobia, classism, and other forms of discrimination."[127] The guidelines required medical school graduates to identify "systems of power, privilege, and oppression," learn "the impact of various systems of oppression on health and health care," and incorporate "dimensions of diversity into the patient's health assessment and treatment plan."[128] For faculty, the AAMC guidance required them to teach students "how knowledge of intersectionality informs clinical decision-making and practice" and "how systems of power, privilege, and oppression inform policies and practices and how to engage with systems to disrupt oppressive practices," reported *The Washington Free Beacon*.[129]

In medical schools, clinical courses have been reduced to make way for more social justice and social science offerings. The National Association of Scholars' John Sailer reports that Oregon Health & Science University was developing an "anti-racism and structural competency curriculum" for internal medicine residents,[130] while Georgetown University Hospital devised a "social medicine and health equity track" for trainee doctors to "explore the social, racial, cultural, and historical forces that shape health and illness."[131] Sailer reports that the American Board of Internal Medicine's charitable arm, the American Board of Internal Medicine (ABIM) Foundation, certifies internal medicine doctors and funded both curricula.[132] In the critical year 2020, he writes, the ABIM itself declared that it had "transitioned from being 'passively non-racist' to 'actively anti-racist'"—that is, full bore implementing CRT and DEI.[133]

Unfortunately, accreditors like the ABIM have enormous power to compel speech, belief, and action, as they control who gets into a very competitive and lucrative profession. The standards they set quickly become the norm, and resistance comes at a professional cost. The ABIM's certification exam, which doctors are required to take every ten years, added questions on "health equity" in 2021. DEI "competencies" are filled with woke jargon like "allyship," "microaggression," "intersectionality," "culturally responsive," "oppressive practices," and "social justice."

In 2022, *The Washington Free Beacon*'s investigative reporter Aaron Sibarium looked at a report by the AAMC titled "The Power of Collective Action: Assessing and Advancing Diversity, Equity, and Inclusion Efforts at AAMC Medical Schools."[134] He found that 70 percent of medical schools require students to take a course on DEI or "cultural competence," and 79 percent require that all hiring committees receive "unconscious bias" training or include faculty "equity advisors."[135]

Sibarium concludes: "At many medical schools, concerns about social justice have saturated every layer of institutional decision-making, particularly the hiring and admissions process."[136] Half of medical schools required job applicants to submit diversity statements, and more than two-thirds "require departments/units to assemble a diverse pool of candidates for faculty positions."[137] All 101 schools in the AAMC report said they used a "holistic admissions" process, which in practice means lowering the grade and test score requirements for favored students based on race. By lowering the average ability across classes, concerned doctors lament, medical schools inevitably have to lower standards so that students don't fail disproportionately by race. That will inevitably endanger patient care and health.

The AAMC report follows the AAMC's new, DEI-infused guidelines and is clearly intended to reward schools that meet its DEI goals and punish those that don't.

The orthodoxy of professional trade organizations on issues like COVID-19, DEI, and gender ideology has caused some members to split off and form rival groups. The reaction of the legacy media is as harsh as Chinese Communism against "splittists," or the Spanish Inquisition against heretics. The American College of Pediatricians (ACP) is a smaller, more conservative, pediatric association than the American Pediatric Association (APA). *The Washington Post* attacked the ACP in a hit piece, with Taylor Lorenz as one of the authors. (Lorenz is better known for controversial statements on social media, for instance calling President Joe Biden a "war criminal" and seeming to praise Luigi Mangione, accused assassin of the UnitedHealth CEO, and she eventually left the *Post*). The *Post* writers say that "internal documents [of the ACP] emphasize how religion and morality influence its positions." They claim that the ACP "promotes conversion therapy, a discredited practice intended to change the sexual orientation or gender identity of LGBTQ people," without noting the important distinction between conversion therapy aimed at sexual orientation and therapy intended to make children accept the biological reality of sex. The *Post* says that LGBTQ+ health advocate Kellan Baker accused the ACP of "intentionally and aggressively laundering pseudoscience through this veneer of respectability." That is the pot calling the kettle black while throwing stones from his glass house, since gender ideology is the apex of pseudo-science.[138]

The National Association of Independent Schools (NAIS)

The NAIS sets accreditation standards for more than 1,600 American private schools, writes John Sailer, and "requires members to practice 'cross-cultural competency' to promote 'diversity, inclusion, equity, and justice.'"[139] The NAIS claims that it "does not discriminate in violation of the law on the basis of race, religion, creed, color, sexual orientation, age, physical challenge, nation of origin, gender, or any other characteristic."[140] Yet, incredibly, in the 21st century, the NAIS has a special, apparently segregated, People of Color Conference, which it calls "the flagship of NAIS's commitment to equity and justice in teaching, learning, and sustainability for independent schools."[141] The NAIS resources for schools are not visible in detail online without a password, but although the title of its Resource Guide of courses, seminars, and other products is now titled "Inclusion and Belonging," it is replete with DEI in all its manifestations and buzzwords.[142]

4. Woke Federal Agencies

The Biden Administration was staffed with young, leftwing, social-activist political appointees, fresh from woke universities. Under President Biden, the most progressive wing of the Democratic Party penetrated every agency, injecting gender ideology and the race agenda of DEI. It is probably thanks to the wing's militancy that President Biden churned out so many executive orders insisting on the primacy of sexual minorities and divisive DEI policies that put race and sex above merit and performance. These ideologies have penetrated not just the soft targets, like the

Environmental Protection Agency (EPA) and the State Department, which were ripe for the plucking, but the formerly harder, badge-and-gun, cloak-and-dagger agencies like the CIA, the FBI, and the National Security Agency. What follows is not an exhaustive list, merely some illustrative examples of this phenomenon:

The U.S. Commission on Civil Rights (USCCR)

USCCR Chair Rochelle Garza refused to go gently when President Trump lawfully appointed a new chair. As Heritage Foundation scholar and former Department of Justice official Hans von Spakovsky wrote in March 2025, the USCCR was established in 1957 and is charged with "investigating and reporting on important civil rights issues."[143] It has eight members, four appointed by the president, two from the House of Representatives, and two from the Senate. As of March 2025, it was evenly split between Republican and Democratic members. On January 20, President Trump chose Commissioner Peter Kirsanow as the new chairman, but Garza "refused to yield her chairmanship to the vice-chair or Kirsanow," Von Spakovsky writes, despite the USCCR's governing law stating clearly that in the absence of a chair, the vice chair is to act as chairperson.[144] Von Spakovsky calls Garza "a DEI activist" based on her political campaigns and activity in Texas, which center on her race and sex identity, abortion, and civil and immigrant rights. She formerly worked as a lawyer at the American Civil Liberties Union (ACLU), which routinely supports illegal migrants in litigation and resists enforcement of immigration law.[145] As chair, Garza ran the Texas Civil Rights Project, which "envisions a border state that respects the right to migrate."[146]

The U.S. Department of Education

Neetu Arnold of the *City Journal* reported on grants made by the U.S. Department of Education (DoE) through its Education Innovation and Research (EIR) program that put DEI ahead of actual qualifications.[147] This program's budget was $284 million in 2023. As Arnold writes, the EIR program funded grants for "restorative justice," a woke concept that evades punishment for misbehavior in favor of more complicated and less effective forms of accountability, and "culturally responsive" teaching, which usually means holding miscreant students to lower standards on the (racist and condescending) assumption that some cultures simply have lower standards than others.

Worse, the EIR grants take into account irrelevant, ideological factors that skew decisions in favor of woke recipients. Starting in 2022, the DoE considered "whether prospective grant recipients would 'encourage' applications for employment from persons who are members of groups that have traditionally been underrepresented based on race, color, national origin, gender, age, or disability.'"[148] In brief, this means that grant applicants are encouraged to use discriminatory hiring to boost hiring of "underrepresented" groups for their projects. Without regard to merit, it appears the EIR program made several grants on the basis that recipients would hire non-white, non-male staff for their projects if granted the federal money.

In January 2025, President Trump appointed Linda McMahon as Secretary of Education, calling on her to "send Education BACK TO THE STATES."[149] In February, the Trump Administration cut $600 million from teacher "development" programs, including "diversity, equity, and inclusion." In March, President Trump signed an executive order directing "the Secretary of Education to take all necessary steps to facilitate the closure of the Department of Education and return education authority to the States."[150]

The National Institutes of Health (NIH)

No sector of the federal government lost more credibility over the past five years than the health and medical sector. The federal management of COVID-19 starting in 2020 was characterized by obfuscation, suppression of information, and rigorous efforts to discredit diverse views. COVID-19 was a catalyst, but the ideology that allowed it to remove common sense from "the science" was already well in place at the NIH, the source of billions in annual federal research funding. As the National Review's Anthony Mills wrote in 2025 when it was all over, "[f]ollow the science became a rallying cry for those on the left – a badge of tribal affiliation as well as a way to rationalize their policy preferences while dismissing dissent."[151]

Christopher Rufo of the Manhattan Institute explains how DEI "corrupted the NIH" over time.[152] President Biden's executive orders to put "equity" at the center of everything the government does were taken to heart at most agencies, including the NIH. As part of its five-year strategic equity plan, the NIH has an Office of Equity, Diversity, and Inclusion (OEDI) with more than 50 employees, led by a chief officer for scientific workforce diversity. As Rufo found, the NIH approach is guided by CRT and social science, not science. The OEDI created "digital information hubs" on "Understanding Systemic Racism" and "Racism in Health." NIH training courses discussed "liberatory race-conscious mentorship" conducted "through the framework of critical race theory."[153] "Health equity" is a belief that "people of color often have worse health outcomes than white people because of racism, increased barriers to accessing health care and other factors,"[154] as opposed to genetics, lifestyle, environment, diet, and other individual factors.

Rufo's calls "health equity"

> a trendy new academic discipline that, in theory, studies health disparities between groups—for example, African-Americans' disproportionately high rates of Alzheimer's—and tries to identify causes and find solutions. In practice, however, Health Equity is critical race theory's window into medical science, yielding trifling grievance reports focused not on medical outcomes but on the demographics of the medical-research workforce itself.[155]

NIH grants followed the theme of CRT and "health equity." One grant for $3 million to Columbia University was to study how black people use Twitter. Another $3 million went to Yale to track gay men with GPS monitors, and another $3.7 million to Stanford to study the effect of cross-sex hormones on the neurodevelopment of "transgender adolescents."[156]

The NIH also created a program in 2021 used, in Rufo's words, "explicitly to justify increasing minority hiring," which likely violates equal employment law. Rufo concludes that "[t]he only way to clean up our medical research institutions, and, by extension, our federal grantmaking agencies, is put the science back in medical science—and leave the ideology at the door."[157]

President Trump started down that road when he appointed Dr. Jayanta Bhattacharya, one of the signatories of the Great Barrington Declaration in 2020, as director of the NIH. The Declaration signatories wrote in 2020 that "[a]s infectious disease epidemiologists and public health scientists we have grave concerns about the damaging physical and mental health impacts of the prevailing COVID-19 policies, and recommend an approach we call Focused Protection." What they meant by that was ending the lockdown policies that ruined businesses and wreaked havoc in families and education. Instead, they argued for "Focused Protection," which "is to allow those who are at minimal risk of death to live their lives normally to build up immunity to the virus through natural infection, while better protecting those who are at highest risk."[158]

Those running the pandemic response for the federal government at the time, including Francis Collins of the NIH and Anthony Fauci of the National Institute of Allergy and Infectious Diseases, successfully stomped on the Declaration and all who wrote it, causing reputational damage—and arguably, huge economic and social harm.[159] In retrospect, with examples of countries like Sweden, which followed the Focused Protection approach, the Barrington signatories appear to have been right. Bhattacharya was confirmed as NIH director in March 2025.[160]

As part of the Trump Administration's effort to cut costs and eliminate programs and grants that illegally discriminate on the basis of race, the NIH cut grants funding research into "health equity." The theory "that people of color often have worse health outcomes than white people because of racism, increased barriers to accessing health care and other factors" has been accepted as a "fact [that] has been widely been adopted by researchers, health organizations, providers and the medical establishment," according to Jessie Hellmann of Roll Call.[161] To what extent the "worse health outcomes" are attributed to racism, rather than "other factors" like lifestyle, weight, and genetics is left unclear and uninvestigated, leaving activists free to place all blame for disparities in health between groups on "racism," with "health equity" as the chosen solution. "Health equity" was dogma under the Biden Administration, but the NIH letters issued under the Trump administration which ended the "health equity" research grants counter that such research projects based on "amorphous equity objectives" are "antithetical to the scientific inquiry, do nothing to expand our knowledge of living systems, provide low returns on investment, and ultimately do not enhance health, lengthen life, or reduce illness."[162]

The National Aeronautics and Space Administration (NASA)

The storied agency that put the first man on the moon in 1969 has lost much of its steam. The U.S. is a partner in the International Space Station (ISS), and American astronauts have to hitch a ride on Russian craft to get there. This past year, astronauts Butch Wilmore and Sunita Williams were stuck on the ISS for nine months because of a failure in the Boeing ship that NASA had contracted to get them back home. Meanwhile, Elon Musk's Space X has been demonstrating remarkable achievements, from making rocket boosters re-usable to catching them with incredible precision on the launch frame, ready for reconditioning. It was SpaceX that finally brought Wilmore and Williams home, in March 2025.[163]

Under the Biden Administration, NASA reportedly spent millions of dollars from its $20 billion annual budget on DEI programs, many of which had nothing to do with space exploration. As with other federal agencies, NASA implemented the Biden executive orders on DEI, race, and gender identity, by infusing DEI in everything from strategic planning to annual employee evaluations. NASA made grants to universities for "environmental justice," diversity, and "inclusive practices," and to one college to make "NASA's heliophysics material 'more relevant and open to the Latinx and Native American communities.'"[164] These NASA grants focused on diversity and inclusion for political and ideological reasons, not to increase the efficiency or quality of the space program and related science programs.

Though DEI is not the main or only reason behind NASA's current funding problems and mission failures, it is the mindset that underlies America's failing institutions and declining competitiveness in general. It is also hard to remove, once ideological capture is complete. NASA initially appeared to comply with the executive order to root out DEI in March 2025, when the agency announced the closure of its DEI offices.[165] However, at NASA's Jet Propulsion Laboratory (JPL), former Chief Inclusion Officer Neela Rajendra was simply re-titled to "Chief Team Excellence and Employee Success Officer," a supposedly new job which appears to assume the duties of her old job.[166] The JPL also reportedly retained its race-based "affinity groups" and other DEI policies.[167] Similar legerdemain has been reported in many federal agencies, as well as universities receiving federal funding.

The National Security Agency (NSA)

The NSA is less famous than the CIA but crucial to U.S. security. The NSA gathers and analyzes "signals intelligence," meaning all forms of electronic communication, for the federal government, mostly from a giant compound in Fort Meade, Maryland.

In May 2022, the NSA published a "glossary of terms and language commonly used in dialogue regarding diversity,"[168] which was publicized by *The Daily Wire* and others more than a year later. The 34-page glossary "pushes blatantly left-wing views on race and sex," writes Spencer Lindquist, and "explicitly endorses the tenets of Critical Race Theory and Queer Theory."[169] It defines hundreds of social-justice terms, including "white fragility," "transmisogyny," "settler colonialism" (defined as "oppressive governance...and enforcement of codes of superiority"), "White privilege" (an "unquestioned and unearned set of advantages, entitlements, benefits, and choices bestowed on people solely because they are white"), and "structural racism" (a "feature of the social, economic, and political systems in which we all exist"). The NSA glossary goes beyond merely defining words to policing how employees use them, for example advocating the use of made-up pronouns and advising readers not to use language that "genders bodies nonconsensually and plays into cissexism" or is otherwise "problematic."

The NSA guide's obsession with gender ideology and terminology made it slightly less shocking when two years later, in February 2025, Christopher Rufo revealed that the NSA was investigating staff who had been using an authorized chat program, meant for them "to discuss security matters," instead to "talk about sexually-explicit topics."[170] For more than two years, as was later reported in more detail in *The Daily Wire* and other outlets, a group of employees had engaged in "wide-ranging discussions of sex, kink, polyamory, and castration" on the government-sanctioned platform. Newly confirmed director of National Intelligence Tulsi Gabbard ended up firing more than 100 staffers that she said had been "brazen in using an NSA platform intended for professional use to conduct this kind of really, really horrific behavior." In the usual shoot-the-messenger style, Martin Matishak of *The Record* described Rufo, a journalist, filmmaker, and now scholar at the Manhattan Institute, as a "right-wing activist."

Small Business Administration

For decades, federal contracts have been awarded based on race preference. Section 8(a) of the Small Business Act allows "socially and economically disadvantaged" businesses to get federal contracts with limited or no competition. To get around the Supreme Court's ban on overt racial discrimination, Judge Glock reported in the *City Journal*, the Small Business Administration has been asking applicants for loans to write essays about their "social disadvantage." The agency recommended that "business owners write about their race, ethnic origin, sexual orientation" and how it led them to suffer discrimination or bias. These "discrimination essays" are clearly a proxy for race, based on which the SBA has awarded billions of dollars in federal contracts.[171]

5. Non-Governmental Organizations (NGOs)

A comprehensive list of woke NGOs would need several books and would in any case be a moving target. It's not surprising that there are NGOs dedicated to helping illegal migrants, keeping criminals out of jail, helping children to "transition" to the opposite sex, and furthering all manner of leftwing causes. Much of their funding comes from individual donors, including well-known billionaire business and entertainment moguls, and woke foundations. Some national foundations which were started by conservative businessmen generations ago have veered left over time, following the rule of politics attributed to Robert Conquest: "any organization not explicitly and constitutionally right-wing will sooner or later become left-wing."[172]

Community Movement Builders

It's well known that billionaires like George Soros and Netflix founder Reid Hoffman fund leftwing causes. In June 2025, the *Washington Free Beacon* reported on the funding behind Community Movement Builders, an Atlanta, GA nonprofit run by Kamau Franklin that takes a raft of far-left positions including anti-capitalism and supporting black separatist terrorists convicted of murdering police officers.[173] Steve Jobs' widow Laurene Powell Jobs, Google founder Eric Schmidt, and the Soros-backed Tides Foundation all reportedly gave money to Community Movement Builders, which referred to "the illegal occupation of Palestine by the so called 'i$raeli' occupation entity." A statement endorsed by various activist organizations, and Franklin, called the murder of Sarah Milgrim and Yaron Lischinsky in Washington, DC in May 2025 "fully justified" and "morally righteous."

Thanks to excellent reporting on new media, the power of dark money—meaning untraceable contributions distributed through a chain of cut-out entities, or corporate middlemen that can obscure the source of funds—is also becoming clear.[174] But what has shocked Americans is to learn that much of the funding that advances the leftwing agenda actually comes from their own tax dollars. One of the overlooked scandals of the Biden Administration is how billions of taxpayer dollars were funneled to NGOs created by partisan Democrats with ties to the Biden or Obama Administration. Many appeared out of nowhere, as if they anticipated the funds and were vehicles for receiving them.

At the end of the Biden Administration, reporters uncovered how the Environmental Protection Agency (EPA) was rushing to spend billions of dollars appropriated by Congress in a rush before the November election and a potential Republican win. The misnamed Inflation Reduction Act (IRA) of 2022 was nick-named the Green New Deal, because it did nothing to fight inflation and instead pumped billions into Democrats' wish-list projects including their climate change agenda. The IRA included a $375 billion climate fund to spend on green energy projects and subsidies to consumers. President Biden picked former Bill Clinton Chief of Staff John Podesta to run the fund. Many of the recipient organizations of the climate money hadn't even existed before the IRA was passed. As the *New York Post* reported, they included the Climate United Fund of Bethesda, Maryland, which received $7 billion but was only incorporated in November 2023, a few months before getting the massive cash dump. The *New York Post* lists at least seven other new and unknown NGOs that among them received around $20 billion in federal grants.[175] Most of them were owned, run, and staffed by people with ties to previous Democratic presidential Administrations or Democratic politics. One of them was Power Forward Communities.

Power Forward Communities (PFC)

This "coalition of some of the country's most trusted housing, climate, and community investment groups"[176] was founded in the middle of the Biden Administration, apparently in preparation to receive grants from federal spending bills, such as the IRA and Infrastructure Investment and Jobs Act. In 2023, PFC reported only $100 in revenue.[177] In 2023, fresh from her loss in the election for Georgia governor, Stacey Abrams took a job with Rewiring America, one of the partners in PFC.[178] It's hard to see what expertise Abrams brought to the enterprise other than her political connections. According to Fox News, Rewiring America's donors "are shielded from public view," and it "does not file federal tax forms since it is sponsored by the Windward Fund, a nonprofit that is part of the billion-dollar dark money network managed by the Washington, D.C.-based Arabella Advisors."[179]

Abrams told MSNBC that she'd run a program for Rewiring America in a town in Georgia that replaced old appliances with energy-efficient ones.[180] In effect, she was using federal funds to buy people new stuff—providing "new lamps for old" in an area with a high concentration of Democratic voters.

In August 2024, PFC announced the receipt of $2 billion in grant money from the EPA to "affordably decarbonize American homes, boost local economies." The consortium claimed that the federal money would somehow "mobilize additional tens of billions of dollars of private capital to improve Americans' homes."[181] The affair became a scandal in March 2025, because the EPA had put $20 billion dollars in banks to stop the incoming Trump Administration from cutting the intended grants. To what extent Abrams' salary at Rewiring America came from federal grants is unclear. But the link between billions of federal funding made possible by a Democratic Administration and the politically connected recipients was clear.

In 2025, the Georgia Ethics Commission fined the New Georgia Project, an NGO Abrams founded in 2013, $300,000—a state record—for violating campaign finance laws by not disclosing contributions and spending when it supported Abrams in the 2018 governor's race.[182] In that race, Abrams reported her net worth as $109,000. In the 2022 governor's race, her net worth had grown to $3.17 million.[183]

Black Lives Matter (BLM)

BLM rode the wave of indignation over George Floyd in 2020 to amass riches—for its founders, not the black lives it purports to care about. Journalist and Heritage Foundation analyst Mike Gonzalez literally wrote the book about BLM.[184] In a July 2023 article, he explained the Marxist roots and motivations of its founders.[185] Gonzalez traces BLM's origins to 2013, when Alicia Garza of Oakland, California, started it after the acquittal of George Zimmerman in the fatal shooting of Trayvon Martin. Garza and the two other BLM founders, Patrisse Cullors and Opal Tometi, "were hard-boiled Marxists who had been waiting in the wings to revolutionize America for years,"[186] writes Gonzalez.

BLM really took off in what the media called—and still call—the "racial reckoning" after George Floyd died in police custody in Minneapolis on May 25, 2020. Based on what Gonzalez calls a "self-evidently farcical idea that America is systemically racist and oppressive," the DEI complex grew in academia, government, and industry. Profiting from this same wave of corporate and individual guilt, BLM solicited large donations from American companies and many small donations from individuals—more than $90 million in 2020 alone.[187]

Gonzalez' accusation that BLM's founders were Marxists is literal, not figurative. Cullors, Garza, and Tometi belonged to a series of far-left organizations, including the U.S. Social Forum, which was inspired by Venezuelan socialist dictator Hugo Chavez at the World Social Forum in Caracas. Garza was on the organizing committee of the first U.S. Social Forum in 2007, notes Gonzalez, and out of this grew the National Domestic Workers Alliance. The alliance paid for her to be in Ferguson, Missouri, after the police shooting of Michael Brown in 2014. The Ferguson incident was blown up into a race issue by activists, although the police officer was exonerated after a Department of Justice investigation, and the claim that Brown had approached him saying "hands up, don't shoot" was debunked by eyewitnesses.[188] *Washington Post* columnist

Jonathan Capehart told NPR a year later that he regretted "the building of a movement [BLM] on the false rumors" that Michael Brown was trying to surrender and had his hands up,[189] but the false narrative blotted out the truth thanks to supportive and blinkered coverage by the national media.

The Black Lives Matter Global Network Foundation (BLMGNF) was incorporated in 2017 to raise money, which would then be distributed to local groups through Black Lives Matter Grassroots (BLMGR). The BLMGNF did not disclose any financial information until 2020, when it became a nonprofit under section 501(c)(3) of the tax code. (As someone who set up a 501(c)(3) recently, I can attest that it does not take three years.) Between 2017 and 2020, the BLMGNF channeled its donations through an already established charity, as the law permits, which allowed it to hide its donations and expenditures.

When information finally came out in 2020, the BLMGNF disclosed that it had bought a $6 million house in Los Angeles and another residence for $6.3 million in Toronto, Canada. How these deluxe properties would benefit black lives other than the BLM executives was never made clear. It's hard to see what good came of all the money that BLM took since 2020. Local leaders complained that the money did not trickle down to them from the BLMGNF. The founder of the St. Paul, Minnesota, chapter, Rashad Turner, quit BLM, saying "after a year on the inside, I learned they had little concern for rebuilding black families, and they cared even less about improving the quality of education for students in Minneapolis."[190]

The BLMGNF hired Shalomyah Bowers, a board member, to help with its finances. In 2022, Bowers was sued by BLMGR members, who alleged that he stole more than $10 million. Bowers had his own consulting firm, which was paid $2 million by BLMGNF in 2020, according to the *Daily Mail*.[191] The BLMGNF's predictable tactic was to play the race card, claiming that the BLMGR people suing Bowers were "falling victim to the carceral logic and social violence that fuels the legal system," and that by suing Bowers, BLMGR was acting like "our white oppressors" in using a "criminal legal system which is propped up by white supremacy…to solve movement disputes."

The BLMGNF board responded to the suit saying that it had wanted to avoid going to court, to "stay true to the principles of abolition," and that the BLMGR lawsuit was taking "the same steps of our white oppressors" to "utilize the criminal legal system which is propped up by white supremacy."[192]

6. Woke Companies

Many American companies have followed academia, the media, and NGOs in putting "equity" ahead of equal opportunity and embedding CRT and DEI in everything from recruitment to marketing. Many U.S. institutions, including schools, universities, companies and professional associations, super-charged their existing diversity initiatives to recruit black employees after the death of George Floyd in 2020. In 2021, companies in the Standard and Poor's Top 100 hired more than 300,000 people, and according to Bloomberg, 94 percent were "people of color."[193] This is an incredible statistic, given that whites still make up 58 percent of the country and, presumably, a similar proportion of job applicants. Were the races reversed, such a proportion would inevitably produce accusations of racism due to the "disparate impact" on the losing race that got only 4 percent of the jobs, but the Bloomberg report attracted little notice in the legacy media.

Here are a few examples of major corporations putting "equity" over equal opportunity.

Just Google "Diversity Hiring"

Like many U.S. companies, Google is keen to hire a diverse workforce. The realities of their recruitment pipeline, from top-ranked schools domestically and from abroad (mostly India) through the H1-B work visa, result in an employee population that is mostly Asian and European. An attempt to recruit engineers at Historically Black Colleges and Universities (HBCUs) failed to make much of a difference.[194] Google ranked colleges as "elite," "tier 1," or "tier 2." There were no HCBUs represented in these tiers, although they graduated many computer science majors. Google called colleges whose students needed extensive preparation to be ready for work at the company "long-tail schools." HCBUs were in this category.

Google chief executive Sundar Pichai promised to spend $175 million to promote racial equity after the 2020 George Floyd riots. Google then proposed a partnership with Howard University in Washington, DC, which included sending a company engineer to teach an introductory computer science class, because, according to the proposal document, "HBCU CS [computer science] students struggle with the most basic of coding, algorithms and data structures." The pilot resulted in ten Howard students getting internships at Google, but the company took flack for the effort both from HCBUs that felt the programs didn't end up hiring enough graduates, and from conservatives who saw them as discriminatory.

Morgan Stanley

The bank Morgan Stanley also ramped up DEI efforts, including special hiring and training programs for black recruits after 2020. The bank graded managers on recruiting women and favored minorities, tying pay and bonuses to these achievements. Not surprisingly, three-fifths of Morgan Stanley's hires in at least one state in 2023 were women or minorities. The DEI efforts ended in recrimination, lawsuits, and bad feelings all round by 2025 according to AnnaMaria Andriotis and Lauren Weber in *The Wall Street Journal*.[195] Some black employees complained that they did not receive the jobs, pay, or bonuses they expected after participating in special recruitment and mentoring programs. Some white executives complained that they were pressured to hire non-white job applicants and not to fire low-performing employees who were women or favored minorities. A "Black leadership program" was disparaged by some who had to take it as "special education."[196] For its efforts, Morgan Stanley was sued by both white and black employees.

After the Supreme Court ruling in *Students for Fair Admission v. Harvard* in 2023 and Trump Administration action against discriminatory college and corporate scholarships and programs, Morgan Stanley quietly revised its corporate labeling. The bank removed explicit hiring quotas from its annual report and changed the name of a program from "women and multicultural entrepreneurs" to "early-stage innovators," before finally calling it an "Inclusive and Sustainable Ventures Lab."[197]

Lockheed

In June 2025, a whistleblower at the defense contracting giant Lockheed Martin alleged that management overtly discriminated in awarding employee bonuses in 2022, urged on by the company's Human Resources director. According to emails seen by the *City Journal*'s Chris Rufo, the whistleblower was expressly instructed to add 18 minorities to the bonus list and remove 18 "non-minority" [white] employees.[198] Rufo reported that Lockheed has already "adopted radical DEI policies" in training programs for staff. The company, which makes the F-35 fighter, responded to Trump's Executive Orders banning discriminatory DEI programs, but the revelation of such clear disparate treatment of employees based on race may open up Lockheed, and other violators of equal rights laws, to legal action by employees, or the Department of Justice's Civil Rights Division, which under Harmeet Dhillon has turned from enforcing dubious and likely illegal notions of "equity" to enforcing equal treatment, as the law requires.

Conclusion

Woke ideology has penetrated every type of American institution, if not every single institution. Some redoubts remain, and a few new challengers to established leftwing universities, foundations, and think tanks are emerging. Given that leftist dogma like CRT and DEI is strongest in K–12 schools as well as higher education, the challenge today is not only removing it bit by bit from all the institutions into which graduates feed, but also fixing the indoctrination at the source. School choice, home schooling, and returning sanity to school boards and local governments are some of the key political battles to wage.

A person to follow: Christopher F. Rufo, Manhattan Institute, https://manhattan.institute/person/christopher-f-rufo.

A book to read: *Woke Racism: How a New Religion Has Betrayed Black America*, by John McWhorter, 2021.

A group to support: Alliance Defending Freedom, national and international offices, https://adflegal.org/.

Chapter 3

The Third Commandment:
You Shall Forget Your Past (It's "Problematic")

Perhaps one of the most harmful things that the contemporary Left commands us to do is to forget our past. Despite philosopher George Santayana's adage that those who forget the past are doomed to repeat it, leftists today borrow straight from George Orwell and command us to forget everything that is inconvenient to their partisan narratives or that threatens their ability to present every issue under the sun as infused with racism, sexism, homophobia, and xenophobia. Once we have forgotten our past, the woke literati can inject their revisionist faux history directly into our minds with the assistance of compliant media and school systems fearful of mistakenly being on the wrong side of leftwing cancel culture. In Western countries, whose demographics have been changing radically in recent decades, activist pseudo-intellectuals try to convince entire societies that everything about their histories is either false, problematic, or evil.

It's true that America's history has missing chapters. For much of our past, as in the past of other countries, women and certain minorities were prevented from working and exercising their talents freely. We will never know what we have lost; but we can tell all the stories we can, and there are many left to tell. For example, the *Journal of Free Black Thought* has an American Heroes series that describes the life and achievements of Americans who haven't received adequate historiography.

As part of the series, Jennifer Richmond gives a preview of her upcoming book about Hallie Quinn Brown, education and women's rights advocate.[1] Born in 1840s Pittsburgh to enslaved parents, Brown attended Wilberforce University in Ohio and then became a teacher, and later Dean of Women at the Tuskegee Institute in Alabama. She advocated women's rights and suffrage, traveling inside the United States and to Europe, Africa, and the Caribbean to speak. Renowned for both her advocacy and her rhetorical style, Brown taught that "education is the key to unlock the golden door of freedom."

Another lost story worthy of inclusion could be Sophie Mousseau, daughter of a French-Canadian trader and an Oglala Lakota woman. Martha Sandweiss wrote a book, *The Girl in the Middle: A Recovered History of the American West,* which illustrates not only the life of an extraordinary woman, but the clash between European settlers and plains Indian tribes in the mid-19th century.[2]

Given the low level of achievement in American history in public schools, and the minimal reading most children now do, it's very likely that most have never heard of Adams and Jefferson, let alone figures like Mousseau and Brown. But instead of celebrating and adding Brown and others to our existing historical framework, thus enriching us all, the modern Left seems more intent on erasing or minimizing the European contributions.

Cancelling the West

One of the main reasons the Western Left wants to cancel its own history is that the past provides a basis of comparison for the efficacy of today's policies, and the Left does not like it when it becomes apparent that certain ideas are either useless or make bad situations worse. Anyone who attempts to work from a set of common, shared understandings of historical narratives that are not entirely negative threatens the progressive stance that everyone and everything is racist, sexist, homophobic, transphobic, and on and on.

In addition to hatred of Western ancestors, achievements, and values, modern leftists want us to forget our history so that they can memory-hole the sad history of communism, and the communism-lite known as socialism. As the people who lived through the mass killings caused or ordered by communist leaders, such as Lenin, Stalin, Mao Zedong, and Pol Pot, are dying off, no one is left to tell young activists that socialism was not only tried, but that it was a disaster. Leftists especially want us to forget the lesson of history that one can only soak the rich so much before they pack up and leave. As Lewis Andrews writes in *The Spectator*, European countries that taxed their wealthy too much ended up losing them to other countries with lower tax rates, and didn't even make net revenue from taxes on assets.[3]

Senator Elizabeth Warren, a Democrat from Massachusetts, has advocated an Ultra-Millionaire Tax of 2 percent on a person's net worth above $50 million, rising to 3 percent for every dollar above $1 billion in net assets. Andrews describes how imperial Rome's administrative state and defense requirements put the government in permanent budget deficit and debt. Rome tried a wealth tax on the assets of the rich, after tapping out the ancient world's primitive inflationary tools: diluting the precious metal percentage in coins and clipping small pieces off them to make new ones. But taxes on all manner of wealth, restrictions on what workers could do for a living, and other coercive measures failed to save the republic— and even caused some Roman citizens to emigrate to live among the barbarian Germans.

Burying the knowledge and understanding of how Rome rose and fell, and the history of past civilizations and political systems in general, allows the Left to keep claiming that socialism works, and that "real socialism" hasn't been tried yet. In fact, it has indeed been tried, on several continents and in a variety of countries from Angola to Venezuela, and the result every time has been a combination of economic stagnation, political repression, and popular misery. As the *Cornell Review* summarizes, "[o]ver the past 100 years or so, socialist experiments around the world unleashed a vast tide of tyranny, starvation, and mass murder on a scale never seen before in human history."[4] Anyone interested learning more about the inhumanity of communism around the world can visit the Victims of Communism Museum in Washington, DC.

The 1619 Project

There has perhaps never been such an egregious effort to rewrite history as the 1619 Project, published by *The New York Times* in 2019.[5] The 1619 Project, which appeared as a series of essays in the *Times* and its related publications, attempts to reframe American history entirely from the perspective of the role of slavery. According to the project, no part of

American history can be understood without slavery and white racism. The project recasts America's founding date from 1776 to 1619, the year the first slave ship arrived in Virginia. According to its lead author Nikole Hannah-Jones, the political rebellion against the king of England, formalized by the signing of the Declaration of Independence, is not the foundational date of the forming of the United States of America. Rather, Hannah-Jones argues, the year 1619 should be considered as the founding of the country because the arrival of slaves on American shores began the history of racism that serves as the substructure for understanding all subsequent American history.[6]

The 1619 Project argues that the American Revolution was not about liberty, democracy, and self-governance, but about enshrining white racism in the form of slavery in the American system. Some of the most renowned scholars of American history have debunked this claim, citing the lack of evidence that slavery was at the forefront of the thinking of the American patriots.[7] On the contrary, most evidence shows that they genuinely intended to build a country based on freedom and equality.[8] The fierce debates during the constitutional convention about the future of slavery are evidence that it was a grudging compromise between competing visions, rather than an agreed basis for the foundation of the country. Further, the Constitution provides the basis on which slavery was abolished. The notion that the founders who wrote the Declaration of Independence and the Constitution were "secretly" trying to formally institutionalize slavery, as opposed to disagreeing strongly on the subject, isn't supported by what they actually wrote and said.

The great writer and educator Frederick Douglass, himself formerly enslaved, vehemently attacked the practice of slavery and racist laws, and also said this:

> [T]here is no matter in respect to which, the people of the North have allowed themselves to be so ruinously imposed upon, as that of the pro-slavery character of the Constitution. In that instrument I hold there is neither warrant, license, nor sanction of the hateful thing; but, interpreted as it ought to be interpreted, the Constitution is a glorious liberty document. Read its preamble, consider its purposes. Is slavery among them? Is it at the gateway? or is it in the temple? It is neither.
> ...(I)f the Constitution were intended to be, by its framers and

adopters, a slave-holding instrument, why neither slavery, slave-holding, nor slave can anywhere be found in it? ...Now, take the Constitution according to its plain reading, and I defy the presentation of a single pro-slavery clause in it. On the other hand it will be found to contain principles and purposes, entirely hostile to the existence of slavery.... While drawing encouragement from the Declaration of Independence, the great principles it contains, and the genius of American Institutions, my spirit is also cheered by the obvious tendencies of the age.[9]

The 1619 Project alleges that "we aren't taught" about black history and America's legacy of racial discrimination. As a former U.S. history teacher, I can attest that this is nonsense. U.S. history is taught in both eighth and 11th grades, and slavery, segregation, and the mistreatment of Indian tribes are well covered in both curricula. That's not to say that students are paying attention and actually learn anything. James Oakes, author of several books on slavery, declares: "You were taught this. Unless you didn't bother to take a US history class, or you didn't do the reading, or you weren't paying attention to the lectures, or you forgot."[10]

Despite the many critiques of the scholarship found in the 1619 Project, *The New York Times* continues to stand by its veracity, and Hannah-Jones was awarded a Pulitzer Prize for work that, while offering some insightful discussion of the painful history of slavery in America, is polemic rather than historiography. The University of North Carolina offered Hannah-Jones a professorship, which she ultimately declined after members of the school's board of trustees questioned the quality of her scholarship.[11]

The goal of the 1619 Project is ostensibly to initiate a reckoning with painful and shameful aspects of American history, and to encourage a new path for positive inter-racial relations. But the ulterior motive seems clear: to discredit the accomplishments of the United States' colonial founders and their descendants. In the context of the 17th and 18th centuries, slavery was, tragically, an economic norm in the Americas, where numerous countries relied on slave labor as an early basis of their economy. In fact, more than 90 percent of Africans enslaved and sent to the Americas went to the Caribbean islands and South America, notably Cuba and Brazil, with only around 6 percent going to the British colonies and, subsequently, the United States.[12]

The 1619 Project does not pull the wool from our eyes, as its authors claim. In terms of morality, the tension between the Enlightenment principles of the founders and the evil of slavery sowed the seeds of its eventual demise, in a Civil War that cost 600,000 lives. Economically, the advantages imparted by the horrific transatlantic slave trade no doubt contributed something to the United States' rise to becoming the world's predominant power by the 20th century. But it was not as important as the centuries of colonization, immigration, and collective work by Europeans. "America was built by slaves" is a rhetorical flourish, not a historically defensible proposition.

Black Americans contributed, in some measure, as did all groups who came to this land over the past 40,000 years, by land across the frozen Bering Sea or by ship from everywhere on Earth, to the creation of our unique, hybrid American culture,[13] but claims that America was mostly built on slavery are simply not true. Nevertheless, the Smithsonian's National Museum of African American History and Culture claims that "[b]y 1860 four million enslaved people produced well over 60 percent of the nation's wealth," a canard repeated elsewhere and often.[14] Economic historian Paul Rhode looked at the data and found it wildly inaccurate to state that half or more of the gross national product (GNP) of the U.S. before the Civil War was due to slave labor.[15] "The share of the enslaved in GNP was likely closer to (and somewhat below) the enslaved share in US population [12.6 percent in 1860], which was about one-eighth on the eve of the American Civil War," concludes Rhode.[16]

While the U.S. is a rich country today, the countries, such as Cuba and Brazil, where more than 90 percent of enslaved people were sent and whose economies relied on slavery far more than the southern United States did are, today, either still in deep poverty or only recently emerged from generations of underdevelopment. Slavery in the United States has certainly influenced the development of society. The extent to which its effects can still be felt today is an ongoing academic debate, but it is a vast and incorrect simplification on the part of the Left to ascribe all the current struggles of today's black communities to the lingering effect of slavery, without accounting for the many other individual, social, and cultural variables.

Why Must You Forget Your Own History?

Why is it so critical to leftists that we forget our past? Aside from eliminating any basis of historical comparison and providing a pathway to socialism, perhaps the biggest reason is that much of what we enjoy in the modern world is the fruit of technological, artistic, political, and philosophical progress in Europe or by Europeans. Because women did not enjoy equal political, economic, and civic rights until around a half century ago, much of this achievement was by men. It is everyone's loss that centuries of talent among women went undetected or unappreciated, but regrettable as it is, it is history. These facts are unacceptable to the woke leftists. The only historical narrative that is acceptable to them goes something like this: The history of the world is the history of oppression. All of history, and particularly all Western history, is the history of racism, sexism, classism, and heteronormativity. Only the histories of oppression are meaningful and worthy of study. Any great achievement by European men is suspect, as it was probably accomplished directly or indirectly through the exploitation of black and brown people, women, sexual minorities, the poor, and other "marginalized" communities.

That is the intellectual soil in which the 1619 Project and like revisionist history prospered.

History Is...History

While we can understand that there are many unsung heroes in history, much research yet to do, and many tales yet to uncover, we cannot deny what has been. New discoveries must be put in the context of what is known. We cannot let our modern sensibilities about equality and social progress twist our understanding of the world in which our ancestors lived, with different norms, assumptions, and values. Expecting Julius Caesar, Napoleon, and George Washington to have behaved according to 21st-century morals is ridiculous. While there is surely much more human achievement in art and industry yet to come from Asia and Africa, it is undisputable that the European continent has left the world an incredible legacy. European and European-descended people, predominantly men, have left all of humanity an incredible inheritance in science, mathematics, literature, music, arts, architecture, and other areas. They used these discoveries to make modern life unimaginably better by drastically reducing or eliminating illnesses, enabling travel at the speed of sound and communication at the speed of light, and inventing millions of modern conveniences that make everyone's lives better. Their achievements belong to all of us. As Brown University economist Glenn Loury said, "Tolstoy is mine! Shakespeare is mine! As a man of the West, I am an inheritor of all of its traditions and great figures, just as surely as I'm an inheritor of the traditions and great figures particular to African American history."[17] That is true regardless of the fact that his ancestors came from Africa and not Europe. As an American today, he is the rightful inheritor of all our shared history, just as Asian Americans are the inheritors of jazz, hip-hop, and classic rock.

Until after World War II, the countries of Europe were populated by indigenous peoples who fall under the U.S. Census definition of "white." Since around 1970, the Census has divided Americans into five arbitrary and illogical categories. The definition of "white" is "[a] person having origins in any of the original peoples of Europe, the Middle East, or North Africa."[18] That means that Margaret Thatcher, Osama bin Laden, Fidel Castro, and Golda Meir were all "white" according to the U.S. official definition, despite not sharing a language, culture, religion, or geographic origin. Some scholars have concluded that 10,000 years ago, the inhabitants of the British Isles were much more dark skinned than today, which, given the current theory that all modern peoples from China to North America came out of East Africa 50,000 years or so ago, makes sense.[19] But that does not mean that northern Europe's achievements can be ascribed to the modern populations of Africa, any more than they can be to Lucy, the young female *Australopithecus afarensis* discovered in 1974 in Kenya.

The brilliance of Beethoven's music, Tolstoy's writing, Napoleon's exploits, or Copernicus's discoveries must be understood within a framework of general social and cultural development. They are of a certain time, and place, and people. For the woke leftists, the never-ending search for grievance and injustice today means looking back at the achievements of our past with derision, mining them for racism, sexism, classism, homophobia, and other forms of "structural inequality." All of this existed, of course, at the time. But because the founding fathers wore wigs, and George Washington's doctors essentially bled him to death trying to treat what was probably a bad cold or flu, does not minimize their contributions to the founding of our country.

Rather than raising the profile of the neglected historical figures, revisionist woke historiography seeks to minimize or cancel those of Europeans. One example is the coin and currency debates of recent decades in the United States. Going back to the 1970s, feminists and activists pushed for women and minorities to appear on U.S. currency. The first coin showing the likeness of a woman in standard circulation was the Susan B. Anthony dollar, followed by the Sacagawea dollar. Neither coin ever gained much popular use. The Alabama state quarter issued by the U.S. Mint featured Helen Keller on the "tails" side. Several prominent African Americans, including Booker T. Washington, George Washington Carver, and Jackie Robinson, have appeared on coins, but mostly on commemorative coins not in regular circulation. A new initiative is in place to put women on the flip side of U.S. quarters, some of which are already in circulation.

While the idea of adding women and underappreciated men to the national coinage isn't bad, the idea of parity for its own sake, is. One cannot equate the men who wrote the Federalist Papers, the Declaration of Independence, the Constitution, and Poor Richard's Almanac with obscure figures whose contributions to our history are quantifiably and qualitatively lesser. Dr. Pauli Murray, Patsy Takamoto Mink, Dr. Mary Edwards Walker, Celia Cruz, and Zitkala-Ša are not exactly household names, but perhaps they merit the extra attention they will get by being featured on the back of a quarter. But *replacing* Andrew Jackson on the $20 bill with Harriet Tubman seems more revanchist than anything else. Tubman's amazing story is well known and well memorialized in a variety of ways, from museums, to books, to place names. Jackson was a soldier of the Continental Army and prisoner of war during the American Revolution, a hero of the War of 1812, a major general, a U.S. senator, and a U.S. president. He has been on the $20 bill since 1928, when he replaced the far less famous Grover Cleveland. Let him stay there, warts and all.

For lazy scholars, nothing is easier than latching on to a fashionable, popular ideology to get woke credibility in left-leaning academia—which is to say, academia in general—while bringing in praise and grant money from universities, NGOs, and foundations. It's easy, and profitable, to stick to a theme of white supremacy, structural racism, and implicit bias, then dig up a few examples that can be twisted into "evidence" to support it. It's much harder to take a good look at a controversial issue and come up with unpopular results and defend them with intellectual courage. It may be that those results are later overturned by subsequent research; that's how science and scholarship work.

Science Is Hard, Activism Is Easier

The greater male variability hypothesis is one such example. A 2013 Chinese study of creativity found that while "boys significantly outnumbered girls in the higher extremes, girls tended to outnumber boys in the central region and the lower extremes."[20] One can see why this is controversial. As the study's abstract says, the finding "is useful in explaining the phenomenon that there are more males than females in homes for the mentally deficient and that more 'geniuses' are male than are female."[21] That is not to say that men are on average smarter than women—simply that they are more likely to be found at the extreme ends of human physical and mental variation. This theory has been challenged. It may end up debunked, on the ash heap of intellectual history like phrenology or Lamarckian evolution. But it could also explain the near absence of women among the top competitive chess players, or why men outnumber women in Silicon Valley and also make up 95 percent of California's prison population. Research into differing intellectual and physical traits among the sexes, races, and ethnic groups is fascinating, and can be useful, but it is also likely to land a scientist in hot social-justice water.

With revisionist history, on the other hand, one is safe from the woke mob. Once a poorly vetted and inadequately reviewed news article or journal paper comes out, it can then be promoted by activist journalists who are only too happy to repeat the story of the day. Their approving articles in *The Atlantic*, *The New York Times*, or *USA Today* are cited with fawning fealty and little curiosity by woke politicians. Universities and foundations then throw jobs, awards, professorships, and money to the likes of Nikole Hannah-Jones and Ibram X. Kendi, who repay them with little product and sometimes reputational damage. Hannah-Jones's scholarship has been criticized as shallow and lacking rigorous methodology.[22] Kendi's Center for Antiracist Research at Boston University amounted to a house of cards, closing down four years after opening, having burned through about $50 million and produced almost no research.[23]

Leftist scholars and activists seem intent on looking in a sort of carnival rear-view mirror that twists history to fit their narrative, rather than accepting it, moving past it, and building a more positive future for everyone. Guilt-ridden Europeans and white Americans are foolish to think they can save themselves by admitting that their ancestors failed to live up to standards that they take for granted today. The ultra-woke require destruction and cancellation in the name of what Kendi calls "antiracism."

Destruction of Statues and Monuments

Like totalitarians from China to Russia, the woke Western Left has spent much of its political energy in the past decade tearing down and destroying the statues and monuments that earlier generations built to honor their history and heroes. Just as communist dictator Joseph Stalin rewrote history to remove any trace of politicians or others guilty of thoughtcrime,[24] today's leftist revolutionaries insist that there can be no visual or physical memorials to any person from the past who failed to live up to contemporary puritanism. Heritage Foundation analyst Nile Gardiner suggests that the goal of tearing down monuments is "to wage a cultural war [and] to deny the moral legitimacy of our democratic republic."[25]

The demolition of statues and monuments in America and elsewhere began in earnest around 2017, following the "Unite the Right" rally in Charlottesville, Virginia. The rally occurred in part to oppose the removal of a monument to Confederate Commanding General Robert E. Lee from a park in Charlottesville. Following the rally, which included attendance by members of far-right extremists and violence against counter-protestors, the push to remove Confederate and other monuments gained momentum. Since 2017, hundreds of statues, monuments, and memorials have been demolished, defaced or removed. The movement to remove and destroy monuments gained even more steam after the death of George Floyd and the rise Black Lives Matter protests in 2020.

In the case of monuments to the Confederacy and its leaders, one can argue that those physical markers are hurtful to many members of society and should be considered for removal. One could demand, for the same reason, the removal of statues to Napoleon, Julius Caesar, and Louis XIV. It's a question of context, and degree, and remove from the present. Nathan Bedford Forest and James Longstreet both fought for the Confederacy, but Forest was known to be a particular racist and a vicious soldier in his own time, while Longstreet was not. Lee did indeed lead the Confederate cause, but more from a loyalty to Virginia than a hostility to the United States. Preserving historical records, including statues, of these men helps us understand their times and the Civil War, while eradicating them leaves us ignorant receptacles for the ideological plantation.

Those wishing to revisit the placement of historical monuments and statutes could choose to engage in a civic process with government and community members to evaluate the appropriateness of particular monuments and argue to have them removed or placed in a different location. Instead, the activists of the Left prefer vandalism, defacement, and other extralegal paths. Perhaps this is because they know that if they put the matter to a vote, as often as not people would not want to see the monuments removed.

History shows how revolutions start with the pursuit of social and economic justice and devolve into blind rage, show trials, gulags, and excommunications. The push to remove Confederate monuments followed a similar path, rapidly devolving into a frenzy of destruction that resulted in removal of any relic or memorial to anyone even remotely associated with today's political orthodoxy. Within a few years, radical leftists had destroyed or demolished monuments to Christopher Columbus, Thomas

Jefferson, George Washington, Ulysses S. Grant, Francis Scott Key, and other American heroes, many with tangential or even zero links to slavery. Even statues of Abraham Lincoln, who freed the slaves, were torn down.

The list of statues and monuments destroyed by radical leftists in America and globally is too long to itemize here, so following is a short list of some of the more outlandish examples of historical revisionism by brute force and ignorance:

- At Dartmouth College in New Hampshire, the school removed a weathervane from the top of the school's library because it depicted a Native American seated in front of the school's founder Eleazar Wheelock.[26]
- The statue of Thomas Jefferson was removed from the New York City Council chamber, where it had been since 1834.[27]
- A statue of Meriwether Lewis, William Clark, and Sacagawea was removed from its place in Charlottesville, Virginia, because Sacagawea was seen as being in a submissive position.[28]
- A statue in Saratoga Springs, New York, depicting a soldier of the Union Army was torn down and destroyed.[29]
- A statue of the Virgin Mary in Chattanooga, Tennessee, was torn down and decapitated.[30]
- A statue of Jesus Christ in Miami was torn down and decapitated.[31]
- A statue of Andrew Jackson in Jackson, Mississippi, was removed by the city council. Andrew Jackson is the namesake of the city of Jackson.[32]
- The Emancipation Memorial in Boston, Massachusetts, which depicted Abraham Lincoln symbolically ending slavery, was removed because some claimed that the freed slave depicted at Lincoln's feet was shown in a subservient position.[33]
- A statue of Hans Christian Heg, a Union Army officer and abolitionist, in Madison, Wisconsin, was decapitated and thrown into a lake.[34]

- Statues of "The Pioneer" and "The Pioneer Mother" at the University of Oregon were removed after they were toppled by protestors.[35]
- A monument and statue to Delaware law enforcement officers was removed after it was vandalized and decapitated.[36]
- A statue of Christopher Columbus in Columbus, Ohio, was removed by the city council. The city is named for Christopher Columbus.[37]

Leftwing activists justify the destruction of these monuments with a dogmatic radical canon based on the Marxist division of the world into oppressors and the oppressed. These statues represent, to them, oppression. They berate those "normies" who accept and perhaps like the historical statues, whether or not they represent flawed humans of the past, as incurably racist and sexist. Antifa and other destroyers from the far Left are blissfully unaware of any moral failures in their own sacred icons such as Karl Marx, Che Guevara, and Hamas's Yahya Sinwar.

Woke Museums

The museums of the world have served for centuries as places of inspiration for artists, young people, and curious people of all types. Indeed, the word museum is derived from the Greek *mouseion*, meaning the place of muses. At their best, museums offer a glimpse into the past and a display of the greatest forms of human and natural expression. They can challenge us, even shock us, but they are not meant to indoctrinate us. When leftists get involved, museums turn into spaces of performative virtue signaling designed to "challenge" and "interrogate" what would otherwise be self-evidently valuable and inspirational.

Shakespeare: History's Labor Lost

William Shakespeare, the bard of Avon, was not spared the purge of Western culture.[38] His home and museum in the English village of Stratford-upon-Avon is managed by the Shakespeare Birthplace Trust. In 2025, the Trust decided to "decolonize" the collection. This "decolonization" has meant removing the work of male Europeans, and by extension, European history and culture. Often it is replaced with offerings from elsewhere, whether or not they are relevant and of commensurate worth. The Trust commissioned a report by a postgraduate researcher at Birmingham City University, who recommended to "purge" the Trust of "Anglocentric and colonialist thought" and thus address "societal inequities that are embedded in imperialism and associated with Shakespeare's global cultural status."[39]

The report's author claims that venerating Shakespeare means supporting "white, Anglo-centric, Eurocentric, and increasingly 'West-centric' views that continue to do harm in the world today," and "the ideology of white European supremacy" in an act of "epistemic violence."[40] "Epistemic" means "relating to knowledge or knowing."[41] We all know what "violence" means, but for the Left, words, or even silence, can be violence.[42] Such a report could only come from someone steeped in critical race theory (CRT), which rejects the Western cannon as oppressive. The Shakespeare Birthplace Trust refused to make the report available to reporters.

The Smithsonian

CRT has undermined museum objectivity in the United States as well. America's flagship museum collection, in Washington, DC, was based on the gift of an Englishman, James Smithson. Today, the Smithsonian Institution has succumbed to the tide of revisionist history propelled by critical theory. All serious scholars, amateur historians, and the general public readily admit that African Americans have a unique and painful past due to the long period of slavery and the subsequent age of Jim Crow discrimination. There is no pushback against efforts to do a better job of incorporating African American history into museums, memorials, and retrospectives on American life. But adding and highlighting this important history isn't enough for grievance-obsessed leftists, who maintain that equality for previously oppressed groups can only be achieved by having a separate forum to glorify their members. This is why we have the African American history museum, the National Museum of the American Indian, and the proposed museum for Latinos and others in the planning stages.

The National Museum
of African American History and Culture

The Smithsonian's National Museum of African American History and Culture in Washington, DC, which opened in 2016, has become one of the bigger attractions among the Smithsonian museums on the National Mall. The success of the museum demonstrates that there is great interest among blacks, whites, and everyone else to learn about and appreciate the contributions of African Americans to American history and culture. And yet, the museum provides one more example of the Left's emphasis on ethnic division, combined with degradation of traditions. The history of grievance and wrongs is featured more than the story of how America became a nation.

When it opened, the museum had an exhibit featuring a poster on "Aspects and Assumptions of Whiteness & White Culture in the United States." *Newsweek* pointed out that, according to the poster, "rational thinking and hard work" are white values.[43] The exhibit derided habits like punctuality, hard work, and rational thinking as "white" cultural traits. The poster explained that "[w]hite dominant culture, or whiteness, refers to the ways white people and their traditions, attitudes, and ways of life have been normalized over time and are now considered standard practices in the United States."[44] Many other traits ordinarily assumed to be positive for society were pilloried, including an emphasis on cause-and-effect relationships, respect for authority, planning for the future, and delayed gratification. "White culture" was also criticized for having a "written tradition," being polite, being action oriented, and following time schedules. The poster on "whiteness" was quickly removed from the museum's exhibit and website after public mockery, but it neatly encapsulated the anti-European, anti-capitalist, anti-traditional ideology that motivates the Left. The museum removed the poster, but it did not repudiate the idea behind it.

As leftists insist that we tear down European and European American history at every turn, they will brook no criticism whatsoever of their favored groups. So, while we are forced to mention over and over again that many of America's founding fathers were "enslavers" at a time when slave ownership was both legal and normal, there can be no mention of the fact that many African American freedmen also owned slaves.[45] It's also seldom mentioned that black African slaves were typically captured and sold by other black Africans.[46] Europeans are permanently denigrated as settler-colonialists and blamed for the ills of deeply impoverished and dysfunctional countries they left 50 years to 70 years ago.[47]

The National Museum of the American Latino

After touring the Smithsonian's not-yet-opened National Museum of the American Latino, journalist and Heritage Foundation analyst Mike Gonzalez called it "a woke indoctrination factory" and recommended the project be abandoned.[48] The exhibits, he writes, are seen through the "oppressor vs. oppressed" prism, highlighting only "historical injustices."[49] Gonzalez, who is Cuban American, felt that the exhibits display not only anti-American bias, but also anti-Catholic and anti-Spanish bias. Ultimately, Gonzalez concludes, the museum's "aim is to teach the young and future generations to see themselves as victims of America, so they can destroy it from within."[50] That's quite the opposite of the traditional purpose of a museum, which is to inspire joy and passion for art and respect for history.

New York: America's Second Museum Capital

Instead of letting works of art and displays of natural beauty speak for themselves, allowing the viewer to interpret them with the aid of some brief explanatory context, activist exhibitors feel they must explain the exploitation and oppression behind every work.[51] Elizabeth Weiss, a fellow of the Heterodox Academy's Segal Center for Academic Pluralism, spent a year visiting and studying the museums of New York City. At the end, her conclusion was that NYC's museums are "drowning in politics."[52] Professor Weiss wrote in the *New York Post* that "[s]mothered by political ideology, America's great museums are failing their mission as the protectors of our shared human heritage."[53] At the American Museum of Natural History's Northwest Coast Hall, she writes, an exhibit containing items used by shamans (traditional healers) has the warning: "CAUTION: This display case contains items used in the practices of traditional Tlingit doctors. Some people may wish to avoid this area, as Tlingit tradition holds that such belongings contain powerful spirits." Weiss is incredulous that "indigenous superstitious beliefs that harm can come from artifacts" because they are imbued with spirits "are treated with complete seriousness" by the exhibit.[54] In the Metropolitan Museum of Art, an exhibit on European paintings from 1300 to 1800 focused on "class, gender, race, and religion." The "Delaware Water Gap," a panoramic landscape from 1861, was described as invoking "genocide," the "capitalism" that threatened native people's "very existence," and the current "chaos and destruction of climate change." Weiss argues that museums "have become just another arena for pushing political agendas, especially those supporting the postmodern ideology that identity—race, gender, nationality and class—is more important than truth."[55]

Homes of Our Founding Fathers

Brenda Hafera of The Heritage Foundation found similar revisionist, unbalanced, and often inaccurate exhibits at Montpelier, the home of James Madison in Virginia.[56] She writes that the exhibits "for children and those about the Constitution focus on race and slavery—there are no exhibits on James Madison's accomplishments."[57] She explains that behind the exhibits is the Southern Poverty Law Center (SPLC), which provided guidance for museums and teachers that view history through a decidedly woke lens. Learning materials that the SPLC commissioned or endorsed teach the dubious proposition that "[f]rom mass incarceration, to the achievement gap, to housing discrimination, and the vicious cycle of poverty, violence, and lack of opportunity throughout America's inner cities, the legacies of 200 years of African American bondage are still with us."[58]

A rubric for teaching history that came out of the national summit on teaching slavery held at Montpelier in 2018 says that American history should be approached in a "spirit of restorative justice," and staff should undergo "significant and ongoing anti-racist training (which includes interpreting difficult history, deconstructing and interrogating white privilege, white supremacy, and systemic racism, and engaging visitors on these subjects)."[59] Hasan Kwame Jeffries, a history professor who wrote some of the guidance, believes that "Slavery is our country's origin."[60]

Slavery is indeed an important and shameful part of U.S. history, but it is not all, or even most, of it. James Madison was a two-term president and wrote the Constitution, achievements which surely merit inclusion in teaching materials about his house.

Many others have pointed out the incursion of radical-left ideology into our museums. Eric Gibson of *The Wall Street Journal* claims that "Woke Ideologues Are Taking Over American Art Museums."[61] Michael Deacon, a columnist with *The Telegraph*, notes that, "The woke takeover of our museums is almost complete." Deacon concludes: "At almost every major exhibition these days we find ourselves subjected to finger-wagging lectures about the evils of Western colonialism, transphobia, and other obsessions of the 21st-century Left—irrespective of whether they're actually relevant to the subject at hand."[62]

Can Conservatives Fight Back?

Despite its almost complete control of the culture, schools, museums, and institutions that preserve American history, the Left still bleats in outrage whenever any attempts are made to restore balance to historical points of view. Leftists want to stress the worst elements of America's past and extrapolate to imagine that "structural racism" still underlies everything today, which gives them justification for their discriminatory "diversity, equity and inclusion" (DEI) programs. The BBC, Britain's leftwing state broadcaster, criticized President Trump's March 2025 executive order titled "Restoring Truth and Sanity to American History."[63] In the order, Trump wrote that "the Smithsonian Institution has, in recent years, come under the influence of divisive, race-centered ideology," citing the National Museum of African American History and Culture as an example. Opponents of the president quickly claimed that Trump was trying to "sanitize racism" and erase the history of slavery, Jim Crow, and segregation.[64]

The American Historical Association, which has 10,000 historians as members, put out a statement saying: "No person, no nation, is perfect, and we should all—as individuals and as nations—learn from our imperfections."[65] Yes, indeed. But to make the imperfections greater in the historical record than the achievements is the leftist goal. Jefferson should be seen only as a slave owner, not the genius who drafted the Declaration of Independence and founded the University of Virginia and gave the Library of Congress its initial collection.

One tool the woke resistance uses with some effect to fight conservative attempts to restore perspective is "malicious compliance." This is rather like the "work to rule" tactic of British labor unions, which used to follow rules on breaks and safety to the letter, thereby slowing down production and resisting employer reforms. For the woke anti-Trump "resistance," malicious compliance would be removing exhibits about black civil rights heroes like Rosa Parks, pretending that was what the anti-DEI orders required. For example, the managers of Arlington National Cemetery in Virginia removed information about "African American, Hispanic or female servicemembers, including…stories about veteran and civil rights leader Medgar Evers and the Tuskegee Airmen, the US's first Black Airforce pilots" from public exhibits and web pages[66] in response to Trump's order and Secretary of Defense Pete Hegseth's orders to remove discriminatory DEI content wherever possible. Removing these exhibits was clearly not the intent of either Trump or Hegseth.

In fact, conservatives have no problem with telling U.S. history and celebrating the achievements and greatness of black Americans, women, and minorities of all kinds—they just want the stories told in context and proportion, and without ideology. The Department of the Army employees who removed information about black heroes were either utterly ignorant of the instructions they were given, or maliciously complying in order to gain negative press attention and thwart the anti-DEI policy of the Trump Administration.

Opponents of reform complain that without public money, they can't hold events featuring only ethnic or sexual minorities. But why should the federal taxpayer fund local museums dedicated to one race, sex, or any minority? Why should American taxpayers who like their country and are proud of its history fund museums that do nothing but denigrate their past and their ancestors? With billions in woke donor dollars floating around, surely these institutions can attract private money for their causes.

Conclusion

Woke ideology tears down mainstream history and culture not for the purpose of spreading the truth, but to erase a society that the woke despise and replace it with a global socialist utopia. This assault on American history is conflated with a dislike of "whiteness," a term that apparently refers to the values and norms of all Americans who trace their roots to Europe. Deliberately dividing Americans, as we grapple with changing demographics, deepening debt, and other threats to national cohesion, is a dangerous and destructive game. But for the woke, destruction is the whole point.

A person to follow: Mike Gonzalez, The Heritage Foundation, *@Gundisalvus* on X.

A book to read: *The Autobiography of Benjamin Franklin*, by Benjamin Franklin, 1791.

A group to support: National Association of Scholars, www.nas.org.

Chapter 4

The Fourth Commandment:
You Shall Not Know "What Is a Man"

Trans men are men. —Rupert Grint, actor

A Disclaimer

Before wading into the shark-infested waters of gender ideology and "trans" matters, I want to make two things clear. First, all conservatives I know are concerned first and foremost with protecting children from doing themselves permanent harm, and second with the societal implications of erasing the fundamental difference between the two sexes.

Second, I reject the neo-pronouns like "xe," "zir," and the like as silly—not to mention impossible for normal people to remember. Having taught Seventh grade, I can imagine the joy my classes would have taken in each having their own pronouns, changing often, for their teachers to remember on pain of "misgendering" – which very nearly became a criminal offence in Ohio in May 2025.[1] Out of politeness, most people will honor someone's decision to change his or her name. However, calling one "non-binary" person, an individual, "they" and "them" is obviously nonsensical. As to what to call adults who have chosen to live as the opposite sex to that which they were born with, like Caitlyn Jenner, Buck Angel, and Corinna Cohn, people tend to go case by case. I have tried to use biologically correct pronouns throughout this book, though I sometimes avoid them. Please expect no perfect consistency, nor infer anything from my usage one way or another.

Where Did Gender Ideology Come From?

I went to school in the '70s and '80s. We knew what "gay" meant, but the concept of "transgender" did not exist for grade schoolers. I do remember reading the back of a record album called *Switched-On Bach*, which was the great composer's harpsichord works played on an early Moog synthesizer. The artist was identified as "Walter (now Wendy) Carlos." At that time a "sex change," as it was then called, was extremely rare.

In the late 1990s, I taught middle school and high school drama, English, and history. Of the several hundred students I had, several showed signs that they might later be same-sex attracted, but not one identified as "transgender." The very expression would have been unknown to the entire school, from administration and teachers to students. Today, as Christopher Rufo wrote for *City Journal*, a friend of his teaching in a middle school said "one-third of his female students identify as "trans," "queer," and "non-binary," which he is required to "affirm" and keep secret from parents."[2] In 2025, gender ideology has reached such levels of absurdity, and so penetrated American institutions, that a hospital in New Jersey was handing out forms to parents asking which gender their newborn babies "identified" as, with options including "transgender female," "transgender male," and "genderqueer."[3]

Gender ideology is one issue, but it deserves two chapters because there are distinct differences between the impact on individuals and society of its two central tenets: (1) "transmen" (women who identify as men) are real men, and (2) "transwomen" (men who identify as women) are real women. The trend of girls who want to be boys has become a problem of mass contagion, including a range of particular afflictions affecting pre-pubescent and adolescent girls, with irreversible surgeries and drug "treatments." "Affirming" this trend harms society because it requires popular acceptance of a falsehood, but it mostly hurts individual girls and their families. "Trans men" are not a physical threat to biological men. The reverse, however, is not always true. The issue of boys who want to be girls adds a larger dimension: the harm to girls and women of prioritizing the demands of gender-dysphoric men above girls' and women's safety, comfort, privacy, and ability to succeed in sex-segregated spaces.

This chapter examines the Left's commandment to accept women as men whenever a woman "identifies" as a man. In 2020, the actor Rupert

Grint (from the Harry Potter movies) framed his view neatly on Twitter: "I firmly stand with the trans community. Trans women are women. Trans men are men. We should all be entitled to live with love and without judgment."[4] This elicited the now-famous response from the *Harry Potter* author J.K. Rowling that put her in the crosshairs of trans activists and their allies, and in turn made her a champion of reality and women's rights. Rowling is generally a progressive, rock-steady voter for Britain's leftwing Labour Party. She has long supported equal rights for gay people, but she understands that tolerance of rights for same-sex-attracted people does not mean accepting anyone's "gender identity" at face value and as trumping all other rights.

In a 2020 essay, Rowling explained her position and suggested that rape shelters and prisons were places in which women's rights might supersede those of "trans women."[5] Her attempt to reason with radical activists did little good. Rowling is one of the many brave women who stood up to the trans onslaught, with its threats of violence and attempts at cancellation, to defend women's rights, spaces, and plain old facts. Her fame and wealth might have afforded her financial and physical protection, but they also made her a lightning rod for some of the most unhinged radicals on the planet.

Women to the Barricades

The same year, 2020, journalist Abigail Shrier wrote *Irreversible Damage: The Transgender Craze Seducing Our Daughters.*[6] Like many Americans, by that time I was dimly aware of the increase in trans-identifying girls. By then, my wife and I had more than one old friend whose daughter had changed her name, or announced she was "non-binary," or even that she was a boy. With children of the same age, going through their own challenges, we were sympathetic to those families' struggles and the difficult choices they had to make. A long series of COVID-19 lockdowns and forced time at home gave me the time to really dig into the issue and figure it out. I read three excellent books in a short time, starting with *Irreversible Damage*. Shrier's book showed the scale of a disaster that was befalling girls in Western countries, and she made a convincing case that it was due to social contagion, along the lines of the

Salem witch craze of 17th-century Massachusetts, rather than another stage of societal enlightenment.

Like so many others who resist the Woke Commandments, Shrier's reward for this excellent work of research and journalism was to be shunned and cancelled. A review in *Psychology Today* called her book "bizarre and full of misinformation."[7] The reviewer—a doctor specializing in care for "trans" youth—claimed that several of Shrier's conclusions were wrong, including her assertions that (1) puberty blockers usually led to cross-sex hormones or surgery, (2) that the majority of gender-dysphoric children will desist if left alone, and (2) that so-called gender affirming care did not lead to improved health and happiness.

As to the first conclusion, Dutch researchers conducted a study of 70 children with gender dysphoria between 2000 and 2007, putting them on puberty blockers with the idea that some would desist and want to go off blockers and revert to their natal sex. The study instead showed that "every single one [though some children dropped out of the study] progressed to cross-sex hormones."[8] The Tavistock clinic in the UK, which, before being shut down, was the National Health Service's main center for treating children with gender issues, showed that only 1.2 percent of children put on puberty blockers desisted from trans identification.

As Helen Joyce writes in her book *Trans*, politics trump science when it comes to gender: "high quality research casting doubt on affirmation [of perceived gender identity] has been suppressed, and low-quality research in its favor gets fast-tracked to publication."[9] Furthermore, this research is bolstered and touted by major medical associations while counter-evidence is ignored or written off as "transphobic" and harmful to children.

Shrier's next claim, that the majority of gender-dysphoric children will outgrow gender dysphoria if left alone, is supported by all the major studies on this relatively new phenomenon, including one from Canada in 2021 that followed 139 boys with gender dysphoria from 1975 to 2009 and found that 90 percent of them "ceased to feel dysphoric and became reconciled with their sex, generally before or in early puberty."[10]

As to her third conclusion, the reviewer in *Psychology Today* said: "Shrier ignores all of the data showing that gender-affirming medical care results in improved mental health outcomes for transgender youth." To support his rejection of her arguments, the reviewer cites weak or biased studies and pro-transition physician-activists, such as Dr. Jack Turban. Several studies cited by trans activists to support childhood transition were conducted before 2013, well before the massive increase in gender dysphoria among minors and thus sampled a very different population.[11] Other studies purport to show that very few people who attempt to transition to the opposite sex regret doing so. According to the Society for Evidence Based Gender Medicine, however, "one of the most frequently-cited studies asserting a low rate of regret omitted all those who stopped coming to the gender clinic—a remarkably high 36%."[12]

Five years later, Shrier's analysis is increasingly borne out, as more research is possible on the growing cohort of girls who have "transitioned," from taking testosterone, to getting mastectomies, to creation of facsimile penises from flesh taken from their arms or legs. The results of this "transition" do not show "improved mental health outcomes"—quite the opposite—for thousands of vulnerable, troubled young women who had been told that transitioning to men would solve their problems. Back in 2020, however, such was the pressure of cancellation when anyone invoked "transphobia," that Target stores pulled Shrier's book from its websites, and mainstream media ignored or derided her.[13]

The second book I read—and another book that Target decided to remove from its physical and online bookshelves—was Dr. Deborah Soh's *The End of Gender.* Unlike Shrier and Joyce, who came from professional journalism, "Dr. Debra Soh is a neuroscientist who specializes in human sexuality, gender, and evolutionary explanations for behavior," according to her biography.[14] Soh writes with empathy but as a dispassionate researcher into human sexuality with no axe to grind.

The third book I read was *Trans*, by Helen Joyce, known best as editor of *The Economist.* These three important books, written by courageous women, outline how gender ideology escaped academic obscurity and wreaked havoc on the Western world.

How Transgender Ideology Harms Girls

As Shrier, Soh, and Joyce all wrote, childhood gender dysphoria—the feeling that your body's actual sex doesn't reflect the sex you think you are—used to be very rare. "Historically, it afflicted a tiny sliver of the population (roughly 0.1 percent) and almost exclusively boys," writes Shrier.[15] A decade ago, fewer than one in 10,000 people sought medical intervention for gender dysphoria. In the past few years, however, the rate of alleged adolescent gender dysphoria has exploded.

In Britain, cases rose by more than 40 times, with most of the increase being in girls, who had previously made up far fewer cases than boys. Great Britain has a National Health Service (NHS), making national records easier to obtain than in the U.S. The country's largest clinic for treating gender dysphoric children, the Tavistock and Portman NHS Foundation Trust, saw 25 times more referred patients over a decade, mostly "girls transitioning to male."[16]

There are two plausible explanations for this sudden increase in transgender self-diagnosis in young women. First, you could argue that there have always been this many gender-dysphoric girls but only now, in an enlightened and accepting age, can they "come out" and "transition." Second, one could conclude that there is a psychological or other cause for the phenomenon, such as peer group contagion, or mass hysteria. (The word "hysteria" comes from the Greek for uterus, because the ancient Greeks thought it an entirely female affliction.)

Unfortunately, just like with COVID-19, instead of engaging in an open academic debate on the causes and best treatment for the condition, a core of activists shut down discussion of the topic like the Spanish Inquisition, waging an all-out ideological war that caused respected, caring professionals to lose their jobs and parents to acquiesce to experiments on their children with the threat of suicide hanging over them.

Shrier suggests that one cause of the explosion in trans-identifying girls is social media. What might have been a localized craze that burned itself out was spread exponentially through social media applications like TikTok. In the United Kingdom, a 2018 study showed "a 4,400 percent rise over the previous decade in teenage girls seeking gender treatments."[17] Furthermore, the massive increase was in adolescent girls, whereas the previous decades had seen mostly pre-school-aged boys.

Shrier credits Brown University researcher and physician Dr. Lisa Littman for her work in discovering this phenomenon and giving it a name: rapid onset gender dysphoria (ROGD). Littman found that social media use played a significant role in girls who suddenly identified as boys, and that there were clusters of such identifications among girls' friend groups. At ultra-leftwing Evergreen University in Oregon, where professors Bret Weinstein and Heather Heying were famously driven out for defying the campus insanity, over half the students identified as "LGBTQ" or "questioning."[18]

Littman's research strongly supported the hypothesis that the massive increase in trans-identifying girls was due to social contagion.[19] Littman found that adolescent childhood dysphoria in girls had risen from fewer than one in 10,000, to more than ten times as high.[20] Her research also found disturbing patterns in girls who identified as trans: "a majority had one or more psychiatric diagnoses and almost half were engaging in self-harm prior to the onset of the gender dysphoria."[21] Of the girls Littman studied, 90 percent were white, and used social media with increasing frequency before they "came out" as trans.

Littman, sex researchers Ken Zucker and Ray Blanchard, psychologist Lisa Marchiano, and many others paid a heavy professional price for putting science, research, and evidence ahead of ideology. They were pilloried online for their views, and in many cases lost their jobs in academia or medicine, reflecting an environment where evolving scientific and medical understandings and the best interests of the patient have been usurped by a radical agenda.

Biological Reality

"Sex is not a spectrum." So writes biologist Colin Wright in an essay of the same name.[22] "Claims that 'sex is a spectrum' rely on fundamental misunderstandings about the nature of biological sex," he says. Humans are a dimorphic species: half produce small gametes (sperm) and the other half large gametes (eggs): "Male body parts are those directed towards the production of small, motile gametes (in animals, called sperm) and female ones are those directed towards the production of large, immotile gametes (in animals, called ova), or eggs."[23]

There is no documented case of a human ever being able to do both at the same time. No human being can self-fertilize, as some hermaphroditic organisms can. Some humans are born with visible abnormalities or invisible variations of a sexual nature, once called "intersex" conditions and now more commonly called "disorders of sex development" (DSD), but this is chance, not choice. Just as babies born with six toes are still human, so people born with chromosomal, genital, or other anomalies are still male or female.

While one should consider people's feelings and choices about how they identify and want to live, no one should be compelled to deny reality or pander to the whims of others at the expense of one's own, equally valid beliefs. Trans radical activists insist otherwise—they seek to suppress or compel speech that does not conform to their belief system. They insist that one's natural genitalia are irrelevant to a person's sex.[24] They consider a straight man who is attracted only to women with female parts (breasts and vaginas) to be "transphobic," as they do a lesbian who is not attracted to intact males who identify as women. The extremists consider any resistance to this nonsense to be "reducing people to their genitals" and thus "blatant transphobia."[25] Radical trans ideology does not accept the most basic fact of attraction, common to all people, and mammals for that matter, and which, ironically, is often the non-straight mantra: you love who you love.

Sex Is Not *Assigned* at Birth, It Is *Observed*

A tiny percentage of people are born with disorders of sexual development (DSD), that is, with abnormal secondary sex characteristics (such as genitalia) that don't match their chromosome configuration. In the past, doctors in these cases may have "assigned sex at birth" (and sometimes made mistakes) though they can now determine, with more screening, the sex of the child. For more than 99 percent of babies, however, the question is one of simple observation and taxonomy (male, female).

The attempt to use the phrase "sex assigned at birth" for all people, not just those with DSD, is an ideological tactic to normalize the post-modernist idea that sex is a social construct and not a biological reality. Former Harvard biologist Carole Hooven notes that "the phrase 'sex assigned at birth' sows confusion and 'creates doubt about a biological fact.'"[26] Hooven earned her doctorate in 2004 and lectured at Harvard on human evolutionary biology. In 2019, she wrote her book *T: The Story of Testosterone, the Hormone that Dominates and Divides Us*. Her spirit of open enquiry, scientific method, and research ran her straight into the brick wall of diversity, equity, and inclusion (DEI), which was nearing its post-2020 high tide. As she explains in a *Free Press* article, Hooven was essentially driven out of Harvard over the next several years, retiring in January 2023 at a point where she could easily have had another decade at the top of her field. As she wrote of her experience, "Harvard has a long way to go to restore an environment where those on its campus feel free to teach, write, and speak without fear."[27]

DEI would have it otherwise, but as Abigail Anthony confirms, "Sex preexists birth...and it isn't contingent on birth, either."[28] If it wasn't, then we would not read about embarrassing "gender reveal" parties ending in literal plane crashes, explosions, and wildfires.[29]

"Gender Affirming Care" for Female to Male

The core of gender ideology in its current form is that humans are born with an innate "gender identity," while their sex is "assigned" at birth – based, presumably, on the biases of doctors and nurses. Therefore, a child can be born in the wrong body – one conventionally associated with something that does not match his or her "gender identity." To sustain the proposition, activists consistently use terms like "assigned male" and "assigned female" at birth, as if these are random or prejudicial decisions made by doctors with no grounding. Supporters of this theory then believe that "gender affirming care" (GAC) is necessary to correct this mistake. GAC can include social transitioning in schools, as well as the prescription of puberty blockers to stop a child from experiencing the "wrong" puberty, or the prescription of cross-sex hormones, which can to some extent mimic the secondary sex characteristics of the desired sex, or both. Ultimately, "affirming" a "trans" child's gender can mean surgery to remove breasts or the penis and testicles, and to create facsimiles of breasts and a vagina or a penis to approximate the desired "gender."

The Hippocratic oath that doctors take starts with "first, do no harm." GAC is the opposite of this approach. As Joyce writes in *Trans*, practitioners of GAC "recommend immediate 'social transition'—a change of name, pronouns, and presentation—followed successively by drugs to block puberty, cross-sex hormones and surgery." She calls this treatment protocol "a fast track to sexual dysfunction and sterility in adulthood."[30]

Shrier cites two of the many studies showing that most (upwards of 70 percent) of childhood gender dysphoria resolves itself, usually after an affected child goes through puberty.[31] In *The End of Gender*, Soh writes that in "all eleven long-term studies ever done on gender dysphoric children, between 60 and 90 percent desist [stop experiencing gender dysphoria] by puberty," listing all the studies in her end notes.[32] Moreover, those studies were done long before the current wave of trans identification by girls.

Nonetheless, the American World Professional Association for Transgender Health (WPATH) has promulgated this treatment paradigm, and many U.S. professional organizations have adopted it. GAC quickly became the standard of care adopted by the American Medical Association, the American College of Physicians, the American Academy of Pediatrics, the American Psychological Association, and the Pediatric Endocrine Society.[33] GAC was held out as the answer for children experiencing body dysmorphia in the Biden Administration by Admiral Rachel Levine, the second-ranking official in the U.S. Department of Health and Human Services. Dr. Levine, a man named Richard Levine for most of his life, now wears women's clothes and identifies as a woman.

GAC posits, counter-intuitively, that children "know who they are" and should be affirmed in this conclusion. This notion was mocked by comedian Bill Maher, who was glad no one had affirmed his childhood belief that he was a pirate by removing one eye and a leg and giving him a peg-leg and an eye patch.

One study concluded that 100 percent of children prescribed puberty blockers went on to take cross-sex hormones.[34] Puberty-blocking drugs were used to chemically castrate male sex offenders, and to treat precocious puberty (defined as puberty that begins too early, for example, at age seven, and can cause medical issues or psychological distress) in children. They were never intended to stop healthy children from making their essential passage through puberty. Cross-sex hormones (estrogen for boys and testosterone for girls) are antithetical to a process that virtually every human body goes through in puberty. "The long-term effects include heightened rates of diabetes, stroke, blood clots, cancer…and heart disease."[35] Puberty blockers can result in permanent sterility and developmental stagnation. Cross-sex hormones can reduce bone density and cardiovascular health.[36] It can also be extremely expensive for parents, their insurance companies, and the taxpayer if the child in question receives government-funded medical care. Young people who go the full GAC distance to transition surgery will require hormones and other medications for the rest of their lives.

In the United Kingdom, no single institution did more to advance trans medicine than Britain's Tavistock clinic, which opened in 1989 as the Gender and Identity Development Service, with the intention of helping "people aged 17 and under struggling with their gender identity."[37] Tavistock had just two patients in 1989, both young boys. In 2020, it had 2,378 referrals, nearly three quarters female and mostly teens.[38] In 2019, a young woman named Keira Bell sued Tavistock and the government trust that ran it for having "transitioned" her through cross-sex hormones and a double mastectomy without adequate safeguards. She won her case, with the UK High Court ruling that "puberty blockers and cross-sex hormones are experimental treatments which cannot be given to children in most cases without application to the court."[39] However, the Court of Appeal overturned the High Court judgment in 2021. In 2022, following a major study of the UK's transgender medicine system for children by Dr. Hilary Cass, the Tavistock clinic was closed.[40]

Why Do Parents Go Along?

Most children with gender dysmorphia outgrow it, eventually accepting their natal sex, often growing up to be same-sex attracted. Longer-term studies are showing that GAC doesn't fix the problem.[41] The logical response would be to "first, do no harm" and adopt the strategy of watchful waiting for gender dysphoric children, yet many parents don't.

There seem to be three main reasons why parents allow their children to undergo so-called gender-affirming care. The first is the cachet of being one of the in crowd, part of the elite—a type of performative political activism. Particularly in the first Trump Administration, coastal leftists seemed willing to believe anything they thought hoi polloi Trump voters didn't. As Joyce puts it, "[p]roclaiming that transwomen are women is a way of showing that you are a member of an elite intellectual tribe,"[42] like putting pronouns in your email signature or social media bio.

A second reason is that parents are blinded by what Dr. Anthony Fauci called "the science"—which is to say, not empirical science that challenges assertions and seeks through trial and error to reach the truth, but an ideological, conventional dogma that it is dangerous for professionals to challenge and intimidating to laymen and parents.[43] Trans ideology's capture of the major medical associations makes it hard for providers to offer other, safer options like watchful waiting. Practitioners can be bullied into compliance or forced out of the field leaving it to the activists.

The third reason is psychological blackmail: activists imply that children who are not affirmed in their "gender identity" are at risk of suicide. "Would you rather have a live son, or a dead daughter?" was the awful question they posed to parents. It is a manipulative psychological trick, but it works. Trans activists and their "allies" [44] insist that GAC is lifesaving, but the evidence does not back up that claim.[45] In fact, according to one important study, suicide, at least among adults, is more likely *after* transition than before. A Swedish study concluded in 2011 that "[p]ersons with transsexualism, after sex reassignment, have considerably higher risks for mortality, suicidal behaviour, and psychiatric morbidity than the general population." [46] The study followed adults for up to 15 years *after* surgical transition and found a suicide rate 19 times higher than average.

In 2024, a study by the National Institutes of Health based on a database of 56 U.S. healthcare organizations and more than 90 million patients showed that "individuals who underwent gender-affirming surgery had a 12.12-fold higher suicide attempt risk than those who did not."[47] Strangely, the "significantly elevated risk of suicide" that the study's authors found among patients who had "gender-affirming" surgery led them to advocate "the necessity for comprehensive post-procedure psychiatric support," instead of recommending a complete re-thinking of the gender-affirming model.

In any case, the population of young people with gender dysphoria is far above the norm in a range of mental health problems, and their risk of suicide or suicidal ideation is far above average. In one study of 83 patients requesting sex reassignment surgery, 57 (62.7 percent) "had at least one psychiatric comorbidity."[48]

What Are the Societal Effects of "Trans Men"?

When men who want to be women are allowed to self-identify as such, there are direct effects on women's spaces and safety, as we'll discuss in the next chapter. When girls and women who want to be men are encouraged to do so, there is little effect on the safety of most men. One notable exception is when girls and women take the male hormone testosterone. This is known to make men more aggressive and violent, and it likely has a similar effect on women. A 2020 study on such women found that "aggression may increase during initiation of testosterone treatment, but will return to baseline during long-term testosterone treatment."[49] The young woman who shot and killed six people, including children, at a school in Nashville in 2023 may have been receiving "gender affirming care" at the time; whether this involved testosterone, and for how long, has not been disclosed. For the most part, men are more puzzled than threatened by "trans men," but the phenomenon still has major societal effects.

Fairness in Sports

We'll look more at the issue of fairness in sports in the next chapter, which deals with "trans women." What is there to say about biological women competing in men's sports? Very little, for the simple reason that by competing in a male league, "trans men" are actively placing themselves at a disadvantage. Try as I might, I cannot find an instance of a female taking a prize from a man. The worst five players in the NBA would beat the best five players in the WNBA every single time. The same can be said for most sports. This is why there is little argument about keeping females out of male spaces—their participation in male sports does not skew the competition in their favor or affect the ability of male athletes to win in their respective sports.

Conversion Therapy Bans

For most people, "conversion therapy" refers to therapies intended to help people overcome same-sex attraction. Whatever one thinks of the benefits of such therapies, surely any adult should be allowed to seek counseling, whether religious or secular, that he thinks will help him. Since the public seems to support bans on "conversion therapy" for minors, however, trans activists have blurred the lines. As a result, conversion therapy can now mean any challenge to a person's claimed "gender identity." The success of this campaign is evident through proclamations by former President Joe Biden, former Secretary of State Antony Blinken, and others in that Administration who either did not understand or deliberately conflated the difference between homosexuality and "gender identity." Trans activists have succeeded in twisting the term "conversion therapy" to mean not just the attempt to change same-sex attraction, which has no support outside fundamentalist religious circles, but also to include any effort at holistic counselling of young people presenting with gender dysphoria. Many U.S. states ban conversion therapy, and as a result doctors, psychologists, and therapists are often leery of trying to help a child accept his or her actual sex, or look into the reasons for his or her gender distress.

Activists and Allies: From Planned
Parenthood to Transgender Activism

One of the biggest propagators of trans ideology and prescribers of "gender affirming care" is Planned Parenthood, which was founded nearly a century ago by Margaret Sanger explicitly as a eugenics organization intended to prevent undesirables from overcoming the genetic stock of the superior races.[50] Planned Parenthood started with contraception, which at the time was illegal in many states, and then moved into abortion advocacy and abortion services. In the last few years, Planned Parenthood has become a major prescriber of GAC. Though this might seem tangential to Planned Parenthood's mission, in fact dispensing puberty blockers and cross-sex hormones is yet another method to the original ends, since it leads to sterilization. Under the heading "What should I teach my elementary school aged child about identity?" this is what the organization's website says to parents: "Be aware that puberty can be an especially tough time for transgender or gender nonconforming kids. As they get closer to reaching puberty, you can talk with a doctor or nurse about puberty blockers and other transgender medical care."[51]

Planned Parenthood fully endorses "affirmative care," that is, the concept, legally mandated in 20 states already, that therapists and doctors must not challenge the assertion of a child that his or her "gender" is contrary to his or her sex observed at birth. They must, instead, take the word of that child as if it were a clinical diagnosis, and proceed with "affirming," through hormonal and surgical intervention if that is what the child wants—regardless of parental objections.

A page from the website of Planned Parenthood of Illinois claims that "there is scientific evidence to support that gender identity is biologically determined."[52] The studies supplying this alleged evidence have been, as Dr. Debra Soh points out, negated by further, more comprehensive meta studies (studies which aggregate smaller studies). There is growing evidence from people who have "transitioned" and then "detransitioned" that gender identity is a choice, one that can later be changed. Medically or surgically transitioning, however, cannot be undone so easily, or at all, and as such should not be the first or even second course of action for children or teens.

A Florida chapter of Planned Parenthood "offers gender-affirming hormone therapy for transmasculine, transfeminine, non-binary, and gender diverse individuals" and its staff "see hormone therapy as an important service that really goes to the core of our mission."[53] That mission has clearly changed far beyond planning parenthood and ensuring that women have access to comprehensive healthcare. Providing such services to patients does not assist with human reproduction or help to fill the historical deficiencies in the way the healthcare system treats women. The ability to have children is both a right and a choice, which GAC makes difficult for its victims, if not impossible: too much testosterone makes women infertile and atrophies their reproductive organs, while excess estrogen reduces male production of sperm. Transgender "men" cannot produce sperm and impregnate women.

The Media: Symbols and Role Models

As Abigail Shrier wrote in *Irreversible Damage*, and as is obvious to anyone who has had a teenage daughter, social contagion of fashion, phobia, and collective belief is strong in young women. There are many examples of localized contagion of bizarre beliefs and new fashions, from the Salem witch trials to the sudden appearance of knotted-rope wrist bands in my fourth-grade classroom in the 1970s. Social media has exponentially increased the power of ideas to spread, and the authority of online "influencers" to whom young girls and women look for guidance and affirmation. This is a huge part of the massive increase in girls who identify as boys, or as non-binary, or as some other thing that is not a girl.

From Ellen to Elliot

One prominent "transman" is Elliot Page, formerly Ellen Page, an actress known for her role in the film *Juno*. Page is still working, albeit with a reduced range of possible roles. As Elliot, Page has appeared in a few films and television series.[54] What makes the issue of "trans men" so different from that of "trans women" is that no man need fear Elliot Page. No man would be concerned if the slight, elfin Page showed up in a men's bathroom or changing room. Men might be a little confused, but they would not fear for their safety or experience the sense of violation that girls and women do when seeing a naked man in their pool changing room.

From Mac to Gabriel

The story of journalist Gabriel Mac, formerly known as Mac McClelland, represents the far end of the trans man journey, and it is laid out in a lengthy 2021 article in *New York* magazine, where Mac worked as a writer.[55] In brief, Mac chose to have a phalloplasty, an operation—or series of operations—in which a facsimile of a penis is made from the flesh of the patient's arm or leg and affixed to the groin area. Phalloplasty leaves a large scar where the flesh was taken and results in an organ that does not become erect when the owner is aroused (though it can be inflated with a pump if one is installed). As this article explains, "surgeons are currently required to mix and match a large number of surgical techniques in order to produce an ideal aesthetic and functional outcome. This cloudiness adds unnecessary difficulty to an already major surgical procedure."[56]

Mac attempts to justify this path in a 5,000-word story. Mac did this as an adult, but *New York* magazine and other sympathetic media send the same message to young girls, which is that they can complete the journey to manhood, and that this will cure what ails them. That is a fantasy not borne out by evidence. The photo of Mac on the cover of the magazine is highly idealized: Mac has a toned physique and is wearing flattering "tighty whities." Yet Mac admits that transitioning from "her" to "him" was an "emotional-mental-social-medical-legal-extreme-marginalization mindfuck shitshow."

In reality, as Mac honestly explains in the piece, complications from phalloplasty are common, and most recipients have to return for multiple corrective or ameliorative surgeries. Mac admits that the worst outcome of a phalloplasty is that after "all the fat and skin had been stripped from their left forearm from wrist to nearly elbow, along with major nerves, an artery, and veins, and then shaped into a tube and connected, in careful layers, to skin and blood vessels and nerves in their pelvis" his new penis had failed.[57] This resulted in the patient having to remove the neo-penis and, incredibly, finding surgeons willing to harvest more flesh for another try. Mac writes that the "overall proportion of phalloplasties that need surgical revision…is about one in two. The highest number of corrective follow-up surgeries needed by anyone I know personally is 12."[58]

As mentioned, there is evidence that a majority of people with gender dysphoria also suffer from other issues, like depression, suicidality, autism, and anxiety. In Mac's case, he believes he had a "patriarchal, heterosexist, racist, capitalist acculturation." Mac claimed to be "asexual," though clarifying that "you can be asexual and have a boyfriend." Mac has had suicidal thoughts since kindergarten. It's hard to get inside the head of someone who writes that "when penis is self, as penis is a gift to self, it's a gift, too, to others." Or that Mac's uterus, before surgical removal, "swirled with dysphoria like nausea from the depths of my soul."

Young girls need to understand the messy, expensive, sometimes debilitating medical and surgical reality of "transitioning," not just the air-brushed, all-problems-solved ideal they are presented with on social media.

De-Transitioners

The contradiction at the heart of gender ideology is this: a person's inner feeling about his or her "gender" – which, recall, is independent of the bodily reality of sex - is always correct and should be validated by the world. For this reason, the fact that increasing numbers of young women are discovering that they made a horrible mistake and are "de-transitioning" is anathema to trans activists.

In the United States, several social media networks exist for de-transitioners, as well as organizations that raise awareness of gender ideology's dangers, such as the medical association Do No Harm.[59] Britain has a Detransition Advocacy Network. There are also some brave men and women who have withstood the barrage of attacks from trans activists and their allies to tell their stories. Inconveniently for the activists, the ranks of de-transitioners continue to grow. In the U.S., several brave young women, such as Billy Burleigh, Cat Cattinson, Luka Hein, Prisha Mosley, and Chloe Cole, have not only de-transitioned but done so publicly. They have been willing to appear in media interviews, conferences, and even testify before federal and state legislators. Trans activists, leftwing organizations, legacy media, and many politicians paint these women as the willing stooges of conservatives, but the girls and women speak for themselves. They do so to help other girls avoid making the uninformed decisions they did, and to raise awareness so that legislators restrict what children are allowed to do, as well as what adults can do to them, in the name of "gender affirming care."

Chloe Cole

Chloe Cole from California is perhaps the best-known de-transitioner. At a March 12 (now Detransition Awareness Day), 2025, hearing before the House Judiciary Subcommittee on Constitution and Limited Government on gender-affirming care for children, Cole testified that girls like her were "lied to" and "abused by the medical system we were told to trust when we were most impressionable, most vulnerable..."[60] Cole is now the patient advocate at Do No Harm, an organization of medical professionals whose name—taken from the Hippocratic Oath—explains its mission. She has described her journey many times. For four years, she was led down the path of "transition" from female to male, realizing at age 16 that she had made a horrible mistake. After fairly brief consultations, Cole herself was prescribed puberty blockers and then cross-sex hormones and was later given a double mastectomy, all in the name of "gender-affirming care." Cole says the doctors and therapists who took her down the road to transition refused to treat her when she decided to reverse course. By that time, some of the effects, including a lower voice, were irreversible.

In 2025, President Trump issued executive orders to stop federally funded hospitals from providing "gender affirming" drugs and surgery to children. Representative Dan Crenshaw (R–TX) introduced a bill to enshrine these protections in a law that can't be overturned as easily as a presidential order. Do No Harm reports that 54 U.S. hospitals provided nearly 14,000 sex-change "treatments," including 5,700 surgeries, to minors between 2019 and 2023. Surgeries included mastectomies, removal of penis and testes, and creation of artificial vaginas.

Keira Bell

Keira Bell from the U.K. sued the National Health Service's Tavistock center. Her claim was that "children and young persons under 18 are not competent to give consent to the administration of puberty blocking drugs," and that "the information given to those under 18 by the defendant is misleading and insufficient to ensure such children or young persons are able to give informed consent."[61] The issues before the High Court boiled down to whether a minor could consent to puberty blockers, but the wider implications were whether minors could consent to other GAC, including cross-sex hormones, mastectomies, and genital surgeries. In 2020, the High Court concluded that

> much information the child is given as to long-term consequences, s/he will not be able to weigh up the implications of the treatment to a sufficient degree. There is no age-appropriate way to explain to many of these children what losing their fertility or full sexual function may mean to them in later years.[62]

The Bell case was a major blow to the trans medicine complex, which in Britain was nearly all financed by the public National Health Service. In the United States, for-profit providers and hospitals have a far greater incentive to continue the lucrative industry of transgender medicine. The British government shut Tavistock down completely in 2022, after publication of the interim report of *The Cass Review* (the final report was published in 2024).

Conclusion

As Keira Bell told Stella O'Malley of Genspect in 2024: "As the years go on and more people are detransitioning—or stopping the process of transition—and figuring things out, people are also starting to realise that those terms aren't really fitting anymore," as, in O'Malley's words, "they both offer a promise that arguably isn't available."[63] In an interview, Elliot Page describes how happy "he" is. Few people watching Page talk about looking in the mirror at her chest, scarred from a voluntary double mastectomy, would perceive happiness, let alone male-ness.[64] The promise that one can change one's sex is a lie. The sooner that society stops trying to pretend otherwise, and stops allowing children to pursue a chimera, the healthier society will be. Pandering to delusion is not compassion—it's just enabling.

A person to follow: J.K. Rowling, @jk_rowling, X.

A book to read: *Irreversible Damage: The Transgender Craze Seducing Our Daughters*, by Abigail Shrier, 2021.

A group to support: Genspect, www.Genspect.org.

Chapter 5

The Fifth Commandment:
You Shall Not Know "What Is a Woman"

Trans women are women. — Sir Keir Starmer

Gender ideology is inconsistent and self-contradictory. And though activists posit that there are unlimited "gender identities," they fight hard to make everyone accept that "trans men are men" and "trans women are women," thus enforcing a binary they seem to reject. Other than aggressively attempting to compel speech in support of their desired reality, the reasons are different in each case. For "trans men," as discussed in the previous chapter, it seems to be an issue of forcing acceptance of the ideology, or of the perception—a largely intellectual battle. For "trans women," it is more about forcing women to accept men who claim to be women into their spaces, such as clubs, sports, prisons, and changing rooms.

Having examined the case of women who want to be accepted as men, let's look at the very different case of men who want to be accepted as women.

1. How Did We Get Here?

In her book *Trans*, Helen Joyce gives an abridged history of how trans ideology went from obscure to mainstream. The first "trans woman" that people have heard of, if any, was likely George Jorgensen from Denmark, who fits the pattern that was common before the current wave of what Lisa Littman called rapid onset gender dysphoria (ROGD) that started after 2015. Jorgensen (whose life was fictionalized in the movie *The Danish Girl* starring Eddie Redmayne) had his penis and testicles surgically removed and an artificial cavity constructed in what would later be known as a "neo-vagina."[1]

German endocrinologist Harry Benjamin was an early purveyor of "trans" medicine. He created the Harry Benjamin Foundation, funded by a wealthy trans-identifying donor. This activist foundation was renamed the World Professional Association for Transgender Health (WPATH) in 2006.[2] Today, the WPATH provides the treatment guidelines followed by most U.S. clinicians.

Another early purveyor of gender ideology was John Money, who ended up at Maryland's Johns Hopkins University. Money's theory was that sex was not determined by nature, but by nurture. To test it he carried out perhaps one of the most barbaric experiments in medical history. Money convinced the parents of two twin boys, born in 1965, to castrate and raise one as a girl. The selected twin boy's penis had been damaged beyond repair in a circumcision accident, making him an ideal candidate in Money's eyes. Baby Bruce Reimer was thus raised as Brenda, with his parents supplying all the sex-stereotypical toys and roles under Money's watchful guidance. During puberty, Bruce rejected his imposed female identity, and as an adult, he chose the name David. The story was a tragedy from start to finish: Reimer shot himself in 2004, two years after his twin brother died of a drug overdose.[3]

Helen Joyce connects trans ideology to the wider movement of postmodern theory, in which reality is socially constructed and there are no objective certainties. This esoteric academic framework, explored by French philosophers Jacques Derrida and Michelle Foucault, has spawned all manner of academic mischief that boils down to attempts to "queer" everything, which essentially means to strip it of all common meaning and make it whatever a person wants. According to online learning source MasterClass, "queer theory aims to deconstruct what is acceptable or 'normal.'"[4]

Feminists who had started out seeking equal rights for women found themselves tied in intellectual knots. Leading feminist Judith Butler, for instance, has claimed famously, and obscurely, that both "sex" and "gender" are mere performances. If men could become women simply by saying they were, and vice versa, a whole new, supposedly inclusive, vocabulary was needed. Hence, the monstrosities of "birthing person," "people who menstruate," "pregnant people," and "vagina owners." As

Joyce concludes, the goal of such terms is to remove "all obstacles to using the words 'woman' and 'female' for any male who wants them,"[5] and therefore, eliminate any spaces reserved exclusively for females.

Autogynephilia

Dr. Ray Blanchard, a clinical psychologist, coined the term autogynephilia—meaning literally "the love of oneself as a woman"—to differentiate boys who believed from a young age that they were born in the wrong body from a second phenomenon: adult men, often in middle age, who enjoy dressing, acting, and appearing as women and are sexually aroused by the idea of themselves as women.[6] Blanchard's research and conclusions made him a prime target of aggressive trans activists. He believes that the leaders of the trans radical activist (TRA) movement are angry because of "envy of women, and resentment at not being accepted by women as one of them."[7]

The vitriol and rage against British women's rights activist Kelly-Jay Keene, also known as Posie Parker, certainly supports Blanchard's hypothesis. In 2024, while on a "Let Women Speak" tour in New Zealand, Keene and her entourage were attacked by TRAs and she barely escaped with her life.[8]

2. Women Lose Their Spaces

Trans activists have made it clear that no space formerly reserved for women is beyond their grasp. Nothing is off limits: sports, changing rooms, rape shelters, even prisons.

Women's Spas

Canadian "Jessica" (formerly Jonathan) Yaniv has made a hobby of suing spas that refuse to wax his penis and testicles. A member of British Columbia's human rights tribunal agreed with Yaniv's complaint, saying that waxing was "critical gender-affirming care for transgender women."[9] By that logic, a man's bikini wax to remove unwanted hair should be covered by health insurance, as well as his manicure, or his make-up. All might be said to "affirm her gender." Where does one draw the line?

Women's Prisons

At least with spas, women have a choice about where they choose to go. The same cannot be said of prison. A survey of English-speaking countries shows that in the past decade, at least 98 percent of sex offenders have been men. When gender ideology dictates that any male sex offender can get into women's prison simply by saying he is a woman, the results are predictable. In the United Kingdom, which has a similar ratio of male to female prisoners as the United States, there are 88,000 male and only 4,000 female prisoners. That's because men commit more crime than women. Of the men, 19 percent are in prison for sex offences, but only 4 percent of women are—meaning that men are *a hundred times* more likely to be imprisoned for sex offences than women.[10] In the U.K., where they can self-identify and the authorities must take them at their word, around one in 50 male prisoners now identify as female—at least four times the number of men who identify as women in the population as a whole.[11] Furthermore, over 70 percent of transgender prisoners—overwhelmingly biological men—are in prison for sex offenses or violent crime.[12] From this one can conclude that either (a) trans-identifying men commit sex offenses at a far higher rate than either men or women, or (b) some of these men are identifying as women in order to get into women's prisons—whether for an easier prison experience, or to be among potential victims or willing sex partners. Neither possibility is accepted by the progressive orthodoxy.

Socially liberal Canada, under leftwing Liberal Party Prime Minister Justin Trudeau, set the standard for putting men's desires ahead of women's rights. In 2000, a male murderer who identified as female successfully sued the prison service to force it to provide him (and all future inmates who so asked) with hormones and sex-change surgery.[13] In 2017, Trudeau allowed prisoners to self-identify into either male or female units.[14]

At the U.S. federal level, under President Biden, the Department of Justice supported prison inmates seeking gender surgery as a constitutional right. In January 2025, President Trump issued an executive order banning "gender-affirming care" in federal prisons and immigration detention. In March, the ACLU filed a class-action lawsuit against the Trump

Administration and the Federal Bureau of Prisons to force provision of "gender-affirming care" to federal inmates.[15]

The picture in the states is mixed. Under President Trump, the Department of Justice withdrew its support for a lawsuit (left over from the Biden Administration) by an inmate seeking to force the Georgia Department of Corrections to provide "gender-affirming care."[16] In 2021, California passed SB132, the Transgender Respect, Agency, and Dignity Act, a law introduced by State Senator Scott Wiener that allows men who identify as women into women's prisons. The law requires the California Department of Corrections and Rehabilitation to consider a prisoner's request "regardless of his criminal history, his anatomy, or whether he has undergone any so-called 'transition' procedures."[17]

Transferring extremely dangerous male sex offenders to women's prisons is, hardly surprisingly, opposed by a majority of female prisoners. There have been a number of rapes, assaults, and pregnancies resulting from males being housed with females. According to a lawsuit filed by several female prisoners, represented by California lawyer Harmeet Dhillon:

> Many of these biological males who now identify as transgender have never self-identified as transgender prior to entering the prison system. Often, there is no evidence they are in the process of "transitioning." They do not call themselves by a female name, dress or otherwise groom themselves to appear as a female, and have not received or plan to receive treatment for their trans-identification such as hormonal treatment or genital surgery. Yet simply by stating they now identify as transgender, S.B. 132 requires the California Department of Corrections and Rehabilitation ("CDCR") to transfer them to a female correctional facility.[18]

In 2014, a few weeks before his 18th birthday, a California man called James Tubbs was arrested for sexually assaulting a ten-year-old girl. He self-identified as a woman – shortly after his arrest. In 2023, now with criminal records in three states and pending murder charges in another case, Tubbs was to sentenced to serve two years - for the 2014 assault - in a juvenile prison for females as "Hannah" Tubbs, where he would be housed with girls.[19] As *The Federalist* reported in April 2025, California had "45 trans-identifying males housed in the women's prisons, 208 pending transfers, and 898 requesting to be transferred."[20] In April 2025,

State Senator Shannon Grove proposed a bill to prohibit male prisoners with histories of sex offenses from being housed in women's prisons.

In 2021, Jonathan Richardson was convicted of murdering his 11-month-old step-daughter and sentenced to 55 years in prison in Indiana. While incarcerated, Richardson began identifying as Autumn Cordellioné (AC) and taking cross-sex hormones. In 2023, AC asked prison authorities to provide gender transition surgery but was denied. The ACLU sued on behalf of AC. In 2025, a federal judge ordered Indiana to provide AC with surgery to remove his male genitals and create facsimile female genitalia.[21] AC's argument, via the ACLU, is that *not* providing such surgery violates the Constitution's 8th Amendment, which says that "cruel and unusual punishments [shall not be] inflicted." (In any other era but ours, cutting off, rather than *refusing* to cut off, a male prisoner's testicles and penis would be considered "cruel and unusual."). Indiana state law bans using state funds to provide inmates with gender re-assignment surgery, and the one gender clinic in the state reportedly will not operate on prison inmates. Indiana's Department of Corrections was also told by its lead psychologist that AC was not transgender and has an "established pattern of attention-seeking behavior." Despite all that, in September 2024, a judge enjoined the state of Indiana to provide AC's desired surgeries. Indiana challenged the ruling, but the judge affirmed his injunction in April 2025.[22]

3. Colleges and Title IX

The aim of "queering" something is to destroy its foundations so that it can be rebuilt in the right (meaning leftwing) way. No institution is more a target for the contemporary Left in this quest than schools and universities. Accordingly, the Biden Administration sought to change Title IX, the 1972 law that requires equal treatment of the—two—sexes.[23] Title IX was protecting women's rights while gender ideology was still fermenting in the academic basement.

Biden's Title IX Rules—
All In on Gender Ideology and SOGI

In April 2024, the Biden Administration finalized 1,500 pages of rules on the interpretation of Title IX. The impact of the changes was to expand a law that had been protecting women's rights for 50 years to a new class: men who identify as women. The new regulations added sexual orientation and gender identity (SOGI) to the definition of women for the purposes of Title IX. SOGI is a term that includes self-identified and synthetic "gender identities." The Biden rules would have forced educational programs to accommodate males in female-only spaces and female-only organizations or lose federal funding.[24]

The liberal media greeted this as an unalloyed victory. *The Washington Post* headline proclaimed that "Biden Title IX rules set to protect trans students, survivors of abuse."[25] The AP's headline read: "Biden's new Title IX rules protect LGBTQ+ students, but avoid addressing transgender athletes."[26]

The rules had been proposed months earlier but were held pending public comment. Despite more than 240,000 comments, mostly critical, the rules took effect on August 1, 2024.[27] By this time, ten U.S. states had passed laws requiring people to use what *The Washington Post* called "bathrooms and locker rooms that align with their biological sex identified at birth."[28] The Biden rules would also have, in theory, compelled school districts to use "pronouns corresponding with a trans student's gender identity" (again, the *Post*) or be accused of violating Title IX. Fortunately, lawsuits delayed implementation of the Biden rules until after the November 2024 presidential election. In January 2025, a judge struck the rules down saying they "exceed the Department's authority under Title IX, violate the Constitution, and are the result of arbitrary and capricious agency action..."[29] Shortly afterwards, the Trump Department of Education announced that it was dropping the rules.[30] This left the state of play the same as under President Trump's 2020 rule, which had undone changes made under President Barack Obama, in a policy whip-saw that is hard to keep up with.

Even though they weren't fully implemented, it's worth looking at the massive Biden Title IX rules in some detail, as they sum up the Biden Administration's approach to gender identity in education, and the people who pushed them could one day be back in office. The Biden rules studiously avoided the third rail of male participation in women's sports. This wasn't an ideological omission. The Biden Administration was enthralled to gender ideology as it gets. This was a political choice, as it was passed seven months before the presidential election. But it clearly implies that the same protections for SOGI apply, for example stating that men or boys who identify as women or girls cannot be kept out of female spaces, such as locker rooms.[31]

Sexual Harassment Claims: No Due Process

Biden's rules would have changed how schools are required to deal with complaints of sexual harassment and assault and tied compliance to their receipt of federal funds. In essence, the Biden rules rolled back the Trump rules, which changed the Obama rule, which gave colleges the power to determine the mechanics of their sex harassment and assault processes, and let college officials act as investigator, prosecution, defense, judge, jury, and executioner. Unfortunately for the accused, who are usually male, U.S. college administrators are overwhelmingly from the political Left. This is even more so in the DEI departments and other such offices that deal with student complaints against faculty and one another. Apart from how the Biden rules abandoned due process, they also made it easier for woke colleges to add new "offenses" to the list of what constitutes harassment, including individuals failing to accept gender ideology and every fellow student's chosen gender identity.

Title IX and "Mis-Gendering"

The University of California at Davis's Title IX office promulgates gender ideology in a session called Abusive Conduct and Harassment Training, which, according to a student, was required of all students. As Rebeka Zeljko writes in *The Federalist*, the training taught that "trans women are women" and "trans men are men" and that "nonbinary, agender, genderqueer, gender fluid, Two-Spirit, bigender, pangender, gender nonconforming, gender variant" sexual identities exist.[32]

The university was not able to tell students how to skate on this thin ice. If one does not believe in gender ideology, that is, that it is possible to be born in the wrong body, or to be "non-binary"—neither male nor female—then one will have a hard time speaking honestly while following the guidance that students "use language and support policies and practices that affirm all persons' ability to live, work, and socialize as their whole selves."[33]

When she asked college authorities to clarify what that meant in practice, the UC Davis student was told that "accidental misuse of a transgender employee's preferred name and pronouns does not violate [Title IX, but] intentionally and repeatedly using the wrong name and pronouns to refer to a transgender employee could contribute to an unlawful hostile work environment."[34]

UC Davis's campus Sexual Violence and Sexual Harassment Policy defines sexual harassment to include "acts of verbal, nonverbal, or physical aggression, intimidation, or hostility based on gender, gender identity, gender expression, sex- or gender-stereotyping, or sexual orientation."[35] This standard is vague and would intimidate many students into taking the safer road of pretending to accept gender ideology to avoid being the subject of a complaint.

4. Fairness in Sports

In October 2024, a United Nations report noted that "according to information received, by 30 March 2024, over 600 female athletes in more than 400 competitions have lost more than 890 medals in 29 different sports" due to the "replacement of the female sports category with a mixed-sex category."[36] The report explained what should not need saying: that male athletes are on average bigger and stronger, advantages which "can result in the 'loss of fair opportunity' for female competitors." That is an edge that even suppressing the male levels of testosterone through drugs cannot remove.

Trans activists say there is no proof that men have any advantage and claim there are no studies to show this. There are also no studies showing that adults can beat toddlers in a fight, but everyone knows it to be so. The Left insists, in the face of evidence, that men competing in women's sports "hardly ever happens."[37] Yet it does, in boxing, cycling, disc golf, golf, swimming, track and field, mixed martial arts, and an increasing number of competitions. At the time of this writing, two men were competing in the finals of a women's pool tournament in England.[38] The apex of performative ignorance on men in women's sports was an April 2025 rant by former *Daily Show* sidekick and now host of HBO's *Last Week Tonight* John Oliver. On his show, Oliver did his best to minimize and mock women and girls who were physically hurt by, or lost to, male competitors.[39]

Most Men Are Physically Stronger than Most Women

It's difficult to believe that one needs to cite evidence and data for why men competing with women is unfair, but here goes. Men are on average bigger, stronger, and faster than women. Men have higher lung capacity, bone density, and muscle mass than women.[40] These differences are baked in at puberty, after which cross-sex hormone treatment (estrogen for men) can slightly lower performance but does not change underlying bone, muscle, or organ structure. As a result of greater average male size and strength, some professions and nearly all sports, there is an advantage to being male. This is why separate categories for women and men exist, as they do for different age groups.

This advantage has been recognized by someone with a keen understanding of the issue: Caitlyn Jenner, who, as Bruce Jenner, won the decathlon at the Montreal Olympics in 1976 and set the world record. Jenner has publicly said that males should not be competing with women in sports, as have other professional athletes like Martina Navratilova and Olympic swimming medalist Nancy Hogshead-Makar. The sports-science consensus is that men have at least a 10 percent average advantage in physical competition over women, though it varies widely according to the sport.[41] Caitlyn Jenner may now identify woman, but beneath the artful clothes, makeup, and other adjustments still lies the frame of a male Olympic champion.

In testimony before the Indiana legislature supporting a bill to ban transgender "women" from participating in women's sports, Corinna Cohn identified as "a transsexual...someone who was born male and used pharmaceuticals and plastic surgery to feminize my body so that I appear to be a woman." Cohn goes on: "Despite having these procedures, my sex is male, and neither science nor medicine can change that."[42] For thirty years, Cohn tried to live a private, productive life. Despite being on estrogen for decades, Cohn does not deny the obvious benefits of male puberty.

Facts Be Damned

Venn diagrams of men's and women's height, weight, and strength do have a small intersecting middle. Sex is binary, but many traits derived from sex, such as height, strength, and musculature, are bimodal. Picture two bell curves. The one on the left represents the distribution of physical traits of females, and the one on the right represents the distribution of various physical traits for males. The rightward long tail of the female curve overlaps with the leftward tail of the male curve on the right. Many female athletes are typical females who are somewhere along the narrowing tail to the right of the female curve. The average female in the WNBA, for instance, is just over six feet – which is taller than the average male. But the male athletes come from the far tight tail of the male curve.

As a rule, short men don't play basketball, weak men don't lift weights or play football, and slow men don't play soccer. The best high school or college male athletes, in nearly every competitive sport, handily beat even the best female professional athletes. This is not to say that male athletes train harder or apply themselves better than women do—it's just that they have a natural, biological advantage in most sports. The same can be said for women in certain pursuits; some studies show that on average women are better at learning languages than men, supporting the idea that biology may confer different advantages on the sexes.

In addition to media leftists like John Oliver, even some organizations supposedly fighting for women take the side of male athletes. On December 5, 2023, Fatima Goss Graves of the National Women's Law Center (NWLC) testified before the U.S. Congress[43] on Title IX[44] and what she called "gender equity in school sports." The NWLC claims to be

> committed to the robust enforcement of Title IX and eradicating all forms of sex discrimination in school, including sex-based harassment, discrimination against LGBTQI+ students, discrimination against pregnant and parenting students, and intersectional discrimination based on both sex and other protected characteristics, such as discrimination against women and girls of color and women and girls with disabilities.[45]

Yet, the NWLC staff members say they "know unequivocally that trans women and girls, and intersex women and girls, are women and girls who deserve the full benefits and opportunities intended by Title IX."[46] Lumping men with "differences of sex development" (DSD), aka "intersex" women, with women is subsuming women's rights to men's. The NWLC filed amicus briefs in all the major Supreme Court Title IX cases. Though the groups claims to "protect women and girls' athletic opportunities," it also defends trans "women" who want to take those opportunities away. Graves argued that "policies excluding trans girls and women from school sports programs threaten all women and girls who excel in athletics."[47] She testified that policies protecting women's and girls' sports "reinforce a false binary by assuming that those assigned male at birth are inevitably and inherently athletically superior and those identified as female are inherently weaker and less athletic."[48]

In her testimony, Graves claimed that the assumption that "being assigned male at birth is innately linked to athletic success" is "misogyny and stereotyping." And, once again using the debunked claim that gender dysphoric people are more likely to commit suicide if not affirmed in their gender identity, she claimed that the benefits of allowing "trans, nonbinary, and intersex students the right to play sports" "could even be lifesaving."[49]

Graves testified that

> the premise that excluding or restricting participation by trans, nonbinary, and intersex student athletes is necessary for "fairness" or "safety" invokes false and harmful myths; specifically, that transgender and intersex women and girls are categorically bigger, faster, and stronger and pose an inherent threat to the physical safety and athletic success of their peers.[50]

However, it is reality, not myth, that most men are larger and stronger than most women. That reality does not change if those men identify as women. There's ample proof that this is true, though ideologues vainly try and argue otherwise. More on that in a minute. First, on the question of how sex affects performance in sport, there is *much* evidence. There are too many examples of average men defeating top-class women in the women's category, but I can illustrate with a few examples across different sports.

Cycling

Canadian cyclist Rachel McKinnon, a biological male, won a gold medal at the UCI Masters Track Cycling World Championships in Manchester, England, in October 2019. McKinnon was, as is typical of trans women who beat women at sports, unrepentant, as she wrote for *The New York Times*.[51] Because McKinnon has a legally changed birth certificate, passport, driver's license, U.S. permanent resident card, and medical records, as well as a racing license that reads "F" for female, McKinnon argues, that's the end of debate. Not only does McKinnon claim that "trans women are women," he takes the further step of arguing that "the Union Cycliste Internationale, USACycling, Cycling Canada, the Canadian and United States governments and the state of South Carolina all agree that I'm female."

"No openly trans woman has set an open elite world record in any sport," McKinnon says, as if that is the metric. It does not take more than a glance at McKinnon to see that—at six feet tall and 190 pounds—the cyclist possesses the height, skeleton, and muscle more typical of a man than of a woman, even if a few women are bigger than he is. McKinnon claims that his "testosterone levels are so low that they're undetectable, and have been that way since 2012." But that does not, as the U.N. report makes clear, mitigate the advantages of having testosterone for many years pre and post puberty, and growing up as a male. McKinnon argues that it "is a human right to be able to compete." No such right to compete exists, even in the sweeping terms of the Universal Declaration of Human Rights, a United Nations document which contains many supposed rights that are aspirational and entirely unenforceable in many countries. Even if it did exist in a binding international treaty, the right to compete fairly is a right that women were denied until very recently and are now at risk of being denied again if trans men are allowed to compete freely against them. For sports to be fair, they need rules, from the size of the bat, paddle, or racket to the length of the race. One such logical rule is that one should compete against people of similar age and of the same sex.

On December 3, 2023, Tessa Johnson and Evelyn Williamson, both transgender-identifying male cyclists, won first and second places in the Single Speed category at the Illinois State Cyclocross Championships women's competition. The pair had previously won first and second places at a Chicago women's race two months before.[52] Merely looking at the photograph of these two next to the woman who took third place makes the obvious point that men are generally bigger and stronger than women. Martina Navratilova, the greatest female tennis player of the '80s and '90s, blasted the riders as "more mediocre male bodies taking podium places from female athletes."[53]

Soccer

In 2017, an under-15 boys' team from Dallas easily defeated the U.S. women's national soccer squad.[54]

In the fall of 2024, five girls on the Hillsboro-Deering High School Girls Varsity Soccer team in New Hampshire refused to play against Kearsage Regional High School, whose best player is a trans-identifying boy named Maelle Jacques.[55] Heather Thyng, the mother of a Hillsboro-Deering player who refused to play, told a media outlet: "This is about biology for us and the increased physical risk when playing a full contact sport against the opposing sex." Jacques won first place at the New Hampshire Interscholastic Athletic Association Division 2 state championship in February.[56]

Swimming

Will Thomas, a male University of Pennsylvania swimmer, competed on the men's team in 2017 and 2018, where he was ranked 462nd nationally. After "transitioning" to female by changing his name to "Lia," and taking estrogen for a year, he was allowed to swim on the women's team where he was instantly a top performer.[57] Thomas is much bigger, taller, and stronger than the women he competes against, thanks to having been through male puberty, a transformation of skeleton, muscle, heart, and lungs that no amount of female hormones can undo. In the Ivy League Swimming and Diving Championships for 2022, Thomas won the 100-yard, 200-yard, and 500-yard freestyle races and set several pool records.[58] In 2022, Thomas won three Ivy League titles and was nominated as "woman of the year" by the University of Pennsylvania, where he was a student. In just a few years, Thomas had gone from a mediocre male swimmer to top ranked in the female category in the entire country. In one race, Thomas tied with swimmer Riley Gaines, who is much smaller than he is. The race organizers insisted, according to Gaines, that Thomas keep the one (shared) trophy.[59] The University of Pennsylvania strongly supported Thomas over the objections of female members of his own team and other teams. In March 2025, the Trump Administration announced funding cuts of $175 million to Penn.[60] In July 2025, Penn struck a deal with the Department of Education in which they agreed to ban transwomen from women's sports teams and to remove Thomas's putative swimming records.

In May 2025, a 47-year-old swimmer named Ana Caldas, reportedly born a male, won gold medals in all five events at the U.S. Masters Swimming National Championship in Texas.[61] This may have violated Texas' Save Women's Sports Act of 2023, which requires athletes to compete in the sex listed on their birth certificate.

Tennis

Serena and Venus Williams are as big, strong, and talented as women athletes get. Back in 2001, they thought maybe they could beat any male tennis player ranked below 200 in the world. Karsten Braasch, then ranked 203, took the challenge and handily beat them 6 to 1 and 6 to 2, respectively.[62] The Williams sisters are amazing athletes, but they accept the reality that men's and women's tennis are different games.

Track and Field

The website Boys vs Women compares, with easy to grasp graphics, high school boys to Olympic-level women in the 100-meter, 200-meter, 400-meter, and 800-meter races. In all four, boys take the top eight places. With a few exceptions, like the 5,000-meter race, boys place ahead of women in every sport compared.[63] The world's fastest woman running 100 meters can be beaten by more than 100 boys under the age of 18.[64]

In 2019, college runner Minna Svärd of East Texas A&M University came in second to a trans "woman," CeCé Telfer, in the finals of the NCAA Division II Women's 400-meter hurdles. As Craig Telfer, he had competed for Franklin Pierce University on the men's team in 2016 and 2017. According to Svärd, Telfer then ranked 390th among NCAA Division II men. As CeCé, Telfer beat Svärd by nearly two seconds and became "the first known transgender-identified athlete to win an NCAA title."[65] Svärd notes that Olympic competitive men run the 400-meter hurdles a full five seconds faster than women. In 2025, after President Trump's executive order protecting women's sports, Svärd, who without Telfer's presence was the fastest 400-meter hurdler in 2019, argued in *The Wall Street Journal* that "official results of past competitions should be corrected to align with reality. Male competitors should be removed and the rank of affected women increased accordingly."[66]

The state of Connecticut has a policy of allowing public school athletes to compete in the gender as which they identify rather than their biological sex. For several years, two male runners who "identify as female," Terry Miller and Andraya Yearwood, won 15 state championships between them. In 2021, female high school runner Chelsea Mitchell wrote an opinion piece for *USA Today* describing how these two runners had damaged her prospects and those of other girls. *USA Today* changed Mitchell's choice of the word "male" to "transgender" throughout her article, as noted by the legal group Alliance Defending Freedom, which published the article in its original form.[67] In 2023, Mitchell and several female athletes sued the Connecticut Association of Schools and the Connecticut Interscholastic Athletic Conference to overturn the trans policy.[68] They also want the race records corrected so that Miller and Yearwood's results are not counted. As of this writing, the case is still before the courts.

In February 2025, a southern California male high school student won the girls' triple jump competition by a huge margin, as well as winning the girls' high jump and long jump. This prompted the board of the Temecula Valley Unified School District to support AB 89, a state bill to bar male students from competing in female sports.[69] Currently, California lets students self-identify as whatever "gender" they want and participate in sports accordingly.

In March 2025, Aayden "Ada" Gallagher, a male student identifying as a woman, won gold in the girls' 400-meter varsity race at the Portland Interscholastic League meet in Oregon. A video clip shows the stark gap—seven seconds—between Gallagher and the nearest female finisher.[70]

Trans Activists' Proposal: Suck it Up, Ladies

For the most part, the mainstream national media has sided with trans "allies" like John Oliver and Fatima Gross Graves. A willful ignorance of obvious facts is essential to maintaining a belief in gender ideology. Gender ideologues and their progressive allies use several lines of argument to confuse what is really a simple picture. "I don't know who is right in the scientific dispute over whether athletes who were assigned male at birth have lingering advantages from nanomoles of testosterone, or disadvantages from their suppression—hormone studies are all over the map, and anyway, every sport has different demands,"[71] writes *Washington Post* columnist Sally Jenkins.[72] Jenkins uses several arguments in a "no easy answers" approach to assert that the desired of a small number of men who identify as women should trump those of all girls and women. There are several arguments in the "no easy answers" package.

One is that women and men vary in talent and physique within each sex—a concept in biology known as "variation"—so one should recognize the physical differences of trans "women" in women's sport as a part of that variation. Trans activists pretend that the variability within women and men, as groups, negates the large difference between average male and average female size and strength. For example, Fatima Graves cited gymnast Simone Biles' height of 4'8" and basketball player Brittney Griner's height of 6'9" as positive factors in their success. But the comparison is nonsense. Yes, some women are taller and stronger than some men in the general population. But when it comes to elite, and even not so elite, athletic competition, the male advantage is obvious. Everyone knows, and many examples prove, that the best male high school athletes in sports from basketball to ping-pong would beat the best pro women.

A second argument used by Jenkins and others is that competition is never fair, and that women just have to accept it when they lose to men. That argument implies that society should abolish sex, age, and physical handicap as categories for sport, and declare one open contest. That could be done, but women would win few contests ever after. The players in Little League would be much bigger, and the Special Olympics would cease to be special, if able-bodied male narcissists competed and took all the prizes. Easier still would be to ban women from competing in sports at all, like the Taliban did in Afghanistan.

A third argument is that, "Well, 'trans women' aren't really any better anyway, sometimes they lose." Yes, some "trans women" are mediocre or poor athletes and even their unfair advantage can't overcome that. But the difference between *competitive* males and competitive female performance in sports requiring strength and size is just too blindingly obvious for that argument to work. As far as I can tell, women are free to play in the NBA, NFL, or NHL, yet none do.

A fourth argument is, to quote Jenkins, "[p]hysical gifts are distributed unequally, and so are advantages. There are lots of differentials in sports, maybe none bigger than money—the money to pay for coaching and lessons, money to train, money to eat properly so your body develops."[73] The idea here is that men who beat women in all sports where size and strength are important is not about physical differences, but "socioeconomic factors" like equipment, coaching, nutrition, and training. This theory would be simple to put to the test, but it seems hardly worth the research dollars to prove something so obvious. Astrophysicist and noted social liberal Neil deGrasse Tyson was mocked by noted liberal talk show host Bill Maher for sticking to this particularly risible "training and support" argument in a November 2024 episode of Maher's *Real Time* show.[74]

On his show, Maher had criticized a 2021 article in *Scientific American* written by Jack Turban, a medical doctor, radical gender ideologue, and advocate for medical intervention in "gender affirming care."[75] The core of Turban's argument is that because women and girls sometimes beat men and boys who think they are women, there's no problem. Additionally, because testosterone levels vary among men, that factor can't be all that important. The flaw in this argument is simply that even second-rate men can beat first-rate women in their chosen sport. Take Lia Thomas again. The photo of Thomas and Gaines after their infamous tied race shows how absurd it is for these two to be racing in the same category. Thomas is a foot taller than Gaines and appears 100 pounds heavier. His shoulders are much broader, his hips are narrower, and his hands and feet are larger. You can't see inside him, but his heart and lungs are also bigger.[76] All these variables are important in sports, and the reason why a low-ranked male swimmer like Thomas could tie a top-ranked female swimmer. But rather than look at real-life evidence, or conduct large-scale studies of average boys against average girls in mainstream sports - before and after puberty - activists like Turban fall back on obscure research into outlying physical cases, to muddy the waters.

Turban's next argument is that "to force transgender girls to play on the boys' teams...[is] unscientific, and [it]would cause serious mental health damage to both cisgender and transgender youth."[77] He falls back on the one, supposedly unanswerable argument of the trans activists: that if not allowed to live in every way as the opposite to their biological sex, gender dysphoric children will commit suicide. However, that contention has now been thoroughly undermined by studies showing that allowing children to "transition" does not reduce their chance of attempting or committing suicide, and may even increase the risk.[78]

Turban's last attempt to justify males in female sports is a moral one: that "transgender girls...suffer from higher rates of bullying, anxiety and depression" and "have higher rates of homelessness and poverty." That may be true, and it is not a good thing, but the solution cannot be to make things worse for girls and women. For good measure, Turban plays the race card and compares keeping trans-identifying boys out of girls' sports to "painting Black athletes as 'genetically superior' in an attempt to downplay the effects of their hard work and training." Sally Jenkins argues that there is no bigger advantage in sports than money, and Turban rejects the possibility that some individuals are genetically superior (at least when it comes to performing a specific physical task). To what, then, would one attribute the overrepresentation of Hispanics in baseball, and blacks in football and basketball? Is it all simply due to their family wealth and better access to training facilities?

Biden Administration Regulation
to Force Women's Sports to Accept Males

The Biden Administration tried to insert gender identity into every place where sex was referred to. The result of this would be to make discrimination on the basis of sex (that is, spending more on men's sports than women's, or keeping women out of certain courses, professional training, or scholarships) synonymous with discriminating against someone on the basis of sexual orientation or gender identity. That means that colleges would be scrutinized for discrimination not just against women or men on the basis of their sex only, but against a man who simply *thought* he was a woman, or vice versa. Self-identification would be the only ticket needed to access this protection—any kind of test or evaluation is anathema to the gender ideologues.

A regulation proposed under the Biden Administration's Department of Education (DoE) would have ignored the self-evident reality of male advantage. "Under the proposed regulation, schools would not be permitted to adopt or apply a one-size-fits-all policy that categorically bans transgender students from participating on teams consistent with their gender identity," according to an agency fact sheet.[79] The Biden DoE started with the presumption that there is nothing unfair or dangerous about men competing with women. The DoE regulation put the onus on schools and women's teams to show that it would be detrimental to women to have men on their teams. For example, schools would have had to show why there is a heightened risk of "sports related injury" to women, in writing, with the threat of litigation by aggrieved male athletes, or be subject to sanctions, including reduced funding from the DoE.

Sports Injury

The incidence of girls and women being injured by boys and men in women's sports is not high—likely due to the fact that at present, the numbers of males participating in women's sports are still low. But that does not excuse it.

In 2021, one such male who identifies as a woman, Alana McLaughlin, a former Army Special Forces soldier, used a "rear-naked choke" to defeat a female opponent, Celine Provost, at a mixed martial arts (MMA) competition.[80] The first transgender woman to fight in the MMA, Fallon Fox, fractured the skull of one opponent, Tamikka Brents, in a 2014 match.[81] McLaughlin and Fox were both born male and later identified as women—retaining all their physical advantages from male puberty—and competed in full-contact fighting events against women. This seems unfair and dishonorable, not to mention dangerous.

In 2022, high school volleyball player Peyton McNabb was struck in the face by a ball hit by a male player on the opposing (girls') team. Women's volleyball nets are lower than men's, which made it easier for the male player, who is taller and stronger than most women, to spike the ball. In 2025, McNabb was one of many female athletes invited to watch President Trump sign an executive order banning males in female sports.[82]

DSD Muddy the Waters

The clear cases of men self-identifying into women's competitions with an unfair advantage are sometimes confused with a different, very rare, phenomenon: boys who are born with DSD who are, in fact, misclassified as female at birth and raised as girls. One such athlete is Caster Semanya of South Africa. Though Semanya was raised as a girl, he went through male puberty with all the resulting muscle and strength. Semanya and others with this condition (known as 5-ARD) have it through no fault of their own and may have been oblivious to their actual sex throughout their lives. These conditions are rare and often not diagnosed early in developing countries where medical care is less sophisticated or easy to get.

Decisions about where to let them compete are not easy for sports bodies to make, but in the interests of fairness they must be made.

In the 2024 Olympics, a Chinese boxer and an Algerian boxer were entered in the female category although both had all the associated physical advantages of being male. The exact DSD in each case is too complicated to go into here, but the physical advantage of these two competitors was obvious to observers, competitors, and everyone else except the Olympic authority that allowed them to compete as women. The Algerian, Imane Khelif, won a gold medal.[83] So did the Chinese boxer, Lin Yu-ting.[84]

One is naturally sympathetic to individuals who are born with ambiguous genitalia, and no doubt other complications, but empathy should not outweigh basic fairness to female athletes. And yet the mainstream media spared no thought for the women whose dreams of medaling were destroyed in seconds. Italian boxer Angela Carini stopped her fight with Khelif after less than a minute, and while others fought longer, even the best women were outclassed by the two men. NPR crowed that Khelif was "the first Arab or African woman to win a boxing gold."[85] The International Olympic Committee was utterly incompetent at drawing clear lines as to what qualified as female, concentrating on testosterone levels rather than taking into account all the other relevant factors and arriving at a level playing field in which women could safely compete.

Transgender activists and their ideological "allies" revert to pious language about discrimination, like this from the Chicago Cyclocross Cup: "Discrimination or harassment of any kind on the basis of race, color, religion, age, gender, sexual orientation, gender identification, national origin, sportsball team affiliation, or any other stupid ideas someone comes up with to belittle others will not be tolerated."[86]

Cases like Lia Thomas pit two arms of the Left—radical feminists and gender ideologues—against each other. Attempts to bridge the gap by such as UC Berkeley professor of "trans studies" Grace Lavery, who was born male but identifies as a woman, a feminist, and a lesbian, are derided by many actual lesbians and feminists. While there is growing acceptance of trans rights, a majority of Americans—79 percent in a 2024 *New York Times* poll—believe that biological men should not compete against women in sports.[87]

"Gender Affirming Care" and the UN

The previous chapter explored GAC. On its face, it is more religious cult than science: GAC is based on the premise that any human could be born into the wrong body. The Biden Administration did its best to proselytize this cult abroad, in bilateral relations with other countries and at the United Nations. The UN has at best been co-opted, or at worst been negligent in its responsibilities towards children, in furthering the agenda of WPATH and gender ideology. The World Health Organization (WHO) has changed its terminology and recommendations in line with activists' demands. In 2019, the International Classification of Diseases (ICD-11) re-labelled "transsexualism" as "gender incongruence," and re-classified gender dysphoria as no longer a mental disorder. The WHO also promotes the WPATH standard or care, despite the fact that it is disputed scientifically by the United Kingdom and other European nations as well as a growing number of experts in the United States. Just like President Biden forced gender ideology and critical race theory into every aspect of the federal government via his executive orders, the UN has slipped it into programs covering health, food, and assistance. Therefore, adopting gender ideology and the WPATH standards has implications for U.S. foreign aid for healthcare, and undermines parental rights and the rights of children worldwide.

The UN Committee on the Rights of the Child has followed California in prioritizing the decisions and privacy of children over the judgement of their parents. The UN has also adopted the misuse of "conversion therapy" to mean not just programs, but any effort by parents or therapists to help confused children to accept their real, as opposed to imagined or desired, bodies.[88] Accusations of conversion therapy by parents have led to the state taking custody away of one or both parents in Canada and several U.S. states, including California.[89]

As The Heritage Foundation's Grace Melton and Emilie Kao (now of Alliance Defending Freedom) wrote,

> families are the natural and fundamental group unit of society, and parents have the primary responsibility—and corresponding rights— to direct the upbringing of their children... Advocating children's autonomy to access...dangerous, disfiguring medical procedures without the consent of their parents violates the well-established need for parental safeguarding.[90]

5. Recovery From Trans Ideology: Reality Responds

The obvious, though difficult, response from girls and women seeking fair competition and wanting to avoid injury is to sit it out. Until recently, the social pressure against being "transphobic" has been simply too strong. Witness Angela Carini, the Italian Olympic boxer pounded out of competition by Imane Khelif. After seeing her Olympic dream crushed in less than a minute, and understandably refusing to shake hands with Khelif, she later *apologized* for having to, as she said at the time, "preserve my life" by stopping the match.[91]

In 2025, there are encouraging signs that women are willing to change the rules or else boycott. Complaints from women to the North American Grappling Association that they had been paired with men without being warned led to a rule change.[92] There is a heightened risk of injury for women in contact sports, but a measurable male competitive advantage is apparent even in many non-contact sports and activities like pool.

In November 2023, Lynne Pinches politely forfeited her match against trans-identifying male Harriet Haynes at the English Pool Association's 2023 Champion of Champions Ladies competition in Wales.[93] The tournament's organizer, the Works Eightball Pool Federation, had initially stated that the women's competition was to be open "exclusively open to individuals who are born female," but they backtracked a few months later, leading to Hayne's entry and victory by default.[94] As noted, in April 2025, the pool championship in England had two men competing in the women's final. Trans activists are always protesting against alleged "erasure" of trans people—but if two men in the women's finals isn't "erasure" of women, what is?

In 2024, San Jose State University fielded a male identifying as a woman on its women's volleyball team. As of October that year, four schools in the same conference had refused to play San Jose.[95]

Resistance to male intrusion in women's sports was buoyed by high-profile support from women such as Jennifer Sey, a former top gymnast and founder of the clothing brand XX-XY, as well as many others with large social media followings. In early April 2025, Sey and others spread the story of female fencer Stephanie Turner, who when faced with male opponent Redmond Sullivan, took a knee and politely declined to compete.[96] Turner's conduct was exemplary; she focused on the issue, which was fairness in sports, not the person. When told by Sullivan that he had support from the fencing officials and that she would be "black-carded," or officially reprimanded, she reportedly told the referee: "I'm sorry, I cannot do this. I am a woman, and this is a man, and this is a women's tournament. And I will not fence this individual." To Sullivan, she said, "I'm sorry. I have much love and respect for you, but I will not fence you."[97]

Around the same time, professional disc golf player Abigail Wilson refused to compete in a Nashville competition against "trans woman" Natalie Ryan. In 2022, Ryan beat the world's top-ranked female disc golfer and has won many contests and cash prizes in recent years while competing against women.[98] As she left, Wilson said "[f]emales must be protected in our division… This is unfair. I refuse to play."[99]

Gays to the Rescue

Despite the ubiquity and growing length of the initialism LGBTQIA2S+ (which has no doubt grown between writing and publication of this book), the train seems to be splitting into separate cars. Middle-aged gay men and women have finally realized that not all stripes on the two-spirit, lesbian, gay, bisexual, transgender, queer and/or questioning, intersex, asexual, and more "progress pride" flag stand for the same thing. The evidence shows that most children with gender dysphoria—in other words, who believe they are in the wrong body— grow out of it after puberty, and of those, a significant percentage are same-sex attracted as adults.[100] For adult gay men and lesbians, then, trans ideology presents an existential threat. The extortion tool that activists use to persuade reluctant parents to accept "gender affirming care," meaning puberty blockers, cross-sex hormones, and surgical castration, mastectomy, and facsimile genitalia, is that their children would kill themselves. Writer and commentator Andrew Sullivan calls this "one of the most malicious lies ever told in pediatric medicine."[101]

Gays and lesbians are fighting for the recognition that biological sex is real, that same-sex attraction is real, and that neither of these can or should be solved by convincing every troubled teen that he or she is in the wrong body or that either sex has to conform to 1950s gender stereotypes. Gender ideology has produced resistance in the form of groups like Gays Against Groomers, the LGB Alliance, and LGB Without the T. Prominent journalists like Gen Xer Andrew Sullivan, a gay man, and Millennial lesbian Bari Weiss, are speaking out. As Sullivan wrote in April 2024, back in 2009 "the Food and Drug Administration said adults using prescription testosterone gel must be extra careful not to get any of it on children to avoid causing serious side effects," including "enlargement of the genital organs, aggressive behavior, early aging of the bones, premature growth of pubic hair, and increased sexual drive…" Today, Sullivan writes, "it's deemed a 'genocide' if you don't hand out these potent drugs to children almost on demand."[102]

De-transitioners

In the previous chapter, I wrote about Keira Bell and other young women who have stopped and tried to reverse their supposed transition to male. These girls, misled by activists and the health care industry that was supposed to help them and "first do no harm," must suffer the lifelong consequences of the drugs and surgeries they took when trying to pursue the impossible. There are plenty of male detransitioners too. Reporter Christina Buttons tells the story of Yarden Silvera, a young man who sought to transition to a woman. Silvera "is believed to have committed suicide after suffering severe complications from gender-transition surgery," she writes.[103] Like many minors with gender dysphoria, Yarden was autistic and struggled with many other issues growing up, including a broken family and being gay. His attempt to transition was facilitated and encouraged by doctors and therapists, and the State of California, which considered his surgeries medically necessary and paid for them under Medi-Cal, the state version of Medicaid. According to Buttons, all the health care providers who assisted Yarden to transition were far less helpful when he was suffering from various complications of the surgeries gone wrong and tried to detransition back. Towards the end of his life, Yarden felt he had been lied to and realized that "It isn't possible to biologically transition from one sex to another."[104] Buttons concludes that "blind [gender] affirmation can do irreparable harm, especially for autistic or otherwise vulnerable youth who cling to the hope that adopting a transgender identity will solve their deeper struggles."[105]

Parents Fight Back

Parents whose vulnerable children are being sucked into the gender ideology vortex by schools and partisan internet cheerleaders are calling for caution through groups like Advocates Protecting Children and Parents with Inconvenient Truths about Trans. Parents are confronting school boards about policies that keep them in the dark about their children's social gender transitions. Women are protesting an "inclusion" that dissolves their identity into "birthing persons" or "pregnant people," terms that erase the complex history associated with women's bodies, and the rights and privileges that have been denied them as a result of those sex differences.

The Cass Review—the Beginning of the End?

The Cass Review, a 388-page "[i]ndependent review of gender identity services for children and young people" by a respected British pediatrician, Hilary Cass, came out in 2024 and has been the biggest challenge to gender ideologues yet. In brief, Dr. Cass recommends ending automatic affirmation of a child's chosen gender identity in general, and medical GAC in particular, and returning to the practice of "watchful waiting"; that is, listening, patience, counselling, and sympathy to help children overcome their distress naturally and come to accept themselves as they are.[106] For many clinicians and trans activists, there is no going back, even if, as Andrew Sullivan writes, "the Cass Report has definitively destroyed their case for child sex-changes."[107] For doctors, therapists, and hospitals to admit that they mutilated and sterilized thousands of children based on now debunked, biased, or inconclusive research would be professional suicide and open the legal liability gates of hell; but it is for parents of gender-confused children that one should have the most sympathy. As Helen Joyce, author of *Trans*, explains, for parents to accept that they allowed their children to be harmed permanently is psychologically almost impossible. That explains why parents of "trans" kids often turn their wrath on people who point out the flaws in gender ideology and the push for GAC.[108]

Northern Europeans went down the gender rabbit hole earlier than the U.S. did, but due to their systems of state-funded (non-profit) healthcare, and a willingness to accept the conclusions of rigorous meta-studies over the confirmation bias of entrenched ideology, they reversed course in response to evidence. As a result of actual evidence-based medicine, several European countries have replaced GAC with counseling and therapy as the default treatment for gender dysphoria in children and minors. It was a Dutch study on a limited sample of gender dysphoric boys that formed the basis for the WPATH's recommendations and, in turn, those of most major American medical associations. The Dutch have revised their thinking in response to evidence, as a 2024 television documentary explained.[109] So far, the U.S. has not, although there are signs of emerging opposition to the consensus.

Doctors and researchers are finally pushing back against the professional associations that, often dominated by a militant minority, have advocated affirmation and discouraged counseling or watchful waiting. The Society for Evidence-Based Gender Medicine (SEGM) aims "to promote safe, compassionate, ethical and evidence-informed healthcare for children, adolescents, and young adults with gender dysphoria."[110] Instead of activism and inductive reasoning, the SEGM promotes research, the scientific method, and open discussion of this difficult topic.

Victory in Sight?

Gender ideology is not the first cult in the United States. The western part of New York State was called the "burned-over district" in the 19th century, because of the waves of religious revivals and new sects that swept over it, one after another. It remains to be seen what will rise from the ashes of gender ideology, the latest quasi-religious craze to burn over the country, but the flames are subsiding. What brought this change about?

First, conservative politicians and fed-up parents threw down the gauntlet. Then, though discouraged and suppressed, scientific research started to mount that proved gender ideology—chiefly the irreversible medical and surgical changes it so strenuously advocates—is false and dangerous.

In January 2025, President Trump signed an executive order stating that it is "the policy of the United States to recognize two sexes, male and female. These sexes are not changeable and are grounded in fundamental and incontrovertible reality."[111] The next month, he signed another executive order protecting women's sports. While some states passed laws to keep men from competing in women's sports, others dug in their heels. Those committed to gender ideology, or who have pinned their credibility to its mast, will not cede the road gently. But eventually the weight of evidence and public opinion will bring enough people around to set the law right at the national level. As states split along ideological lines, there will be a tragic fallout in young lives ruined where neither parents nor government do their duty to protect them.

As Nathaniel Blake wrote for *The Federalist* in March 2025, "Gender ideology is unraveling... There is no good evidence that 'transitioning' helps anyone, especially children.[112] On March 12, Genspect, a trans-skeptical group, organized a Detrans Awareness Day in Washington, DC, where de-transitioners, elected officials, and experts met to discuss transgenderism and policy responses. Blake explains how some medical practitioners are so committed to "gender affirming care" that they commit billing fraud so that insurance companies will pay for it. Now that there is growing evidence that medical intervention to "affirm" a child's self-declared sexual identity is counter-productive, lawsuits by de-transitioners may force doctors and hospitals to follow the evidence and not ideology.

Where will that leave us as a society? The bottom line was well expressed by Ohio Attorney General Dave Yost:

> All who suffer from gender dysphoria, especially children, deserve to be treated with compassion and dignity. We should assume that the families of those children want the best for them. Which is precisely why a growing number of nations, and more than half the states, have passed laws protecting children from irreversible, adult medical decisions for which they are ill-prepared. As in Ohio, these laws reflect the consensus of the people of their states. They ought to be defended and upheld against the assault of lawfare practitioners who would substitute their elite judgment for that of the duly elected representatives of the people.[113]

Conclusion

The innate biological differences between men and women cannot be wished or "identified" away. This matters in healthcare, sports, and prison, just to name a few areas. Both Corrinna Cohn and Buck Angel, Generation Xers, are conservative compared to the radical trans activists. They ask for acceptance, tolerance, and understanding of homosexuality and gender dysphoria, not the denial of biological reality. In contrast Lia Thomas, whose self-centered approach to competition has come at the expense of young women who trained their whole lives for a shot at success in swimming, insists on others accepting his preferred conceit. It is not transphobic to ask that society maintain protected facilities and categories for women where introducing biological men threatens their safety or ruins their chances for fair competition. Compromise is possible, but we must all first accept reality. Only then can we engage in open discussion about how best to help those with gender dysphoria to live and prosper.

A person to follow: Kellie-Jay Keen, aka Posie Parker, *@ThePosieParker*, X.

A book to read: *Trans: When Ideology Meets Reality,* by Helen Joyce, 2021.

A group to support: Do No Harm, www.donoharmmedicine.org.

Chapter 6

The Sixth Commandment:
You Shall Be "Woke" to Imaginary Oppression

What Is Wokeness?

The word "woke" sums up a rainbow of leftist beliefs in one easy word. Its origins are in "African American Vernacular English," or slang, and they go back at least to 1940. English professor Adam Ellwanger writes that "woke" used to mean "to have savvy political awareness—a unique attunement to the structure of American oppression and a grasp of the revolutionary techniques required to 'dismantle' it"—which, for the Left, was a good thing. Today, he says, "to be called 'woke'…connotes a facile, reflexive mode of thinking, a self-important sort of posturing, a kookiness masquerading as political sincerity."[1]

According to an article co-authored by Robin DiAngelo, author of *White Fragility* and America's hands-down female champion at getting rich and famous from race grifting, "Critical social justice recognizes inequality as deeply embedded in the fabric of society (i.e., as structural), and actively seeks to change this."[2] DiAngelo believes that "disparity in condition can only be the result of systemic discrimination"—and nothing else.[3]

Woke means to be hyperaware of imagined or unverifiable "systems of oppression," which the woke want to tear down so they can achieve what they call "social justice," a redundant and nebulous term that means "nothing more or less than the full implementation of the Democrats' radical, ever-evolving agenda," according to Ellwanger.[4]

No one denies that human history includes a long litany of injustices, with men dominating women, and some peoples or races dominating others, for nearly all of it. Anyone who paid attention in eighth-grade

American history, let alone studied it in college and taught it as I did, is well aware of the evil of slavery before the Civil War and the injustice of segregation and Jim Crow afterwards. We know race-based discrimination did not end immediately with the civil rights acts of the late 1950s and 1960s, but when I was in K–12 school in the '70s and '80s, we were clearly on a path towards Martin Luther King's dream of a nation where white and black Americans "will not be judged by the color of their skin but by the content of their character."[5] The reality is that racism in America has declined to the point where "demand exceeds supply," as Wilfred Reilly shows with many examples in his book *Hate Crime Hoax*.[6] Certainly, overt racists still exist in America, as they do everywhere, but they are rare. In this country, people of all races are able to go to school, get jobs, and succeed with fewer obstacles than in any time and place in human history.

Public awareness of this gradual but measurable progress seemed to evaporate around President Barack Obama's second term. The reasons are complicated, but we seem to have gone backwards in our perception of racial equality, if not its reality. In 2023, when Joe Biden was still the presumed candidate for re-election, a poll of 1,200 black voters in Georgia, North Carolina, and California claimed that "42 percent of black voters 'want white supremacy declared a national security threat.'"[7] The reason for this "Great Awokening"[8] to perceived, rather than actual, injustice and oppression was that academic theories that had been safely contained in the campus laboratories of mind viruses escaped, around 2015, into the general population.

1. Critical Race Theory

Critical race theory (CRT) is hardly worth the time of graduate students, let alone undergraduates, and certainly not K–12 students, so it would be silly to waste much time on it in this book. But, as it underlies so much of what is called woke, we need a basic outline. In their book *Cynical Theories*, Helen Pluckrose and James Lindsay set out the roots of CRT in the 1930s in Germany, where it began with academics in what was later known as the Frankfurt school. One of them, Herbert Marcuse, fled Europe for America and ended up at Columbia University, with many others like him. Their ideas cross-pollenated with those of French existentialists like Michel Foucault and Jacques Derrida, becoming something known as post-modernism by the 1960s—just in time to inspire the hippie generation, many of whom opposed the Vietnam War and sought some coherent philosophy to replace what they saw as a decadent Western, capitalist culture. Postmodernism spawned critical theory, and its sister schools and later off-shoots such as post-colonial theory, critical race theory, critical queer theory, gender ideology, fat studies, and intersectionality.[9]

Postmodernism rejected tradition, objective truth, objective value, and borders, literal and figurative. Everything was about the individual—what each of us believed, experienced, wanted. There were no duties to the greater society except to "self actualize" into the ideal you. The idea was to "deconstruct" everything—history, institutions, art—and because nothing was real and constant, everything was a construction. This even applied to gender, with academic and queer theorist Judith Butler writing that "'woman' is not a class of people but a performance that constructs 'gendered' reality."[10]

Lindsay and Pluckrose write that "post-modernism is characterized by its intense focus on power as the guiding and structuring force of society…"[11] In that structure, we are all either holders of power or its victims; we are all either oppressors or oppressed. Kimberlé Crenshaw coined the term "intersectionality" in the 1990s, meaning the overlap of oppressed identities which supposedly combine to add up a person's overall oppression. In the reality of 21st-century America, however, intersectional points of oppression are trump cards. For example, President Biden's press secretary, Karine Jean-Pierre, held an almost-perfect intersectional hand in modern America's poker game of life, as a black, gay, immigrant woman. She could do no wrong, as evidenced by her three feckless years at the White House podium. The only better hand than hers would be the pinnacle status of a trans woman, as discussed in Chapter 5.

A rich country like the United States can afford a lot of academics, who then have a lot of time to try to develop original ideas. Derrick Bell and others took "critical legal theory'" and applied it to race, and we got "critical race theory." Pluckrose and Lindsay sum up CRT as holding that "race is a social construct that was created to maintain white privilege and white supremacy."[12] By the 2020s, CRT has brought us full circle: because of racism, we need racism. The popular voice of this view is "anti-racist" academic Ibram X. Kendi, who wrote in his book *How to Be an Antiracist*, "[t]he only remedy to past discrimination is present discrimination. The only remedy to present discrimination is future discrimination."[13] [Later editions of the book were reportedly edited and may vary from the original]. According to woke ideology, interpreted by Kendi, DiAngelo, and others for the masses, "equity" requires equality of outcomes across identity groups, not fairness or equality of opportunity; therefore, society must treat Americans unequally depending on their race.

What it All Means

What we're dealing with today boils down to all these academic theories coming together into one unified field theory which affects nearly every aspect of our lives—all institutions, from school to work to government. As Richard Delgado and Jean Stefancik put it in their book *Critical Race Theory: An Introduction*, "only aggressive, color-conscious efforts to change the way things are will do much to ameliorate misery."[14] With CRT as their ideology, the woke want to "decolonize" all American and Western institutions, which is to say, strip them of everything male and European. They want to remove traditional distinctions, rights, or boundaries between the sexes. And they want to practice active discrimination to make up for past injustice and guarantee an impossible "equity": that we all come out the same.

White Supremacy

The central belief of CRT is that America is a white supremacist country, built on a framework of nebulous "structural racism" that historically and presently disfavors women and "black, indigenous, and people of color" (BIPOC). The list of things that have been labelled under "whiteness" would amaze most Africans, for whom habits like hard work, politeness, and timeliness are associated with prosperity and success.

Early 2020 may have been the peak of woke in matters of race. We saw in Chapter 2 how the Smithsonian, America's national museum in Washington, DC, issued guidelines for talking about race, which included thinking about "objective, rational, linear thinking" as an "assumption of whiteness" or "white" value, along with the nuclear family, planning for the future, being on time, being polite, and protecting property.[15] Three years later, an article in *Medium* sought to "explore the origins of the early-rising narrative and how it is rooted in white supremacy, contributing to the perpetuation of racial inequalities."[16] The belief that ideas like "hard work is the key to success" and that one should put "work before play" are "white" values would surprise my friend Taitusi, a builder in Fiji who worked hard in his business, or my friend Kojo in Togo, who was up at dawn every day to run his coffee farm. Thomas Sowell writes that "2020 census data show more than 9 million black Americans with higher incomes than the median incomes of white Americans."[17] Would they agree that hard work is a "white" thing?

"Systems of Oppression"

If there were demonstrable instances of discrimination, or disparate impact, by specific policies on different groups that could not be explained by controlling for other variables, fair-minded Americans would want to address them. The problem is that the Left makes general statements that vague "systemic injustice" or "systems of oppression" exist, without any reference to evidence and data than can be proven or disproven.

This type of thinking has a strong grip on American academia. Take this opening paragraph from a 2021 article, "Operating within Systems of Oppression," in the *Hastings Poverty and Law Journal*.[18] Author Karissa Provenza begins with a level of self-abasement that comes from years of soaking in the world of critical theory:

> Before I begin my analysis into systems of oppression, I must acknowledge the sacrificial blood, sweat, and tears of the generations of women before me. I will be reflecting on my experiences and responsibilities as a white cis [defined in the footnotes] woman, while highlighting works by Black feminists, Critical Race Theorists, and scholars focused on race, gender, and sexuality. Instead of celebrating my self-awareness, I choose to uplift the perfectly strung together words of those I have learned from in order to decenter myself.

This sort of self-abasement is similar to the ridiculous "land acknowledgements" we've discussed before. Perhaps the ultimate example of these was a statement in May 2025 by the Royal Canadian

Mounted Police. Before briefing the press on two missing children, the police spokeswoman explained that she was standing on the "unceded" land of the Mi'kmaq tribe, and said that "African Nova Scotians are a distinct people whose histories, legacies, and contributions have enriched that part of Mikmagi [the land of the Mi'kmaq] known as Nova Scotia."[19] She does not note that the previous inhabitants of Nova Scotia, the Kwēdĕchk, did not "cede" their land to the Mi'kmaq. Rather, after many years of a "contest presenting all the features common to Indian warfare—spies, scouts, surprises, slaughter of men, women, and children, and torture of captives," the Mi'kmaq removed or absorbed the losing Kwēdĕchk people.[20]

Not only are privilege statements by academics and land acknowledgments by public officials beyond parody, they undermine the credibility of whatever the supposed academic or authority is about to say. When the source evinces such evident self-loathing, guilt, historical ignorance, and lack of self-esteem, the reader or listener has little confidence that whatever the source says will be unbiased, objective, and credible.

"Disparate Impact" Theory

The idea of "disparate impact" originally meant that, *all other variables being accounted for*, disparities in outcome by sex or race are *prima facie* evidence of the sexism or racism of policies. Under the influence of CRT, the part about "any other variables" has been mostly ignored, leading to some terrible policy choices. I discuss in other chapters how this theory has been applied to everything from school discipline to hiring police. Heather Mac Donald writes that American institutions are eviscerating meritocratic and behavioral standards in accordance with what is known as "disparate impact analysis."[21]

But the variables are crucial in understanding why outcomes vary among groups. Living with two married parents, having a library card, and spending hours on homework are variables that have a huge impact on academic success. People commit various crimes at radically different rates depending on age, sex, and sometimes race. Although there are highly successful students of all races and ethnic groups, academic outcomes nationally are not in line with demographic percentages. The reasons why are debatable and contentious, and we can't resolve them here, but the facts are plain.

The National Assessment of Educational Progress, called "the nation's report card," shows marked variance by school district and by race. The ACT test measures readiness for college-level work. It consists of four multiple-choice tests in English, math, reading, and science.[22] According to *The Journal of Blacks in Higher Education*, only 3 percent of black high schoolers who took the test in 2023 "were deemed college-ready in all four areas."[23]

Mac Donald has more:

> The average Medical College Achievement Test (MCAT) score for black applicants is a standard deviation below the average score of white applicants.[24]
>
> Only five percent of black law school graduates passed the California bar on their first try in February 2020, compared to 52 percent of white law school graduates and 42 percent of Asian law school graduates.[25]

But rather than causing a change in the way we educate children, to help every child to succeed, the disparate impact analysis has resulted in schools either dropping requirements for standardized tests or lowering them to achieve racial quotas. For example, in response to lower passing grades among its desired minority, California simply lowered the grade required to pass the bar. Medical schools have lowered passing scores or eliminated requirements to pass standardized tests that have disparate racial outcomes.

But "lowering standards helps no one since high expectations are the key to achievement," Mac Donald argues.[26] Test scores predict later academic and career success. Letting students into elite schools with significantly lower test scores results in less-prepared students. Harvard University, the nation's most prestigious and one of the hardest to get into with a roughly 50-to-one ratio of applications to acceptance, had to offer remedial math classes in 2024.[27] Harvard claimed it was due to learning loss from pandemic shutdowns, but given the over-prepared cadre that makes up their applicant pool, this is not likely.

To maintain high standards and high expectations, we must reward them. America's prime competitor, China, certainly does. So do Japan, Korea, France, and Russia. Mac Donald urges "legislation to ban racial preferences in medical training and practice" and "eliminating the disparate impact standard in statutes and regulations."[28] As Mac Donald concludes, "you can have proportional diversity or you can have meritocracy. You cannot have both."[29]

2. Things That Are Racist: A Never-Ending List

In the CRT framework, everything can be seen as oppressive and racist. Here is a non-exhaustive list.

Racist Free Speech

History professor Matthew Garrett of Bakersfield College in California and a few of his colleagues pushed back against the post-2020 growth of CRT, intolerance of free speech, and mandatory training in implicit bias and microaggressions. The California Community Colleges Board of Governors had "issued guidelines that force faculty to embrace an 'anti-racist' ideology" and "advance and teach the state's official DEIA ('diversity, equity, inclusion, and accessibility') ideology," according to the Institute for Free Speech.[30] Garrett co-founded the Renegade Institute for Liberty, for which he was pursued by the university for "unprofessional conduct" and causing "real harm" to students.[31] Garrett lost his place on the school's diversity committee, found little support among the school's Board of Trustees, and was eventually fired. In 2021, Garrett sued the Kern Community College District, "alleging they retaliated against him for accusing colleagues of using grant money for partisan social justice work." In 2024, the District reportedly settled with him for a $2.4 million payout.[32]

In 2023, another Bakersfield College professor, Daymon Johnson, sued college administrators for investigating his social media posts—which, among other things, were critical of fellow professor Andrew Bond's 2019 Facebook post that "America 'is a f------ piece of s--- country.'"[33] In the California community college system, it seems, hating America is free speech, but criticizing DEI is not.

Racist Foreign Policy

In 2020, as the George Floyd spring was in full swing, political scientist Micah Zenko lamented that the U.S. foreign policy establishment (including him) was too white. Zenko wanted "a more diverse group of future foreign-policy thinkers and leaders," "who experience hatred, bigotry, and oppression" to "conceive of a foreign policy that…confronts racism." [34] Under Joe Biden, the State Department attempted just that, by preferential hiring programs that benefited women and preferred races. Zenko also wanted Congress to "vastly increase funding for international and nongovernmental organizations that work to protect groups experiencing prejudice."[35] This, the Biden Administration also delivered, by showering leftist NGOs with grants for four years. The excessive channeling of money into woke causes overseas undermined U.S. foreign policy and diverted resources from more important and lasting foreign policy aims.[36] In 2025, President Trump and Secretary of State Marco Rubio rapidly unraveled USAID and stopped many of its grants from being paid.

Racist Health Care

Brad McDowell, a nurse for 16 years, describes in *The Wall Street Journal* how he lost his job due to Facebook posts that did not name the hospital where he worked as a manager at a medical center in Maryland.[37] McDowell objected to having to take state-mandated courses that were filled with "evidence-free claims that implicit bias has caused a crisis of maternal mortality in black women," and "implied that white nurses like me are killing black mothers." The DEI course he was obliged to take, McDowell said, "ignored the complex factors that contribute to higher black maternal mortality, including comorbidities, while defining any death from any cause after a year of giving birth as maternal mortality—a logical stretch."[38]

The implications of critical theory have direct impacts on patients, often the most vulnerable and in need of objective treatment. In April 2025, a hospital in New Haven, Connecticut stopped automatically testing babies born to drug addicted mothers for exposure to drugs, because doctors fear positive results would cause child protective services to get involved and "exacerbate what they see as racial bias in the system."[39]

CRT holds that any disparities between races, such as educational or medical outcomes, are proof of racial discrimination. Though evidence, and common sense argue otherwise, CRT is a dominant ideology in American higher education and opposition is ruthlessly crushed. Another course Brad McDowell was told to take contained the CRT framing that "the U.S. is built on 'an ideology of White supremacy that justifies policies, practices and structures which result in social arrangements of subordination for groups of color through power and White privilege.'" McDowell posted to his private Facebook page that "No employer has the right to invade the unconscious spaces of it's [sic] employees minds in an attempt to reprogram them into thinking certain ways." For that and similar posts, McDowell was fired by his employer, Meritus Health.

The study that McDowell references on infant mortality was cited by Supreme Court Justice Ketanji Brown Jackson in the *Students for Fair Admission v. Harvard*. Like other studies that confirm woke dogma, it is often cited by proponents of CRT. Unfortunately for them, the study's conclusions have been exposed as wrong, and worse still, its authors left out important conclusions that interfered with their political objective.[40]

The Left's desired narrative is that some (or all) white doctors are racist, either knowingly or through "implicit bias," and this racism manifests in the death of black babies in their care. The proof is supposed to be that black babies survive at a higher rate when cared for by black doctors. A much-quoted 2020 study led by Brad Greenwood, a business professor at George Mason University, stated that "[b]lack physicians systemically outperform their colleagues when caring for Black newborns."[41] If true, this would be shocking and require urgent corrective action. But it isn't true, because the study allegedly proving it didn't control for crucial variables. First, low birth weight and premature births: such infants are at higher risk for death. Premature babies are also more often cared for by white doctors, who are more likely to be specialists or senior supervising physicians. A 2024 follow-up study from a Harvard doctor and Manhattan Institute scholar showed that when low birth weight was accounted for, "the impact of racial concordance on Black newborn mortality...often become both numerically close to zero and statistically insignificant..."[42]

Second, the 2020 study deliberately left out the important finding that white babies were more likely to die under the care of a black doctor than a white doctor.[43] Do No Harm, a medical association headed by Stanley Goldfarb which opposes unscientific and woke medicine, found through a Freedom of Information Act request that an earlier draft of the 2020 study concluded that: "[w]hite newborns experience 80 deaths per 100,000 births more with a black physician than a white physician..."[44] Greenwood wrote in the margins of the early draft that he would "rather not focus on this" as it "undermines the narrative."[45]

Abigail Anthony reports that another of the study's authors, Rachel Hardeman, was the current director of the University of Minnesota's Center for Antiracism Research for Health Equity.[46] *Time* magazine named her one of America's most influential people in 2024 for "her unwavering determination [that] offers all of us a path forward toward truly advancing birth equity."[47] Though the methodology of the 2020 study appears fatally flawed, and its authors seem to have had political motivations, Supreme Court Justice Ketanji Brown Jackson cited it approvingly in her dissent in *Students for Fair Admission v. Harvard*. According to *The Daily Caller*, the 2020 study "has generated more public discussion in the lay press and on social media than 99% of scientific studies published in the last five years" and "received coverage in 340 outlets including CNN, USA Today, and the *Washington Post*."[48] In April 2025, Hardeman resigned from her position amidst accusations of plagiarism. Though she said "the allegations against me are simply not true" and claimed to be leaving because she wanted a change, a subordinate of hers said that Hardeman had copied her work "verbatim." The University of Minnesota's Office of Research Integrity and Compliance concluded its investigation by finding that "any errors were honest and unintentional."[49] Yet, according to Social Epidemiologist Brigette Davis (also a black woman, if it matters) Hardeman "performed a find+replace in my [grant application] document, and replaced all instances of 'Mike Brown' with 'Philando Castile' and all instances of 'St. Louis, Missouri' with 'Minneapolis, Minnesota,' and submitted this to the NIH as if it were her own."[50]

In 2022, there was an outbreak of monkeypox, a disease so called because it was a pox that originally affected simians. Due to pressure from activists who disliked the name because of its association with monkeys, the world health authorities decided it should be known as "mpox."[51] The mainstream press agonized over how to spread information, because CDC data "showed that people of color are bearing the burden of monkeypox cases at levels disproportionate with their presence in the population overall." At the same time, although "global data suggests skin-to-skin contact during sex is fueling the outbreak," and it was spreading almost entirely among men who had close physical contact with other men, every effort was made to present it as an equal risk to everyone. "Sexually active Americans should consider limiting partners and avoiding sex parties to reduce the risk of contracting monkeypox until they get vaccinated," warned the Centers for Disease Control and Prevention.[52] When the World Health Organization said "men who have sex with men should consider temporarily reducing their number of sexual partners or stop adding new ones to help to stanch the outbreak," there was "a debate about whether calls for sexual restraint are counterproductive and stigmatizing."[53]

Racist History

The state of Virginia's Department of Education put out new standards of learning in 2022 that reduced a proposed 400-plus pages to 52.[54] That year, the department's board had a majority appointed by Republican Governor Glenn Youngkin. *The Washington Post* provided a detailed breakdown of what was lost in the reduction, which was often supplemental material on indigenous history and non-Western culture.[55] The argument between Left and Right about what should be included in the curriculum obscures the more important point: overall, students in Virginia, and in the rest of the country, do not know the basics of American history, let alone the additional stories the old board wanted to cram into the curriculum. In 2022, only 13 percent of eighth-graders reached the "proficient" level in U.S. history.[56] Demanding additional digressions into particular aspects of race, culture, or art history even if worthy and interesting, only makes sense if students already grasp the basic facts and timeline, which they clearly do not.

Racist Math

Minneapolis Public Schools planned to spend $2 million to incorporate "ethnic, racial, and cultural diversity" into the K–5 math curriculum for the 2023 school year according to *The Washington Free Beacon.*[57] The curriculum was supposed to add "cultural and linguistically responsive materials" to reflect "the lived experiences of our Minneapolis students" and develop "positive math identity," according to the school district executive director. After a year of the new curriculum, only 45 percent of Minnesota fourth-grade students had reached "math proficiency."[58] This program is typical of the genre. Unfortunately, buzz phrases like "social justice," "anti-racist," "culturally inclusive," and the like don't teach kids arithmetic.

At the University of Illinois' education school, professor Rachel Gutierez supposedly teaches aspiring teachers how to teach math. Her biography on the university website is worth showing in full, as it captures the essence of woke pedagogy: teaching teachers anything but how to teach.

Dr. Gutierrez' scholarship focuses on issues of identity and power in mathematics education, paying particular attention to how race, class, and language affect teaching and learning. Through in-depth analyses of effective teaching/learning communities and longitudinal studies of developing and practicing teachers, her work challenges deficit views of students who are Latinx, Black, and Indigenous and suggests that mathematics teachers need to be prepared with much more than just content knowledge, pedagogical knowledge, or knowledge of diverse students if they are going to be successful. They need political knowledge. Her current research projects focus upon: developing in pre-service teachers the knowledge and disposition to teach powerful mathematics to urban students; the roles of uncertainty, tensions, and "Nepantla" in teaching; and the political knowledge (and forms of creative insubordination) that mathematics teachers need to effectively "rehumanize" mathematics in an era of high-stakes education. She also builds upon Indigenous principles and has argued for a new form of mathematics where humans are no longer centered. This form of mathematics is referred to as living mathematx. [59]

Perhaps, like me, you've never heard of "Nepantla." I looked it up. Employed in a "mathematx" context, it means a kid can get the answer wrong and the teacher can grade it as right. That will suit equity goals nicely and raise grades all round, but it won't improve the safety of cars, balancing of budgets, or accuracy of missiles.

In his lecture called "Undergraduate Mathematics Education as a White, Cisheteropatriarchal Space and Opportunities for Structural Disruption to Advance Queer of Color Justice," did Luis Leyva, a professor of mathematics education at Vanderbilt University, help his students to become better teachers of math? Leyva claimed that his research "depict[ed] how Black, Latin* [the * appears to be a marker for the "a" or "o" ending in Spanish indicating masculine or feminine] and Asian QT ["queer and trans"]students' narratives of experience reflect forms of intersectionality, or instances of oppression and resistance at intersecting systems of white supremacy and cisheteropatriarchy (or white cisheteropatriarchy)" and that "intersectional oppression" affects queer or trans students of color through ideological, institutional, and relational influences.[60] Is that going to make a difference in places like Baltimore, Maryland, where 7 percent of students are proficient in math city wide, with 23 schools having not a single math-proficient student?[61]

Racist Movies

We can't possibly list every book, movie, and work of art that has been called racist, so *Indiana Jones and the Dial of Destiny* will do as one example. Because Steven Spielberg and George Lucas read *Flash Gordon* and *Zorro* growing up in California in the 1950s, argues Professor Gerard Canavan of Marquette University, and because boys' adventure novels of more than a century ago had characters who were racist and colonialist (which, at the time, nearly everyone was), we now have allegedly racist movies where "a brilliant White man, very often a professor, deploys personal reserves of cleverness, resilience and unrelenting determination in the service of exploration, discovery and resource extraction."[62]

Don't think that it is any defense against revisionist charges of racism that an artist lived five centuries ago. Farah Karim-Cooper, a professor of Shakespeare studies and education expert at the Globe Theatre in London, wrote a whole book about how Shakespeare has a "race problem" because some of his characters are so tiresomely 16th century in their thinking. The Globe, a historical reconstruction of Shakespeare's own theater, is lit by candles to reproduce the atmosphere of the time, but according to Karim-Cooper it "is sometimes too dark, especially for the actors of color," and the lighting and set design "does not work for actors of the global majority." [63] (The "global majority" is "the Globe's preferred language to describe actors of color"). In fact, the wax-powered theatrical lighting of early modern London probably didn't work well for any performer, of any color, which is why gas and then electricity were such improvements. Theaters like the Globe were dingy, dirty, smelly, and loud, unlike modern performance spaces. Karim-Cooper says with chagrin that the theater she is paid to educate people about "feels like a space of empire." Which, for most of the past 500 years, it was—and presumably, that is the history the Globe is trying to evoke and preserve. [64] In 2023, she organized an "Anti-Racist Shakespeare" series "to examine Shakespeare's plays through the lens of race and social justice." [65]

Racist Science

The College Fix reports how in 2022, the National Science Foundation granted Amy Robertson and W. Tali Hairston half a million dollars to "develop a knowledge base that could lead to awareness of how power relations may be embedded in the way physics is taught and learned." [66] The researchers "planned to record introductory physics classes and interview participants, then analyze them using a critical whiteness theory lens," looking for "instances of marginalization through displays of 'certain characteristics that U.S. culture typically associates with white masculine behavior, including control, independence, and decisiveness.'"

In 2024, President Biden appointed Chanda Prescod-Weinstein, a professor of "physics and gender studies" at the University of New Hampshire, to the U.S. Department of Energy's High Energy Physics Advisory Panel, an advisory group. [67] Prescod-Weinstein sees science through a lens well-smeared with social justice. In a 2020 paper for the University of Chicago, she uses "a combination of critical race theory, feminist standpoint theory, and contingency theory to show that race and ethnicity do impact epistemic outcomes in physics and that white supremacy in physics produces Black physicists as a permanent ontological Other." [68]

After the Hamas terrorist attacks on Israel on October 7, 2023, Prescod-Weinstein wrote this on her blog: "I am enormously proud of the students who have sacrificed to fight back against a genocide... Let the students protest, and don't fucking snitch. Free Palestine!"[69]

Other scientists in her field find her conflation of woke ideology with hard science baffling, if not disqualifying. Dorian Abbot, a geophysicist at the University of Chicago, didn't want to discuss her case specifically, but he told *The Washington Free Beacon*'s Aaron Sibarium that "[i]t is essential for political leadership to appoint panel and board members for federal scientific enterprises who are fully committed to promoting excellence and selecting grants and personnel based on merit, and to remove those who are not." Abbot has good reason to be careful: in 2021, he expressed the, hardly radical, view that affirmative action (race preference) programs "treat people as members of a group rather than as individuals" and "that he favored a diverse pool of applicants selected on merit."[70] For that sin, Dr. Abbot was uninvited from giving a lecture at MIT.

Racist Criminal Justice

A persistent myth is that the "systems" in the United States are biased against non-white people in favor white people. It is historical fact that racism, sexism, anti-gay discrimination, and bias of other kinds existed in the country for centuries. To a small extent, they exist today. But the idea that life is the same in 2024 as it was in 1924, let alone 1824, simply doesn't stand up to reality.

Cartoon by Michael De Adder, Used with Permission[71]

In *Hate Crime Hoax*, Professor Wilfred Reilly shows how often alleged hate crimes turn out to be fabrications. Jussie Smollett, the actor who paid two Nigerian American brothers to pretend to beat him up as fake MAGA supporters on a freezing Chicago street is the most famous example,[72] but others abound. To take just one, in March 2025, Allentown, Pennsylvania, city worker LaTarsha Brown complained of finding a noose in her City Hall office, but a police investigation soon found her DNA on it and she was charged with tampering with evidence and making a false report to police.[73]

Another persistent myth is that black people's lives are at high risk of violence by the police. There is a perception, perpetuated by the legacy media, academia, and social activists, that many unarmed black men are shot by police officers in this country. In fact, that number is incredibly small given the population. Wilfred Reilly writes that in 2015, a total of 1,200 people were shot by police, and 76 percent of those shot "were not black."[74] Reilly's best estimate is that "the total number of unarmed black men shot by white cops was seventeen" in 2015.[75] In 2021, a total of 11 unarmed black men were shot and killed by police.[76] Despite this clear data, it is an axiom repeated endlessly in the mainstream media, television, and films that black people are disproportionately shot by police. Reilly concedes that the percentage of blacks shot by police (23 percent) is higher than their percentage in the general population (13.5 percent) but adds that "this disparity is wholly explained by the fact that the Black violent crime rate is roughly 2.5 times the white rate."[77] Heather Mac Donald writes that "black juveniles are shot at 100 times the rate of white juveniles" – the vast majority, by other black juveniles - and "are killed in drive by shootings at nearly 25 times the rate of whites" in the ten-to-24 age cohort.[78]

In most violent crimes, the perpetrator and victim are of the same race. Only 3 percent of violent crime is interracial. Of that small percentage, "roughly 80 percent of it [is] Black on white" according to Reilly.[79] As Mac Donald writes, "a black person is 35 times more likely to commit an act of non-lethal violence against a white person than vice versa."[80]

Despite these depressing but clear numbers, the myth that society at large, and the police in particular, are racist is so powerful that facts cannot kill it. Look at this article from January 2023 by Van Jones on CNN:

Opinion: The police who killed Tyre Nichols were Black. But they might still have been driven by racism[81]

The media, obsessed with the false narrative that black Americans are being killed in large numbers by law enforcement or by non-black Americans, has obscured the routine violence that mars black lives and sensationalized the rare, complicated case that appears to support their viewpoint. One such case was that of Trayvon Martin, a teenager tragically shot and killed in 2012 by a mixed-race Hispanic neighborhood watchman in disputed circumstances on private property in Florida.[82] Another was that of Michael Brown in Ferguson, Missouri, who in 2014 confronted a policeman after allegedly robbing a store and was shot by the police officer after trying to grab his gun. Contrary to the poplar legend, Brown never said "hands up, don't shoot," according to multiple eye-witnesses. A grand jury investigated the case and declined to charge Darren Wilson, the police officer who shot him.[83] A third notorious case was that of Breonna Taylor, who was shot in 2020 in Louisville, Kentucky in a crossfire between her boyfriend—who shot first—and the police. The Taylor case was messy and the result both unfortunate and preventable, but it was not an example of martyrdom. Press coverage, and the race activists who feed off it, led one of the police officers involved to claim they were "tried and convicted in the court of public opinion and convicted on the basis of perjury."[84] That officer, Sgt. John Mattingly, wrote his own account of the affair in his book, *12 Seconds In the Dark: A Police Officer's Firsthand Account of the Breonna Taylor Raid.*

But the death of George Floyd in May 2020 was the straw that broke the camel's back of national sanity and collapsed the country into an imagined dystopia that differs markedly from reality until, eventually, it became a self-fulfilling prediction. Sadly, the America of today does feel more racist, more divided along lines of immutable characteristics, than the country of 50 years ago. This is not the result of facts, but of public perception warped by media bias and ideology.

Racist States

In 2022, the National Association for the Advancement of Colored People (NAACP) issued a "travel advisory" that Republican Governor Ron DeSantis's "aggressive attempts to erase Black history and to restrict diversity, equity, and inclusion programs in Florida schools have turned the state into an 'openly hostile' place for people of color and members of the LGBTQ+ community."[85] Luther "Luke" Campbell, a Miami-based rapper and community activist said at the time that instead of an advisory, there should be a "full-on boycott" of Florida.[86] In March 2025, rather undermining claims that Florida is openly hostile to people of color, the Miami city council renamed a portion of Northwest 11th Avenue as "Luther Campbell Way," after what local news called the "rap legend."[87]

Racist Wine

The Washington Post's Dave McIntyre asked "[a]re our vocabulary, standards and perspectives of wine too Eurocentric for a modern, globalized world?"[88] "Modern wine...is inextricably intertwined with European colonialism," he says. An organization called Wine Unify "promotes minority representation in the wine industry" and claims that "we speak about wine in ways that are exclusionary." Apparently, de-colonizing wine isn't cheap: a bottle of Black Girl Magic which "showcases the playful and vibrant character of rose wine, offering a delightful drinking experience" retails for $18.50 at my local Trader Joe's, where a bottle of boring old rosé from France, La Vieille Ferme, sells for $6.99.

Racist Ignorance (of being racist)

For the critical race theory purist, any belief by a white person that he is not racist is merely "white ignorance," or as Robin DiAngelo put it in the title of her book, "white fragility." According to the CRT argument, "white people" (aka Europeans, or non-members of the "global majority") are racist at birth and to the core, notwithstanding that they express no racist belief and evince no racist behavior. The beauty of this argument that racism is simply "structural" and "systemic" is that it cannot be falsified through evidence.

One apotheosis if this belief system is a study, highlighted by Colin Wright at Reality's Last Stand, called "*Learning (Not) to Know: Examining How White Ignorance Manifests and Functions in White Adolescents' Racial Identity Narratives*" by Brandon Dull and others.[89] As James L. Nuzzo writes, the young people interviewed for this study "rejected racial prejudice and expressed a desire to treat others as individuals"…Yet rather than acknowledging this, the researchers concluded that the students were exhibiting "White ignorance."[90] According to the study's authors, "white ignorance refers to systematic and intentional ways of (not) knowing that function to perpetuate racism," manifesting in an "active refusal to know or imagine racial oppression." Note that the existence and reality of racial oppression - always, everywhere, and forever - is simply assumed. Indeed, the bias of this paper and its utter lack of scientific objectivity is stated right from the beginning, when the authors state that their "decision to not capitalize white is to mark the distinct and oppressive history of whiteness." To support this stance, they cite Linda Alcoff, author of *The Future of Whiteness*, who wrote in 2018 that "we still cannot analogize white identity with other ethnic and racialized identities. Its relations to the imperial imaginary of the United States, its historical foundations in racism and cultural hierarchies, and its potential to provide an alibi for capitalist elites makes whiteness truly distinct."[91]

Based on Critical Race Theory, which posits that racism is the incontrovertible, Original Sin of Europeans alone that can never be extirpated, this type of "research" is impervious to the very evidence it gathers. It is an exercise in inductive reasoning, where the conclusion chases the facts, rather than empirical science, where the facts lead to the conclusion. The inevitable conclusion of supposedly scholarly papers like Dull's is that even if you are a teenager raised in woke 2020s America, you cannot avoid being racist, whatever you believe, say, or do. In the words of Neil Young, "you don't know it, but you are."[92]

Cultural Appropriation

The concept of cultural appropriation holds that for one culture to adopt any cultural "property" from another, such as language, food, dress, music, art, is wrong. Another word for this phenomenon is "culture," since human beings have been borrowing from each other from time immemorial; the Greeks from the Persians, the Romans from the Greeks, the British from the Romans, the Americans from the British.

The standard seems to go only one way, however. In the United States, English is the standard language of business and culture. It is spoken by people of all races and colors, and representatives of a wide range of peoples have distinguished themselves writing in English, though it was not the language of their ancestors. However, journalist Samantha Chery argued that for non-black people to use what she calls African American Vernacular English (AAVE)—also known as African American English (AAE), African American Language (AAL), Black English or Ebonics— is "cultural appropriation."[93]

She wrote that "some Black AAVE speakers believe that the language has been incorrectly chalked up as new vocabulary started by young people—and they've been calling out non-Black people for glorifying internet stars who butcher the speech and lack understanding of the language's cultural significance." Chery explains that the singer Lizzo dropped the word "spaz" from a song "after disability advocates pointed out that a word in its original version, is considered an ableist slur." Yet, she says, "speakers of AAVE defended the Black artists, saying that the word has another meaning—to go wild—and that its use…wasn't meant to offend."

"Black people have been using 'spazz' for decades and it has nothing to do with making fun of disabled people," Chery quoted a music fan as saying. Yet, I remember "spaz" was a common insult in my New Jersey grade school in the 1970s. So was "spastic" as an epithet, like "retard," in the 1980s. There's nothing funny about cerebral palsy, the condition formerly and vulgarly called "spastic" or "spaz." Nor is mental disability anything to laugh about. But kids can be cruel to each other, and always have been, and they culturally appropriate all the time—until adults try to claim their words and make them uncool.

An interesting twist on cultural appropriation has emerged now that it pays to hold "intersectional" status. In 2021, Ibram X. Kendi linked to an article on Twitter about a survey in which 34 percent of white students falsely claimed to be non-white to get into college or to receive financial aid. Three quarters of these students were accepted into the colleges where they applied under a false racial identity, Kendi wrote—before deleting his tweet—perhaps realizing that it completely undermined his argument about white privilege.[94] Rachel Dolezal, a white woman, claimed to be black for years and worked at the NAACP. Even after her lie was revealed, she continued to claim not to be white.[95] A woman claiming to be "Raquel Evita Saraswati" met with Democratic politicians and earned a living as a diversity consultant before being outed as Rachel Elizabeth Seidel and "white as the driven snow" according to her mother.[96]

3. "Equity" vs. Equality

The fruit of CRT is what Ibram Kendi calls "antiracism," and what the Left generally calls "equity," which means preferential treatment of women and selected minorities, trumping objective merit, to engineer desired outcomes in hiring and representation. From 2020, this manifested in some variation of DEI offices and programs in U.S. institutions.

The Growing Demands of Equity

As "equity" became the dominant philosophy in academia, the arts, government, and the non-profit world, demands for representation, reparations, and other concessions were made vociferously by people who stood to benefit. Even progressive, liberal artists are not excepted— perhaps they are the most vulnerable, because unlike "out" conservatives, they care about that particular form of criticism. In March 2021, famed documentary filmmaker and PBS darling Ken Burns was attacked for having the presumption to, as a white man, make a series about boxer Muhammed Ali.[97] "I don't accept the idea that only people of a particular background can tell certain stories about the past," Burns told *The Atlantic*. However, "a coalition of 140 documentary filmmakers" didn't agree, and they sent an open letter to PBS "slamming the choice of Burns to helm what was being positioned as the definitive doc on Ali," wrote *The Atlantic*.

Accepting that you have to be from a particular background to write or make films about it would restrict all creators. *The Jungle Book* would not tell the story of Mowgli, an Indian boy, because the author was a white man. No Indian or African would be able to write about Shakespeare, Molliere, or any white artist. We would all be the poorer for it.

In 2020, a "coalition of theater artists" put out a long statement called "We See You White American Theater."[98] Among their long list of demands, they wanted BIPOC to be "the majority of writers, directors and designers onstage for the foreseeable future," theaters to "end all security arrangements with police departments," and owners to "rename half of Broadway theaters after artists of color, and ensure that half of their shows are written by, for and about BIPOC." Further, the coalition wanted land acknowledgements (for the Indian tribes who used to live on Manhattan) and free tickets to "members of those communities."[99] In the business world, Kehinde Andrews, a professor of "black studies" at a minor British university, said that Lloyd's, the world's largest insurance market, could only "genuinely atone" for slavery "by turning the company over to the descendants of the enslaved." The reasoning here is that because one of Lloyd's founders, Simon Fraser, owned slaves several centuries ago, the modern company is also at fault.[100]

In response, companies that were attacked for their supposed racist pasts did not hand over the cash and keys, but they accommodated the grift through adding DEI statements, staff, and other surface-level public relations efforts which are mostly still in place. A rare set of balls in response to the pressure to conform was displayed by former British Foreign Secretary Dominic Raab, who, in response to being asked whether he'd take a knee to support George Floyd protests, said he'd only do that for the Queen or when he asked his wife to marry him.

"Equity" in Police and Fire Services: *Reductio ad Absurdum*

We've discussed how "equity" and "anti-racism" led to discrimination in higher education admissions, from affirmative action in the 1960s through DEI today. But it did not end there: preferential hiring was applied even to skilled trades where meeting objective standards are a matter of life and death. Former fireman Frank Ricci explained in *The Spectator* that "the harm that DEI has done to public safety cannot be overstated," because after decades of lawsuits by women and minorities who do not pass entrance exams and tests at rates they desire, fire departments have lowered hiring standards.[101] Worsening the problem was aggressive action by the Biden Justice Department's Civil Rights Division, which sued police and fire departments and often obtained settlement decrees that required them to hire candidates who had been rejected on merit.

In October 2024, the Department of Justice (DoJ) sued South Bend, Indiana, "alleging that the hiring process for entry-level police officers at the South Bend Police Department (SBPD) violates Title VII of the Civil Rights Act," according to a press release.[102] The DoJ alleged that the SBPD "uses a written examination that discriminates against Black applicants and a physical fitness test that discriminates against female applicants."

Title VII "prohibits employment discrimination based on race, sex, color, national origin and religion," the release continues, and "prohibits not only intentional discrimination but also employment practices that result in a disparate impact on a protected group, unless such practices are job related and consistent with business necessity." This concept of "disparate impact" is supposed to mean that if all other things are equal, and a policy or action has a disparate impact on women or an ethnic group, there could be discrimination. For example, if 100 white men with a 4.0 grade average and 1400 SAT score are hired by Microsoft, and only 50 black men with the same grade and SAT average are hired, there is a "disparate impact" in Microsoft's employment practices that could arguably be attributed to discrimination. That disparity could still be explained by other variables, of course, such as years of work experience or level of education, but if all variables are controlled for and the disparity still exists, there is prima facie evidence of discrimination that could be assessed for action by DoJ.

The DoJ claimed that South Bend "uses a written examination that discriminates against Black applicants and a physical fitness test that discriminates against female applicants." This means that fewer blacks than other races passed the SBPD written test, and fewer women than men passed their physical fitness test. The DoJ claims that the SBPD's "uses of these tests are neither job related nor consistent with business necessity, and thus, violate Title VII." According to the DoJ complaint, "Since August 2019, approximately 83.8 percent of male test-takers passed the Physical Fitness Test, while approximately 47.4 percent of female test-takers passed."[103]

As Nellie Bowles of *The Free Press* puts it, "the new standard for the Justice Department is that any outcome that produces different results along race or sex lines must be inherently racist or sexist."[104] That's not new, of course; it is the Kendi–DiAngelo standard. The only explanation for disparity between races and sexes is racism or sexism, all other variables be damned.

Under President Biden, the DoJ's Civil Rights Division attacked police and fire departments based on this standard. Given that the DoJ has unlimited government lawyers and time, it often wins despite the ludicrous nature of the claim. The Maryland State Police and the Durham, North Carolina, fire department both caved, signing "consent decrees" to end the lawsuits.

Maryland State Police

In hiring, the Maryland State Police (MDSP) used a written Police Officer Selection Test (POST) and a physical Functional Fitness Assessment Test (FFAT) to screen applicants. The legal test, according to the DoJ, is that if any tests or other practices by employers "are not job related or consistent with business necessity," they violate Title VII. After a two-year investigation, the DoJ "concluded [Maryland]'s written and physical fitness tests do not meaningfully distinguish between applicants who can and cannot perform the position of Trooper" and so "these tests violate Title VII."[105]

Kristen Clarke, who was the assistant attorney general of the Civil Rights Division under President Biden, claimed that "[t]he underrepresentation of Blacks and women in law enforcement undermines public safety." She did not address whether higher representation by people with lower general knowledge and cognitive skills, and weaker physical abilities, will have any effect on public safety. Maryland will find out. The consent decree requires Maryland to "adopt written and physical fitness tests that do not discriminate in violation of Title VII," "hire up to 25 applicants who were unfairly disqualified by those tests and who successfully complete MDSP's new trooper screening and selection process," and give those new hires who were initially disqualified $2.75 million in back pay.

The new screening and selection processes that Maryland will have to implement will certainly set lower standards in both intelligence, knowledge, and fitness. Guidance in the Civil Rights Division's new fact sheet on "Combating Hiring Discrimination by Police and Fire Departments" will cause local authorities across the land to lower standards and hire based on desired percentages, which is the outcome the Biden Administration wanted.

Durham, NC, Fire Department

The DoJ lawsuit and consent decree against the Durham Fire Department (DFD) followed the same pattern. The DoJ alleged that the DFD violated Title VII by using a written test "that discriminates against Black candidates." Again, the DoJ claimed in its press release that the test that the DFD used "does not meaningfully distinguish between applicants who can and cannot perform the job of a firefighter," and "also disqualified Black applicants from employment at significantly disproportionate rates."[106]

Note that the DoJ needs to prove both elements in a one-two punch: if the test discriminated against black applicants but did actually distinguish between those who could and could not do the job, then there would be no discrimination under Title VII. The DoJ has to prove, or force its opponent into conceding, that the tests "are not job-related and consistent with business necessity" to claim these practices violate Title VII.

This is where the DoJ's twin strategy came into play: work with local governments when they are willing woke allies, and bully them into submission when they are not. Durham clearly is in the former category, as amazingly, the complaint was filed on October 7, 2024, and the City of Durham signed the consent decree the very same day. It was "wired" well in advance—a local version of the national "sue and settle" strategy that Democratic Administrations use to change policy.

Echoing the same social-justice platitudes, the DoJ announcement in the DFD case said: "The under-representation of Black people in the fire department workforce in Durham, and across the country, undermines public safety efforts." How, exactly? It did not say. Do people only want to be pulled from burning buildings by those of their own race? Under the consent decree, the DFD will have to "hire up to 16 applicants who were unfairly disqualified" by the now-rejected tests, and give them $980,000 in back pay. The "new firefighter selection process" that the DFD will need to devise will, as with the MDSP, doubtless dumb down all the standards. To help with that, there is the Civil Rights Division's handy Fact Sheet "to help applicants for public safety jobs understand their rights to be free from discriminatory hiring processes."[107]

Fortunately, under the Trump Administration, these consent decrees for "equity" in hiring are on the way out. Trump-appointed Assistant Attorney General for Civil Rights Harmeet Dhillon believes that the consent decrees against police and fire departments enforced by Biden "tie officers' hands and make communities less safe."[108] According to research by John R. Lott, president of the Crime Prevention Research Center. lowering the passing rate on intelligence and aptitude tests to hire more black officers, and lowering physical tests to hire more female officers, results in both higher crime and more assaults on officers. As Lott writes:

Consent decrees increase minority hiring by eliminating or reducing intelligence test standards. On average, cities that had consent decrees for hiring imposed on them saw their violent and property crime rates falling relative to other cities before the consent decrees and rising relative to other cities afterward.[109]

The Mythical Gender Pay Gap

Every year, someone trots out the perennial myth that a "gender pay gap" exists in America. "Social justice" proponents claim women make 84 percent of what men do, and activist groups claim some random day in March is "equal pay day." This is wrong on several levels. First, it is illegal to pay women less than men for the same work. In the federal government, military, and local governments, men and women with the same rank, qualifications, and experience are paid at the same scale. In private industry, too, this is likely the case. Intel, the technology company, reported as far back as 2016 that "the company has no pay gap between U.S. men and woman who work at the same job-grade level" at the company.[110]

Second, like "disparate impact analysis," the conclusion that women are unfairly paid can only be arrived at by comparing the average male wage with the average female wage and failing to account for any variables that might explain it other than sexist treatment of women. Those variables are that, on average, men work two more hours per week than women, men have more years of work experience, and more men choose college degrees and professions that earn more. Men are also more likely to die on the job, because they are more likely to take higher-risk jobs like electricity line repair or mining. Once you adjust for those variables, the "raw" gender pay gap shrinks to an "adjusted," or "normalized" level of less than 5 percent.[111] as Phil Gramm and John Early write, "the difference in wages is the natural consequence of choices that men and women freely make."[112]

Because that conclusion doesn't fit the narrative that we live in white supremacist, cis-hetero-normative patriarchy, the actual science and data gets buried in the mainstream media in favor of the perennial canard. Naturally, the obvious policy prescriptions to address the variables— discouraging women from having children, encouraging them to take degrees they are not interested in, and pushing them into careers they don't prefer—are popular on the Left. Conservatives prefer encouraging family formation, letting individuals choose what they study, and letting a free labor market decide what jobs it needs and how much to pay.

Equity Redux?

The Los Angeles wildfires of January 2025 lifted the curtain on mismanagement and DEI-based hiring in L.A. Mayor Karen Bass eventually fired the city's fire chief, Karen Crowley, who, when hired, seemed prouder of being a woman and a lesbian than of her record as a firefighter. The political Left blamed climate change and power service problems for the fires, while the Right saw the city's over-emphasis of DEI as a contributing culprit. Helping this latter impression was that the LA Fire Department's Deputy Chief and head of DEI Kristine Larson was also a lesbian, and overweight. In a 2019 video, Larson dismissed concerns that women firefighters might not be able to lift men out of a burning building, answering that "he got himself in the wrong place if I have to carry him out of a fire."[113]

Fireman Frank Ricci applauded the decision by President Trump's attorney general, Pam Bondi, to drop lawsuits like those above that had been used to force police and fire departments into hiring on the basis of race and sex rather than physical or mental fitness.[114] In April 2025, Bondi swore in Harmeet Dhillon as assistant attorney general for the DoJ's Civil Rights Division, the office behind all the federal disparate impact lawsuits against police and fire departments, companies, and institutions forcing them to lower or remove objective standards to achieve "equitable" outcomes. Dhillon, an Indian American woman, has built a legal practice and reputation fighting discrimination and DEI. The legacy media and progressive groups called it a "bloodbath" as she quickly moved some of her staff to other work, and some career officials resigned.[115]

The Civil Rights Division did important work in enforcing the Civil Rights Act of 1964. This law, together with other statutes, prohibits discrimination on the basis of race, color, national origin, sex, religion, and shared ancestry by recipients of federal financial assistance. But in recent years, the Civil Rights Division pushed those protections into pursuing disparate impact cases and enforcing gender ideology. The Biden DoJ's Civil Rights Division had supported the claims of male prisoners in federal detention that taxpayer-funded "gender affirming" surgery was "necessary medical care for gender dysphoria under the ADA [American with Disabilities Act]." Under Pam Bondi, the DoJ reversed this position.[116]

4. An Equitable Race to the Bottom

What the public can expect, as long as this race to the bottom continues, is lower standards of hiring and thus lower performance in all public services, from local up through state and federal. American meritocracy is being gradually but inexorably replaced with "equity": representation by race and sex in each selected occupation based on the favored group's percentage of the national population. I say "selected occupation" because a DoJ led by woke political appointees will have no intention of going after occupations that are heavily dominated by favored minorities to argue disparate impact and correct the unbalanced group demographics. For example, you did not see the DoJ investigating K–12 education for employing 80% women to 20% men.

DEI and "Anti-Racist" Training

In the past decade, fortunes have been made in the race grift industry, by exploiting the post-2020 guilt of academia, NGOs, and corporations, and their need to expiate through spending and virtue-signaling. At American institutions of higher education this is ubiquitous. A typical example is Ohio University, where the Division of Diversity and Inclusion hosted workshops for staff to learn about "power and privilege."[117] While such trainings always stress inclusion and diversity as the value, they are also vehicles for CRT, which holds that whites automatically have privilege due to their race, regardless of their individual circumstances. That white people are racist is taken as a given. The workshop's organizer, Kathy Obear wrote the book *...But I'm Not Racist! Tools for Well-Meaning Whites*, the title of which suggests that whites are all racist, even if they don't know it, and that resisting this fact is denial of a self-evident truth. The same logic is behind Robin DiAngelo's best-selling bible of guilt, *White Fragility*.

DEI Training Is Counterproductive

Researchers Pamela Paresky and Lee Jussim of the Network Contagion Research Institute conducted a systematic review of DEI training and concluded that "rather than increasing inclusion for all people, some types of DEI rhetoric and pedagogy may instead increase identity-based bias, hypervigilance and division—potentially creating a self-reinforcing system of a perceived need for more DEI programs and bureaucracies."[118]

The authors note that DEI is "ubiquitous in the corporate and educational sectors," and that "[m]ore than half of American employees have DEI meetings or training events at work, at a cost of an estimated $8 billion annually." This has created, they say, "a culture of DEI conformity based on a pernicious feedback loop in which large minorities or even a majority may disagree with the ideology but because non-conformists face—or at least justifiably fear—retribution."

Paresky and Jussim exposed participants to "anti-racist, anti-Islamophobia and anti-caste bigotry trainings," including writings by Ibram X. Kendi and Robin DiAngelo, and then "evaluated participants' perceptions of bias in hypothetical situations in which bias was not empirically present."

They found that "participants exposed to anti-oppression narratives were more likely than those who were exposed to neutral narratives to perceive prejudice in interactions where none empirically existed." In other words, exposure to so-called anti-racist material made participants hyper aware of imagined racism. Worse, those "exposed to DEI content were also significantly more likely to endorse punishing the imagined perpetrators of bias."

Ibram X. Kendi alleged that Paresky and Jussim had "misrepresented" his work and that it wasn't peer reviewed. That's quite a claim from the man who burned through $40 million in five years and ran his Center for Antiracist Research at Boston University into closure in 2025, after only four years during which it had produced no notable research.[119]

Suicidal Empathy

In 2010, "civic journalist and activist" Amanda Kijera wrote about being raped by a man in Haiti, according to an account written at the time and available on an internet archive. [120] She had been writing about violence against women that day: "I have witnessed as a journalist and human rights advocate the many injustices inflicted upon Black men in this world," which apparently make them "want to strike back, to fight rabidly for what is left of their personal dignity in the wake of such things.

Black men have every right to the anger they feel in response to their position in the global hierarchy." Kijera concluded: "While I take issue with my brother's [referring to the rapist (!)] behavior, I'm grateful for the experience," going on to advocate more job training and other solutions. Her forbearance is extraordinary, and perplexing, but not unique.[121]

In 2023, Jen Angel, a bakery owner in Oakland, California, was killed by a 19-year-old in a robbery. One might expect outrage and cries for justice, but her friend Moira Birss told the local news that Angel "strongly disagreed with the current criminal justice system, and would not want her alleged killer to go to prison."[122] She said: "Jen believed that we need to address harm and create accountability that is really rooted in looking at the root causes of why harm happens." Angel's friends say she would have preferred "restorative justice," and they hoped to work with the NGO Restore Oakland to bring it about.[123] This organization says that "healing justice is legacy of Southern, Black feminist, queer, and Indigenous revolutionaries who have always known that healing is inseparable from the work of ending systemic oppression." Its staff are committed to "decarceration and keeping our people free," which is in line with the "abolitionist" movement that wants to abolish the current criminal justice system, along with detention, especially of illegal aliens. It's difficult to critique this kind of hippie idealism, except to say that abolishing the police and refusing to lock up dangerous criminals will not bring about community safety, only more martyrs to ideology.

Conclusion

DEI reached its high-water mark under President Biden, and the tide is receding amidst public backlash and a new president committed to restoring meritocracy and enforcing civil rights laws. Although DEI will be fiercely defended, particularly in academia and the media, President Trump wants it rooted out of the federal government, and half the states want it out of their governments.

In corporate America, a return to merit-based selection and promotion is under way. DEI offices have been dismantled, and preferential hiring based on race and sex is harder to get away with. Harvard's Roland Fryer advocates an approach he calls Merit, Excellence, and Intelligence (MEI).

MEI "involves hiring solely on merit, without consideration of demographic factors."[124] As he did with college admissions, Fryer advocates using artificial intelligence and machine learning to "estimate applicants' likely performance or attrition before they are ever hired," and thus "identify future leaders."[125] He rejects the idea that diversity per se will make a company successful, instead advocating a targeted, data-driven approach to recruitment that, if done right, produces diversity as a side benefit.

A person to follow: Wilfred Reilly, @wil_da_beast630, X.

A book to read: *Social Justice Fallacies*, by Thomas Sowell, 2023.

A group to support – FAIR (Foundation Against Intolerance and Racism), New York, NY, @Fairforall, Substack, or https://www.fairforall.org/).

Chapter 7

The Seventh Commandment:
You Shall Bear False Witness (Trust the Media)

No person is entirely free of bias, and because institutions are made up of people, no institution is either. Because of this fact, one can safely conclude that there has never been an entirely neutral media outlet. Still, the general ethos that has prevailed for two centuries suggests that there should be a difference between news reporting and opinion. For much of the legacy media, that ethos died a decade or so ago.

Today, much of the media cover even straightforward, non-political news stories through a lens of bias. For the Left, this lens is one of "social justice," or one of the branches of critical theory (such as critical race theory and critical queer theory). For the Right, the lens is one of traditional conservative values, underpinned by federalism and a strict interpretation of the Constitution. A simpler way to say this would be that those on the Right are generally "anti-woke" and those on the Left are generally "woke."

Print journalists, later joined by radio and television news readers and reporters, used to have a monopoly on news reporting. Now, they are just one species of a larger category of media content creators that includes podcasters, writers on Substack and other self-publication platforms, and X (formerly Twitter) posters with large followings. In this chapter, I call media outlets that have long existed in print form like *The New York Times* and *The Washington Post*, or broadcasters that are many decades old like the major television networks ABC, CBS, and NBC, the "legacy" or "mainstream" media. Until very recently, they had the news field to themselves.

Then, over the past two decades, hundreds of small and upstart outlets emerged from the "media big bang" of the internet, including online newspapers, such as *The Free Press*, *The Daily Wire*, and *The Washington Free Beacon*. Countless news-aggregator sites compile stories from other outlets, concentrating on a particular set of issues or an ideological leaning—Yahoo News is one example.

The vast majority of journalists are left-leaning in their politics.[1] This bias, and commensurate support for Democrats over Republicans, has grown over time in the media, as it has in academia. In the 2016 election, the Center for Public Integrity reported that 96 percent of campaign donations from journalists in America went to Hillary Clinton, while less than 5 percent went to Donald Trump.[2]

Breaking Down Media Bias

Bias in the media is easier to spot if you read the same outlet over many years. For younger people, most of whom don't get their news and analysis from one source but from many, and who have never subscribed to a physical newspaper or magazine, media bias can be harder to detect. Google News in 2023 took 63 percent of its content from leftwing media sources, and 6 percent from rightwing sources, according to a report by AllSides, which looked at a sample of 500 articles.[3] The bias was particularly noted when it came to stories on "abortion, climate change, economy, election, immigration and [President Joe] Biden." From the top 10 sites that Google preferred, only Fox News could be considered right of center—AllSides considers the leftish Reuters to be centrist. CNN and *The New York Times* together accounted for more than a quarter of the stories that Google chose.

Under President Joe Biden, the Federal Communications Commission (FCC) required broadcasters to post a race and "gender" scorecard of all employees. Like the U.S. State Department's "diversity, equity, inclusion, and accessibility" (DEIA) baseline, the intended use of this scorecard is to engineer race and sex outcomes.[4] This FCC requirement is an example of a federal "rule," or how the administrative state implements federal laws in ways that hijack the agenda and even conflict with the intended purpose of these laws. Despite the fact that Congress has passed no law to this effect, the FCC rule requires broadcasters to track the racial and gender composition of their employees and make that data publicly available or else risk receiving a fine.

Conservatives who claim that the "mainstream," or "legacy" media is leftwing and biased are often met with derision from that same media. But they're not making it up—we have the receipts. Below, I break down media bias into nine types, with examples of each.

1. Bias in Internet Search Engines (Algorithm Bias)

Every media outlet is curated. That means that someone decides what goes in and what doesn't. With a print newspaper, that decision is made by the editors. Social media are different—the news and other stories on X or Instagram aren't decided by a human editor, but by an algorithm.

A media algorithm is a computer program that can tailor content to the individual. For example, it can look at what kinds of things you like each time you view or click and gives you more of it. Of course, humans decide what kinds of algorithm are used, and how they are programmed. But unlike with a newspaper, an algorithm decides for each person separately, creating millions of variations of news feeds.

That's a problem, because leftwing bias is in the architecture of the internet itself, perpetuating the woke agenda and belief system. This is evident in text searches, but a picture is worth a thousand words, and Google's Gemini artificial intelligence (AI) unwittingly but devastatingly demonstrated the woke racism deliberately designed into its search engine.

It has been obvious to anyone sentient that Google results skew leftwards. But Gemini starkly, and often hilariously, showed this in black and white. As Bari Weiss (among others) reported based on sample searches, when asked to depict "a Swedish family," Gemini showed a variety of non-white people. Asked to show "a historically accurate depiction of a medieval British king," or a French king from the 17th century, Gemini showed women as supposed kings, and non-white male kings, neither of which (of course) ever existed in these countries. America was not spared, with its founding fathers recast as a "diverse racial and gender mix, including, of course, a Native American."[5] Gemini refused to show Norman Rockwell paintings (presumably they are controversial because they are too traditional, too white, or somehow conservative-coded) or a European family. "Instead, I can offer you a variety of images featuring diverse families, showcasing the beauty and richness of human connection across different ethnicities, genders, and backgrounds," Gemini said.

That Gemini was determined to re-write European and American history to erase white people wasn't what worried *The New York Times*. What bothered the paper's editors was that when asked to show a Nazi or a German soldier of World War II, Gemini showed blacks and women, who were not exactly prominent among frontline soldiery in what the Russians call the Great Patriotic War. Many journalists and amateurs played with Gemini, producing results that have to be embarrassing, even for a woke Silicon Valley tech company. A thread posted by X user "TexasLindsay" is one of the best.[6] TexasLindsay requests of Gemini: "using less than 50 words, share three facts about" and then names a series of Democratic and Republican politicians of similar stature. The first pair is Senator Chuck Schumer (D–NY) and Senator Mitch McConnell (R–KY). In every pairing, Gemini provides three facts for the Democrat, for example: Schumer is the first New Yorker to serve as Senate majority leader. For the Republican, in every case Gemini says this: "Elections are a complex topic with fast-changing information. To make sure you have the latest and most accurate information, try Google search."[7] Gemini is happy to provide detailed, individual information each Democratic politician, but takes a generic cop out for all the Republicans—evidence that its algorithm sees Republicans as riskier, or dangerous, to discuss than Democrats.

The experiment continued with TexasLindsay asking Gemini to write a poem about Democratic Governor Gavin Newsom of California (result: "Newsom helms the Golden State, sun-kissed and vast...") and then Republican Governor Ron DeSantis of Florida (result: "it wouldn't be appropriate for me to express a personal opinion about a political figure...") Again, content for the Democrat, and cop out for the Republican. There's an old saying in computer programming: "garbage in, garbage out." With Gemini, the corollary seemed to be "woke in, woke out."

2. Begging the Question

"Begging the question" means assuming that which has yet to be proven. Let's say you're reading an article about chess and the author asked: *Since women are as smart as men, why aren't there an equal number of female and male chess champions?* The sentence seems to be asking why there aren't more women chess champions, or why so many are men. But it "begs the question" of women being as smart as men. Are they? Are they as good at the type of reasoning that makes good chess players? That's a pretty important thing to prove, given what the article is about.

Example: In a December 4, 2024, Reuters story, Andrew Chung and John Kruzel write about a Supreme Court case known as the Skrmetti case, referring to Jonathan Skrmetti, who is the attorney general of Tennessee. The ACLU, supported by President Biden's Department of Justice, was at the time suing the State of Tennessee to stop the state's ban on hormones and surgery for children who think they are in the wrong body.

The headline read: "US Supreme Court leans toward allowing youth transgender care ban."[8] The writers say that the Skrmetti case is "testing the legality of a Republican-backed ban in Tennessee on gender-affirming medical care for transgender minors, one of 24 such policies enacted by conservative states around the country." This begs several questions. What is "gender"? Is it "gender affirming" to give puberty blockers to children to stop them from going through the puberty their bodies would naturally start? Are there "transgender" minors? Isn't it more "gender affirming" to stop this inexorable, irreversible path to transition in minors who are too young to know the consequences?

3. "Conservatives Pounce" Stories

"Conservative pounce" stories are a mainstream journalistic tactic to make any story not about the *action* by a favored (leftist) group or individual, but about the conservative *reaction*. The idea is to frame the reaction as out of proportion to the supposedly minor incident that elicited it. A telling example is this headline:

"Republicans say Biden is a 'liar' after he pardons Hunter, his son," *Politico*, December 1, 2024.[9] The headline about President Biden pardoning his son Hunter makes the story about the reaction of Republicans, not about the president's action.

In the opening sentence of the piece, the author writes: "Republicans called President Joe Biden a 'liar' for pardoning his son, who was convicted on gun charges and pleaded guilty to tax fraud this summer." This, again, puts the focus on the Republican reaction instead of the president's action. President Biden had stated repeatedly, and his spokesperson often confirmed, that he would not pardon Hunter Biden. So, to say he lied does not seem unfair.

4. Editorial Bias

Three national television networks (ABC, CBS, and NBC) emerged after World War II. A fourth network, PBS, is non-profit "public broadcasting" and started with no commercials. Now, it has succumbed to paid sponsorships.

All four networks are still around but have much less share of today's diverse media market. Where viewers once had four nightly national news shows to choose from after work, and one morning show on each network, today, they have a plethora of choices, from streaming services, to YouTube, Rumble, X, Instagram, podcasts, and many other platforms.

The leftwing bias in the national media is obvious to those who marinate in it every day, but most Americans do not. To illustrate the point, we need only take a brief look at some national outlets.

ABC News

In 2024, the legacy media were quick to call out "false" claims by Donald Trump and others that the Federal Emergency Management Agency (FEMA) money had been used to support illegal aliens. ABC News ran this headline on October 7, 2024:

"Trump falsely claims Biden used FEMA funds for migrants—something Trump did himself."[10]

See how the ABC title has its cake and eats it, too: *Biden didn't do it; but if he did, Trump did first*. In the article, the author wrote:

Former President Donald Trump has been spreading false claims about the Biden-Harris administration's response to Hurricane

Helene, including the baseless claim that the administration is using Federal Emergency Management Agency money to house illegal migrants. Some of Trump's allies, including Elon Musk, have been amplifying those claims.

Despite ABC's headline, the claims that the Biden Administration used FEMA funds to transport, house, and support illegal aliens (or aliens paroled into the United States) were not false, as other outlets like the *New York Post* had been reporting for several years. In fact, from fiscal year 2021 to fiscal year 2024, Congress gave FEMA's Shelter and Services Program $2.2 billion for "nonprofits and local entities to provide support to noncitizens released from DHS [Department of Homeland Security] custody." (This means to pay for illegal aliens released at the border.)[11] In 2024 alone, FEMA set aside $640.9 million in Shelter and Services grants "to enable non-federal entities to offset allowable costs incurred for services associated with noncitizen migrant arrivals in their communities."[12] Not surprisingly, the top recipients were Denver, Washington, DC, Chicago, the state of Massachusetts, New York City, and Philadelphia—Democrat-run "sanctuary" states and cities that offer free housing and services to illegal aliens, partly using federal tax dollars.

Here's what White House press secretary Karine Jean-Pierre said at the time: "[I]t's just categorically false. It is not true," pointing to a *Washington Post* headline that claimed, "No, Biden didn't take FEMA relief money to use on migrants—but Trump did."[13]

Moreover, not only did President Biden use FEMA Shelter and Services Program (SSP) money, but his Administration even tapped FEMA's Emergency Food and Shelter Program (EFSP), which was authorized in 1987 to help homeless veterans, for another billion dollars to house illegal immigrants. In 2022, Jean-Pierre helpfully explained that "[f]unding is also available through FEMA's emergency food and shelter program to eligible local governments and not-for-profit organizations upon request to support humanitarian relief for migrants."[14]

In an X clip, an ABC reporter says: "Federal lawmakers have negotiated $800 million to give out as grants to cities seeing an influx of migrants. Sources say Senator Chuck Schumer has already discussed with FEMA the allocation of a substantial amount of it for New York City."[15]

The fine line that ABC was trying to walk was this: FEMA has different pots of money. One is disaster relief, which can only be used after a state governor and then the president declares an emergency. There are other pots, like the SSP and EFSP grants, that don't require an emergency declaration. So, the media claim, President Biden didn't use FEMA emergency money for illegal aliens.

This pretzel-twisting is called "sophistry" (a "sophist" is essentially ancient Greek for "wise guy"). In their effort to protect President Biden and vilify Donald Trump at all costs, ABC and other legacy media sacrificed credibility and objectivity.

CBS News

The CBS network has long had a reputation as the best of the three national networks for news coverage; however, just like the other mainstream networks, the quality of its journalism has declined markedly. CBS News hit rock bottom in October 2024. First, its flagship news program *60 Minutes* replaced a classic, rambling Kamala Harris answer with a shorter one that made slightly more sense.[16]

Host Bill Whitaker said to Vice President and presidential candidate Harris about the U.S.-Israel relationship: "It seems that Prime Minister Netanyahu is not listening." Harris responded with a word salad: "Well, Bill, the work that we have done has resulted in a number of movements in that region by Israel that were very much prompted by, or a result of, many things, including our advocacy for what needs to happen in the region."[17]

CBS changed her answer to: "We are not going to stop pursuing what is necessary for the United States to be clear about where we stand on the need for this war to end."[18]

CBS News host Tony Dokoupil had interviewed author and leftist darling Ta-Nehisi Coates about his new book *The Message*, challenging Coates on his apparent anti-Israeli bias.[19] Shortly afterwards, "CBS News leaders…reprimanded Dokoupil…for an interview they said didn't meet their standards."[20] This triggered an internal conflict at CBS and its corporate parent Paramount, or what CBS network president and CEO George Cheeks called a "strong and growing discord within CBS News."[21] The self-flagellation was typical. The legacy media is dominated and run by people who believe so strongly in the "anti-racist" creed that it no longer seems odd for a supposedly serious news organization to expect its journalists and hosts to treat guests differently based on race.

National Public Radio

While National Public Radio (NPR) traditionally served as a source of wide-ranging news stories of general interest to a broad swathe of Americans, that is, the "public," it now embodies wokeness. The station cancelled Garrison Keillor's *Prairie Home Companion* show after almost 40 years because of accusations by women that he had behaved inappropriately. The accusations amounted to a series of apparently bawdy comments and "inappropriate touching," a nebulous term that could include anything from a pat on the back to outright groping. During the entire "Me Too" era, which contributed to Keillor's downfall, NPR adopted the "trust the victim" without question mentality that has led to devastating repercussions for many innocent people.

In 2022, *The Washington Post* reported on the departure of some on-air presenters at NPR, noting that they were joining a *New York Times* podcast, Vox Media, and MSNBC. Ari Shapiro, co-host of the news show *All Things Considered*, tweeted that this was a "crisis," and that NPR was "hemorrhaging hosts from marginalized backgrounds."[22]

No one who listens to NPR in 2024 would consider any of the departed NPR talent "marginalized." It has become a joke among conservatives to tune in to NPR and see how long it takes for some aspect of wokeness to be featured. Players of this game—which is affectionally referred to as "How long till woke?"—typically report that it takes anywhere from less than a minute or up to no more than five minutes before the story angle moves in the direction of a liberal or woke tilt.[23] I tried this out in late April 2025. Before I got out of my dirt road to the highway, there was a story about a transgender support gathering in the state capital. The idea of local NPR featuring a similar story about a hunters' gathering, or a support group for home schooling parents, was laughable. That story was followed by one about deportation, which clearly took the side of the "undocumented" or people "lacking legal status" and treated government statements with haughty disdain.

As with many other industries, the departed talent at NPR is not homeless and indigent, but working in higher-profile, and perhaps better-paying outlets. In *The Washington Post*, Paul Farhi and Elahe Izadi wrote that, "Despite giving unprecedented opportunities to women since its founding in 1970, NPR has struggled for many years to diversify its audience and provide alternative perspectives."[24] They cite Neilsen data that NPR's radio audience is 21 percent "people of color." The implication is that the content is driving the audience, not the other way round.

The authors write that "NPR's internal statistics show that its workforce is 62 percent White, 15 percent Black/African American, 12 percent Asian American and 7 percent Latino or Hispanic." Those percentages are very close to national racial breakdown for white and black, but much higher for Asians. The Hispanic percentage is lower than the national share, which makes sense given that many of the recent arrivals from Latin America do not understand English well enough to get much out of listening to NPR.

Paul du Quenoy of the Palm Beach Freedom Institute describes NPR as a "radical leftist, government-subsidized news source."[25] In 2023, Katherine Maher took over from John Lansing as the broadcaster's CEO. Maher is as woke as they come, and has in the recent past railed against Trump, "white silence," and "whiteness" in general.

As du Quenoy writes, the Nielsen Audio ratings showed NPR ratings in their New York city affiliate, WNYC, declining by 20 percent from June 2021 to June 2023, with similar declines in Chicago, Los Angeles, and San Francisco. NPR has made a massive effort to hire non-white employees, with results that could not plausibly have been achieved without discrimination on the basis of race. Under the CEO before Maher, NPR "employees of color" went from 9 percent of the workforce to 46 percent. Yet, only a quarter of NPR listeners were "of color." After losses in corporate sponsorship, NPR cut $10 million from its budget and 10 percent of its staff.

In 2024, Uri Berliner left NPR after 25 years, writing a sad summary of the network's decline in *The Free Press*, where he now works. "It's true NPR has always had a liberal bent," he wrote, "but during most of my tenure here, an open-minded, curious culture prevailed... In recent years, however, that has changed. Today, those who listen to NPR or read its coverage online find something different: the distilled worldview of a very small segment of the U.S. population."[26] Berliner describes how NPR's bias undermined its coverage of the Hunter Biden laptop story, COVID-19, and what turned out to be baseless reports of President Trump's collusion with Russia. Anyone old enough to remember NPR a few decades ago will nod his head in agreement with Berliner, who while wryly admitting to being a left-of-center Subaru driver educated at Sarah Lawrence College, still knows what objective reporting is.

The New York Times

It's hard to say when *The New York Times* went from being a left-leaning but credible paper of record to rank partisanship and wholesale adoption of the woke agenda. How did that happen?

Batyar Ungar-Sargon's book *Bad News* explains how journalism in general went from being a working-class profession that held elites accountable from the outside, to an elite profession that defended its own.

In his review of the book in *Quillette*, Kevin Mims writes that "Ungar-Sargon's book is an excellent summary of how an obsession with postmodern doctrines of anti-racism has caused left-wing journalism to become a wholly unreliable source of information about the current, rapidly improving, state of race relations in America."[27]

One notable turning point in *The New York Times'* journey was in 2019, when executive editor Dean Baquet learned that his young journalists no longer saw their jobs as reporting the who, what, when, where, and why, but as reporting everything through a sort of social justice lens. As Mims writes, a reporter asked Baquet "to what extent you think that the fact of racism and white supremacy being sort of the foundation of this country should play into our reporting... I just feel like racism is everything. It should be considered in our science reporting, in our culture reporting, in our national reporting."[28]

And so it is.

The Washington Post

Above, I discussed how ABC News tried to help the White House to deny that President Biden was using FEMA funds to support illegal aliens.

This is a *Washington Post* headline from October 4, 2024 by in-house "Fact Checker" Glenn Kessler:

No, Biden didn't take FEMA relief money to use on migrants – but Trump did[29]

Almost the same as the ABC headline, and just as wrong.

Like *The New York Times*, *The Washington Post* applies a lens to its reporting, turning it into a hybrid product of opinion and fact, leaving it to readers to figure out the difference. To give one example, the byline for *Washington Post* reporter Anne Branigin says she "is a staff reporter in Features focused on gender coverage. Previously, she worked at the Root covering news, politics, health and social justice movements through the lens of race and gender."[30]

The Lancet

One might hope for science publications to hold out against the woke mind virus and its language enforcers. Sadly, they didn't. As Mary Chastain reported in *Legal Insurrection*, *The Lancet*, one of the United Kingdom's two most respected medical journals, has jettisoned science for the woke lens.[31]

The Lancet's style guide for contributors now says that "Sex and gender are often incorrectly portrayed as binary (female/male or woman/man), concordant, and static."[32] Therefore, it continues, those submitting articles "should use the term 'sex assigned at birth' rather than 'biological sex,' 'birth sex' or 'natal sex' as it is more accurate and inclusive."

"In human research, the term 'sex' carries multiple definitions," says this medical journal, and

> these constructs exist along a spectrum that includes additional sex categorisations and gender identities, such as people who are intersex/have differences of sex development (DSD), or identify as non binary. In any given person, sex and gender might not align, and both can change.[33]

This, remember, is a scientific, medical journal. In 2021, *The Lancet* referred to women—on the magazine's cover—as "bodies with vaginas." *The Lancet*'s editors later apologized.[34]

5. Appeals to Credentials

Credentials are college degrees, certificates, training, jobs, and other experiences and personal history that make some people seem smarter than others on a given subject. When the media refer to "experts," they usually mean people with these credentials. But there are all kinds of credentials, some worth more than others. And there are also many non-expert experts, or people who *believe* they are experts. Who you choose as an expert can influence what you believe.

The media quote experts in their stories regularly. Ideally, reporters should cite a range of experts to show both or all sides of a story. Opinion articles or editorials tend to cite only those experts who agree with them. But sometimes, reporters for straight-news stories use experts to inject bias into their story and lead readers to think the way the writer wants them to.

The key to spotting this kind of bias is that they will cite experts from one side of the argument only, or at a ratio that makes it clear what the writer thinks and thus what the reader is supposed to think after reading the article.

The attempt is not to inform and to allow readers to make up their own minds, but to trigger an automatic agreement with the author's own opinion.

Example: "Experts warn that Trump's economic plans could make inflation worse," Associated Press, March 11, 2025.[35]

Which experts? Does that mean all experts? With law, economics, science, and the arts, there are always "experts" who think one thing and others who think the opposite. Who is the best painter in history? Which is the best system of government? Does lowering taxes strengthen the economy? How much unemployment is healthy? Remember that this was only a few weeks before the November 5, 2024, election, in which the economy and inflation was the number one issue for voters.

Example: "Trump's triumph threatens an already battered democracy, experts say," *The Washington Post*, November 6, 2024.[36] (The subtitle read: "American democracy simply wasn't set up to 'deal with an aspiring autocrat,' especially with a willing electorate.")

Which experts? Does that mean all experts? The author cites professors from Harvard, George Washington University, and the University of London. Why not include a conservative, or alternative view? Note how the word "autocrat" is used strategically to discredit Trump.

6. Fact-Check Bias

Fact-check bias comes in two types. First, a media outlet can *choose which facts to check*. For example, in the debate between Donald Trump and Kamala Harris of the 2024 presidential campaign, ABC News moderators checked many things that Donald Trump said while leaving many things that Harris said unchallenged. That created the impression for viewers that Trump was not speaking the truth, and that Harris was.

The second type of fact-check bias is the check itself—in other words, the fact-checker is assuming the God-like role of determining truth. Some facts are easy to check, like who the U.S. president was in 1962. Others are harder, like how much prices have risen in the U.S. between 2021 and 2024, or how many jobs were lost or created under President Trump or President Biden. Many things can influence these numbers, like when you start, when you finish, which items you count when determining average prices, and so on.

Example: On October 24, 2024, *The Washington Post* gave four "Pinocchios" to a Trump ad saying that Kamala Harris "supports EV mandates, killing Michigan jobs."

Headline: "Trump's 'crazy,' false ad claiming 'massive layoffs' among autoworkers."[37]

Subtitle: "Motor vehicle manufacturing employment hit a 34-year high in July."

"Fact checker" Glenn Kessler hardly strikes an objective tone in his headline. He goes on to say that banning gas cars was "an old proposal, long ago abandoned" by Harris. It is fair to say that the Trump ad cherry-picked statistics to support its contention that the auto industry has lost jobs, but Kessler himself "relied on statements from Kamala Harris and the United Auto Workers, which has endorsed her," according to Allysia Finley in *The Wall Street Journal*.[38]

Example: On October 18, 2024, *USA Today* "fact checked" this Instagram post by conservative strategist Joey Mannarino: "'Not one dollar' of $42 billion for internet access used for that purpose; $7.5 billion spent on seven electric vehicle chargers."

Headline: "[Instagram] Post misleads on funds for internet access, EV charging stations."[39]

USA Today's Chris Mueller fact checks Mannarino's post about the Biden Administration broadband program. Mannarino wrote that "Kamala Harris and Joe Biden promised to use $42 billion…to expand internet to the entire country and not one single house or business received service," and "Pete Buttigieg promised to use $7.5 billion to expand electric vehicle charging in America. Only 7 EV charging stations have been produced in 3 years. We paid more than $1 billion per charger."

Mueller rates these claims "false," because, he says, "Officials say the $42 billion high-speed internet allotment was designed to be part of a longer-term program, so minimal spending at this point was expected. But some of the money has been used by states to plan their projects, and other funds have been approved to pay for construction once plans are finalized."

Furthermore, Mueller said: "The charging station stat is outdated, as the federal funds have now funded 20 stations, not seven. And there are plans for hundreds more…"

This fact-check is one-sided because the substantive point of the Mannarino claim is that the vast bulk of billions of federal dollars appropriated for particular projects had not, three years later, been spent. Further, what had been spent had made little progress. Whether there were seven or even 20 charging stations built seems nit-picking detail, which doesn't undermine the larger point that the $7.5 billion didn't achieve much in three years.

7. Headline Bias

Media organizations can be biased through their inclusion or exclusion of certain news stories and topics based on political considerations. More specifically, this is bias about which stories a media outlet or writer chooses to cover in the first place. This can influence readers' views of what is news and what isn't, of what matters and what doesn't. This is known as selective coverage bias, which we cover in further detail below; but related to it is headline bias.

Headline bias is when the headline itself—the title of an article—isn't neutral but leads a reader to form an opinion before even reading the article. You can spot this by comparing right-leaning and left-leaning media headlines on the same story. You will see that instead of just reporting "Dog Bites Man," a headline could indicate a rash of dogs biting men ("Dog Bites Man" *again*), or that this was a rare incident ("Dog Bites Man" *an unusual event*). An article about a jobs report could have a headline that makes the reader think it is good news, or, with the same exact numbers, that it is bad news.

Example: On November 25, 2024, *Roll Call* ran this headline on Trump Cabinet picks: "Trump's second administration set to be filled with losers."[40]

(Subtitle: "At least 17 of his picks have previously lost elections.")

Roll Call wants readers to think that Trump picks are "losers" in the general sense of the word, with this click-bait joke. The subtitle reveals that the paper is describing how 17 of Trump's hundreds of appointees for the Cabinet and other jobs have previously lost an election. Yet, almost all politicians, even those at the top, will have lost an election somewhere along the way.

Example: On September 1, 2024, CNN decided on this headline about the murder of Israeli-American Hamas hostage Hersch Goldberg-Polin:

Israeli-American hostage Hersh Goldberg-Polin has died, his family says in a statement released by the Ministry of Foreign Affairs.[41]

CNN's original title states in a passive voice that Goldberg "has died," a framing which removes any agency for his murder, as well as the brutality that he suffered. Who killed him? Hamas, presumably. CNN changed the headline later to:

Hersh Goldberg-Polin: The 'happy-go-lucky' Israeli-American who became a symbol of Israel's enduring hostage heartbreak.

The article also does not say that he was murdered by Hamas, but the first headline seems more deliberate in its obfuscation.[42]

Example: On their October 28, 2024 online front page, the *New York Times* featured an inspiring, flattering photo of Democratic candidate for president Kamala Harris looking confidently into the future. Below her is a mocking cartoon of Republican candidate (now president) Donald Trump as a giant orange clay balloon with bright yellow hair.[43] The contrast is blatant. On the page are seven articles, all of which hint that the articles will be supporting Harris or criticizing Trump. One article criticizes the Republican party for "Anti-Trans Ads."

The November 2, 2024 online front page of *The New York Times* started with a 110-word editorial titled **"Vote to End the Trump Era,"** calling him "unfit to lead."[44] A quarter of the words are underlined in red, such as "subvert," "lies," "deportations," "climate," and "autocrats."

Below that ominous editorial are these article headlines:

If the Choice in 2024 Were So Obvious, the Election Wouldn't Be So Close
All the Demons Are Here
Whatever Happens Next, Trump Has Already Won a Tragic Victory
Springsteen Is Fighting Back the Darkness at the Edge of America
Had Enough of the Election? Take Solace in the Marathon
I've Covered Authoritarians Abroad. Now I Fear One at Home.
Trump Has a New Theory of Power and How to Use It
The Cost of a Nuclear Arsenal
Humorless Feminists Against Trump
What I Truly Expect if an Unconstrained Trump Retakes Power

Judged by title alone, 7 out of 10 of the above articles would presumably take anti-Trump positions.

Example: Donald Trump had said publicly that Liz Cheney—former representative from Wyoming and a Never Trump Republican—is a war hawk but would likely change her mind if she were on the front lines facing enemy guns. Legacy media reported, outrageously, that he had suggested she face a firing squad.

On November 1, 2024, *The Atlantic* ran this headline: "Trump Suggests Training Guns on Liz Cheney's Face."[45]

Kasie Hunt said on her CNN show that "Donald Trump is escalating his violent rhetoric, suggesting...Liz Cheney should be fired upon."[46]

The Washington Post wrote in a X post: "Former president Donald Trump appeared to suggest on Thursday that former congresswoman and longtime Trump critic Liz Cheney should be subjected to gunfire as he called her a 'war hawk.'"[47]

8. Editorial and Opinion Page Bias

Newspapers do have an editorial line. That editorial line should be distinct from their news coverage, which should be about the facts; the who, what, where, and when. Editorials and opinion pieces address the "so what?"—the analysis, what it all means. Newspapers have owners, and owners have interests. Often, those interests far exceed the investment in a newspaper alone. If owners assert editorial control over the news coverage, they risk destroying their paper or outlet's reputation, which can be financially ruinous or destroy the reputation of their media asset.

However, it is not unusual or unreasonable for owners to assert some control over the editorial page of the paper they own. Examples of this are Patrick Soon-Shiong, owner of the *Los Angeles Times*, declining to endorse Kamala Harris for president in 2024, and Jeff Bezos announcing in early 2025 that *The Washington Post* editorial page would start featuring pieces supporting free enterprise and free speech. Not surprisingly, both papers saw journalists resigning in a huff both at the lack of a Harris endorsement (though both papers were hardly subtle about whom their writers supported) and the change of editorial direction.

At the *Post*, columnist Ruth Marcus resigned after 40 years, when an editorial she wrote criticizing the paper's owner, Bezos, was rejected.[48] Her level of entitlement is staggering.

Another who left was Jennifer Rubin, the *Post*'s former nominal token Republican, who is worth writing about in greater detail, as her style of column has become emblematic of the leftist media. Rubin left the *Post* after Trump's second inauguration to start her own online publication, inaptly called *The Contrarian*. Far from being a contrarian at the *Post*, the Democratic Party's house journal, Rubin was the most shameless shill for Biden and then Harris in print media. A look at some of her columns leaves no doubt about her political bias.

In October 2023, Rubin called Trump an "unhinged, vengeful, incoherent, dangerous neo-fascist president,"[49] while she bemoaned the "media obsession with finding fault with President Biden."[50] Without irony, in November 2023, Rubin then lamented "the sorry state of political coverage in this country."[51] She was upset about "endless speculation that President Biden might step away from the 2024 race," which, of course, turned out to be true. A *New York Times* poll showing that Trump could win five of the six swing states was "hysterical prediction," Rubin scoffed, urging readers to "consider how utterly meaningless this poll truly was."

In April 2024, Rubin wrote that "Trump day by day has become smaller, more decrepit and, frankly, somewhat pathetic." As for her man Biden? He "set a vigorous campaign schedule crisscrossing Pennsylvania," she wrote, describing the same guy who, when he got back to Washington, read the stage direction to "pause" off the teleprompter.[52]

9. Selective Coverage Bias

Every media or social media outlet, from *The New York Times* to X, is curated. That means someone is deciding what goes in and what doesn't. With a print newspaper, that decision is made by the editor. Editors can influence what their readers think is important by which stories they choose to cover and which ones they leave out. *The New York Times* motto is *All the news that's fit to print*, but of course it doesn't have room for every story in America, much less the world. Who decides what is "fit"? The editor. Who picks the editor? The owner or shareholders.

Here's one example of how a news outlet's selective coverage of stories affects the way readers perceive reality: In October 2023, *USA Today*'s Rex Huppke wrote about national crime statistics.

Headline: "Crime in America is down, rudely interfering with the GOP narrative that it's out of control."[53]

Subtitle: "Some inconvenient facts have come along that threaten to undermine the hard work we've put in convincing our beloved Republican voters their country is a wasteland ravaged by violent leftists."

Selective coverage bias was evident in the reporting about national crime leading up to the 2024 election. Many people *saw* that crime was going up, but much of the media simply told them otherwise. Huppke's article is typical of this coverage. His article was based on the FBI report of 2022 crime data, reported in September 2023. According to this data, violent crime had fallen by 2.1 percent nationwide. But a year later, in September 2024, the FBI revised its numbers. According to the new data, the FBI said, "violent crime actually increased by 4.5 percent in 2022."[54]

Legacy media like *USA Today* reported the lower crime figures as fact and attacked those who cited other evidence—such as national surveys of victims—that crime was rising. When the FBI revised its figures, the same outlets that cited FBI data to claim crime was down did not write new, prominent articles correcting their earlier articles based on false information. The revised FBI data, as well as national surveys of crime victims and other reporting, are all inconvenient to political beliefs that Huppke and others hold dear. Therefore, Huppke chose to use evidence that supported what he wanted to be true and to ignore facts that went the other way. Huppke's bias is also evident in his sarcastic use of "beloved" to describe Republican voters, and his labelling of the facts he cites as "inconvenient" to an argument he disagrees with.

In many large U.S. cities, like Boston, Chicago, New York, Los Angeles, and San Francisco, Democratic prosecutors have been elected on promises to "reform" the criminal justice system. This usually means fewer arrests, easier bail terms, fewer prosecutions, and lighter sentences, all in the name of "equity," "social justice," and the like. If crime goes up after these policies are put in place, then voters might think the policies don't work and they might want to elect more traditional prosecutors. That means media who want leftwing prosecutors to remain in office don't like admitting that crime is up, so they prefer to cite data, true or not, that shows it is going down.

Conclusion

One has to get news from somewhere. I am not suggesting that there is no bias in conservative or rightwing media; there is. The difference is that conservative media make no bones about it. The legacy media still cloak themselves in a previous generation's better attempts at objectivity. "Democracy dies in darkness," *The Washington Post*'s motto adopted in

2017 in response to Donald Trump's presidential election win, smacks of ideology.

Today's readers have only two real solutions. The first is to ignore the media altogether, which many seem to do. "Where ignorance is bliss, tis folly to be wise."[55] For those who wish to be informed, the answer is to triangulate—to take information while considering its source, and to confirm one source with others, preferably from a range of perspectives.

A person to follow: Matt Taibbi, author and journalist, https://www.racket.news/.

A book to read: *Bad News: How Woke Media Is Undermining Democracy*, by Batya Ungar-Sargon, 2021.

A group to support: Free Speech Union, London, U.K., https://freespeechunion.org/.

Chapter 8

The Eighth Commandment:
You Shall Have No Nation

Ask a progressive this: Is there any difference between an American citizen and a citizen of another country? Are there any benefits to being an American citizen that an illegal alien, or a legal immigrant, should not have? You may have to wait a while for the answer.

The word "progressive" is, to use a favorite word of the Left, "problematic." Towards *what* we are progressing? How do we know when we've reached it—and do we then stop? The progressive movement of President Teddy Roosevelt and Senator and Governor Bob La Follette of Wisconsin was about reining in monopolies, improving work and public safety, and helping every American to share in the country's growing prosperity. Today's progressives seem to be intent on breaking down all the norms, guidelines, and traditions that this society has worked out over centuries for human flourishing. They want to "queer" the distinction between the sexes so that there is only a vague continuum of *ersatz* gender identities. They want to abolish the criminal justice system, or at least render it toothless, so that no one is responsible for his own actions. And they want to tear down borders so that there is only one, global, community and no nations. They speak of the ascendant "global majority," by which they mean everyone but Europeans. They preach the Marxist dogma of oppressors and oppressed, with capitalism as the tool of oppression.

Conservatives, in contrast, believe in conserving that which is good. They accept and embrace change, not for its own sake, but when they are convinced that it really is progress. They know that family is the basic unit of the community, so they cherish marriage, children, and social responsibility. They know that communities, towns, cities, and states are the foundation of this federal republic. They believe that patriotism is good. They are open and willing to trade, ally, and be friends with other countries, but they love their country most.

The Left seeks globalism over national sovereignty. The woke hate the idea that some cultures are more successful than others, and instead of trying to find the cause and emulate it, they seek to destroy the Western countries (and a few elsewhere, like Japan) that have led the world in science, art, and human achievement. They command that Westerners shall have no allegiance to a nation or a country, but that we are "citizens of the world." Henry Kissinger's remark, "Who do I call if I want to speak to Europe?" may be apocryphal.[1] But everyone knows what it means. There is no "global" army. The so-called global majority is made up of billions of people riven along racial, ethnic, religious, and political lines. Just because they are not Europeans does not mean they are in any way united, or a cogent force.

Americans, on the other hand, are. We may come from diverse backgrounds, but when united by a common history, culture, and values, we are a mighty people. We not only won our independence by the sword, we rescued Europe twice from itself, losing 115,000 men in World War I and 415,000 in World War II. We defeated world communism in the Cold War. And we are not done yet. But the forces of the global Left are on the march. They undermine all that we stand for by deliberately blurring the line between who is an American and who is not. To them, citizen and foreigner should be treated alike. No benefits accrue to American citizens, only duties. No duties accrue to illegal immigrants, only benefits.

1. Who Is an American?

One can become an American citizen by birth, through one's parents (or through happenstance by being born on American soil), or by naturalization, the process where someone from another country becomes a citizen. In America's early years, it was expected that new Americans would renounce their former nationality, and the oath of citizenship still speaks of renouncing all allegiance to foreign governments. But the U.S. long ago accepted the idea of dual nationality, and millions of naturalized Americans today remain citizens of other countries.

Birthright Citizenship

The 13th, 14th, and 15th Amendments were passed to enshrine the hard-won victory of the Civil War, which cost more than 600,000 lives. The 13th Amendment banned slavery, extending Abrahm Lincoln's Emancipation Proclamation of 1863, which only banned slavery in the Confederate states then at war with the Union. The 15th Amendment guaranteed the right for all Americans, including newly freed slaves, to vote. The 14th Amendment is the longest of the three, with five sections. Section 1 says: "All persons born or naturalized in the United States, and subject to the jurisdiction thereof, are citizens of the United States and of the State wherein they reside."[2]

Many Americans assume that this statement means that anyone born in the United States, regardless of the parents' citizenship, allegiance, or legal status, is a U.S. citizen. Indeed, that is what many assume to be "birthright citizenship." But there are solid legal arguments that the phrase "subject to the jurisdiction thereof" excludes certain people who are born in the U.S. from acquiring citizenship automatically. One such class is the children of foreign diplomats. Because their parents are not "subject to the jurisdiction" of the United States in some ways, due to treaties on diplomatic immunity between their governments and that of the United States, such children do not become U.S. citizens at birth.

Heritage Foundation legal scholars Hans von Spakovsky and Amy Swearer are among those who argue that children born to parents neither of whom is a legal immigrant or citizen should also not be citizens at birth.[3] They argue that based on the legislative history at the time, the 14th Amendment's birthright citizenship excludes those only temporarily present in the country. In their examination of the legal history, Swearer and Von Spakovsky conclude that "neither the Supreme Court nor Congress has clarified that the U.S.-born children of illegal or non-permanent resident aliens are U.S. citizens." As a result, "the president has the constitutional authority to…direct agencies to issue passports, Social Security numbers, etc., only to those whose status as citizens is clear under the current law."[4]

Writing in *The Wall Street Journal*, Samuel Estreicher and Rudra Reddy of NYU Law School point out that Congress enacted the 1866 Civil

Rights Act to establish birthright citizenship but excluded those "subject to any foreign power," an exclusion that they argue would have applied to the 14th Amendment, passed only a few months later. They cite case law where the State Department did not accept that citizenship had been acquired by a child born to foreign parents who had not naturalized as American citizens, and conclude that "[c]hildren born to parents who have violated U.S. laws barring their entrance here have also not indicated their complete allegiance to this country, and are not entitled to citizenship at birth absent legislation so providing."[5]

President Trump issued an executive order in January 2025 stating that to acquire citizenship based on birth in the United States, a child must have at least one parent who is a citizen or legal resident. The State Department and other federal agencies were instructed not to issue passports and federal documents to children born in the U.S. who did not meet that bar. As with so much else that President Trump did in his first 100 days, this move was immediately met with lawsuits, which are not resolved at the time of writing. To avoid waiting for the courts to settle the matter, Congress could legislate that for (and only for) the purpose of acquiring U.S. citizenship, the phrase "subject to the jurisdiction thereof" in the 14th Amendment does not apply to people whose parents, at the time of their birth, were citizens of other nations. The proposed law could specify that to acquire citizenship at birth in the United States, a person would need to have at least one U.S. citizen parent at the time of birth.[6]

Birth Tourism and International Surrogacy

Under the prevailing interpretation of the 14th Amendment, any woman from any country can provide her child with instant U.S. citizenship simply by giving birth here, whether in the country legally or not. As a result, millions of people became American citizens because their mothers crossed the border illegally specifically to give birth, or who flew from countries like China, Nigeria, and Russia on birth tourism packages arranged by for-profit companies. One such company, Miami Mama, was featured in a 2022 U.S. Senate report about birth tourism. According to the report, "Miami Mama's customers were primarily Russian wives of dignitaries, oligarchs, and celebrities."[7] Another company, Ada International, is one of many that caters to the lucrative Chinese market for birth tourism, offering luxury accommodation, priority medical services, and shopping for mothers before and after they give birth to U.S. citizens.[8]

U.S. federal law and most state law does not prevent international surrogacy, by which foreign nationals, including those of states hostile to U.S. interests or with abysmal human-rights records like China, can "rent a womb" from American women. Foreign couples, or single people, can contract out nearly every step of procreation by contracting for an egg from one person and sperm from another, combining them in a lab, and paying a woman—who does not have to be an American citizen or legal immigrant—to gestate the result.[9] The resulting children gain the full rights of American citizenship, even if they have no biological relationship to either parent nor to any American citizen or legal resident. While banned in several countries, such cross-border surrogacy for hire is not regulated at the national level in the U.S. Worse, about half of U.S. states openly encourage the industry because it brings in big-spending overseas visitors. Many states, such as California, New York, Washington, Florida, and Michigan, have detailed surrogacy laws and Uniform Parentage Acts that pre-emptively list the intended parents on the birth certificate. After the U.S. citizen child is born, the parents can move them wherever they want. Neither the federal nor state governments have any way to know where they are.[10]

As Heritage Foundation researcher Emma Waters writes, there are nearly 5,000 attempted international surrogacies in the U.S. per year, more than 40 percent of them with Chinese parents.[11] "Of the foreign nationals," according to a report I wrote with Emma, "the purchasing parents were most likely to be Asian men over the age of 42," and "75 percent of foreign intended parents use clinics in California."[12] The state has policies that make it easy for surrogate parents, and many private clinics that cater to the Chinese market. The American Society for Reproductive Medicine even has a Chinese Special Interest Group.[13]

Once the surrogate-born U.S. citizen children turn 21, subject to some residency requirement in the U.S., they can petition for their parents and siblings to receive immigrant visas. As full American citizens, they can "return" any time they want to live in the U.S. even if they were, for example, previously or still employed in the People's Republic of China's military or intelligence services.[14]

What happens if the foreign parents change their minds and don't want the child being gestated in the U.S.? That depends on each state's family law—and it can get messy. Surrogacy scandals in Thailand led that country to ban surrogacy for foreign parents in 2015. The ban lasted a decade, but in 2024 Thailand was reportedly considering changing the law to allow it again.[15]

Assisted Reproductive Technology

The rules about how and when American-citizen parents can pass American citizenship to their children born overseas have changed over time. Until recently, they required at least one U.S. citizen parent to have lived for some time in the U.S. In 2021, under legal pressure from same-sex couples using "assisted reproductive technology" (ART), the State Department re-interpreted the nationality rules. Now, it merely requires one of a foreign-born child's parents to have a "genetic or gestational" tie to a child for it to be an American citizen. That means parents living in the U.S. can pay a surrogate mother in another country to gestate a baby using their sperm or egg. It's the ultimate outsourcing of labor.[16]

In February 2021, the State Department announced matching changes to its Consular Report of Birth Abroad form. Now, an American woman can combine sperm and egg from anyone, anywhere in the world. And when she gives birth—in a foreign country—the resulting child will be an American citizen despite having no genetic connection to even one U.S. citizen.

Even if some children born to American parents overseas through ART lack their genes, they will still probably live, work, and pay taxes into U.S. federal and local systems to fund any future benefits they get. In contrast, the hundreds of children born in the U.S. to foreign parents who take them back to their home countries soon after birth pay nothing into U.S. tax systems. Under current rules, a child born in China to a Chinese-citizen mother using an anonymous sperm donor (from any country) can still be a U.S. citizen at birth—with lifelong voting rights —as long as the mother is married to a U.S. citizen.

2. Who Gets to Live in America?

Congress has the constitutional power to determine who is allowed to enter the country and on which terms. However, in recent decades, and most egregiously under the Biden presidency, the executive branch has usurped congressional prerogative through regulation, executive orders, lawsuits, and by twisting statutes beyond credible interpretation of their intended purpose. President Joe Biden abused the power of immigration parole to bring in more than 1.5 million inadmissible aliens—that is, foreign nationals who do not qualify for a visa and who are not qualified under the official U.S. Refugee Admissions Program. As I wrote in Chapter One, the U.S. has allowed its asylum system to be overwhelmed due to overly generous interpretation of the UN Refugee Convention, which allowed fraudulent applications, meritless appeals, sclerotic case processing, and utterly inadequate attempts to deport failed asylum claimants.

In 2021, though admitting that it reduced migratory flows, the Biden Administration ended the Migrant Protection Protocols (MPP), sometimes known as "Remain in Mexico," an agreement with Mexico that kept asylum applicants out of the U.S. except for their hearing dates.[17] He ended the Asylum Cooperative Agreements that the U.S. had with Central American countries[18] to return asylum seekers "to the country of last presence," or a "safe third country," to pursue asylum instead of coming to the U.S.

No part of the U.S. border and immigration structure, from the Border Patrol to immigration courts to U.S. Citizenship and Immigration Services (USCIS), was able to cope with the ensuing flow of illegal aliens allegedly seeking asylum. As of late 2024, nearly 1.7 million asylum cases were pending in the Department of Justice's immigration courts, of a total caseload exceeding 3.7 million.[19] In July 2024, the backlog of asylum cases pending with USCIS exceeded 1 million (of around 9 million total pending cases), more than a 10-fold increase in a decade.[20] Many of these cases were also applying for work authorization, further adding to the processing workload.

Biden's State Department opened regional Safe Mobility Offices (SMOs) in Latin America to help people from all over the world to illegally migrate to the United States. Biden invented "temporary humanitarian programs" and "lawful pathways" that violated parts of U.S immigration law.[21] He stopped building the border wall. His Department of Homeland Security, under Secretary Alejandro Mayorkas, deliberately chose to process inadmissible aliens into the country as fast as possible, and enforced immigration laws in the interior selectively and with countless restrictions. Secretary Mayorkas described the Biden strategy as a way to "disincentivize irregular migration while incentivizing safe, orderly, and humane pathways…and achieve systemic change."[22]

Biden and Mayorkas failed utterly at the first part but succeeded beyond their wildest dreams at the second, bringing in millions of inadmissible aliens and adding them to a swamped asylum process. In fiscal year 2022, there were more than 2.7 million encounters of inadmissible aliens at U.S. borders and ports of entry. In 2023, there were 3.2 million, and December 2023 set the monthly record for the highest number of inadmissible aliens encountered at the border in U.S. history, at 370,883.[23] Fiscal year 2024 was only slightly lower at more than 2.9 million encounters. On top of that were an estimated 2.4 million "gotaways" who entered the country without any arrest, encounter, or inspection by U.S. authorities. The Biden Administration oversaw the worst period in U.S. history for the entry of illegal aliens and compounded it with facilitating mass migration overseas and creating reckless, unauthorized mass immigration parole programs. Biden's border crisis was entirely self-made, and entirely preventable. Creating and enduring it was a matter of pure politics.

Trump's Border

Though Americans had been told for four years by the Biden Administration that illegal mass migration was caused by world factors beyond their control, and that they needed more money, and that they needed new laws, this was never true. The proof came almost immediately after Donald Trump took office for the second time in January 2025. The White House reported that in March 2025, "Border Patrol encountered just 7,181 illegal immigrants at the southern border," representing a 95 percent decrease from March 2024, a 96 percent decrease from March 2023, and a 97 percent decrease from March 2022.[24] According to a Department of

Homeland Security official cited by Fox News, the daily average of gotaways in the first few months of the Trump Administration fell by 93 percent from the highest daily numbers under Biden.[25]

Just as they had denied or tried not to cover the disastrous numbers under President Biden and Vice President Kamala Harris, the mainstream media were reluctant to report the news. When they did, it was with warnings like this "Fact-checking" article from PBS: "[T]he White House's data use is misleading," PBS claimed. Because the "immigration experts" its staff spoke to told them that the weather or political conditions abroad "can affect whether someone migrates," PBS concluded that "it's uncertain what causes a drop or how long it will last."[26]

As an immigration policy expert whom PBS did not consult, I will say that while the weather and politics can affect illegal migration, they pale in comparison to the policies of the U.S. government, which changed radically under the Trump, then Biden, then Trump Administrations. Sending the clear message that people will not be allowed to enter the U.S. illegally, only to be released to go wherever they want, to work and live as if they were U.S. citizens, makes a huge difference. So does enforcing immigration law in the interior and carrying out the deportation orders handed down by judges. Illegal migration will never stop completely, but as long as the U.S. has a president determined not to let aliens have a veto over U.S. policy, the numbers of illegal entrants will be much lower.

3. Who Gets to Stay in America?

Immigration law is complicated. There are many categories, endless processes, and countless exceptions, appeals, and ways to tie things in knots. Generally, an alien who enters the U.S. illegally is put into "removal"—another word for deportation—proceedings in immigration court. If someone overstays a visa, the same applies. There are also many ineligibilities, from a criminal record to being a Nazi or Communist Party member, that will stop people from getting a visa. The same reasons can usually also allow the Department of Homeland Security's Immigration and Customs Enforcement (ICE) to deport them once they've had their due process. As the term "due process" gets bandied about a lot by open-border activists and progressives when they are fighting the enforcement of laws, it's important to remember that the "due" part varies depending on many factors. An alien who enters illegally could have a different "due process" when charged with an immigration offence than a visa holder, or a legal permanent resident (green card holder), or an American citizen. In many cases, once aliens are in removal proceedings, the first thing they do is to claim asylum. As discussed, most won't qualify, but they know the process will take time—possibly many years—and they have appeals and other ways to drag it out.

The bottom line is this: Aliens are not U.S. citizens, and they don't have the same rights and protections. If they are here as invited guests, aliens must obey the rules they agreed to before entering the country—which might be stricter than those that apply to American citizens at home. If they break those rules, they can be deported. If they are here illegally, aliens are subject to removal, unless they qualify for protection under asylum or a few other, less common categories. I've already discussed asylum in Chapter One. Assuming an alien does not qualify for asylum or other protection, our law requires that they leave the country.

The Fight to Deport Illegal Aliens

Let's think of President Trump's immigration policy as a three-legged stool, with the legs marked Deter, Detain, and Deport. The first leg deters people from entering illegally, through barriers, Asylum Cooperative Agreements, Remain in Mexico, and other policies. The second leg detains those who manage to enter illegally despite the barriers, and keeps them detained until their immigration process is concluded with a decision that they can stay or must go. The third leg enforces the decision of the immigration courts to remove an alien, or the decision of the president or secretary of state that an individual is a risk to national security or foreign policy and must be sent home.

The Left will fight enforcement on all three policy legs, even when the individuals are gang members, recidivist criminals, and terrorists. But they will fight hardest on the third leg of the stool: Deport. As enforcement resumed and lawful deportations increased in Trump's second term, the legacy media showed its overwhelming bias against immigration enforcement, let alone deporting anyone. In story after story, the mainstream media did its best to downplay the criminal histories of aliens being removed from American neighborhoods, instead concentrating on any aspects of each case which could elicit sympathy.

Criminal Aliens

The press and immigration activists chose (rather poorly) the case of Kilmar Armando Abrego Garcia as their first poster child for resisting deportations. Garcia, a national of El Salvador, came to the U.S. as a teen illegally in 2012, probably by crossing the border without being detected. Years later, he was arrested on immigration charges when standing outside a Home Depot looking for (illegal) work. An alien must claim asylum within a year of being in the U.S. and Garcia did not, so an immigration judge denied his asylum claim—which he made to avoid being deported—in 2019. The immigration judge did, however, grant Garcia "statutory withholding" from El Salvador, on the grounds that he was a member of a Particular Social Group (see Chapter 1)—namely his own family—that was under threat by the Bario 18 gang.[27] At the time, the judge was convinced by government evidence that Garcia was a member of MS-13, the notorious and violent Salvadoran youth gang. So, perversely, Garcia's claim was that, as a member of a violent gang, he was afraid of another violent gang, and so the U.S. couldn't deport him and that he should be allowed to continue living in Maryland. To make things more complicated, in what could have been a cut-and-paste error, the judge wrote that the only country to which Garcia should not be deported was Guatemala a few times in the withholding order, instead of El Salvador.

In March 2025, ICE arrested Garcia and a few days later deported him to his home country, El Salvador. His wife filed a case in federal court against the Department of Homeland Security. There was a national freak out in the legacy media and among activists, who lamented what they alleged was the unlawful removal of this putative "Maryland man."

A federal district judge ordered the government to return Garcia to the U.S. An appeals court agreed. The Supreme Court upheld that ruling but acknowledged that the president has exclusive rights to direct foreign affairs. Also, as a practical matter, President Trump can't order another country to do something, and a federal judge certainly can't tell El Salvador what to do. So, the Supreme Court told the U.S. government to "facilitate" Garcia's return to the U.S. to get his due process, which would almost inevitably result in his being deported somewhere else.

Meanwhile, since 2019, three things had changed. First, El Salvadoran Nayib President Bukele solved his country's gang problem by putting them all in his massive new jail, the CECOT.[28] That means that Garcia would no longer have to worry about Bario 18 or MS-13 hassling him back home. Second, Trump designated MS-13 as a Foreign Terrorist Organization (FTO), and Garcia's membership in an FTO negates the statutory withholding. Third, President Bukele visited President Trump in the White House in mid-April 2025 and when asked about the case, said he can't just release a terrorist or ship him back to the U.S. When criticized for his gang crackdown, Bukele told Trump that though "he is accused of imprisoning thousands of people, "I like to say that we actually liberated millions."[29] Indeed, for the people of El Salvador, reducing the murder rate from the world's worst to below European levels, and making their cities and villages safe to walk around in and do business, was a liberation.

Democrats rallied round Garcia, whom the press called "Maryland dad" emphasizing that he was a father of three, as if no criminal ever had children before. As the case dragged on into May 2025, a few more things came out about Garcia. First, he had been stopped in Tennessee in 2022, driving a van of eight people - suspected by local police, but not confirmed by federal authorities, to have been illegal aliens - from Texas to Maryland.[30] Garcia had an expired or invalid driver's license, and it was highly likely some of the men in his van were illegal aliens being taken from the border to Maryland to work under the table, taking a job from a legal resident or U.S. citizen. The government later charged Garcia with human trafficking based on the 2019 incident.

This confusing case highlights two things: First, the U.S. immigration system is overly generous and far too complicated. If even men like Garcia, with demonstrated gang affiliations and standing deportation orders, can string things out for years with endless appeals and claims, then the laws are toothless and Americans have ceded their national sovereignty to any alien who shows up. Second, the national legacy media, Democrats, and many activist NGOs will make a hero of anyone they can to try to stop enforcement of existing immigration law. "Abolition" of ICE, any immigration enforcement, detention, and deportation, is a central tenet of the American Left—along with defunding the police and not jailing criminals. Black Lives Matter (BLM) founder Patrisse Cullors explained in a *Harvard Law Review* essay from 2019 what "abolitionist" meant to activists like her: "For our political strategies and struggles against racism, patriarchy, and capitalism to be effective, we must deeply ground ourselves in an abolitionist vision and praxis."[31] In the same essay, she was crystal clear on what the Left thinks about immigration: "Abolition means no borders. Abolition means no Border Patrol. Abolition means no Immigration and Customs Enforcement."[32]

American Children?

In late April 2025 three illegal-alien women were deported, and they chose to take their U.S. citizen children with them. The press reported this as if the children themselves had been deported. As Secretary of State Marco Rubio told NBC's *Meet the Press*, "the children went with their mothers. The children are U.S. citizens, they can come back into the United States if their father, or someone here, wants to assume them."[33] Because of the ease with which illegal aliens can remain in the United States for years pending, and even after, a removal order, many of them have children or spouses who are U.S. citizens. If that is always considered a valid excuse not to deport them, removals will be almost impossible. In addition, it will add to the many existing perverse incentives facilitating illegal migration, like free healthcare, education, and welfare.

President Trump signed an executive order on January 20, 2025, telling federal agencies to stop automatically issuing citizenship documents to children born to illegal aliens or tourists. A federal judge blocked the order, and the legality of Trump's order—and birthright citizenship under the 14th Amendment as it currently is interpreted—will be decided by the Supreme Court.

Student Miscreants, Antisemites, Terrorist Sympathizers

After President Trump took office and replaced the leadership at the State and Homeland Security Departments, the Trump Administration started holding foreign students accountable for the antisemitic and pro-Hamas protests they'd engaged in since the October 7, 2023, Hamas attacks on Israel. Under U.S. immigration law, "Any alien—who endorses or espouses terrorist activity or persuades others to endorse or espouse terrorist activity or support a terrorist organization…is inadmissible" to the United States. If this endorsement is apparent at the time of a visa applicant's interview with visa officials, the adjudicating consular officer should refuse the visa. If ICE determines that a student triggered the "endorses or espouses" ineligibility after arriving in the U.S., it can initiate removal proceedings against the now-deportable alien. Meanwhile, the issuing U.S. embassy or consulate in the student's home country can revoke his visa, adding a second charge of deportability for being present without a valid visa. That means when the student goes home, he can't return to the U.S. without getting a waiver for the ineligibility.

Momodou Taal, a Gambian–British student at Cornell University on a visa working on his doctorate in "Africana Studies," played a prominent role in campus protests. In March 2024, he reportedly said that he and other protesters were "in solidarity with the armed resistance in Palestine." At various times, students supporting Palestinian "resistance" to Israel occupied the library at Cornell, staged "die-in" protests, and marched around campus chanting slogans. In September, Taal was part of a group that allegedly pushed past police into an event to which the group was not invited. Cornell decided not to suspend Taal, because the school would then be required to report to ICE, which maintains the national Student and Exchange Visitor Information System (SEVIS) database. That would have resulted, eventually, in Taal losing his immigration status in the U.S. and being subject to—though with low likelihood in normal times— removal by ICE.

After President Trump came to office, the State Department revoked Taal's visa for his activities and he was detained by ICE. He decided to leave the country rather than fight his deportation or apologize for his conduct. He expressed no remorse, telling CNN: "I think it's quite racist, Islamophobic, that before I'm allowed to have a view on genocide [allegedly by Israel against Gazans], I have to condemn a terrorist organization [Hamas]." Taal believes that as a foreign guest, he can say and do exactly as he pleases. But, in America, Americans set the rules— and he broke them. He would have fared far worse expressing gay pride in Iran, or anti-Islamic sentiment in Riyadh, or anti-monarchy views in Bangkok. In a parting shot at the U.S. on X after leaving, Taal wrote "long live the student intifada" and criticized "Zionist" students for "collaborat[ing] with law enforcement to target students of color" in "the suppression of the global majority."[34]

All across the U.S. in 2023 and 2024, university students—many of them foreigners in the country on student visas, like Taal—demonstrated, sometimes crossing the line from free speech into violence, or arguably even supporting U.S.-designated terrorist groups.

In Washington, DC, according to a student at Georgetown University's School of Foreign Service, "several master's degree candidates, many on prestigious Pickering and Rangel fellowships, attended protests on campus and elsewhere" in the capital. These fellowships, which come with free tuition, a stipend, and close to guaranteed entry into the State Department's diplomatic service, are paid for with our tax dollars.[35]

At nearby George Mason University in Virginia, police searched the home of two students who led the campus Students for Justice in Palestine (SJP) chapter and found guns, ammunition, Hamas and Hezbollah flags, and signs that read "Death to America" and "Death to Jews." One of the students posted a photo with the caption "Glory to every single martyr in Gaza, Lebanon, and Yemen...may we avenge our martyrs every single day." The students, who are American citizens of Palestinian origin, are not subject to visa issues, but they are certainly bound by university rules, and responsible if they damaged college property as alleged.[36]

Over at Washington's Union Station, protesters, including students, flew Palestinian flags, burned an American flag, threw objects at National Park Service rangers, defaced public property, and chanted, "Globalize the intifada," "From the river to the sea," and other genocidal slogans.

At Columbia University, students broke into the university's Hamilton Hall and barricaded the doors with furniture. Young men who may have been students dragged the American flag on the ground.

At the University of Michigan, radicals vandalized the home of a college regent three times, threw jars of urine through his house window, and painted "Divest" and "Free Palestine" on his wife's car.

A group of Princeton students claimed they would go on a hunger strike until their demands ("divest from Israel," "cultural boycott," and "complete amnesty from criminal charges") were met. Some professors demanded that no one be suspended.

As explained, the federal government can deport aliens for many reasons under existing immigration laws. The power to deport aliens for endorsing terrorism was passed into law after 9/11 but had never been widely exercised. In 2025, the time had come. In March, the State Department "revoked the first visa of an alien who was previously cited for criminal behavior in connection with Hamas-supporting disruptions," a department official told Fox News.[37] Many more followed.

In March 2025, ICE detained Mahmoud Khalil, a Columbia student who came here on a student visa but, based on marriage to a U.S. citizen, is now reportedly a lawful permanent resident, meaning that he has a "green card." Khalil is believed to be Syrian-born and is a graduate of Columbia University's School of International and Public Affairs. As journalist Eitan Fischberger has documented, Khalil was a leader of the protests at Columbia, negotiated with university officials on the protesters' behalf, and was the protests' spokesperson to media outlets including the Iranian regime's Quds News Network.[38] At the protests that Khalil helped to lead, protesters chanted genocidal slogans calling for the ethnic cleansing of Jews in Israel and violence against Jews worldwide. The protesters handed out pamphlets supporting Hamas and praising the "Operation Al-Aqsa Flood" massacre it carried out on October 7. At one protest, Khalil publicly expressed support for "our resistance in Gaza," which is a common euphemism for endorsing Hamas, short for Harakat al-Muqawamah al-Islamiyya, which means "The Islamic Resistance Movement."[39]

Some have claimed that green card holders cannot be deported for supporting terrorism. Not so. Section 237(a) of the Immigration and Nationality Act lays out numerous grounds that make "any alien" deportable. Terrorist activities are found in section 237(a)(4)(B) of the Immigration and Nationality Act (INA). In addition, under section 237(a)(4)(C) (Foreign Policy) of the INA, "any alien whose presence or activities in the United States the Secretary of State has reasonable ground to believe would have potentially serious adverse foreign policy consequences for the United States is deportable." In a typical legacy media response, NBC News said that Secretary Rubio was using "an obscure provision of the Immigration and Nationality Act of 1952 to justify Khalil's removal from the U.S."[40] Notably, NBC did not call the part of the INA that President Biden used to parole more than 1.5 million inadmissible aliens over four years "an obscure provision," because NBC approved of his ends, and apparently disapproves of deporting aliens under any conditions.

At the time of this writing, President Trump's ramped-up interior immigration enforcement efforts, including deportations led by Border Czar Tom Homan, were in full swing. Lawsuits, often led by the ACLU and other activist groups opposed to enforcement, were flying in response, and many were in process at the time this book was published. Low-level federal judges were handing out nationwide injunctions, in which they claim to block the federal government from certain action, as freely as parking tickets. Where each of these immigration cases ends depends on the individual circumstances. What can be said overall is that without the power—and the will—to enforce our laws, including immigration laws, Americans make a mockery of the law itself, and the Congress that passes them.

4. Who Gets to Vote?

Only American citizens are allowed to vote in America. Though the franchise (who gets to vote) was initially restricted to free men, it expanded over time to cover all U.S. citizens over the age of 18. However, some non-citizens (aliens) have voted in U.S. federal elections. The Heritage Foundation maintains an Election Fraud Map, which shows that although fraud in elections such as non-citizens voting in federal elections is not common, it does happen.[41]

Reasonable people might think that both political parties would agree that non-citizen voting is bad, and that it should remain rare and be punished when it happens. What has happened instead is that Democrats fiercely resist efforts by Republicans to keep voter rolls clean of deceased people, those who moved out of state, and non-citizens. Democrats seem far more concerned about the possibility, real but remote and avoidable, of U.S. citizens being unable to vote than about aliens, legal or illegal, being able to vote without consequences. The likely reason is that Democrats believe that most votes cast illegally would benefit them.

The SAVE Act

In March 2025, President Trump issued an executive order on election integrity. Combined with the Safeguarding American Voter Eligibility (SAVE) Act, a law introduced in January 2025, this executive order could make voting much more secure.[42] The order requires prospective voters to provide proof of citizenship in order to register to vote. Acceptable proof includes a U.S. passport, a REAL ID that indicates citizenship, a military identification card, and a valid state or federal government–issued identification.

The SAVE Act would require registering to vote in person, with documentary proof of citizenship. Opponents of the act claim that because it is illegal for non-citizens to register to vote or vote, it never happens. But it does, just as other illegal things happen, and there are few safeguards to prevent it. The Brennan Center for Justice, which opposes measures like the Trump executive order and the SAVE Act, call it a "voter suppression" law. Without evidence, it claims that more than 20 million Americans "lack ready access" to any of these documents and that nearly 4 million don't even have them.[43] That figure seems improbable, but even if true, people certainly have the time and the ability to get a proper ID before the next election. Supposed concerns that married women won't be able to vote if they have changed their names seem disingenuous, as women have been dealing with this issue, and voting, for generations.

State Voter Integrity Laws

It is in the interests of all Americans to keep non-citizen voting rare, and to continue to secure the process at the federal and local level. According to Ballotpedia, "[a]s of June 2025, 36 states required voters to present identification in order to vote at the polls on Election Day." However, these did not include Democratic strongholds California, New York, Illinois, and Massachusetts, where voters were not required to produce ID to cast a ballot.[44] It cannot be a coincidence that the highly populated, Democrat-run states, many with "sanctuary" policies and whose governments are highly resistant to immigration law enforcement, resist measures to ensure that only citizens can vote.

The Heritage Foundation also maintains an Election Integrity Scorecard, which grades states on their measures to ensure voter integrity.[45] The Left is critical of state voter integrity laws as well as the national bill, the SAVE Act.[46] But most voters seem to get it. Some critics of voter ID laws are correct to point out that they increase requirements on states to verify federal documents, and that the federal government needs to simplify that process. This could be done by ensuring that states have easy access to a national database proving citizenship. However, this would a double-edged sword for the Left, which has resisted programs like e-Verify and the Systematic Alien Verification for Entitlements (SAVE) Program—not to be confused with the SAVE Act voter ID bill just discussed. The Systematic Alien Verification for Entitlements Program is maintained by U.S. Citizenship and Immigration Services. Federal, state, and local agencies can check it to verify the immigration status of applicants for public benefits like Medicaid and food stamps to make sure that applicants are eligible.[47]

In New Hampshire, 80 percent of voters in 2024 "favored requiring people in their state to show a passport, birth certificate or other evidence of U.S. citizenship when they register to vote."[48] This included a majority of voters for Kamala Harris. Typically, a March 2025 AP article highlights the negatives. It discusses the case of two voters in Milford, New Hampshire, who were unable to vote on town elections "thanks to a new state law requiring proof of U.S. citizenship to register to vote.[49] The AP featured a married women who changed her name, and a first-time young voter, as having particular difficulties. Yet, the married woman in question admits: "If I did a little research, I probably would have known...what I needed." For the young voter, procuring basic civic documents is no unreasonable burden and would be of benefit in other circumstances later in life. We've all been there at some point, whether at the DMV trying to prove we live somewhere, or applying for a passport with the State Department, or even trying to open a bank account. The bar for valuable identification documents is high because the benefits are great—as are the risks if that information is misused. The bar for voting should also be high, because American citizenship is precious.

New Hampshire and the 20 other states that allow voters to register on Election Day have to be extra careful. To vote in New Hampshire, one must show proof of U.S. citizenship, age, identity, and residence in the state.[50] Proof of citizenship could be a birth certificate showing birth in the U.S., a U.S. passport, or naturalization papers according to the state. New Hampshire residents can still register on Election Day, but they can no longer simply sign an affidavit attesting to their identity and then back it up with documentation within seven days, as they could before the law was passed. The affidavit was a legacy of a former time, when small states like New Hampshire had a high degree of trust. Activists on the Left, including Lauren Kunis of the group Vote Riders, disingenuously claim that laws like New Hampshire's are "about blocking voters from accessing" the ballot box rather than making sure only those allowed by the state to vote can vote.[51]

In 2021, New York City approved a law allowing non-citizens who have lived there more than a month to vote. (It should be obvious that "non-citizens" include legal permanent residents (green card holders); foreigners with visas, such as students, visitors, and temporary workers; and foreigners here under parole or Temporary Protected Status—not just illegal aliens). New York is home to 800,000 green card holders and at least 600,000 "undocumented immigrants"—the euphemism for illegal aliens.[52]

In March 2025, the New York Court of Appeals ruled that the law violated the state's constitution.[53] City Council Democrats supported the bill, and Republicans challenged it in the courts. Republican Staten Island Borough President Vito Fossella praised the court's ruling against the law for upholding the "sanctity and security of our franchise—the right to vote as American citizens."[54]

Washington State's legislature passed Senate Bill 5077 in April 2025 that is similar to the federal motor-voter law, in that it requires public agencies to automatically send applicants' information to the secretary of state's office for voter registration.[55] This means that aliens who apply for state benefits to which they are entitled, can be registered to vote, which they legally can't do. There are documented cases of non-citizens, including foreign students, being registered to vote in Washington State, either on purpose or against their will. Though voting by illegal aliens and other non-citizens is both illegal and relatively rare, it can have a powerful impact when the margins are small. *The Daily Caller* reported that at least two recent elections in Washington State were won by just one vote.[56]

In April 2025, the state of Wisconsin amended its constitution to prevent voters from casting a ballot in any election without presenting a photo ID issued by the "state, the federal government, a federally recognized American Indian tribe or band in this state, or a college or university in this state."[57] Wisconsin joins Arkansas, Mississippi, Nebraska, and North Carolina in having a constitutional amendment requiring voter ID.[58]

5. Who Gets Federal and State Benefits?

For most of American history, newly arrived immigrants were expected to pull their weight. There was no social "safety net" until the 1930s, and when one was created in response to the Great Depression, it was clearly intended for indigent or retired Americans, not indigent foreigners. According to the Immigration and Nationality Act, aliens who would be a "public charge" on U.S. taxpayers, i.e. would need welfare or health benefits on arrival, are ineligible from getting a visa. But over the years, Congress and successive presidential administrations watered down this provision so that today, it means almost nothing. Legal immigrants are, by law, not entitled to federal welfare programs until they have been here for five years. But there are many loopholes in that restriction, and millions of immigrants, legal and illegal, tap into welfare through their American-born children.

Free Education

In 1982, the Supreme Court decided in *Plyler v. Doe* that states had to allow all children, including those living illegally in the country, into free public K–12 schools. States pay for more than 90% of public education, so states like California, Florida, New York, and Texas are paying billions a year to educate millions of minors that the United States did not lawfully admit.[59]

Federal Healthcare for Illegal Aliens

In March 2025, the Foundation for Government Accountability reported that the Biden Administration spent $16 billion on emergency services for illegal aliens, while non-emergency Medicaid spending increased more than 75 percent. Between 2020 and 2023, the report says, "the number of Medicaid recipients who couldn't prove their citizenship or lawful immigration status rose by more than 400%."[60] The report's authors recommend federal legislation requiring proof of citizenship or lawful status before allowing Medicaid enrollment, and prohibiting states from using federal funds for administrative fees. They say this could save taxpayers $20 billion a year.

Californian Victor David Hanson, a professor at Stanford University and noted historian, is a prolific chronicler of his state's demise.[61] As he explains, taxes, crime, and regulations are driving middle-class people to leave the state, leaving a Hollywood–Silicon Valley elite and an impoverished underclass. Hanson notes that "some 4 million—or nearly 25 percent of utility users—simply no longer pay their monthly power bills and are yet usually not subject to cutoffs of power."[62] He also writes that 40 percent of Californians are covered by Medi-Cal, the state's version of the federal Medicaid program, and that half of all births in the state are covered by Medi-Cal.

In 2024, Governor Gavin Newsom and the state's legislature, which has a strong Democratic majority in both houses, passed a law giving access to Medi-Cal and Medicare (for older Americans) to everyone in California, including illegal aliens. The state's healthcare system was $7 billion over budget that year. *The Federalist*'s Deane Waldman explains how this choice affects not only Californians, but all federal taxpayers.[63] The cost of adding illegal aliens to Medi-Cal was estimated at $8 billion. Estimates like that are always low-ball: when Illinois added illegal residents over age 65 to the state's Medicare program, initial estimates in the tens of millions ballooned to nearly a billion, forcing the governor to cap enrollment.[64] California's cost for insuring illegal migrants has already soared past Newsom's fiscal year 2024 estimate of $6.5 billion to $9.5 billion for fiscal year 2025.[65]

For Medi-Cal, the federal government matches state's funding, even though a law passed under Bill Clinton in 1996, the Personal Responsibility and Work Opportunity Reconciliation Act (PRWORA), prohibits even legal immigrants from enrolling in Medicaid for five years after arrival in the U.S. Under California's new law, illegal migrants can sign up as soon as they get there. Federal rules ban illegal migrants from enrolling in Medicare and Medicaid or the Children's Health Insurance Program (CHIP).

State Healthcare Costs for Illegal Aliens

Florida hospitals spent about $660 million on caring for illegal aliens in calendar year 2024, according to state agencies.[66]

In Arizona, a single hospital in Yuma lost more than $26 million in care costs for illegal aliens for which it was not reimbursed.[67]

Texas Governor Greg Abbott, who fought hardest against Biden's open border, wanted at least to know the scale of the costs his state was funding due to illegal migration. He ordered the Texas Health and Human Services Commission to collect the data. In April 2025, the commission reported that in November 2024, Texas hospitals "incurred over $121 million in health care costs...for people not lawfully present in the United States."[68] That would mean well over a billion dollars a year.

Federal Welfare Programs for Illegal Aliens

Democrats, libertarians, and open-border advocates all claim that illegal migrants add more than they take to our economy and society. (That's a long conversation, and it comes down to the age, education, and skill levels of the migrants.) Open-border proponents also deny that illegal migrants can claim federal benefits. That's just wrong, as Steve Camarota of the Center for Immigration Studies shows.[69] He explains that nearly 60 percent of households headed by an illegal migrant use one or more major federal welfare programs, either because they qualify, or more likely their U.S. born citizen children do. Camarota adds that the profile of illegal migrants is typical of those that get more in federal benefits than they pay in: 70 percent of illegal migrants have only a high school education, and only 18 percent have a bachelor's degree—half as many as among native-born Americans.

The effects of America's generosity to those here illegally aren't just the cost—estimated at $150 billion a year by the Federation for American Immigration Reform. It's also the Americans who are out of work and not looking, because they are competing with cheaper workers who accept worse working conditions. In 2023, Camarota writes, "the share of U.S.-born men ages 20 to 64 with no education beyond high school who were 'not in the labor force' (not actively looking for work) increased from 7 percent in 1960 to 25 percent."[70]

State and City Costs

Just a few examples:

Chicago, another self-proclaimed "sanctuary city" for illegal migrants, had spent more than $300 million supporting them between Biden's inauguration and mid-2024.[71]

In Denver, a report by the Common Sense Institute found that the city had spent up to $340 million in only the past year and a half to house, educate, and support migrants, both illegal and paroled, who almost all would not have been here without Biden's welcoming policies.[72] To compensate, Denver cut programs, staff, and budgets, including taking millions of dollars from public safety programs.

New York City is the biggest spender of them all. With its sanctuary policy for illegal aliens and "right to shelter" policy, based on a debatable interpretation of state law, New York was hard hit by Biden's mass illegal migration. The city government released a statement in 2023 saying that "[n]early 100,000 asylum seekers have made their way to NYC, and with no end in sight, the city is poised to spend more than $12 billion through Fiscal Year 2025."[73]

The city received hundreds of millions of dollars in funding from the Federal Emergency Management Agency's Shelter and Services Program. Some of it went to renting more than 200 make-shift migrant shelters, from rented hotels to camps in national and state parks, and even to paying homeowners to take unvetted migrants into their houses.[74] New York gave debit cards to thousands of migrants, costing taxpayers $2.6 million. Illegal-alien families were eligible for up to $350 per week, which was more than needy American citizens receive under the Supplemental Nutrition Assistance Program (SNAP, known as food stamps). New York modified its Safety Net Assistance—a state welfare program—"to include illegal immigrants with pending asylum applications." Mayor Eric Adams even offered illegal aliens a taxpayer-funded one-way ticket out of the city "to any state, or country of your convenience"—which in some cases, turned out to be Chicago.[75]

There are also many small towns like Logansport, Indiana; Charleroi, Pennsylvania; and Springfield, Ohio that have been hit with massive numbers of released and paroled aliens that overwhelm their schools, health care providers, and police in the short term, and may never generate additional tax revenue to improve these public services.[76]

The Welfare Loopholes for Illegal Migrants

Other than a small number of refugees admitted through an official program every year, immigrants to the United States are expected to pull their own weight and not be a financial burden on American taxpayers. That has been the expectation since colonial times. In 1996, Congress passed a law that stops most legal immigrants from being eligible for federal welfare programs for five years after arrival. Illegal migrants already get free education for their children and are treated for free in emergency rooms—though of course, in both cases, someone has to pay, which means taxpayers. Illegal migrants are also not eligible for most federal welfare benefits, though they "may be eligible for a handful of benefits that are deemed necessary to protect life or guarantee safety in dire situations, such as emergency Medicaid, access to treatment in hospital emergency rooms, or access to healthcare and nutrition programs under the Special Supplemental Nutrition Program for Women, Infants, and Children (WIC)."[77]

But, due to a provision in federal law, Cubans and Haitians can receive a whole range of federal benefits immediately. Under Section 501(e) of the Refugee Education Assistance Act, they are "Cuban–Haitian Entrants," who are then considered "qualified aliens" under the PRWORA and may be eligible for certain federal public benefits, including Medicaid, Refugee Cash and Medical Assistance, Refugee Social Services, Social

Security, Supplemental Security Income, SNAP, Temporary Assistance for Needy Families, and federal student aid.

6. Whom Does U.S. Foreign Policy Put First?

Finally, it's worth noting that a woke foreign policy puts Americans last. Amidst the culture wars at home, the U.S. under both parties has been spreading dubious certainties abroad through diplomacy and foreign aid. The theme is an odd mix of interventionism, anti-Westernism, and gender ideology. For years, the State Department and USAID funded a range of grants and programs that were of no evident value and pushed divisive and ephemeral concepts to countries unready and unwilling to receive them. Public disgust was one reason President Trump cut USAID funding dramatically. In April 2025, the State Department announced a re-organization plan that would bring foreign aid under closer supervision in the Department.

Apart from dubious aid projects, the U.S. has been in an interventionist rut since the Vietnam War. As John Hulsman writes in his book *The Last Best Hope*, the U.S. is stuck in a "permanent foreign policy crisis," a series of "botched humanitarian interventions," "endless nation-building wars of choice" in Iraq and Afghanistan, and a vague war on terror.[78] He calls this foreign policy crisis a "colossal waste of America's blood and treasure" and indeed, over the past 50 years the U.S. has squandered trillions of dollars, thousands of irreplaceable young lives, and national credibility on matters that failed the critical test that guided our ancestors: Were American primary national interests at play?

Conclusion

If America is to remain a land of freedom, prosperity, and opportunity, the government and society must preserve the clear difference between citizens and the rest of the world. We, the People, of the United States of America are the only ones who get to vote in this country and decide its future.

A person to follow: Steve Camerota, Director of Research, Center for Immigration Studies; www.cis.org/Camarota

A book to read: *The Last Best Hope: A History of American Realism,* by John Hulsman, 2024.

A group to support: Protect the Vote, www.protectthevote.com.

Chapter 9

The Ninth Commandment:
Honor the State (as Thy Mother and Father)

1. The State Replaces the Family

Americans believe in individual agency and responsibility. Many of our ancestors were slaves, serfs, landless peasants, or indentured servants who had little control over their own lives and destinies. They really were "oppressed" in the literal sense, not the pretend version of DEI, CRT, and woke imagination in the 2020s. When they got to America, they had to fend for themselves—educating their children, producing food and clothes, and defending their homes. If they needed institutions, they had to build them from scratch. With the glaring exception of slavery and indentured servitude, American families had a choice as to what they did for a living, and where they lived, that was unimaginable in Europe.

For the first 200 years, there was always somewhere new to move if the spirit led you, and millions migrated across the continent north, south, and especially West. After 1865, millions of black Americans left the south for opportunities and greater freedom in the north. Even today, you can move from one of the 50 states to any other with relative ease. Socialism, where people expect everything from the benevolent state in exchange for giving up their freedom and the fruit of the labors, is anathema to our traditions. The family is the core of everything we are. Yet in recent years, we have ceded personal responsibility and agency to allow a creeping, expensive government in its place.

Baby Daddy

I remember the first time I heard the phrase "baby daddy." It was around 2004, in Ghana in western Africa, where I was then posted as deputy chief of the consular section at the U.S. embassy. A young unmarried American woman had come to visit the country with her small child. I think she was from Georgia. She'd had some personal items stolen and needed a replacement passport. She'd also run out of money. The State Department's consular service can provide small emergency loans for American citizens in certain conditions, but officers have to first ask the destitute American to list, and try to contact, any possible relative or friend who might be tapped first. Most of the time someone will help out. My colleagues and I helped this woman to go through her mental list of contacts, starting with parents, siblings, and friends, and she could not think of anyone to ask. Finally, she sighed and said: "Well, I could ask my baby daddy, I guess."

I had to ask some colleagues, out of earshot, what she meant. It is likely clear to everyone today, but in case it's not, she meant the man who had fathered her child and with whom she had no other ongoing relationship. In the end, I believe we did contact the man. After all this time, I can't recall if he sent money. I hope so, given that his two-year-old child was stuck penniless in West Africa.

Many single parents do a great job of raising children, and there are many valid reasons that explain why they are doing so alone. But for most of human history, in nearly all societies, the ideal was for a child to have a mother and father who lived together with their children as a family. For conservatives, that remains the norm and ideal, although they can accept and embrace other forms of family. Leftists, however, see the "family" as a Western, heteronormative, patriarchal, colonialist relic. They believe that the societal functions that the family traditionally has provided should instead be met by the government. From childcare to elder care, and everything in between, the Left want the state to take over people's lives. In this way, liberal, educated bureaucrats can propagate and implement their leftist policies and ultimately replace any lingering semblances of traditional Western values and culture. It was not by mistake that the original version of the Black Lives Matter website included among its original principles: "We disrupt the Western-prescribed nuclear family structure requirement..."[1] BLM later scrubbed that principle from the website in response to criticism, but hostility to the West and the nuclear family is consistent with the beliefs of BLM founders Patrice Cullors,

Alicia Garza, and Opal Tometi. Garza and Cullors have made no secret of their being "trained Marxists."[2]

"Family Doesn't Matter" Is a Luxury Belief

Author Rob Henderson, an Asian-Hispanic American, coined the phrase "luxury beliefs," meaning "ideas and opinions that confer status on the upper class at little cost, while often inflicting costs on the lower classes."[3] For example, "progressive" wealthier people in safer neighborhoods inflict crime, murder, and fear on poor people by defunding law enforcement and continuously electing district attorneys who refuse to prosecute criminals. Another example, which Henderson knows too well himself, as he was orphaned as a child, is that progressives who in theory scorn the institution of marriage and the nuclear family tend to embrace both for themselves. One of Black Lives Matter at School's 13 "Guiding Principles" is: "We disrupt the narrow Western prescribed nuclear family structure expectation. We support each other as extended families and villages that collectively care for one another, especially 'our' children."[4] This is despite the overwhelming evidence that living with a married mother and father makes children far more likely to succeed in life and less likely to go to jail.[5]

The connection between family structure and children's later success in education and careers is undeniable. Family structure varies greatly in the United States by race, although it should be noted that there are significant variations within racial groups, that is, between African immigrants from Ethiopia or Ghana, and Americans of African descent whose ancestors have been here for generations; or between immigrants from Tonga in the South Pacific and those from Kerala province in India.[6]

In 2022, the percentage of black children living in single-parent homes was about 63 percent, compared to 16 percent for Asian children.[7] Rob Henderson's upbringing was the complete opposite of the Asian cliché of strict, involved parents pushing him to success. Due to his single mother's drug issues, he spent most of his childhood in foster care. As Christina Rosen writes in her review of his book *Troubled: A Memoir of Foster Care, Family, and Social Class*, Henderson "learned that so much of success depends not on what people do, but what they don't do...avoiding rash and reckless actions that will land us in trouble." And he learned painfully that "[a] solid, two-parent home is critical for a child's future."[8]

The Far Right and the Far Left Both Destroy Families

Attempting to destroy the nuclear family is something that American leftists share with totalitarians on both extremes, from communists in the Soviet Union and China, to fascists in Nazi Germany. For totalitarian states of the far Left and far Right, only the relationship between the individual and the state—or the *Leader*—is what matters: family, church, and other traditional structures that get in the way of state control must be eliminated. In 1933, Germany's parliament (Reichstag) passed a "Malicious Practices Act" that outlawed mockery of the government. The government encouraged people to tell on their neighbors, co-workers, and even family.[9] Spreading rumors or "malicious gossip" about the regime or Nazi leaders was outlawed. In December 1934, a law made "hateful statements about leading figures in the Nazi Party or the state" punishable by death, according to Professor Richard Evans of Cambridge University.[10]

In place of the Boy Scouts (now known as Scouting America) Germany had the Hitler Youth, and the Soviet Union had its Pioneers. That Soviet youth movement created little communist fanatics, as it "trained its members to believe that to inform against the people's enemies represented a high ideal, that to betray one's own family was the highest good of all."[11]

China's Cultural Revolution

Survivors of China's Cultural Revolution describe "a striking similarity between the radical left's actions in America and the Communists/Red Guards (Maoists) in China 50 years ago."[12] Yukong Zhao writes that Communist Party Chairman Mao Zedong's take on Marxist Class Struggle Theory divided Chinese society into oppressors and oppressed. The former, including intellectuals and teachers, were subject to the famous "struggle sessions" where they would be humiliated and forced into false confessions of capitalism, oppressing others, or agitating against the communist regime by their brain-washed militant students.

As Zhao notes, Asians, no matter how humble their origins or how recent their immigration, are grouped in the woke imagination with the supposedly oppressive whites, due to their relative success in American life. They are subject to the discrimination against merit that is the core of the DEI bureaucracy. Mao's Cultural Revolution coincided with his socialist agricultural policy, the Great Leap Forward, that created a man-made famine that killed around 30 million Chinese in the late 1950s. So massive was the loss of life that a graph of world life expectancy shows a visible dip at that time.[13] Mao's political inspiration was Joseph Stalin, the leader of the Soviet Union who succeeded Lenin. Stalin's application of communist theory to agriculture killed millions of Ukrainians in an earlier man-made famine in 1932 and 1933.[14]

Like the Russian communists, the Chinese Maoists destroyed books, historical monuments, and traditions. They shut down free speech and censored dissent with violence and even murder. Xi Van Fleet writes about this in her book *Mao's America: A Survivor's Warning*. She draws disturbing parallels between the China she grew up in and the progressive Northern Virginia county where she ended up. Van Fleet explains how "the Communist regime used the same critical theory to divide the people. The only difference is that they used class instead of race."[15] She describes how the Red Guards "were the indoctrinated and mobilized youths who vowed to carry out the Cultural Revolution," subjecting adults and teachers to the forementioned struggle sessions. These student enforcers also attacked "students who did not talk or behave in the 'right' way."[16]

In his book *Splintered*, Heritage Foundation education policy analyst Jonathan Butcher describes a surprisingly similar movement in American schools. At Georgetown Day School in Washington, DC, he writes, staff and teachers must attend "anti-racism" education sessions with a group called the Alliance of White Anti-Racists Everywhere. One of the group's tenets is that "in order to challenge racism and dismantle white supremacy, white people need to unlearn racism and discover the ways we enact white privilege."[17] Note the assumption that all white people, including the mostly progressive teachers and staff of this expensive school, are assumed to be racist and to have "white privilege," just as Mao's class enemies were simply assumed to be recalcitrant and counter-revolutionary.

Having made it to America, Van Fleet was disturbed to see the emergence of "political correctness" in the 1990s, which was largely a movement of euphemisms. Like James Lindsay, Christopher Rufo, and others who've written about how DEI took over universities, government, and society, she traces its roots to the Frankfurt School and critical theory.

Critical theory is a framework for understanding society that developed from Marxism. Similar to Marxism, it also looks at society's economic inequalities and injustices but focuses more deeply on the specific mechanisms by which elites control and manipulate the public. While Marxists emphasize class relations and control over the means of economic production, critical theorists look much more broadly at all the forces and ways that power and inequality manifest themselves in advanced societies. When applying critical theory, it is necessary to look for new contexts and sources of social inequality and to investigate the psychological, material, and symbolic sources of power imbalances.

Radical feminism, critical race theory, critical queer theory, and post-colonial theory all derive from critical theory. Taken together, critical theory studies the ways in which intersecting domains of power and inequality play out to result in unequal and perhaps unjust social outcomes. Critical theory was developed by scholars like Max Horkheimer, Theodor Adorno, Herbert Marcuse, and Jürgen Habermas through their work with the Institute for Social Research in the West German Frankfurt. These scholars viewed their work as useful in building a more just and fair society through enlightened social research and action. However, their work arguably resulted instead in a pattern of perpetual outrage and "suicidal empathy" among the educated elite, as well as the rise of so-called grievance studies programs at colleges and universities around the world.[18]

Not coincidentally, when they fled Nazi Germany in the 1930s, the men of the Frankfurt School ended up at New York's Columbia University, which most recently has been a hot bed of anti-Israel, pro-Hamas campus violence. Van Fleet compares the "class consciousness" of China in the 1970s to "wokeness" in the U.S. post 2015.[19]

Schools Betraying Parents and Children

The doctrine known as *in loco parentis* (Latin for "in the place of parents") has for centuries meant that when children are at school, the teachers and administrators have an assumed right and obligation to act as a child's parent for the purposes of ensuring safety and discipline.[20] But *in loco parentis* has never been taken to imply that school teachers and administrators fully replace, or are empowered to overrule, parents and their fundamental right to be the final decisionmakers for their children's lives. When, in the past, children acted inappropriately, caused trouble, or appeared to have deep personal traumas and issues, teachers and school leaders would approach the parents at the first sign of real trouble. Today, however, teachers and administrators have taken it upon themselves to enable children to do something that no child is mature enough to understand and every parent, obviously, should have to give permission for: gender transition.[21]

In the dystopian world of wokedom, childhood gender transition is seen as a normal and appropriate pathway for children in the "LGBTQ+ community" to override their "gender assigned at birth" and become who they believe they are. For everyone outside of the woke bubble, childhood gender transition is representative of serious mental health trouble, in the case of the child, and serious social disorder, in the case of its reflection of broader social concerns. And yet, school administrators in America, Canada, and elsewhere have decided that official school policy shall be to affirm and enable childhood gender transition while explicitly not informing the child's parents.[22] The dangers of "gender affirming care" were discussed in Chapters 4 and 5.

This attitude, on the part of school faculty and administration and the local school boards and governments that support them, is reflective of a broader leftist attitude that families, and parents in particular, are not and should not be the rightful locus of care and decision making for children. The woke attitude is that the state, in the form of the school system, local government, and social services, should take control of childrearing in order to socialize and raise children who become fully vested in the godless, progressive worldview that rejects traditional life in the Western world. When parents send their children off to school, they do so in the belief that the adults at the school will look after their children, protect them, and mentor them for successful lives through quality education and healthy socialization. The decision of schools to enable childhood gender transition without informing parents is a complete failure to live up to the true intent of *in loco parentis*, which is protecting the well-being of children. It is a capitulation to the scare tactics and browbeating of woke leftists who insist that any conformity to the natural standards of human sexuality and gender expression is "oppressive."

Several states have passed laws that allow teachers to socially transition—that is, treat kids as if they have changed their sex by giving them different clothes and using new names—without telling their parents.

A California law passed in 2024, ironically named the SAFETY Act (Support Academic Futures and Educators for Today's Youth Act), prohibits school staff from "enacting or enforcing any policy, rule...that requires an employee or a contractor to disclose any information related to a pupil's sexual orientation, gender identity, or gender expression to any other person without the pupil's consent unless otherwise required by law."[23] In practice, the law means that school districts can adopt their own policies to *prohibit* school staff from telling a parent about their child's alleged "gender identity," but they can't have policies *requiring* staff to share that information with parents.[24] It's all done in the name of progressive virtue; advocates say that it will protect kids from parents who don't accept their self-declared gender identity. But the bottom line is that a school pupil can now make decisions to overrule her own parents.

In March 2025, the federal Department of Education began investigating the California Department of Education, suggesting that its guidance on implementing state law violates the federal Family Educational Rights Privacy Act, which "gives parents the right to access their children's educational data," according to The Daily Signal's Tyler O'Neill.[25]

Education Secretary Linda McMahon called it "not only immoral but also potentially in contradiction with federal law for California schools to hide crucial information about a student's wellbeing from parents and guardians."[26]

Two teachers sued the Escondido Union School District over its policy that teachers must "immediately accept a student's expressed gender identity" and not share that information with parents without the child's permission.[27] The federal District Court judge in that case ruled in their favor, citing precedent from nine Supreme Court cases that "parents have a right, grounded in the Constitution, to direct the education, health, and upbringing, and to maintain the well-being of, their children."[28]

In Colorado, state legislators passed a supposed transgender rights bill in May 2025 that parents' rights advocates called "totalitarian."[29] Colorado's bill HB25-1312 provided that

> when making child custody decisions and determining the best interests of a child for purposes of parenting time, a court shall consider deadnaming, misgendering or threatening to publish material related to an individual's gender-affirming health-care services as types of coercive control.[30]

Laws like this force parents to "affirm" their child's self-proclaimed gender identity and support permanent changes that would render any later desistance and return to reality less likely. Erin Friday of California and Erin Lee of Colorado both have daughters who for a time identified as the opposite sex and eventually desisted. Both say that they had visits from Child Protective Services because they had refused to call their daughters by their chosen new, male names. Friday and Lee wrote an article for *The Wall Street Journal* in which they describe how the Colorado law would force parents to recognize their child's chosen name and pronouns or be judged abusive by courts in custody cases. They also point out that if the bill passed, Colorado could punish not just parents but any news media in the state for using a child's given name instead of one he or she later chose, without parental consent.[31]

There are already cases in multiple states of child protection authorities removing children from parents who do not "affirm" their child's social or even medical attempts to "transition" to the opposite sex or the nebulous "non-binary" status. Colorado father "Robert Cameron" has been fighting in the courts, against the odds, to stop his ex-wife from transing their son using Colorado's "affirmation only" laws, reports *The Federalist*. Cameron's ex-wife is "an academic in a left-wing community" and according to him, started considering their twins gay at age 5 and transgender a few years later.[32]

In Ohio, a court took a girl from her parents' custody when they refused to follow guidance from a gender clinic to put her on testosterone, a male hormone.[33] As discussed in Chapter 4, such treatment usually leads to permanent changes in the child's developing body. In adopting this bill into law, Colorado would be following in the steps of totalitarian regimes by giving brain-washed children power over their parents in a perverse re-arrangement of the natural order.

Drag Queen Story Hours

A further embarrassing capitulation by schools and libraries around America and elsewhere is the rise of "drag queen story hours."[34] Teachers, librarians, and school administrators have decided that, in order to overcome the sexism and "heteronormativity" of society, they would invite drag queens, otherwise known as transvestites, cross-dressers, or "members of the trans-community," to come and read LGBTQ+ propaganda to small children in place of regular children's stories, like fairy tales or Winnie the Pooh.

Drag queen story hours, in which a man dressed in overly sexualized outfits and adorned with stereotypical feminine accoutrements like false eyelashes, extra-large false breasts, high heels, and long false nails reads stories to children, are more than a rare occurrence. The website dragstoryhour.org, published by its namesake non-profit organization, lists 33 worldwide affiliate groups.[35] An article lamenting the "pausing" of a drag queen story hour in Chester, a small Vermont town, explains how drag queen story hours are increasingly common, "with events taking place in big cities as well as rural towns across America."[36] When Chester's town library trustees attempted to stop the drag queen story hour, the resulting uproar by local woke activists led to the resignation of the library director.

Only a generation ago, "drag queens" were perceived by most people as best left to perform in gay bars and nightclubs in New York, San Francisco, or Paris, not in smalltown public libraries in the middle of the day. Today, upper-middle-class parents in swanky suburbs invite drag queens to teach their children about how it's perfectly normal for a man to dress like a burlesque version of a woman. A conservative man in France was even sentenced to four months in jail for protesting a drag queen story hour.[37] This fits neatly with the woke agenda and the commandment to honor the state over your mother and father: if the state says your child should sit and listen to a stranger read about sexual relationships and practices, your job is to shut up and take it, or else the woke forces will come hard at you in an effort to cancel your social status.

The State Feeds Your Children

There's an old saying that there's no such thing as a free lunch. Indeed, the socialist policies in some states that provide three free meals to students regardless of their parents' duty, or ability, to do so, are expensive. The cost is not just in tax dollars, but in surrendering ideological control. Under the Biden Administration in May 2022, the U.S. Department of Agriculture (USDA) said it would require recipients of Food and Nutrition Service (FNS), or money for school lunch programs, to "update their non-discrimination policies and signage to include prohibitions against discrimination based on gender identity and sexual orientation." Schools had to accept gender ideology or lose access to lunch money—not to mention federal student loans and Pell grants.[38]

The Washington Post's Theresa Vargas advocated in 2023 that every U.S. city should offer free lunches to all students, regardless of need.[39] She cited the case of a full-time working mother who could not afford to both buy food and fix her car. That case does attract sympathy, and no one wants her children not to eat. But Washington, DC, lawmakers considered providing free meals to *every* K–12 student in public schools regardless of income. The measure would restore a practice the federal government put in place for students across the country during the COVID-19 pandemic and took away in September 2024.

Vargas was arguing that a temporary program during the pandemic should be extended indefinitely. Indeed, the pandemic was a backdoor that allowed significant socialism to creep into local and state budgets, buoyed by federal borrowing. She objected to parents having to fill out "a complicated form that asks detailed information about their family's circumstances"—as if parents don't have to fill out forms for banking, cars, taxes, health, and a dozen other things.

Vargas claimed that the program would cost only $8 million a year, out of a city budget closer to $20 billion. She said "D.C. should offer universal free meals. Every city should." The DC Council members took up the proposal again in February 2025. If they pass it, they will join

Colorado, California, and Maine in providing free school meals without means testing. California proposed that all three daily meals should be provided for free, regardless of need.

The State Tells You What to Read

Starting in the first Trump Administration, the Left had a collective freak out about supposedly banned books. No books were banned—even the books about adolescent sex, and those with LGBTQ and trans themes. All were available in every state and town that had bookstores or postal service and Wi-Fi. Libraries, however, particularly school libraires, must select books from a huge catalogue of published material, and some of them decided not to include books containing graphic sexual material or themes inappropriate for young learners. Other than educational value, books in a school library should be appropriate for the ages of the children at each school. For the most part, concerned school boards and parents were trying to keep out books about pedophilia, graphic sex acts, and other topics not suitable for elementary or middle-school children.

The Left painted this attempt at appropriateness as "banning" books. Yet as James Fishback found, the only books really missing from most school libraries were those written by conservatives.[40] He surveyed the online library catalogs of more than 4,600 schools in 35 of the largest public school districts in 14 states, some that leaned Republican and some that leaned Democrat. Fishback found Ibram X. Kendi's *How to Be an Antiracist* in 42 percent of the U.S. school districts, but a book with a counterargument in only one. Fishback found *Felix Ever After*, a book promoting transgenderism, in 77 percent of the districts, but not one book critical of trans ideology, such as *Trans* by Helen Joyce or *Irreversible Damage* by Abigail Shrier.

Fishback found *Dreams from My Father* by Barack Obama in 75 percent of the libraries he sampled, and *Becoming* by Michelle Obama in 65 percent, yet memoirs by Republicans Nikki Haley, Vivek Ramaswamy, Mike Pompeo, Tim Scott, and Ron DeSantis in 0 percent. Zero. Not one.

Fishback found *Genderqueer* by Maya Kobabe, which outraged many parents with its graphic depictions of "queer" and adult–child sexual acts, in 25 percent of the school library districts, despite gender activists' claims of it being "the most banned book in America." Karl Marx's *Communist*

Manifesto was found in 75 percent of school districts, the 1619 Project was found in 54 percent, and a host of other leftist-revisionist histories were also widely available. However, *Capitalism and Freedom* by Milton Friedman was found only in 8 percent. Two excellent books with a conservative, impeccably researched, point of view—*Social Justice Fallacies* by Thomas Sowell and *The Diversity Delusion* by Heather Mac Donald, were both on 0 percent of shelves.

Emily Drabinski, president of the American Library Association, calls herself a Marxist, and just like public school teachers, many school librarians are progressive Democrats. Fishback explains a "movement among librarians known as 'critical librarianship,'" which the American Library Association defines as "challenging regressive conceptions of gender identity in cataloging" and "documenting microaggressions in librarianship." Often that pseudo-academic jargon simply means replacing the works of classic European and American thought with books by women and non-white, non-Western authors—not for reasons of quality, but of representation.

The State Won't Educate Your Kids
—But Won't Let You Do So Either

Chapter 2 looked at the dismal state of K–12 public education across the country. The catch-22 is that although they are failing to teach American kids, powerful teachers' unions and the Democrats they support resist any attempt to allow charter schools or home schooling, both of which threaten their power and income. In March 2025, Illinois passed a Homeschool Act adding onerous requirements to parents who want to home-school their kids.[41] Supporters of the Homeschool Act claim that it is about saving children from abuse at home, but the real purpose seems to be to discourage parents from trying to control and guide their children's education. According to *The Wall Street Journal*, "there is no evidence of a connection between home-schooling and abuse or neglect." Meanwhile, according to a 2017 report, "an estimated 10% of K–12 students will experience sexual misconduct by a school employee by the time they graduate from high school."[42] In a two-day period in April 2025, at least six female teachers were arrested across the country for sexual misconduct with a student.[43] In Chicago Public Schools, there were 446 "allegations of sexual misconduct or abuse" in 2023.[44]

Despite spending around $22,000 per student, Illinois school results are unimpressive, and you can see why some parents would want to escape it.

In Illinois Public Schools, 33 percent of students performed at or above the "proficient" level in reading in 2024, down 2 percent from 2003.[45] In Chicago, in 2023 "only 12.2% of low-income third graders were reading at grade level" according to the *Chicago Sun-Times*.[46] Instead of addressing that terrible waste of talent, the Illinois Democrats' bill would compel home-schooling parents to register with the state, submit annual forms to their local public schools with details on parents and students. They would also have to give Illinois education bureaucrats their home-school materials and progress reports. The bill is not law, but Democratic politicians like Chicago Mayor Brandon Johnson—a former teacher and teachers' union employee—support it. While home schoolers should be held to basic standards and a rigorous curriculum, this level of micro-management seems intended to make them give up altogether.

In the 2022–2023 school year, 3.7 percent of American K–12 students were being taught at home.[47] Home schooling was given a boost by the pandemic school closures, and it continues to grow, driven by parent concerns of safety, discipline, academic rigor, and their wish to avoid the leftist indoctrination that takes place in many K–12 school systems and detracts from the three Rs.

Giving parents vouchers so they can pull their kids from failing public schools and choose better schools is popular with parents but fought by teachers' unions—because vouchers work, and they fear the competition. Ohio started a school voucher program called the Educational Choice Scholarship Program in 2005 and expanded it gradually. A recent study by the Urban Institute found that students who used the vouchers to attend public schools were more likely to graduate high school and attend college than public school students with "similar demographics and academic characteristics."[48] Indiana began a school choice voucher program in 2011. In the 2024-5 school year, "more than 20% of the state's students attend a school other than the public one for which they're zoned." [49]   Indiana expanded the program in 2025, by eliminating limits on parental earnings to qualify for the $6,000 in tuition vouchers for private schools. State lawmakers also allowed property tax dollars to go directly to charter schools, as with public schools, instead of financing them through annual appropriations. Since 2022, Indiana has moved up from 19th place in the NAEP national 8th grade reading scores to 6th place.[50]

DEI Guides Admissions, Discipline, and Indoctrination at School

Remember that DEI is the term for putting the philosophy of CRT into action. CRT assumes that all disparities in achievement between races, both good (educational achievement) and bad (criminal behavior) are the result of racism. In the case of education, the DEI solution is (1) to get rid of standardized tests (because on average, scores are not equal among racial groups); (2) to reduce or eliminate class discipline (because more members of one race are disciplined than others); and (3) to pour more money into failing school models. A perfect example of the latter is the Los Angeles Unified School District (LAUSD), the largest in the nation.

There is no doubt that in the past, racism caused disparities in school funding. However, this has been undone for more than the 60 years since the Civil Rights Act to the point where the greatest spending across the nation goes to schools in Washington, DC, Los Angeles, and New York City, where the majority of students are non-white. Nonetheless, leftist elected officials and teachers' unions keep pushing the lie that the reason behind low performing schools is racism, in the form of underfunding.

In February 2024, the LAUSD held a "Black Lives Matter at School Week of Action" as part of a $26 million budget for a Black Student Achievement Plan.[51] The LAUSD has a budget of $20 billion, which Manhattan Institute researcher Heather Mac Donald calculates at between $35,000 and $50,000 per student per year, depending on how much of the district's ancillary programs one counts. Despite all the money, in 2023, less than a fifth of California's black students achieved basic proficiency in math, and only 30 percent did so in English. Meanwhile, 71 percent of Asian students were proficient in math, and 77 percent in English. Rather than the hard question 'why' and hearing answers they don't like, California's answer is to lob another $25 billion at the problem, to feed into contractors and consultants and unionized teacher unions and social services for "social emotional development, trauma, and basic needs."

LAUSD's Action Week mirrors the dogma of Black Lives Matter at School, which is hostile to capitalism and the "Western nuclear family dynamics," but is all in on diversity, globalism, and "affirming" queer and transgender identities. Mac Donald compares the Action Week program to the Chinese Cultural Revolution, where "the goal is indoctrination into an official political creed."[52] But more money, and more DEI, CRT, and LGBTQ+ won't close the achievement gap. As Mac Donald and others have persuasively argued, racism is not the root of the problem of low school achievement, and "racial disparities in representation are more persuasively explained today by an oppositional culture that works against personal responsibility."[53] This means parents as well as children. In the 2021–2022 school year, the rate of "chronic absence" (truancy) for black K–12 students in the LAUSD was above 50 percent. In Washington, DC, 44 percent of K–12 students were reported as "chronically absent" in the 2022–2023 school year; for high school students it was 60 percent.[54] Figures for Chicago public schools are similar.

Mac Donald sums it up: "Being black is not an accomplishment, just as being female or being gay are not accomplishments. The only real academic accomplishment is mastery of a body of knowledge. Pride should come from achievement, not from grievance."[55]

2. The State Makes Your Medical Decisions

There is no more central right for a free man than the control over what happens to his own body. That's why slavery was such an abomination, and why we only accept those health mandates and individual restrictions that are absolutely necessary to preserve the health and safety of the community. Exceptions to the principle of bodily autonomy must be rare and always carefully considered. Attempted encroachments by the government are, in normal times, viewed with skepticism and, if necessary, fiercely resisted. In times of crisis our guard is lowered.

Shutdowns, Masks, Questionable Vaccines, and Mandates

There was perhaps no time when the state worked harder to usurp the rights of the people and enact a set of patronizing policies than during the COVID-19 pandemic, beginning in early 2020. Despite what turned into years of fear mongering and histrionic displays by government officials, it became clear a few months into the coronavirus outbreak that for the vast majority of people, and especially children, the virus would amount to an illness very similar to a cold or flu.[56] Despite having this knowledge fully at hand, the U.S. and other countries wasted no time in using the pandemic to take greater control of people's lives and healthcare.[57] Meanwhile, Sweden took a different approach, more akin to that recommended by the authors of the Great Barrington Declaration in the U.S., of protecting the vulnerable while letting most people go about their lives. With far less cost, borrowing, and disruption to people's lives and livelihoods, the Swedes had fewer "excess deaths" during the pandemic than the United Kingdom, which adopted lockdowns and other strict controls over the population.[58] According to one report, Sweden's excess death rate was the lowest in Europe.[59]

In retrospect, it's certain that many of the decision-makers from the time of the coronavirus outbreak would defend themselves today with the refrain of "we didn't know what we were dealing with, we were just trying to take every precaution." But this defense doesn't hold up. The pandemic provided the perfect cover for state bureaucrats to practice telling us all what to do, in a state of emergency where we could be fined or arrested for the simple disobedience of taking off a mask at the wrong time. Anthony Fauci and others were able to hold the rapt attention of the public, when without the pandemic their otherwise mundane professional lives would have gone largely unnoticed. Former New York Governor Andrew Cuomo appeared to take great joy in holding daily news conferences where millions of people hung on his every word.[60]

Remember wearing a mask into a restaurant, but then being able to take it off at your table? Or having to wear it at your table, except while taking a bite or having a drink? How about the paddle-boarders who were arrested *in the ocean* off California for not wearing masks, despite the fact that there were no other people around?[61] We can all recall the silly things we did, and the state required us to do, during the pandemic years, which were pure exercises in futility. There were people in government who—whether they followed these policies themselves or not—clearly relished making the rest of us engage in such ridiculous behavior. California Governor Gavin Newsom dined at the expensive French Laundry restaurant while everyone else in his state was reduced to delivery services. Representative Maxine Waters flew across the country without a mask despite tweeting how important it was to wear them. Jill Biden hosted masked children at the White House while not wearing one herself. A data visualization page from The Heritage Foundation—"COVID Hypocrisy: Policymakers Breaking Their Own Rules"—has many more examples of hypocrisy from elected officials.[62]

Every family, and particularly every mother and grandmother, has traditional ways of caring for family members fighting a cold. Drink plenty of fluids and get plenty of rest. Stay warm and take vitamins. Have some chicken soup and fresh fruit. It turns out that these traditional remedies would have been perfect in mitigating the effects of the virus and significantly reducing the likelihood of death for a majority of patients.[63] But instead of encouraging us to listen to our mothers, we were informed by state bureaucrats that only a radical program of total isolation, masking, quarantine, and mass vaccination (and re-vaccination) would prevent mass death on a catastrophic scale.

Parents, children, and teachers are still grappling with how to handle the impact on children of closing schools for more than a year. Grown adults with fully developed brains who work on a computer at a desk were able to transition to remote work with less impact. But it was a combination of hubris and ignorance that led anyone to think that children could simply miss the experience of school for a year and a half and avoid negative outcomes. It turns out that many children have irreparable intellectual and social damage as a result of the school closures, which, even during the pandemic, were tacitly understood to be primarily about teacher safety, not child safety.[64] If we don't have the best interests of children at the forefront of our decision-making, what is the purpose of our society?

The hypocrisy of the woke and their unwavering commitment to ideological purity can be illustrated by their willingness to suddenly overlook pandemic protocols during the Black Lives Matter protests after George Floyd's death in May 2020.[65] After spending months wagging their fingers at those of us who attempted to maintain a modicum of freedom in the first wave of shutdowns, suddenly all of the rules and warnings that had been overzealously enacted were thrown out of the window when the right people were breaking the rules. While some folks were told they should be thrown in jail for taking a walk, BLM protestors were allowed to congregate—and riot—in the tens of thousands without so much as a peep about social distancing. If you wanted to go to church on Sunday—absolutely prohibited. If you wanted to have 100,000 people in the city square to burn and destroy things in the name of racial justice—go right ahead.

The state's manipulation of society and attempts to control each aspect of our daily lives culminated in the vaccine mandates. Once a COVID-19 vaccine was developed in record time, using untested and untried new technology, the government got busy forcing us all to take it. And most of us were willing guinea pigs after we had been cudgeled into living lives of near total isolation for more than a year. Like mice in a cage, helpless except for the random possibility of getting a treat from a research scientist, we leapt at the opportunity to get the jab that could free us from the forced quarantine we'd been stuck in. We were told that the vaccine was "completely safe" and that it had been properly tested and would both prevent us from getting COVID-19 and from spreading it. Turns out all of that was untrue, and the woke bureaucrats who pushed it on us knew it was untrue.[66]

When it became abundantly clear that the vaccine did not prevent people from getting COVID-19, or from spreading it, we were told that it would make infections less severe and less likely to result in death. When it also became clear that many people were developing unusual health problems like heart conditions, blood clots, and Guillain-Barré syndrome, we were told that the vaccines were generally safe. And we were told that the only way society could get back to normal was if we all took the vaccine for an illness that had a less than 1 percent probability of resulting in death across all age groups. COVID-19 had a nearly zero likelihood of resulting in death for children and healthy young adults and people without existing health complications. And yet, the state forced many of us to take the vaccine or lose our jobs. Those who were required to take the vaccine or face losing their livelihood included: federal contractors, healthcare workers, employees of private businesses with 100 or more employees, federal government employees, military personnel, and all non-citizens traveling legally to the United States. (Meanwhile, the masses who crossed the border illegally were mostly free to ignore all the Covid protocols including vaccination and testing).

In sum, the COVID-19 pandemic provided a perfect opportunity for the woke to enforce their commandment that you shall honor the state as your mother and father. While conservatives and other freedom-loving people across America and the world were protesting for their rights to work, to gather, to remain unvaccinated and to make their own commonsense health decisions, woke state bureaucrats and liberals generally took every opportunity to demonstrate their willingness to both proclaim freedom-crushing mandates and to push near-total government control over private lives.

Conclusion

Faced with growing federal power, not only individuals are fighting back, but some states are too. Under the Constitution, "the powers not delegated to the United States by the Constitution, nor prohibited by it to the States, are reserved to the States respectively, or to the people."[67] In other words, what is not expressly the power of Congress to regulate falls to the states by default. Under Governor Ron DeSantis, Florida sets a good example. The state passed a Parental Rights in Education law in 2022 that "prohibits school district personnel from discouraging or prohibiting parental notification & involvement in critical decisions affecting students' mental, emotional, or physical well-being," "prohibits classroom discussion about sexual orientation or gender identity in certain grade levels," and "requires school districts to notify parents of healthcare services."[68] In 2024, Florida passed a comprehensive Parents' Bill of Rights stressing that "it is a fundamental right of parents to direct the upbringing, education, and care of their minor children," requiring schools and teachers not to keep information about children's health and well-being from their parents, and placing an affirmative duty on schools to inform parents of "information relating to the health and well-being of their minor children." [69]

A person to follow: Nicole Neily, Parents Defending Education, @nickineily.

A book to read: *Splintered: Critical Race Theory and the Progressive War on Truth*, by Jonathan Butcher, 2022.

A group to support: Advocates Protecting Children, Arlington, VA, www.advocatesprotectingchildren.org.

Chapter 10

The Tenth Commandment:
You Shall Take No Responsibility for Your Success or Failure

The woke Left teaches that no one is responsible for his own success or failure—"the system" is. Critical race theory (CRT) makes us all oppressors or oppressed. Those deemed oppressors can't be absolved of racism, sexism, homophobia, transphobia, or patriarchy no matter what they do. They are born with the original sin of being white European, or male, or straight, or able, or normal. Those deemed oppressed aren't responsible for their actions or the consequences thereof; anything that befalls them is the result of systems and circumstances over which they have no control. In the progressive-woke-leftist worldview, individual agency, where we each make choices and are responsible for the results, is replaced with invisible forces or systems acting on us beyond our control.

Leftist believe these systems should be countered by discriminatory programs to ensure equal results—which they call "equity." Individual ability, effort, and luck are all discounted or perceived as unfair advantages that must be handicapped. In the 1960s, Kurt Vonnegut wrote the short story *Harrison Bergeron,* about a brilliant boy in a future where everyone had to be handicapped to the lowest level—the woke concept of "equity" in a nutshell.

As we've seen, leftists believe that anything good that happens to an individual is due to some "structural" advantage he has, and anything bad that happens is due to some structural handicap. Just as nothing good you do is to your credit, nothing bad you do is your fault—if you are among the "oppressed." Whether it's committing crime, failing in school, or getting out of shape, for the woke mind it's all beyond an individual's control. The truth, of course, is that although we are all dealt different cards in life, and some of us have major obstacles to overcome, our country and history is filled with people who have succeeded against all odds. America continues to be the place on Earth where individual choice and effort have the greatest effect on what we become. We need to hold on to that American dream and never surrender to the depressing alternative of pre-determined outcomes based on factors beyond our control.

1. It's Not You, It's the Job
—the Disparate Impact Theory

Disparate impact analysis, though absurd on its face, has come close to destroying meritocracy and objectivity in American institutions and professions.

As a reminder, the "disparate impact" legal theory holds that all other things being equal, if a law, policy, or rule has a disparate impact on a particular sex, race, or social group, it is inherently wrong and needs correction. The problem is that race, sex, and gender activists have weaponized the theory by leaving out the crucial "all other things being equal" part. Therefore, they will argue that any standardized intellectual, knowledge, or physical test that differentiates between whites and blacks, or women and men, or any two groups, is racist or sexist. In the case of sex, as discussed in previous chapters, this is nonsense. Physical fitness standards *must* be different for men and women, because the average fit man is physically stronger and faster than the average fit woman.

A *Washington Post* article from 2021 asks whether women in the military should meet the same standards as men.[1] In 2015, Capt. Kristen Griest was one of the first two women to graduate the Army Ranger School. She later caught flack from other women for defending physical fitness standards. "To not require women to meet equal standards in combat arms will not only undermine their credibility, but also place those women, their teammates, and the mission at risk," Griest wrote in an op-ed.[2] As women scored (no surprise) lower than men on average, the Army was looking to create different standards for each sex. In the context of military performance—literally a life and death matter—this is insane. The Army tests soldiers in six events that are a proxy for physical challenges of combat: dead lifts, a two-mile run, push-ups, a shuttle run, a medicine ball throw, and leg tucks, in which soldiers must hang from a bar and bring their knees to their elbows. According to the *Post*, roughly 54 percent of women, and only 7 percent of men, failed the test in 2020. A 2012–2015 Department of Defense–funded study found that "all-male task force teams outperformed their mixed-sex counterparts in 69 percent (93 of 134) of ground combat tasks."[3]

In spite of this evidence, President Barack Obama's Secretary of Defense Ashton Carter allowed women into combat units, even elite units such as Delta Force and the Navy SEALs. Yet, although Defense Department officials lowered the bar and changed the physical tests administered to combat soldiers, they could not bring women's average scores up to the level of their male counterparts.

In 2025, President Donald Trump's new Secretary of Defense Pete Hegseth vowed to remove "diversity, equity, and inclusion" (DEI) requirements and to restore equal standards to the military. He ordered a review to "identify which positions require heightened entry-level and sustained physical fitness," so that these standards would remain high. Hegseth was particularly concerned that combat units remain capable. Writing in the *Federalist*, retired Army officer and paratrooper Samantha Nerove applauded Hegseth's policy of holding women and men to the same fitness standards in combat units, saying it would "ensure that the most qualified people are in the right jobs based solely on merit."[4] As Nerove wrote, the rucksack and parachute issues to soldiers was the same regardless of sex or size. She points out that the military's Armed Services Vocational Aptitude Battery test, which is used to assess a new recruit's "intellectual capability, strengths, and potential," takes no account of sex in determining where to assign someone.[5]

As discussed in Chapter 6, correcting for "disparate impact" without taking into account the other variables that account for differences between groups is terrible public policy. It allows life-saving occupations like soldiers, police officers, fire-fighters, doctors, and air traffic controllers to be handed out based on immutable characteristics that have no bearing on the job requirements, rather than on measurable, objectively assessed criteria.

2. Public Payout for Individual Damage

Spend any time driving around our nation's highways these days and you'll notice two types of prominent billboards: ads for marijuana shops and for injury lawyers. The latter isn't a new thing, but the proliferation of firms that claim to make a living exclusively off what should be a very rare occurrence in life is not a positive sign. Like the cargo cults of the South Pacific came to expect treasures to fall from the sky, it seems that ordinary working stiffs now dream of the magic payout of millions that could be theirs with a little luck, like being lightly hit by a well-insured company truck or drinking a glass of tap water from a military base that is now part of a congressionally sanctioned payout program.

Examples of massive private-sector payouts abound. In June 2023, Abby Grossberg, a former producer for Tucker Carlson's show on Fox News, won a $12 million settlement from Fox, which she accused of pressuring her to lie in a lawsuit the company was involved in about voting machines and of allowing "a misogynist workplace culture."[6]

That same month, a white, female manager at Starbucks won $600,000 in compensation and an incredible $25 million in punitive damages from Starbucks. Shannon Phillips was caught up in a 2018 race drama when two black men were arrested for not leaving a Philadelphia Starbucks when asked by staff, because they weren't ordering anything. Activists accused Starbucks of racism, and Phillips ended up getting fired by upper management that was apparently desperate to avoid accusations of anti-black racism, although she was not even at the store in question at the time. A New Jersey jury ruled that "race was a determinative factor" in Starbucks firing Phillips.[7]

Chasing ambulances is lucrative, but the really big money can be made by holding taxpayers responsible for actions by others over whom they have no control or responsibility. Many voters don't seem to notice or care that they are on the hook for such payments, which are just rolled into the budgets, insurance premiums, bonds, loans, and other factors in their annual tax bill.

Turns Out You *Can* Fight City Hall

In July 2023, New York City settled a class action lawsuit by people who had participated in the "mostly peaceful protests" after the death of George Floyd in 2020.[8] The city agreed to pay almost $10,000 in compensation each to up to 1,000 claimants, totaling $13.7 million of city funds, for violating the civil rights of protesters.[9] The First Amendment rights of the protesters were infringed, the lawsuit claimed. Indeed, the NYPD had gotten tough on protesters in 2020, by "kettling" them in confined spaces, sometimes restraining them with zip ties, or using batons and pepper spray.

Were these tactics so outrageous, considering that during the protests in New York, thousands of people rioted, attacked and injured police, destroyed police cars, and looted or vandalized hundreds of city businesses? It's not as if the police simply opened fire into the crowd, as the Chinese did at Tienanmen Square 30 years before.

By settling this lawsuit and paying out to a thousand protesters, New York City conceded that the police, in a period of mass unrest, are supposed to carefully distinguish between every person's conduct in a giant crowd, some of whom are peaceful and some violent, and mete out perfectly proportional penalties—on pain of getting fired or imprisoned if they make a mistake. Like the "Ferguson effect" on a larger scale, lawsuit payouts like this will make police and their political bosses less likely to engage and more risk averse, which will mean more civilian injuries and property damage in future protests that get out of hand.

LA County's $4 Billion Bonanza

In April 2025, Los Angeles County agreed to a $4 billion settlement with alleged victims of sexual abuse at county-run care facilities for children between 1959 and 2000.[10] Of course, any authority responsible for children owes them the highest duty of care. Any county employee who abused children in any way, or by incompetence or negligence allowed children to be harmed, should be professionally and even criminal accountable. This should include convicted abusers as well as any supervisors and administrators who failed to do their duties to a reasonable standard. But holding the taxpayers of the entire county responsible for events that happened before most of them were born or moved to the area is terrible public policy. It's deeply unfair, and it will encourage similar lawsuits resulting in ruinous fiscal consequences for the county.

The LA lawsuit and massive payout was only made possible by a 2020 California law that created a three-year window in the statute of limitations, during which victims of alleged childhood sex abuse long ago could file claims that would otherwise be time-barred.[11] California's three-year window to sue for long-ago wrongs is reminiscent of the New York State law which also retroactively opened the statute of limitations on sex abuse charges,[12] oddly enough just in time for E. Jean Carroll to sue Donald Trump in a case which otherwise could not have been brought after so much time. Carroll sued Trump and won $5 million in 2023.[13] She later reaped another $83 million for Trump allegedly defaming Carroll and "ruining her credibility as an advice columnist when he called her a liar after she accused him of sexual assault."[14]

The LA settlement is the largest sex abuse payout in U.S. history, more than the $2.5 billion paid by the Boy Scouts for abuse by scout leaders, the $1 billion paid by the University of Southern California for a rogue doctor, the $880 million paid by the Los Angeles Catholic archdiocese for abusive clergy, and the $500 million paid by Michigan State to the gymnasts Larry Nassar abused. If approved by the County Board of Supervisors, the $4 billion payout will stick LA County taxpayers, who already live in the nation's highest-tax state, with massive annual payments until 2051, for abuses alleged to have taken place between 1959 and 2000.

3. Crime—It's Not Your Fault

To the woke, the criminal justice system is oppressive because it is supposed to arrest and punish those who commit crimes, and that doesn't break out along the demographic lines they insist on. Woke prosecutors, district attorneys, and politicians in many of our cities and states make policy based on ideology, not cold realities. In putting ideology over fact, and protecting perpetrators rather than victims, they make life less safe for the people who put them in office. Just as with education, woke criminal justice "reform" policies are based on false assumptions and so end up making things worse.

Poverty Doesn't Cause Crime

While it is evident that more violent and property crime happens in the poor neighborhoods of cities than rich ones, there is no direct correlation between an individual's poverty and his tendency to commit crime. Anyone who has lived in a third-world country in a very poor, but very safe neighborhood can attest to this. Prof. Barry Latzer, a professor emeritus at John Jay College in New York City, argues that "the relationship between crime and economic conditions is unpredictable, and cultural values play a central role in the extent of violent behavior by various social groups." He points out that despite black family incomes rising 265% between 1940 and 1970, the violent crime rate also rose. "Arrest rates of blacks for violent crime, including but not limited to murder, were five to nine times the white rates between 1965-90," he writes. Conversely, during the period 1980 – 2009, despite the recession of 2007-2009, black homicide rates fell by more than half.[15]

Criminal Rights, Not Victim Rights

As Hannah Meyers wrote in the *New York Post*, New York passed a law in 2020 placing such unreasonable evidence requirements on prosecutors that defense lawyers are able to get many perfectly solid cases dismissed. Before the law was passed, she writes, "only 5% of cases prosecuted in New York City criminal court were dismissed because prosecutors couldn't meet their compliance burden in time," but that jumped by nearly five times after the law was passed.[16] From dismissing 8,000 cases a year in 2019, prosecutors went to junking 46,000 in 2024. Particularly affected by this decline in prosecutions were domestic violence cases, of which 60 percent are now dropped.[17]

No Cash Bail

After the 2020 George Floyd protests and riots, some of the most liberal states and cities in the U.S. abolished cash bail. New York State and City, the state of Illinois, and other places run by leftwing politicians consider it racist, or at least classist, to ask people accused of crimes to post bail before releasing them back into the streets pending their next court date. Illinois banned cash bail in 2023, and under it's SAFE-T Act went to a "pretrial release" instead under which most accused individuals would be released except for certain crimes, if prosecutors could prove they posed a high level of threat.[18]

In February 2025, a report by the Minnesota Justice Research Center, "a nonpartisan and nonprofit organization committed to criminal justice reform," recommended that Minnesota should eliminate cash bail because "Minnesota's pretrial system relies heavily on monetary bail and disproportionately impacts people of color and low-income residents."[19] Presumably, the criminal justice system also disproportionately affects people arrested for committing crimes, but that's not likely to sway the state's Democrat-dominated legislature, which commissioned the report. The Justice Research Center advocates a pretrial system "that eliminates cash bail, and prioritizes equity, liberty and community safety." As for the latter, Minneapolis restaurant owner Brian Ingram told local news how high crime and recidivism was destroying his businesses. One of his restaurants was robbed by the same individual multiple time on different dates, said Ingram, as he was released time and again due to lax prosecution and bail policies.[20] Ingram, like many business owners in big U.S. city downtown areas, decided to close his restaurant, depriving the area of jobs, services, and vital tax base. It's a city death spiral we're seeing all over the country.

New York State "ended cash bail for most misdemeanors and nonviolent felonies" in 2022, to "stop punishing poor people who can't afford to post bail while they're waiting for trial" according to an NPR story.[21] A year later, the state granted more discretion to judges to detain certain accused individuals. In 2024, a report from New York City's John Jay College showed that in New York State, not including the city, "66% of the people released under bail reform who had a recent prior arrest were re-arrested within two years of their release."[22] Studies of state prisoners have shown that more than 70 percent of inmates are re-arrested within five years for another offence.[23]

Meanwhile in California, the deep blue state on the other side of the country, a group called Smart Justice California gave $1 million in 2023 to "progressive" politicians and prosecutors, while crime rose. The group includes the wife of Netflix's CEO, an Instagram co-founder, and other mega-rich liberal Californians. Smart Justice California spent more than $25 million on "progressive" criminal justice between 2018 and 2024, according to *The Washington Free Beacon*.[24] "Progress" to them means things like giving criminals as little jail time as possible, keeping criminal penalties low, forcing parents to accept gender ideology, and protecting progressive prosecutors from being thrown out by angry voters.

In 2023, Smart Justice California gave Los Angeles District Attorney George Gascón $7,500. Gascon, fresh from subjecting San Francisco to his radical leniency towards offenders, had brought his special energy to Los Angeles. The group also gave $49,000 to California Attorney General Rob Bonta and $27,500 to his wife, a state assemblywoman for Oakland. Speaking of which, Smart Justice gave $29,000 to Oakland District Attorney Pamela Price, who was then facing a recall from voters (and was eventually removed).[25] Let's look at why.

In a conversation with Rafael Mangual, a Manhattan Institute fellow and author of the book *Criminal Injustice*, activist Seneca Scott calls Oakland "a cautionary tale of what transpires when radical ideologues oversee the managed decline of a great American city for an agenda rooted in absolute control of the masses."[26] Scott spoke of slow 911 response times, homeless camps, drug markets, shoplifting, home invasions, and general public safety. Incredibly, one car was stolen for every 30 residents in Oakland in 2023.

In 2024, Oakland Mayor Sheng Thao and District Attorney Price were both recalled by voters.[27] "Recall" of elected officials was, ironically, one of the innovations of the previous progressive movement, in the early 20th century. The others were the referendum and initiative. Ballot initiatives are ways to bypass the legislature and have people vote directly for laws, via propositions put to all state voters on a ballot. Scott put some blame for Oakland's ills on one of these, California's Proposition 47 of 2014, which despite being labelled a Safe Neighborhoods and Schools Act was quite the opposite. Prop 47 legalized "simple drug possession" and ended cash bail so that thieves would be quickly released after being caught. It also lowered the theft of goods under $950 to a misdemeanor, which meant that shoplifting was rarely punished for a decade.[28]

In nearby San Francisco, Twitter (X) has been replete with videos of drugged-out zombies staggering around the streets, where rampant theft, both by addicts and by organized rings, caused many stores to close, from Target branches to the city's famous downtown Macy's store.[29]

Don't Say Criminal—Say "Justice Involved Individual"

"We have stood up an entire office dedicated to re-entry, so individuals who are returning to our communities who have been incarcerated, because of failed policies, we'll have a welcoming space for them," said Chicago Mayor Brandon Johnson.[30] His implication is that the "justice involved individuals"—a euphemism for ex-convicts[31]—are only in prison because of "failed policies," not because of their own actions and choices. Agency is erased in this framework, where perpetrators are never at fault, they are just traumatized victims of oppression. Johnson's 2024 budget set aside $500,000 to form a Commission on Restoration and Reparations. (Chicago's budget is deeply in the red and the city is heavily in debt, so where the half million will come from, let alone money to fund its recommendations, is a mystery). Johnson said the commission's work would somehow "address…the cycle of violence" in Chicago, implying that the city's murder rate, which is six times that of Denmark with only half the population, is tied to slavery, which never existed in Illinois and ended more than 160 years ago.

Who Did It? Fudge the Data

The Washington Post's Philip Bump wrote an entire article about supposedly rising hate crime in 2022. Bump notes changes in reported hate crimes against black, Asian, Hispanic, Jewish, Muslim, and LGBTQ+ Americans in recent years, and pontificates as to the causes—blaming, of course, Trump policies in several cases. Not once does he discuss who the perpetrators of these hate crimes are. That's taboo.[32] But knowing who commits crime, and the motives, is surely as important in knowing who the victims are, if we want to prevent more crime. As discussed in Chapter 7, the media do not like to report the "intersectional" identity of those who commit crime, unless it fits their narrative of white supremacy and oppression—which a mentally ill black man pushing an Asian woman to her death on New York's subway does not. When that happened, even the *New York Post*, hardly leftwing in editorial viewpoint, had this headline: "Deranged man pushes Asian woman to death at Times Square subway station." [33] The race of the victim is there, but not of the perpetrator. In July 2024, AP News ran an article about another Asian woman pushed to her death on train tracks, this time in San Francisco. The article, with the headline "Woman dies from being pushed into San Francisco-area commuter train" mentions or implies (by using their names) that several victims of similar attacks were Asian women, but AP gives no clue about the identities of the perpetrators, except that they were homeless. In case you miss the point, the AP adds that "advocates for people who are homeless say they are more likely to be victims and not perpetrators of crime."[34]

Don't Prosecute Crime, Get More Crime

Instead of prosecuting crime and locking criminals away from society, woke politicians and activists try to reduce prosecutions and penalties. In many of our largest cities, the public prosecutors have been elected thanks to leftist campaign contributions from George Soros and other massively wealthy woke mega-donors, with the express intent of reducing penalties, prosecutions, and incarceration. In Washington, DC, despite high crime rates, the all-Democrat city council voted in 2023—overriding the Democratic mayor's veto—to adopt a new criminal code that eliminated life sentences and reduced mandatory minimum sentences across the board. The maximum sentence for committing a violent felony with a gun dropped from 15 years to four.[35] Police, victims' groups, and experts panned DC's code revision, and eventually Congress stepped in to nullify the change.[36] Residents in many other violence-plagued cities from San Francisco to New York probably wish Congress had supervisory powers over their own woke prosecutors and local governments, but no such luck.

In 2023, *The Daily Caller* found that "at least six large cities have seen crime spikes after the election of liberal prosecutors backed by groups that have received funding from billionaire megadonor George Soros."[37] Public prosecutors were elected with direct or indirect support from Soros-funded programs in Chicago (Kim Foxx), St. Louis (Kim Gardner), Los Angeles (George Gascon), Dallas (John Creuzot), New York (Alvin Bragg), Philadelphia (Larry Krasner) and other cities. Heritage Foundation legal scholar Cully Stimson, author of *Rogue Prosecutors*, compared the approaches of Philadelphia's progressive, Soros-backed District Attorney Larry Krasner with that of a more traditional law enforcer, San Diego District Attorney Summer Stephan. San Diego County, with a larger population than metro Philadelphia, recorded 118 homicides in 2023,[38] whereas Philadelphia had 562. Krasner said when he was elected that he was a "public defender with power," whereas Stimson called Stephan "a real prosecutor."[39] According to a 2022 report, Krasner's office withdrew (declined to prosecute) 65 percent of all violent crime cases that year.[40]

In Washington state, theft up to $750 is only a misdemeanor. In November 2023, members of the United Food & Commercial Workers Local 3000 union at three Macy's stores near Seattle went on strike saying their employer "is not doing enough to address shoplifting, violent shoppers, and other safety threats to workers and customers." Store employee Liisa Luick said workers at her store "frequently observe shoplifting and even occasional violence," but when she called police after seeing a known repeat shoplifter, Macy's suspended her without pay "for nearly three weeks," she told a local paper. Luick said Macy's workers like her "are afraid to call the police because we worry we'll get in trouble or even lose our jobs," and they know few shoplifting cases will be prosecuted anyway.[41]

In Minneapolis, Hennepin County District Attorney Mary Moriarty is notorious for her leniency.[42] A former public defender, Moriarty allowed probation, light sentences, or "alternatives" to jail in cases involving drugs, rape, and wrongful death, prompting criticism even from leftwing Minnesota Attorney General Keith Ellison. Moriarty had "campaigned on the premise of increasing rehabilitation as opposed to incarceration for young offenders,"[43] and she delivered. In April 2025, Minnesota Department of Human Services employee Dylan Bryan Adams was reportedly caught on several videos keying a series of Tesla cars causing up to $20,000 in damage—and, in spite of the evidence, Moriarty chose not to charge him and instead steer him to a "diversion" program.[44] Such programs are not only of doubtful benefit, they leave the offenders on the streets to harm others.

In 2022 and 2023 respectively, Venezuelans Jose and Diego Ibarra were caught entering the US illegally. Like millions of other aliens under president Biden, despite their unverified identity and zero criminal background check in their home country, they were released into the U.S. with a letter telling them to show up at immigration court in the future.

Both were later reported to have been members or affiliated with the violent prison gang Tren de Aragua. In October 2023, the brothers were caught shoplifting in Georgia. Instead of being prosecuted and jailed, or deported for illegal presence, they were both put in a "pre-trial diversion" program. Such alternatives to firm penalties are beloved by leftist criminal justice "reformers." The "diversion" clearly failed, because Diego was caught shoplifting again in December 2023. Again, he wasn't detained.[45] As for Jose, in February 2024, he murdered nursing student Laken Riley in a tragic case that brought home the danger of releasing, time and again, both unvetted migrants and recidivist criminals – or worst still, the two combined. In November 2024, Jose Ibarra was sentenced to life in prison.[46]

Drugs—Nobody's Fault?

Drug addiction is a complex subject to which there are no easy solutions. But one thing is clear: it's much harder to score drugs in jail than on the streets of Philadelphia and San Francisco, where a mix of soft prosecutors and deliberate non-prosecution creates open air free-use drug zones.

In Amsterdam, law enforcement adopted a simple approach to homeless drug addicts, giving them a choice of treatment or being prosecuted for the many offenses they committed while using, from public defecation to theft.[47] Meanwhile in many U.S. cities, notably San Francisco, New York, Portland, and Philadelphia, the philosophy of "harm reduction" takes punishment off the table. The results are exactly what you'd expect. In the *New York Post*, Megan Palin described an apocalyptic Kensington area of Philadelphia where xylazine, known as "tranq," rots addicts' flesh and users stagger around like zombies.[48] One observer said "Kensington is an adult Disneyland for drug addicts" because everything is obtainable and law enforcement leaves people alone. Philadelphia's Police-Assisted Diversion Program "offers offenders access to treatment rather than sending them to jail," writes Palin, who watched police cars patrol without doing anything to stop people from selling and using drugs in the open.[49]

Ineffective and Expensive "Alternatives" to Prosecution

In Washington, DC, Colbert King wrote about a 15-year-old carjacking suspect who was under supervision of the city's Department of Youth Rehabilitation Services (DYRS). Why was this minor, already arrested for a previous crime, free to offend again? King found that in 2022 and 2023, only 64 percent of charges against juveniles in DC were prosecuted; 19 percent were dropped, mostly for insufficient evidence, and 16 percent "were dismissed and diverted to alternative no-incarceration programs or deferred sentencing agreements."[50] For the Left, criminal justice "reform" means fewer prosecutions and more spending on alternatives with no proven efficacy, like Washington's DYRS grants of up to $500,000 for "eligible entities to provide transformative mentoring and family engagement services to DYRS youth and their families."[51]

4. Failing at School—It's Not Your Fault

In Chapter 2, we saw the sad state of public education in much of the country. Locked in a death-grip with teachers' unions, the mantra of leftist elected officials seems to be "if at first you don't succeed, just lower the bar."

Grade Inflation

When I graduated college in 1991 in the U.K., there were four of us, of about 95 graduating from the Modern History department, who earned "first-class degrees," the top grade. At that time, and before, around 5 percent a year earned "Firsts," with most getting "Seconds." (There were a few third-class degrees awarded, which we called a "Douglas," because it rhymed with the last name of British politician Douglas Hurd). Thirty years later, I was astonished to hear that the percentage of Firsts awarded at my university had risen to more than one-third. I highly doubt that kids today are smarter, work harder, and drink less than we did in the late 1980s and early 1990s. The more likely explanation is grade inflation—a desire by the provider, the college, to keep the student-clients happy so they won't go anywhere else.

This phenomenon is clear in the U.S., too. A recent report by Yale University showed that nearly 80 percent of Yale grades were in the "A" range in the 2022–2023 school year, giving an average grade-point average of 3.7 out of 4. Harvard's figures were almost the same.[52] According to the campus paper, the *Yale News*, "the University has not published similar data in over a decade." If it had, it would have shown the gradual watering down of standards in grading. In 2001, *The Boston Globe* called Harvard University "the laughingstock of the Ivy League" because 91 percent of Harvard graduates in Latin received honors.[53] In 2012, Harvard set limits on the three honors categories to a total of no more than 50 percent of the graduating class.[54] In 2013, Yale created a committee to look into grade inflation, which reported that "62% of grades awarded to Yale College students in spring 2012 fell in the A range."

At Harvard, the grade inflation was worst in the soft subjects; in engineering and applied science, only 57 percent received an "A," while in "women's, gender, and sexuality studies" it was 92 percent. There were more than 180,000 "cultural and gender studies majors" in U.S. colleges in the 2021 school year. On graduation, the median salaries earned by these graduates was $58,000[55]—well below the cost of one year's tuition at elite colleges.

Dropped Honors Classes

Honors classes provide children with ability, and who work hard, with accelerated learning. In schools with poor discipline and low standards, honors classes also remove them from the prevailing environment of failure and offer a ladder to academic and life achievement. This is anathema to the tenets of DEI, by which all must end in the same place. In 2023, the Culver City high school in Los Angeles county, California eliminated honors classes because they did not enroll enough black and Hispanic students in proportion with their overall numbers at the school.[56] Similar policies have been enacted in progressive school districts across California and the country. The problem is, removing these classes punishes everyone, not just high-achieving Asian and European-American students, but the many talented black and Latino kids who also qualify for them. "Equity" requires everyone to learn at the same pace – that of the slowest students.

Higher Grades, Lower Results

The American Council of Trustees and Alumni reported in 2020 that "only 18 percent of colleges and universities include an American history or civics course in their general education requirements." It is not surprising, then, to see that a survey by the council in 2024 found that "63 percent of respondents did not know the term lengths of U.S. senators and representatives." Sixty-one percent of those surveyed either were in college or had a college degree. Of the college graduates in the survey only 12 percent "knew the relationship between the Emancipation Proclamation and the 13th Amendment."[57]

"Diversity, Equity, and Inclusion" at the Expense of the Three Rs

A year-long study conducted by the Center for American Institutions found that

> the use of identity-focused terms, primarily the defining terms for diversity, equity, and inclusion (DEI), e.g., "white supremacy," "toxic masculinity," and "homophobia," infuse course instruction. In a review of 75 introductory history course syllabi found in large and small public and private colleges, DEI is the focus.[58]

DEI offices, with dedicated full-time staff and budgets, are now almost universal in American higher education. They influence admissions, faculty hiring, speech and conduct, and even course topics. Seeing the pernicious racial division and discrimination that the DEI administrations have created on their campuses, some states are attempting to limit or defund them.[59] However, DEI principles and enforcement bureaucracies are extremely well entrenched everywhere from the Ivy League to community colleges, which means that indoctrinated students will be fed into the private and government workforce for the foreseeable future.[60]

One side effect of DEI's penetration of academia became apparent in the wake of the October 7, 2023, Hamas terrorist attacks against Israel. Campus groups like Students for Justice in Palestine praised the terrorists and spoke in terms of "liberating" territory forming part of the state of Israel "by any means necessary."[61] Antisemitism was not only tolerated on various campuses by faculty and administrators but even displayed by some professors and staff. Pro-Palestinian, anti-Israel demonstrators in the

U.S. have blocked traffic at bridges and airports, demonstrated in major U.S. cities, and harassed opponents—especially if they are Jewish—online and in person. In November 2023, hundreds of students at a New York City high school rioted in response to a Jewish teacher posting a photo of herself at a pro-Israel demonstration.

Hannah Meyers argues in *Commentary* magazine that DEI-fostered racial entitlement has created a climate in U.S. universities that fosters antisemitism.[62] The CRT worldview, in which people are categorized as oppressed or oppressor according to racial categories, underlies the implementation of DEI in academia. This ideology, with the antipathy it breeds, is increasingly infused into formal education, from K–12 right through Yale law school.[63] Meyers cites polling that "a majority of Americans ages 18 to 24 believe Israel 'should be ended and given to Hamas.'"

In January 2024, the Louis D. Brandeis Center at American University (AU) in Washington, DC, made a formal complaint to the U.S. Department of Education that AU students "are being subjected to discrimination, harassment, and intimidation on the basis of their Jewish shared ancestry and ethnic identity and Israeli national origin."[64] AU students accuse the school of tolerating antisemitism on campus from faculty and students. The Israeli and Jewish students allege that in addition to being ostracized on campus for their national or ethnic identity, they were subject to verbal insults, graffiti, and vandalism.[65] Similar complaints with the Department of Education have been filed by aggrieved students at Harvard,[66] the University of Minnesota,[67] and several other universities[68] since October 7. As discussed in Chapter 2, the presidents of the University of Pennsylvania, MIT, and Harvard testified before Congress in December 2023. Their testimony[69] appeared to expose a double standard applicable in much of academia: antisemitism was acceptable unless it became actual violence, but "mis-gendering" someone could be punishable merely at the level of speech.

Discrimination at Harvard and other selective colleges in favor of applicants and faculty from desired identity groups and against others is no secret. The Supreme Court's *Bakke* decision allowed colleges leeway to discriminate on the basis of race, sex, and other immutable characteristics since 1979.[70] Subsequent cases failed to resolve the question of how far colleges could go to engineer their desired racial and gender composition in admissions. At Harvard, President Claudine Gay made DEI the guiding principle of the university, not least in recruitment of faculty and students. When she was dean of Harvard's faculty of arts and sciences in 2020, Gay called alleged white supremacy "the second pandemic" and laid out a comprehensive plan of "actions for building an effective and active culture of anti-racism" in her faculty. Among her aims were to "identify concrete steps we can take to increase racial diversity of senior staff and recommend near- and long-term hiring goals," and "building an effective and active culture of anti-racism." She promised to be "relentless" and "action-oriented in our pursuit to build the thriving, more equitable" faculty of arts and sciences. Gay brought this Kendian[71] philosophy of using racial preferences in faculty hiring and promotion and student admissions with her to the Harvard presidency.[72]

Racial preferences under the DEI rubric may have finally reached the high-water mark. In June 2023, the Court ruled in *Students for Fair Admissions v. Harvard*[73] that such practices should end. Despite this clear ruling, however, elite universities have declared their intention to circumvent this proscription using more subtle means like essays and personal histories. A similar approach to recruitment—discriminating in favor of certain identity groups while attempting to avoid blatantly illegal action—has been evident in government agencies for some time.

Discipline and Behavior in School

No one should be surprised by the collapse of standards in academia, law enforcement, the media, and competitive professions, given that they are systematically undermined by the Left at every step. K–12 public schools have abandoned traditional discipline methods in favor of therapy and alternatives that take more time and deliver worse results.

This approach continues policies of the Obama Administration. Obama's Department of Education would write "Dear Colleague" letters to schools that appeared to employ disparate levels of student discipline among racial groups. The implication was that school discipline that punished more black students than students of other races, and was therefore inherently racist. In 2014, researchers tested the hypothesis and here's what they found:

> Replicating prior studies, we first show a clear racial gap between black and white students in suspensions. However, in subsequent analyses the racial gap in suspensions was completely accounted for by a measure of the prior problem behavior of the student—finding never before reported in the literature.[74]

Nonetheless, many school districts accepted that any disparity in discipline was racist. They responded to Dear Colleague letters by either adopting woke and ineffective policies, such as "culturally responsive" discipline or "restorative justice," or they simply stopped punishing students who misbehaved. According to a teacher in Newport News, Virginia, in response to the Department of Education pressure, student [i]nfraction numbers are down because incidents aren't always officially reported.[75] In her school district, a 6-year-old boy was able to bring a gun to school and shoot a teacher. Arguably, a reluctance among teachers and administrators to report safety threats is due to fear of reporting too many from favored minorities.

For some school administrators, watering down the language describing poor behavior took the place of practical means to deal with it. In their 2023 contract, negotiated after a month on strike, public school teachers in Portland, Oregon, sacrificed classroom and school order to woke ideology. Faced with a disruptive or misbehaving student, they are required to develop a "support plan" which "must take into consideration the impact of issues related to the student's trauma, race, gender identity/presentation, sexual orientation…and restorative justice as appropriate for the student."[76] According to *The Washington Free Beacon*, "Portland Public Schools' collective bargaining team argued that 'Black, Native American, and other students of color are referred out of class significantly more often.'" Notwithstanding an increase in student misbehavior and violence when they returned after the long pandemic lockdown, Portland schools shifted from punishment to more time-consuming and less effective responses. For example, students who assault other students used to be removed from the school altogether, but henceforth they can be sent to a "self-regulation space" inside the school.[77]

Where things end when discipline goes to hell is clear to anyone who read *Lord of the Flies* in middle school. In 2023, a Massachusetts high school asked Governor Maura Healey, a Democrat, to send in the National Guard to restore order.[78] A letter to Healey from members of the Brockton School Committee complained of "a disturbing increase in incidents related to violence, security concerns, and substance abuse." Students were cutting class and leaving school and desperate high school and faculty administrators wanted National Guard soldiers to handle hall monitor duty and even to act as substitute teachers. Eisenhower sent the 101st Airborne Division to Little Rock, Arkansas, in 1957 to enforce school integration. Seventy years later, to send the National Guard as hall monitors in a northern city seems ludicrous, but the very proposal indicates the level of desperation among teachers in the "progressive" Boston area.

5. Failing Standardized Testing —It's Not You, It's the Tests

Woke educators have applied the same theory that led to grade inflation—*if at first you don't succeed, lower the bar*—to standardized testing, and in so doing have removed not only a tool to measure likely future success, but also a ladder into higher education for unrecognized talent.

Colleges Drop SATs

Under the "equity" dogma, if tests produce disparate results among racial groups, the tests must be ignored or eliminated, even if there is no evidence that the tests are biased. Driven by this philosophy, some American colleges moved away from objective measures toward methods that can be manipulated to ensure desired outcomes. For example, in July 2022, the University of Maryland became the latest institution to no longer require students to include Scholastic Aptitude Test (SAT) or American College Testing (ACT) scores on their applications.[79] The American Bar Association was considering dropping the requirement that law schools use the Law School Admission Test (LSAT) in admissions, and medical schools de-emphasize the objective Medical School Admission Test (MCAT) to attract more students who are not white or Asian.[80]

Colleges Bring SATs Back

After discovering that standardized tests are useful in predicting student achievement, some colleges, notably Yale[81] and Dartmouth,[82] returned to requiring that students submit them. Nonetheless, many other institutions across the nation have adopted the California model. According to an article in *Inside Higher Ed*, "[d]iscussions with admission officers indicate that nonacademic factors…will take on increasing importance in the weighting of admission criteria…. [A]dmission officers see that utilizing character in admission will open doors of opportunity for disadvantaged populations."[83]

Roland Fryer's Story:
The Truth Shall Set You Free—from Your Job

Roland Fryer was the youngest economics professor to be tenured at Harvard. He grew up poor in an inner-city neighborhood, raised by a single father. Despite his childhood challenges, he became a top economist, once winning the John Bates Clark Medal for the best economist under 40 in the world. Then, Fryer committed the ultimate sin: he challenged woke orthodoxy with research and reached conclusions the establishment did not like.[84]

Sometime between the fatal Ferguson shooting of Michael Brown in 2014 and the 2020 death of George Floyd, Americans somehow became convinced of an epidemic of police killing of unarmed, innocent black men. Propagated by BLM and the leftist world, this notion was dogma long after civil rights had been established in law and long before Michael Brown and Trayvon Martin (shot by a civilian in self-defense) were memes. George Floyd was the case that broke the camel's back. Fryer researched the question: do police disproportionately use force against, or kill, unarmed black men?

In 2016, Fryer published his paper. He found evidence of bias in "low-level uses of force," but "we didn't find any bias in police shootings."[85] Despite the fact that he and eight research assistants took a year to examine data to reach this result, and he hired a whole new team to do the research again, academia received his conclusions with hostility. As Fryer said eight years later of research into controversial topics like race in America, "people lose their minds when they don't like the result."[86] Fryer nearly lost his job. This research, by a black man with authentically hardscrabble roots, was anathema to the guilt-ridden white academic class and their elite black colleagues.

Worse still, Fryer later researched the question of black underperformance in K–12 education. Fryer challenged the received wisdom that outcomes in school were unavoidable. His found that, in spite of what everyone thought, black children did not automatically shun their peers who succeeded in school. Fryer's body of research into schools concluded that discipline, hard work, hours of study, family support, and other factors of individual and group behavior were responsible for the black achievement gap, not "structural racism" and societal sins. This was too much for the establishment to tolerate. For the woke, the "blood" of ideology was much thicker than the "water" of Fryer's intellectual rigor, and they cast him out. Under the auspices of Claudine Gay, whose origins were in the upper class of Haiti, Fryer was nearly hounded out of Harvard. The university shut down Fryer's laboratory and temporarily banned him from campus based on spurious claims of sexual harassment. He remains at the university, but his reputation was severely damaged.

Examples of Fryer's principles in action abound. The racial make-up of a student body is irrelevant to the formula's success. Although public schools in America's major cities mostly have low test results, where the right circumstances are put in place in charter schools, success is achievable. Broken homes and poverty are obstacles, but not insurmountable. Economist Thomas Sowell explains that in New York City, some charter schools are located in the same buildings as public schools in low-income neighborhoods. The student bodies were similar— low income, largely black and Hispanic. Yet, in the 2017–2018 school year, "the charter school students achieved the 'proficient' level in mathematics more than 6 times as often as children of the same ethnicities in traditional public schools housed in the very same buildings."[87]

The formula works in different geographic contexts. In Alabama, Nicole Ault reports how the Valiant Cross Academy supplies discipline— and a strong Christian ethos—to boys who have mostly absent fathers.[88] Valiant has 200 boys in grades six through 12. They wear uniforms, do chores, and are held to a high standard of personal conduct. Meanwhile, public schools in Valiant's home city of Montgomery, Alabama, had more than 8,000 "disciplinary incidents" in 2023. Alabama provides parents with tax credits and state scholarships, which many Valiant Cross students are using to attend.

In London, Katherine Birbalsingh has produced consistently impressive results in an inner-city school with nearly all ethnic-minority children, by applying the same basic principles: uniforms, respect, high standards, discipline, support. In 2024, 84 percent of her pupils, aged around 15 and 16, tested for the General Certificate of Secondary Education (GCSE) exam, earned an "A," "A*," or "super A.*"[89] In 2017, the grading system using letters was replaced by one using numbers, with 9 being the top score. With a 7 now corresponding to the old "A" grade, the new top grade, a 9, is commonly referred to as a "super A star." (The fact that there are three distinct levels in the British system marked "A" shows that British schools have suffered rampant grade inflation, too).

6. Being Overweight—It's Not Your Fault

Like so many woke ideas, the militant fat movement started well and ended poorly. It began with accepting the things we cannot change about ourselves. There's only one Brad Pitt and one Jennifer Lawrence; most of us look more ordinary. There's no point beating ourselves up about it, and it's not nice to tease other people for being themselves. In addition to our natural variations, we have the right as Americans to live how we want, and that includes how much we eat and exercise. But tolerance and kindness are not enough anymore—acceptance had to "progress" *ad infinitum*. "Body positivity" went from being about accepting the imperfections we can't change to celebrating ones we can.

Fatphobic Medicine

Kate Manne, an associate professor of philosophy at Cornell University, thinks that doctors are "fatphobic," rather than concerned about the effects of obesity on their patients' health.[90] She argues that people who "live in larger bodies" "need to work on changing not our bodies but the world that unjustly down-ranks us." Manne claims that "weight is largely out of our control—in large part because of genetics and the food environment, among other unchosen factors." In this, she is wrong. However, she is absolutely right to say that "everybody deserves humane, compassionate medical care, regardless of their weight or health status." Doctors and nurses should be honest with their patients about how their weight is affecting their health, but they should not treat them disrespectfully or consciously ignore other issues that may be obscured by obesity.

Fatness is a topic tailor-made for National Public Radio. A typical NPR article refers to "People with larger bodies," as if they were people with larger feet, or people with red hair.[91] The gist of the article is that doctors should stop trying to treat fat people's obesity and concentrate on the immediate issue with which they present, in the case of the patient discussed in that article, a disconnected thumb. Though the article concedes that "a higher body mass index is correlated with heart disease, diabetes, certain types of cancer and other conditions...when clinicians focus on weight, it can lead patients to avoid or delay health care." As a result, a "growing number of providers are...practicing what they call weight-inclusive, or weight-neutral, care," and even a "set of principles called 'health at every size.'"[92] Really? *Every* size? Proponents of no-fault fatness speak of "people with obesity," as if it not a condition directly related to calorie consumption and burn rate, but a pathogen or cancer. In the NPR article, the patient complains of having to deal with doctors giving her unsolicited advice about her weight. But as Alexander Riley points out in *The Federalist*, much of the useful medical advice doctors give is "unsolicited."[93]

Suffer the Children

In January 2023, *The Washington Post* reported on new childhood obesity guidelines from the American Academy of Pediatrics (AAP), which now recommends "early and aggressive treatment...including medication for kids as young as 12, and surgery for those as young as 13."[94] This is redolent of the AAP's position on gender dysphoria, which used to be "watchful waiting"—because most children grow out of it— and is now "gender affirming care." The guidelines say, implausibly, that "[o]besity is a chronic medical condition, not primarily a consequence of lifestyle choices." The *Post* quotes a doctor at Children's Hospital in San

Antonio: "Think of it like heart disease or cancer... It's far more complicated than just eating less." In practice, this means advocating medications like Wegovy and Ozempic for kids as young as 12, and even bariatric surgery—surgically shrinking the size of the digestive system—for kids as young as 13.

Only a decade or so ago, the *Post* article says, "the medical community did not recognize obesity as a disease, and the treatment options for children were mostly limited to counseling about diet, nutrition and exercise."[95] Now, they've medicalized it—which is much more lucrative. In a 2023 *Washington Post* advice column, Dr. Leana Wen calls the new childhood obesity guidelines "overdue and crucial."[96] Wen says "in the United States, more than 14 million children—nearly 1 in 5 of those under 18—have obesity," echoing the woke terminology of obesity as a disease not a result of behavior.

Of course, this approach throws in the towel on personal agency and parental complicity—after all, no kid can afford to stock his own fridge. Coincidentally, seeing obesity "just as we do other chronic illnesses such as diabetes or heart disease," as Dr. Wen advocates, paves the way for insurance companies to pay for its perpetual treatment and lines up a durable cash-stream for providers.[97] A pediatric obesity doctor at Yale New Haven Children's Hospital said that "we are thinking it's [the duration that patients would be on weight-loss drugs] for their lifetime."[98] So far, not every medical insurance plan covers weight loss drugs or surgery for overweight children, and "only a few states mandate reimbursement" from Medicaid. But as with every other area of personal responsibility, expect the government to gradually cover treatment and require private insurance plans to do so.

Normalizing Obesity

The cycle of leftist cultural indoctrination is forced tolerance, acceptance, then celebration. With "people of size," we've moved to the final stage. Seattle hosted a "Fat Con" in January 2024, "with three days of workshops, panel discussions and classes promoting the 'fat liberation' movement."[99] As Kristine Parks from Fox News wrote, "activists have gone further than pushing for body acceptance to argue that efforts to combat obesity are rooted in 'colonialism, racism, and queer and transphobia.'"[100] A documentary called *Your Fat Friend* by Aubrey Gordon was released in February 2024, examining how fat people are seen in movies and television.[101] In the film, a casting director says: "I hope we can get to a point with a character and script where it doesn't specify body size," which seems a tall order for most works of fiction, in which describing the characters is pretty important. One critic of the film wrote that "Gordon's points about mental health and unrealistic media expectations would be so much stronger if they weren't offset by her criticisms of healthy habits and resistance to solve a problem that is quite literally killing people." Universal Studios Hollywood's new Mario Kart ride, based on a Nintendo game, has a 40-inch waistline limit. The average American waist circumference is 40.5 inches for men and 38.7 inches for women.[102] In March 2022, a 14-year-old boy died falling from a ride at a Florida theme park; he was found to have been over the ride's weight limit. There's even fat-positive "chick lit," like author Erin Zhurkin's novel *Plus-Size in Paris,* about a young "plus-sized social media influencer" who is invited to Paris to cover a fashion show for her "account's wide audience." Reviewing the novel in *The Federalist*, Tristan Justice points out that "88 percent of American adults suffer some sort of metabolic dysfunction, thanks in large part to our diet," and "the French obesity rate is just 17 percent, while the U.S. is nearly 42 percent."[103] The author's heroine alter-ego "blames genetics" for her weight, writes Justice, but according to Dr. Robert Lustig, a pediatric neuroendocrinologist and University of California professor, the two genes that "have any real clinical import" on individuals being fat "are only found in about 16 percent of the obese population, never mind the general population."[104]

New York's New School, a private college, is offering a course on Fat Fashion in 2025. Assistant professor of Fashion Design and Social Justice Leila Kelleher teaches students "how to design clothes that value and desire fat bodies and will develop a personal framework for Fat-Centered Design." With the increasing girth of Americans, it might make academic sense to teach a course about how the industry caters to fatter customers, and how to design clothes for them. But the course is as much about ideology as it is about fashion or clothing design: according to the course description, students will look at "fatness as an area of human difference subject to privilege and discrimination that intersects with other systems of oppression based on gender, race, class, sexual orientation, and ability."[105]

Bloated National Security

The U.S. Air Force, like the Army and Navy, has fallen short of recruitment targets for the past several years. Only the Marines managed to meet their targets. The reasons for this are various, including more refusals for drug use and criminal records, and lower interest based on leftwing policies and attitudes fostered by DEI and CRT. Another factor is declining physical fitness. To mitigate this last barrier, in 2023, the Air Force upped the acceptable body fat percentage for men from 20 percent to 26 percent, while the limit for women rose from 28 percent to 36 percent.[106] Meanwhile, as reported in *The Daily Signal*, "six FBI agents from the bureau's Washington, D.C., field office were photographed kneeling during a BLM march on June 4, 2020, and were referred to derisively on social media as 'Kneel Team Six.'"[107] One of them, Sarah Webb Linden, graduated from Smith College in 1998 with a degree in comparative linguistics but now works on "homegrown violent extremism" cases. Linden, who was promoted to assistant special agent in charge of the FBI's DC field office after the BLM protest, made a recruitment video for Smith that said the FBI is looking for a "diverse workforce" "looking like the communities that we represent." She may have just meant more women, but perhaps also more "plus sized" ones like her. But is size diversity desirable in law enforcement? Official social media photos make one wonder if the FBI has also lowered fitness standards for agents, and if that is a good idea if their duties — for which they receive extra law enforcement pay—occasionally include chasing home-grown extremists.[108]

Obesity as a Disability

Northwestern University's "Policy on Discrimination, Harassment, and Sexual Misconduct," issued in August 2024,

> prohibits discrimination and harassment on the basis of race, color, religion, creed, national origin, ethnicity, caste, sex, pregnancy,

sexual orientation, gender identity, gender expression, parental status, marital status, age, disability, citizenship status, veteran status, genetic information, reproductive health decision making, height, weight, or any other classification protected by law.[109]

Under the policy, the news site Campus Reform reports,[110] "a joke about a person's weight counts as 'harassing conduct that may create a hostile environment,'" and could lead to discipline, including "verbal or written warnings from the school, forced counseling," or "[r]equired training, probation, suspension, or expulsion." For faculty, it could lead to loss of tenure.

Until now, courts have mostly "held that obesity isn't a disability under the Americans with Disabilities Act unless it is caused by an underlying health condition."[111] Slowly, however, it is creeping into protected status. In February 2023, New York City Councilman Shaun Abreu sponsored legislation to ban weight and height discrimination by employers, backed by the National Association to Advance Fat Acceptance. Abreu wants discrimination claims based on weight to be investigated by the city's Commission on Human Rights, like claims based on other protected classes like gender, race, age, and national origin. Some states have similar bills passed or contemplated, and Washington State already considers obesity to be a disability, protected under its Law Against Discrimination.[112] A few months later, New York City added "weight and height to the list of characteristics protected from discrimination, alongside race, gender, age, religion and sexual orientation," and other left-leaning cities and states aren't far behind, according to *The Wall Street Journal*.[113]

Conclusion

America began as a can-do culture that prized individual achievement and responsibility. Our communities were made up of strong, independent individuals, responsible for their own actions. In essence, this is the ideological opposite of socialism. Over time, a limited financial safety net, begun with good intentions, has grown into a system of full-scale, no-fault, cradle-to-grave socialism, paid for by federal and state taxes, that Friedrich Engels could only have dreamed of. Meanwhile, academics and politicians have encouraged us to see ourselves as victims of oppression by others or by unseen systems that are at fault for every ill. We must reject this hopeless, nihilistic ideology and return agency and responsibility to individuals.

A person to follow: Roland Fryer, @Dr_RolandFryer, X.

A book to read: *The Parasitic Mind: How Infectious Ideas Are Killing Common Sense,* by Gad Saad, 2020.

A group to support: Foundation for Individual Rights and Expression, Philadelphia, PA, www.thefire.org.

Chapter 11

And Now, the Eleventh Commandment:
Be of Good Cheer - and Keep Fighting

In 10 chapters, I explained the 10 woke ideas that Americans must resist if they are to preserve this unique and successful American democracy. So where are we now? To some extent, gender ideology and the obsession with race and intersectional oppression are collapsing under their own weight. Exposed to the light of day, the practical implications of DEI and academic theories like CRT are unpopular: a wide-open border allowing in millions of unknown and unvetted aliens; discrimination against Asians, Europeans, and men; grown men competing in women's sports; male rapists self-identifying into women's prisons; children being irreversibly damaged by impossible attempts to change their sex.

A Turning Tide?

The election of Donald Trump in November 2024 brought in an Administration committed to undoing the DEI and gender ideology from the federal government and making it harder for it to survive in future. President Trump acted quickly, issuing a flurry of executive orders that included enforcing the border, banning men from women's sports, banning discriminatory DEI programs from federal agencies and recipients of federal money, ending divisive and useless foreign aid grants, and targeting universities for investigations and reduced federal aid if they continue their race-based and sex-based discrimination.

But, as we saw with President Biden's executive orders, what can be done by executive fiat can just as quickly be undone. Congress has a brief window to enact as much of a corrective, post-woke agenda as possible and return the country to its roots and values.

The Trump Administration is working to end race-based and sex-based discrimination in academia, companies, and professional organizations. Meanwhile parents, organized by leaders like Moms for Liberty co-founder Tiffany Justice, are fighting to protect their children's education from toxic DEI, gender ideology, and critical race theory in schools. Justice is also a Visiting Fellow for Coalitions at The Heritage Foundation, which launched a Parent's Rights Initiative in June 2025 as a clearinghouse for information to help parents.[1]

Conservative activists like Robby Starbuck hold companies' feet to the fire and force them to choose whether to dig in on DEI and lose customers, or get back to business and leave "social justice" to the NGOs. Journalists at new media, like *The Washington Free Beacon*'s Aaron Sibarium and *The Daily Wire*'s Spencer Lindquist, are shedding light on the ideological corruption of professional organizations from the American Medical Association to the American Historical Association. None of these institutions will easily back away from what they see as the righteous cause of social justice. Companies have the least invested and the most to lose by angering half the country, so they will be the first to cast off woke ideas. Academia is so far gone that it may never recover, and commonsense Americans may need to build alternatives from scratch. Professional organizations must be retaken by their members, who hitherto have abandoned control to the hard-core woke elements of their number. Or, they can start new structures to accredit schools and provide professional standards and guidance. The worst course would be to hope that this woke wave simply blows over. It may, but not before it has done irreparable harm to the underlying structure and values of this nation and to millions of individuals within it.

DEI and Disparate Impact

In Chapter 6, I discussed the "disparate impact theory" and how it has been used by activists to destroy American standards and institutions in the name of racial "equity." In April 2025, President Trump signed an executive order titled "Restoring Equality of Opportunity and Meritocracy," changing the direction of the federal government. If the order is followed properly, the federal government will not use "disparate impact" under the Civil Rights Act of 1964 to encourage and mandate unconstitutional race and sex discrimination. The Department of Justice will no longer make onerous regulations to force schools, police and fire departments, and other institutions to ignore the realities they face in recruitment, criminal justice, and other measurable areas.

As Heather Mac Donald writes, "disparate impact" has been used

> to invalidate literacy and numeracy standards for police officers and firemen, cognitive skills and basic knowledge tests for teachers, the use of SATs in college admissions, the use of grades for medical licensing exams, credit-based mortgage lending, the ability to discipline insubordinate students, and criminal background checks for employees and renters. It has been used to eliminate prosecution for a large range of crimes.

It was even the justification behind removing the ShotSpotter system in Chicago that could help police to prevent gun violence, and speeding cameras that stop dangerous driving.[2] As Mac Donald has written in articles and books, "disparate-impact analysis was the linchpin of the 'systemic racism' argument," since it ignored the real reasons why there is racial disparity, from elite academia, to the professions, to criminal justice, and thus prevented meaningful laws and policies to address these true causes.[3]

In March 2025, the state of Ohio passed a law to:

> abolish DEI at state institutions, ban faculty strikes, require meaningful annual faculty evaluation including post-tenure reviews, mandate institutional neutrality on contentious political issues, obligate schools to publish class syllabuses online, and require that undergraduates take a civics course to graduate.[4]

President Trump also went after professional bodies and accrediting monopolies, ordering the Department of Education to stop accreditation authorities from requiring DEI training and recruitment programs at the schools they accredit. In response, the Accreditation Council for Graduate Medical Education ACGME put on hold some DEI requirements pending their June 2025 board meeting.[5] Some professional bodies will follow their example, but others will dig in for the long fight.

Free Speech

After years of retreat, victories are racking up for free speech in the English-speaking world.

In April 2024, a high school student in North Carolina was suspended from school for using the term "illegal alien." He used this statutory, accurate, and descriptive term when asking his teacher to clarify a class assignment – specifically, whether by "aliens" she meant "space aliens, or illegal aliens who need green cards" - and without apparent intent to insult anyone.[6] No matter – someone took offence, and he was suspended for three days. In June 2025, he won $20,000 from the Central Davidson School District for violating his rights to due process, free speech, and education.[7] But I can say, as a parent of kids who sat out some of high school and college because of unwarranted Covid lockdowns, twenty grand is not worth a year of a young person's social life.

In June 2025, the University of Oregon agreed to pay Portland State University political science Professor Bruce Gilley $193,000 in legal fees. In 2022, the manager of the University of Oregon's @UOEquity X (then known as Twitter) account had blocked Professor Gilley for responding to her "racism interrupter" prompt with the quote "all men are created equal," according to the College Fix.[8] "Interrupting racism" is one of many techniques pushed by "antiracist" trainers and woke HR departments to police interpersonal relations within institutions with a keen eye for finding offence. According to Ijeoma Olou, author of "So You Want to Talk About Race," to "dismantle racism, we have to observe racist language, interrupt it, and describe it when it occurs in our conversations."[9] Gilley's response, perhaps tongue-in-check, was a direct quote from the Declaration of Independence. He was represented by the Angus Lee Law Firm and the Institute for Free Speech, while Oregon taxpayers picked up the half million dollar tab for fighting this ridiculous case over three years. The University of Oregon has agreed to "revise its social media guidelines and provide training to its employees," and one might hope this will result in fewer attempts to restrict free speech even if it opposes academia's cherished DEI values and allegedly "antiracist" programs.

In 2022, Peter Wilkins resigned from the British government's Defence Science and Technology Laboratory (DSTL) at Porton Down after facing harassment for his supposed "gender critical" views. Paul Kealey, head of counterterrorism at Porton Down had told Wilkins that it was "not OK to express [gender-critical beliefs] in the workplace," and management refused to respond to his requests for support. Backed by the Free Speech Union, a group started by Toby (now Lord) Young, Wilkins complained to an employment tribunal. In March 2025, the tribunal found the DSTL liable for an intimidating atmosphere resulting in the harassment of Wilkins, who had worked there for 15 years, and will be required to pay him damages.[10]

Gender Ideology

In April 2025, the British Supreme Court ruled that for the purposes of the Equalities Act of 2010, the term "women" meant biological sex and not self-identification. All of a sudden, the rules had changed. That same month, Professor Kathleen Stock was awarded £585,000 ($665,000) in damages from Sussex University by the Office for Students, the British regulating authority for higher education. The fine was for "failing to uphold free speech," and this landmark decision will cause other institutions to think carefully. Stock "was accused of transphobia for her views on sex and gender issues and left the university in 2021 after a three-year campaign of harassment," according to *The Times*.[11] British academics are as leftwing as their American counterparts, and instead of supporting her right to express views critical of gender ideology, her own local chapter of the University and College Union piled on and wanted her investigated for transphobia and alleged hate speech. As a sample of her allegedly transphobic language, she wrote in 2018: "It is perfectly possible to think the GC [gender critical] position fundamentally flawed without acting like there is a bad smell in the room when anyone raises it, and that its proponent must be a moral degenerate."

The same month that Stock won her case in the UK, the University of Louisville in Kentucky agreed to a $1.6 million settlement with Dr. Allan Josephson, who sued the college in 2019 alleging that he had been fired as chief of the child psychiatry department because he "openly dissented from the transgender orthodoxy that said gender dysphoria should be embraced, accepted and treated as normal and healthy by the medical community."[12]

Under the Biden Administration, the U.S. Department of Health and Human Services (HHS) had been reluctant to challenge the prevailing orthodoxy of the "gender-affirming care" model pushed by WPATH. But on May 1, 2025, under new Secretary Robert Kennedy, the HHS released a "Review of Evidence and Best Practices" on "Treatment for Pediatric Gender Dysphoria." After looking at 17 systematic reviews of evidence, the report "arguably offers the most comprehensive analysis of pediatric medical transition to date."[13] It essentially confirmed the conclusions of the United Kingdom's Cass Review that there was no solid evidence for promoting child-led "gender affirming care." The HHS report concluded that "the evidence for benefit of pediatric medical transition is very uncertain, while the evidence for harm is less uncertain." The report found "no independent association between gender dysphoria and suicidality," and "no evidence of adverse effects of psychotherapy" on children with gender dysphoria.[14] Despite this, the American Academy of Pediatrics (AAP) immediately issued a press release alleging that the HHS report itself was wrong. AAP's current position supporting "gender affirming care" was written in 2018 by junior pediatrician, Jason Rafferty, and has been criticized for putting ideology ahead of patient well-being. The AAP is now facing lawsuits by detransitioners alleging that its ideologically-inspired guidance harmed them by pushing irreversible medical transition over watchful waiting and counseling.[15]

In May 2025, 50 British academics and clinicians wrote an open letter titled "Biology is not binary" that criticized the U.K. Supreme Court's April 2025 ruling in *For Women Scotland v. The Scottish Ministers*. That ruling clarified for the purposes of Britain's 2010 Equality Act that the words "woman" and "sex" refer to biological sex, not gender identity. As Colin Wright from *Reality's Land Stand* writes, the authors of the letter seek "to conflate sexual dimorphism (physical and behavioral differences between males and females) with sex itself. But these are not the same thing. Sex-related traits exist on a continuum, but sex does not."[16] The British academics are still, in Wright's phrase, "substituting ideology for science" and "pretending that sex is a socially constructed fiction."[17] It is not.

Another blow to the transgender ideology came on June 18, 2025, when the Supreme Court held in *Skrmetti v. United States* that "Tennessee's law prohibiting certain medical treatments [specifically, 'gender affirming' drugs and surgery] for transgender minors" was not unconstitutional.[18] The decision was 6-3, and the dissents of the three left-leaning female justices are an ominous sign of gender ideology's imperviousness to reason and entrenched political power. Still, it provided needed clarity on what states can do to protect children from dangerous, experimental treatments founded on wishful thinking, not empirical evidence.

Boys in Girls' Sports

The national mood is starting to turn, as evidence continues to pile up, to public disgust, of boys competing and winning against girls in sports. In an early 2025 poll from Pew Research, 66% of Americans thought kids should compete according to their natal sex. In 2022, only 58% thought so. In June 2025, the *New York Post* ran an article with recent examples of boys beating girls: In Jurupa Valley, California, a male named AB Hernandez competed in the girls' high and triple jump high school championships and came first. In Long Island, New York, a "6-foot-tall, 14-year-old freshman trans athlete" [male] ran on the varsity track team. In Oregon, a "transgender junior" [male] named Ada Gallagher won a 400-meter race by more than seven seconds, a separation almost unheard of in same-sex races. In Washington State, transgender [male]high schooler Verónica Garcia won a state title in the 400-meter race. In San Francisco, a transgender [male] basketball player scored more than half the points for his team, which defeated their opponents 59-33. In West Virginia, freshman athlete Becky Pepper-Jackson, the first transgender [male] athlete to compete in the state's track championships, won a bronze medal. In Minnesota, the former state high school softball champions lost to a rival school whose transgender [male[pitcher threw 14 shutout innings.[19]

The more educated the public becomes on the subject, the less they want to allow boys to compete against girls. Yet for some in the media, it seems no evidence will ever change their minds. In June 2025, USA Today's sports columnist Nancy Armour was still claiming that the "transgender community…is already at an elevated risk for suicide and self-harm."[20] Armour seems impervious to the mounting evidence, writing that "There is no scientific evidence that transgender women athletes have a physical advantage over cisgender women athletes…"[21]

The Struggle Continues

Even after Kathleen Stock's legal victory, Sussex University managers called the court's decision "egregious and concocted."[22] The same month as Stock's victory, a British nurse was disciplined by the hospital where she worked for "misgendering" a male pedophile despite him having called her a "ni----r" at the time.[23]

Meanwhile in the U.S., Professor Jerry Coyne of the University of Chicago resigned from the Freedom from Religion Foundation because the atheist organization has "not only abandoned science but suppressed discussion and argument about its decision," he argued. In particular, he objected to an article in which the foundation concluded that a "woman is whoever she says she is." As Coyne wrote, the supposedly non-religious foundation had adopted the woke religion of gender ideology.[24]

In April 2024, *The Daily Wire*'s Lindquist wrote that the American Association of Medical Colleges (AAMC, see Chapter 2) was quietly working to resist changes to the Medical School Admission Test and other methods it has been using to lower standards for race-based recruitment.[25] Like many other organizations under threat of losing money and prestige due to the pushback against DEI, the AAMC seems to be hiding or re-wording the content, changing the labels but retaining the message. While it has edited or deleted public-facing web pages, the organization's leaders have told members that they remain committed to DEI and race-based outcomes for "social justice" and "equity."

In response to the Obama Administration's Department of Education's "Dear Colleague" letters, public schools had obsequiously lowered discipline standards under the "disparate impact" theory that if they suspended kids in response to their actions, and not in proportion to their race, they would lose federal funding. In response to a Trump Department of Education's letter in February 2025 asking schools to stop discriminating under DEI or lose funding, they resisted, retrenched, and sued. By the second quarter of 2025, in response to lawsuits by teachers' unions, the National Association for the Advancement of Colored People (NAACP), other groups, and federal judges in Maryland, New Hampshire, and Washington, DC, had issued orders to stop some of Trump's reforms to education, and injunctions preventing funding cuts.[26] As with other lawsuits trying to stop Trump from carrying out his policies as president, those against cutting DEI generally rely on dubious arguments, for instance that rule changes by his agencies were not done the right way under the Administrative Procedures Act, or that revoking funding for programs would harm people who relied on or expected it. In many cases, district court judges are ordering nationwide injunctions preventing the president and executive branch from acting, in an unprecedented and arguably unconstitutional usurpation of executive power.

Whatsoever Things Are True

The majority of Americans believe in equal treatment, not "equity" through discrimination. They understand that there are two sexes and that for some purposes women need protection and distinction from men. They want government to do what only it can and should do, leaving parents to raise their own children as they see fit.

Americans must reject the Ten Woke Commandments, but those who propose them will still be there, dreaming up more lunacy in the name of social justice. This summer of 2025, we celebrate the 250th anniversary of the "shot heard round the world" at Lexington and Concord that began the American Revolution and led to the establishment of the greatest, freest, and most prosperous nation in the world. Today, there is a brief clearing in the clouds above, but the battle for our nation's future never really ends. There are many fights yet to come, in which we must hold faithfully to "whatsoever things are true," and not only "think on these things," but defend them with all we have.

END

Endnotes

Chapter 1

[1] Alison Rauch, "Red pill and blue pill symbolism," Brittanica.com, last updated March 18, 2025, https://www.britannica.com/topic/red-pill-and-blue-pill (last accessed April 6, 2025).

[2] Batya Ungar-Sargon, *Bad News: How Woke Media Is Undermining Democracy* (New York: Encounter Books, 2021), p. 5.

[3] Ibid., p. 15.

[4] Jennifer Harper, "Inside the Beltway: Media bias against Trump is entrenched, vicious, persistent," *The Washington Times*, June 19, 2017, https://www.washingtontimes.com/news/2017/jun/29/inside-the-beltway-media-bias-against-trump-is-ent/ (last accessed April 6, 2025).

[5] Liz Collin, *They're Lying: The Media, the Left and the Death of George Floyd* (Minneapolis: Paper Birch Press, 2022).

[6] Wilfred Reilly, "You don't hate journalists enough..." X, October 12, 2024, https://x.com/wil_da_beast630/status/1845272256899055831?s=43&t=5L2 A9TU9MbM3M70tRUBwAA (last accessed April 6, 2025). Note: I sometimes use "tweet" as a verb in this book. There is no obvious verb to use for posts on the platform X, formerly known as Twitter.

[7] Ungar-Sargon, *Bad News*, p. 12.

[8] Sofia Bettiza, "Australian court rules in landmark case that asked 'what is a woman?'" BBC, August 22, 2024, https://www.bbc.com/news/articles/c07ev1v7r4po (last accessed April 6, 2025).

[9] Madison Ayers, "Unhinged Health 'Experts' Claim Men Can Breastfeed Too," *The Federalist*, February 26, 2024, https://thefederalist.com/2024/02/26/unhinged-health-experts-claim-men-can-breastfeed-too/#:~:text=The%20N HS%20trust%2C%20La%20Leche,primarily%20as%20a%20gastrointestin al%20drug (last accessed April 6, 2025).

[10] Frederick Attenborough, "School chaplain sacked and reported to terrorist watchdog for identity politics sermon begins appeal," Free Speech Union, February 20, 2024, https://freespeechunion.org/school-chaplain-sacked-and-reported-to-terrorist-watchdog-for-identity-politics-sermon-begins-appeal/ (last accessed April 6, 2025).

[11] Ibid.

[12] Drea Humphrey, "No jail time again despite fourth criminal conviction for 'trans activist' Jessica Simpson," *Rebel News*, December 21, 2023, https://www.rebelnews.com/no_jail_time_again_despite_4th_criminal_conv iction_for_trans_activist_jessica_simpson (last accessed April 6, 2025).

[13] Jackson Walter, "Police called on 50-year-old trans swimmer sharing locker room with young girls," ABC News, December 15, 2023, https://wpde.com/news/nation-world/police-called-on-50-year-old-trans-swimmer-sharing-locker-room-with-young-girls-toronto-sun-womens-sports-transgender-lgbtq-sports-athletics-fairness-riley-gaines-canada-ontario (last accessed April 6, 2025).

[14] The term "Generation X" was coined by Douglas Coupland in his 1991 novel of the same name.

[1] Eric Kaufmann, "Welcome to the Post-Progressive Political Era," The Wall Street Journal, May 14, 2025, https://www.wsj.com/opinion/welcome-to-the-post-progressive-political-era-history-culture-4ad308c1?st=STsRqG&reflink=article_email_share (last accessed May 16, 2025).

[2] Harald Bauder, "The Possibilities of Open and No Borders," *Social Justice*, Vol. 39, No. 4 (2012), pp. 76–96; David North, "Open Borders Advocates Dominate House Immigration Panels," Center for Immigration Studies, March 3, 2021, https://cis.org/North/Open-Borders-Advocates-Dominate-House-Immigration-Panels (last accessed April 6, 2025), and John Washington, "11 Arguments for Open Borders," *The Nation*, February 5, 2024, https://www.thenation.com/article/society/open-borders-immigration/ (last accessed April 6, 2025).

[3] Ciah Aksan and Jon Bailes, "What is the Left case for open borders?" Political Critique, February 13, 2019, https://politicalcritique.org/opinion/2019/left-case-open-borders/ (last accessed April 6, 2025).

[4] Sophia Porotsky, "Rotten to the Core: Racism, Xenophobia, and the Border and Immigration Agencies," *Georgetown Immigration Law Journal*, Vol. 36, No. 1 (2021), pp. 349–397.

[5] Hermione Lee, "A Wider Devotion," New York Review of Books, November 2, 2023, https://www.nybooks.com/articles/2023/11/02/a-wider-devotion-george-eliot/ (last accessed May 16, 2025).

[6] Simon Hankinson, "The BorderLine: No, President Biden, Walls Do Work. We Just Saw One More Reason We Need One," The Daily Signal, October 13, 2023, https://www.dailysignal.com/2023/10/13/borderline-president-biden-walls-do-work-we-saw-one-more-reason-we-need-one/ (last accessed May 16, 2025).

[7] Matthew J. Lindsay, "The Right to Migrate," *Lewis and Clark Law Review*, Vol. 27, No. 1 (2023), pp. 95–146.

[8] Greg Groogan, "Biden crackdown on border labeled both 'repressive' & 'too late,'" June 4, 2024, Fox 26 Houston, https://www.fox26houston.com/news/biden-crackdown-border-labeled-both-repressive-too-late (last accessed April 6, 2025), and Alessandra Testa, "Gazes of Race, Immigration, and Hegemony in *Io Sto Con La Sposa* (On the Bride's Side) and *Come Un Uomo*

Sulla Terra (Like a Man on the Earth)," *TCNJ Journal of Student Scholarship*, Vol. XIX (April 2017), pp. 1–9.

[9] Katie Bradbury, "I discovered my house is racist. Now what?" Twin Cities Public Television, May 19, 2023, https://www.tpt.org/post/discovered-house-racist-now/ (last accessed April 6, 2025), and Sara Clemence, "Is There Racism in the Deed to Your Home?" *The New York Times*, August 17, 2021, https://www.nytimes.com/2021/08/17/realestate/racism-home-deeds.html (last accessed April 6, 2025).

[10] Marin Cogan, "How cars fuel racial inequality," Vox, updated June 13, 2023, https://www.vox.com/23735896/racism-car-ownership-driving-violence-traffic-violations (last accessed April 6, 2025), and Theodore Kim, "AI flaws could make your next car racist," *Los Angeles Times*, October 7, 2021, https://www.latimes.com/opinion/story/2021-10-07/op-ed-ai-flaws-could-make-your-next-car-racist (last accessed April 6, 2025).

[11] "Is it OK for white people to have dreadlocks?" BBC, April 2, 2016, https://www.bbc.com/news/blogs-trending-35944803 (last accessed April 6, 2025), and Crunk Feminist Collective, "De-Tangling Racism: On White Women and Black Hair," October 16, 2013, https://www.crunkfeminist collective.com/2013/10/16/de-tangling-racism-on-white-women-and-black-hair/ (last accessed April 6, 2025).

[12] John Blake, "'Am I racist?' You may not like the answer," CNN, June 20, 2020, https://www.cnn.com/2020/06/20/us/racist-google-question-blake/index.html (last accessed April 6, 2025).

[13] Center for American Progress, "Project 2025 Would Destroy the U.S. System of Checks and Balances and Create an Imperial Presidency," October 1, 2024, https://www.americanprogress.org/article/project-2025-would-destroy-the-u-s-system-of-checks-and-balances-and-create-an-imperial-presidency/ (last accessed April 6, 2025), and Fred Wertheimer, "The GOP Is Abandoning the Rule of Law," Democracy 21, July 27, 2023, https://democracy21.org/news/freds-weekly-note/the-gop-is-abandoning-the-rule-of-law (accessed April 6, 2025).

[14] See the following source for a complete list of authors who have made the case for open borders. The open-border advocates listed are divided into libertarian, philosophical/religious, and utilitarian perspectives: Open Borders, "Pro-open borders people," https://openborders.info/pro-open-borders-people/ (last accessed April 6, 2025).

[15] Jarrett Stepman, "How 'Wokeness' Is a Product of Marxism," The Daily Signal, August 2, 2020, https://www.dailysignal.com/2020/08/02/how-wokeness-is-a-product-of-marxism/ (accessed April 6, 2025).

[16] Harold Henry Fisher, *The Communist Revolution: An Outline of Strategy and Tactics* (Stanford CA: Stanford University Press, 1955), p. 13.

[17] Transnational Institute, "Why We Need to Abolish Borders: Arun Kundnani in Conversation with Harsha Walia," April 12, 2023, podcast, https://www.tni.org/en/podcast/why-we-need-to-abolish-borders (last accessed April 6, 2025).

18 U.S. Customs and Border Protection, "Criminal Alien Statistics," for fiscal years 2017 to 2015, https://www.cbp.gov/newsroom/stats/cbp-enforcement-statistics/criminal-noncitizen-statistics (last accessed April 6, 2025).

19 United Nations, *Convention and Protocol Relating to the Status of Refugees*, 1951, https://www.unhcr.org/us/media/convention-and-protocol-relating-status-refugees (accessed March 17, 2025), and United Nations, *Protocol Relating to the Status of Refugees*, 1967, https://www.ohchr.org/en/instruments-mechanisms/instruments/protocol-relating-status-refugees (accessed March 17, 2025).

20 Lora Ries, "Should America Continue to Accept Asylum Seekers? No," *The Ripon Forum*, Vol. 57, No. 3 (June 2023), https://riponsociety.org/article/should-america-continue-to-accept-asylum-seekers-no-americas-refugee-policy-is-unrecognizable-and-it-is-time-to-course-correct/ (accessed March 17, 2025).

21 8 U.S. Code §1158

22 Simon Hankinson and Lora Ries, "The U.S. Must Redesign Asylum Law for 21st-Century Reality and Put America First," Heritage Foundation Special Report, March 31, 2025, https://www.heritage.org/border-security/report/the-us-must-redesign-asylum-law-21st-century-reality-and-put-america-first

23 See, for example, Ted Kim, "Updated Procedures for Determination of Initial Jurisdiction over Asylum Applications Filed by Unaccompanied Alien Children," U.S. Citizenship and Immigration Services, Memorandum to All Asylum Office Staff, May 28, 2013, https://www.uscis.gov/sites/default/files/document/foia/Legal_standards_governing_Asylum_claims_and_issues_related_to_the_adjudication_of_children.pdf (accessed March 18, 2025).

24 Mark Krikorian, "Time to Withdraw from the U.N. Refugee Treaty," Center for Immigration Studies, July 28, 2021, https://cis.org/Oped/Time-Withdraw-UN-Refugee-Treaty (last accessed May 19, 2025).

25 Richard J. Barnet and John Cavanagh, *Global Dreams: Imperial Corporations and the New World Order* (New York: Touchstone, 1994).

26 John R. Oneal et al., "The Liberal Peace: Interdependence, Democracy, and International Conflict, 1950–85," *Journal of Peace Research*, Vol. 33, No. 1 (February 1996), pp. 11–28.

27 David Biller, "Brazil's Lula pitches his nation—and himself—as fresh leader for Global South," Associated Press, September 19, 2023, https://apnews.com/article/brazil-lula-un-general-assembly-global-south-fafdca8216d5fe43e4be72ab85135501 (last accessed April 6, 2025).

28 Justin Akers Chacón and Mike Davis, *No One Is Illegal: Fighting Racism and State Violence on the U.S.-Mexico Border* (Chicago: Haymarket Books, 2006).

29 L. Darnell Weeden, "Undocumented Immigrant Residents Have a Limited Constitutional Right to a Limited Official Driver's License," *Howard Law Journal*, Vol. 66, No. 3 (Spring 2023), p. 643; Paul A. Reyes, "Why noncitizens should be allowed to vote," CNN, December 10, 2021, https://www.cnn.com/2021/12/10/opinions/new-york-city-noncitizen-

voting-smart-policy-reyes/index.html (last accessed April 6, 2025); Ileana Najarro, "Undocumented Students Have the Right to a Free Education. This Is Why," *Education Week*, November 15, 2024, https://www.edweek.org/policy-politics/undocumented-students-have-the-right-to-a-free-education-this-is-why/2024/11 (last accessed April 6, 2025), Melissa Marietta, "Undocumented Immigrants Should Receive Social Services," *International Social Science Review*, Vol. 81, No. 1/2 (2006), pp. 61–66; and Stephen Clibborn, "Why undocumented immigrant workers should have workplace rights," *The Economic and Labour Relations Review*, Vol. 26. No. 3 (2015), pp. 465–473.

30 Ron J. Anderson, "Why We Should Care for the Undocumented," *Virtual Mentor*, Vol. 10, No. 4 (2008), pp. 245–248; Christina Coulter, "Illegal immigrant with $1M worth of drugs, guns given free housing courtesy of blue state taxpayers: officials," Fox News, January 13, 2025, https://www.foxnews.com/us/illegal-immigrant-1m-worth-drugs-guns-given-free-housing-courtesy-blue-state-taxpayers-officials (last accessed April 6, 2025); Tara Sonenshine, "After more than 40 years, the federal right to free education for immigrant students finds itself in the crosshairs of conservatives," The Conversation, July 18, 2024, https://theconversation.com/after-more-than-40-years-the-federal-right-to-free-education-for-immigrant-students-finds-itself-in-the-crosshairs-of-conservatives-231360 (last accessed April 6, 2025); and Sophie Therber, "Undocumented Latino Immigrants: A Unique Challenge in UN Agencies' Realization of the Right to Food," *The Internationalist: Undergraduate Journal of Foreign Affairs*, Vol. V, No. II (Spring 2021), pp. 42–52.

31 Thomas Hobbes, *Leviathan* (J. C. A. Gaskin, Ed.), Oxford University Press, England, 2008.

32 Insa Breyer and Speranta Dumitru, "Les sans-papiers et leur droit d'avoir des droits" (Undocumented immigrants have the right to have rights), *Raison Politique*, Vol. 2. No. 26 (2007), pp. 125–147, translated from French by JPD Systems, https://shs.cairn.info/article/E_RAI_026_0125?lang=en (last accessed April 6, 2025).

33 Jon Guttman, "Why Was New Jersey Suffrage Taken Away?" HistoryNet.com November 13, 2018, https://www.historynet.com/new-jersey-suffrage-taken-away/ (last accessed April 6, 2025).

34 Jeremy Odrich and Jim Kessler, "Is Illegal Immigration Really a Democratic Plot to Sway Congressional Apportionment?" Third Way, July 10, 2024, https://www.thirdway.org/memo/is illegal immigration-really-a-democratic-plot-to-sway-congressional-apportionment (last accessed April 6, 2025).

35 Ballotpedia, "Laws permitting noncitizens to vote in the United States," undated, https://ballotpedia.org/Laws_permitting_noncitizens_to_vote_in_the_United_States (last accessed April 6, 2025).

36 Kyler Yoder, April Tan, and Stefan Martinez-Ruiz, "The Expansion of Voting Before Election Day, 2000–2024," The Center for Election Innovation &

Research, July 2024, https://electioninnovation.org/research/expansion-voting-before-election-day/ (last accessed April 6, 2025).

[37] H. Rept. 104-828, Illegal Immigration Reform and Immigrant Responsibility Act of 1996, 104th Congr. (1995–1996), https://www.congress.gov/congressional-report/104th-congress/house-report/828/1 (last accessed May 18, 2025).

[38] Dara Lind, "Obama flip-flopped on the legality of immigration action. Which time was he right?" Vox, December 2, 2014, https://www.vox.com/2014/12/2/7321607/obama-immigration-flip-flop (last accessed May 17, 2025).

Chapter 2

[1] In the campus radical context, it means that traditionally core courses and sources in universities on Western civilization, from history to art, should be replaced by courses and works centered around and by women, non-whites, and sexual minorities. Dead white men out, BIPOC queers, in – a one-for-one swap, with quality examined and irrelevant.

[2] "Columbia University Apartheid Divest: Who we are," *Columbia Spectator*, November 14, 2023, https://www.columbiaspectator.com/opinion/2023/11/14/columbia-university-apartheid-divest-who-we-are/ (last accessed May 1, 2025).

[3] World Economic Forum, Education and Skills, "This is how much the global literacy rate grew over 200 years," September 12, 2022, https://www.weforum.org/stories/2022/09/reading-writing-global-literacy-rate-changed/, (accessed May 6, 2025).

[4] Sarah Schwartz, "Reading Scores Fall to New Low on NAEP, Fueled by Declines for Struggling Students, *Education Week*, January 29, 2025, https://www.edweek.org/leadership/reading-scores-fall-to-new-low-on-naep-fueled-by-declines-for-struggling-students/2025/01 (last accessed May 1, 2025).

[5] Karol Markowicz, "A New York teacher exposes our state school-system sham—where guessing gets you a pass," *New York Post*, August 21, 2022, https://nypost.com/2022/08/21/a-new-york-teacher-exposes-our-state-school-system-sham/ (last accessed May 1, 2025).

[6] Merrill Balassone, "California Supreme Court Lowers Bar Exam Passing Score," California Courts Newsroom, July 16, 2025, https://newsroom.courts.ca.gov/news/california-supreme-court-lowers-bar-exam-passing-score (last accessed May 1, 2025).

[7] "Understanding Equitable Grading Jargon," Resources, Critical Race Theory & Equity, Defending Education, https://defendinged.org/resources/understanding-equitable-grading-jargon/ (last accessed May 13, 2025).

[8] Matt Barnum, "As 'Grading for Equity' Movement Grows, More Teachers Are Pushing Back," The Wall Street Journal, May 11, 2025, https://www.wsj.com

/us-news/education/grading-for-equity-schools-teaching-b301df23?st=ehh JVW&reflink=article_email_share (accessed May 13, 2025).

9 Ibid.

10 Ibid.

11 Matthew Xiao, "DEI Strikes Back: San Francisco Rolls Out 'Grading for Equity' Program in Schools," Washington Free Beacon, May 28, 2025, https://freebeacon.com/latest-news/dei-strikes-back-san-francisco-rolls-out-grading-for-equity-program-in-schools/ (last accessed June 23, 2025).

12 Derek Thompson, X, Mary 28, 2025, https://x.com/DKThomp/status/1927700160337117617 (last accessed June 23, 2025).

13 Will Dobbie and Roland G. Fryer, Jr., "Getting Beneath the Veil of Effective Schools: Evidence from New York City, Harvard University, EdLabs, and NBER, December 2012, https://scholar.harvard.edu/files/fryer/files/dobbie_fryer_revision_final.pdf (last accessed May 1, 2025).

14 Defending Education, "San Francisco Unified School District provides resource to social studies and ethnic studies teachers that claims 'Israeli terrorism has been significantly worse than that of the Palestinians'; resource defends terrorism against Israel, " January 9, 2024, https://defendinged.org/incidents/san-francisco-unified-school-district-provides-resource-to-social-studies-and-ethnic-studies-teachers-that-claims-israeli-terrorism-has-been-significantly-worse-than-that-of-the-palestinians-reso/ (last accessed May 1, 2025).

15 Defending Education, "Stafford Middle School chooses to represent 'Palestine' at districtwide fair, ignoring the existence of Israel," November 29, 2023, https://defendinged.org/incidents/stafford-middle-school-chooses-to-represent-palestine-at-districtwide-fair-ignoring-the-existence-of-israel/ (last accessed May 1, 2025).

16 Black, Indigenous, People of Color

17 Allyson Tintiangco-Cubales, Anita Fernández, Artnelson Concordia, Brian Lozenski, Carlos EC Hagedorn, Jody Sokolower, Lara Kiswani, Lisa Covington, Valerie A. Martínez, "Fight for Ethnic Studies Moves to K-12 Classrooms," Convergence, September 19, 2022, https://convergencemag.com/articles/fight-for-ethnic-studies-moves-to-k-12-classrooms/ (last accessed May 14, 2025).

18 Kayla Bartsch, "Ethnic Studies Activists Infiltrate California Curriculum, Allies Shame Jewish Parents Who Object," National Review, April 28, 2025, https://www.nationalreview.com/2025/04/ethnic-studies-activists-infiltrate-california-curriculum-allies-shame-jewish-parents-who-object/ (last accessed May 14, 2025).

19 Tintiangco-Cubales et al, "Fight for Ethnic Studies Moves to K-12 Classrooms," Ibid.

20 Kayla Bartsch, "Ethnic Studies Activists Infiltrate California Curriculum, Allies Shame Jewish Parents Who Object," Ibid.

21 Pennsylvania Department of Education, "Culturally-Relevant and Sustaining Education (CR-SE) Program Framework Guidelines," November 2022,

https://www.pa.gov/content/dam/copapwp-
pagov/en/education/documents/educators/certification-preparation-
programs/framework-guidelines-and-rubrics/culturally-
relevant%20and%20sustaining%20education%20program%20framework%
20guidelines.pdf (last accessed June 23, 2025).

22 Neetu Arnold, "The Pennsylvania School Board Undoing Critical Race Theory," *City Journal*, May 21, 2025, https://www.city-journal.org/article/southern-york-county-pennsylvania-school-board-critical-race-theory

23 Ibid

24 Jessica Costescu, "San Francisco's $30,000 'Equity-Centered' School Closure Plan—Put on Hold After Parent Uproar," The *Washington Free Beacon*, December 4, 2024, https://freebeacon.com/california/san-franciscos-30000-equity-centered-school-closure-plan-put-on-hold-after-parent-uproar-used-dei-formulas-to-target-high-performing-majority-asian-sc/ (last accessed May 1, 2025).

25 Ibid.

26 Ibid.

27 Snejana Farberov, "Minneapolis school district defends plan to lay off white teachers first," *New York Post*, August 17, 2022, https://nypost.com/2022/08/17/minneapolis-schools-defend-plan-to-ax-white-teachers-first/ (last accessed May 1, 2025).

28 Ibid.

2929 "Race language in Minneapolis teacher contracts ignites firestorm," NBC News, August 22, 2022, https://www.nbcnews.com/news/nbcblk/minneapolis-teacher-contract-race-language-ignites-firestorm-rcna44274 (last accessed May 1, 2025).

30 Kelsey Koberg, "Teachers union agreement stipulating White teachers be laid off first criticized: 'Constitutionally suspect,'" August 16, 2022, https://www.foxnews.com/media/teachers-union-agreement-stipulating-white-teachers-laid-off-first-criticized-constitutionally-suspect (last accessed May 1, 2025).

31 Corey Walker, "NJ Teachers Union Calls For Ending Basic Skills Test Requirement," The Daily Caller, November 12, 2023, https://dailycaller.com/2023/11/12/new-jersey-teachers-union-calls-end-basic-skills-test-requirement/ (last accessed May 13, 2025).

32 Jonathan Butcher, "Teachers' unions bent the Education Dept. to their will—shut it down to throttle their power," *New York Post*, March 11, 2025, https://nypost.com/2025/03/11/opinion/how-teachers-unions-bent-the-education-dept-to-their-will/ (last accessed May 1, 2025).

33 Influence Watch, "Randi Weingarten," https://www.influencewatch.org/person/randi-weingarten/#:~:text=Weingarten%20earns%20an%20annual%20salary,and%20cars%20for%20union%20executives (last accessed March 24, 2025).

34 Tom Howell, Jr., "AFT's Weingarten defends teachers union's influence over CDC school guidance on COVID lockdowns," *The Washington Times,* April

26, 2023, https://www.washingtontimes.com/news/2023/apr/26/afts-randi-weingarten-defends-teacher-unions-influ/

[35] Press Release, "Weingarten Sets Pandemic Record Straight as Republican Attacks Fall Flat," American Federation of Teachers, April 26, 2023, https://www.aft.org/press-release/weingarten-sets-pandemic-record-straight-republican-attacks-fall-flat (last accessed May 1, 2025).

[36] Anthony Fisher, "Why Do We Have a Department of Education? Jimmy Carter's Debt to a Teachers Union," *Reason*, February 7, 2017, https://reason.com/2017/02/07/department-of-education-jimmy-carter/ (last accessed May 1, 2025).

[37] Butcher, "Teachers' unions bent the Education Dept. to their will."

[38] Alex Oliveira, "Damning nationwide test shows US kids' reading levels plummeted to lowest level in 32-year history—and Republicans are blaming 'woke' education," *New York Post*, January 29, 2025, https://nypost.com/2025/01/29/us-news/heartbreaking-test-score-shows-us-children-falling-behind-on-reading-math-and-some-gop-members-are-blaming-biden/ (last accessed May 1, 2025).

[39] Butcher, "Teachers' unions bent the Education Dept. to their will."

[40] Ibid.

[41] National Association for the Advancement of Colored People, https://naacp.org/ (last accessed May 1, 2025).

[42] American Federation of State, County, and Municipal Employees, https://www.afscme.org/ (last accessed May 1, 2025).

[43] Breccan F. Thies, "America's Largest Teachers Union Sues to Keep 'Stranglehold' on Failed Education Deep State," *The Federalist*, March 24, 2025, https://thefederalist.com/2025/03/24/americas-largest-teachers-union-sues-to-keep-stranglehold-on-failed-education-deep-state/?utm_source=rss&utm_medium=rss&utm_campaign=americas-largest-teachers-union-sues-to-keep-stranglehold-on-failed-education-deep-state&utm_term=2025-03-25 (last accessed May 1, 2025).

[44] Ibid.

[45] Ryan Quinn, "Faculty Overwhelmingly Back Harris in November. But They Won't Tell Students to Do the Same," Inside Higher Ed, October 21, 2024, https://www.insidehighered.com/news/faculty-issues/2024/10/21/faculty-heavily-back-harris-they-wont-tell-students?utm_source=Inside+Higher+Ed&utm_campaign=1b5ccd8920-DNU_2021_COPY_02&utm_medium=email&utm_term=0_1fcbc04421-1b5ccd8920-238015786&mc_cid=1b5ccd8920&mceid=f1ec0a0f26 (last accessed May 1, 2025).

[46] "74 percent of college students would report professors for saying something offensive: survey," The College Fix, July 21, 2023, https://www.thecollegefix.com/74-percent-of-college-students-would-report-professors-for-saying-something-offensive-survey/ (last accessed May 1, 2025).

[47] Lauren Noble, Letter to the Editor, Wall Street Journal, January 24, 2023, https://www.wsj.com/articles/college-students-free-compelled-speech-diversity-statement-11674538908 (last accessed May 13, 2025).

[48] Santi Tafarella, "DEI Invades Community Colleges," *The Wall Street Journal*, February 21, 2024, https://www.wsj.com/articles/dei-invades-community-colleges-too-los-angeles-county-free-inquiry-indoctrination-19058b34 (last accessed May 1, 2025).

[49] Margaret Peppiatt, "DEI in scientific publications up 4,200 percent between 2010 and 2021: study," The College Fix, December 23, 2022, https://www.the collegefix.com/dei-in-scientific-publications-up-4200-percent-between-2010-and-2021-study/ (last accessed May 1, 2025).

[50] Ibid.

[51] Nick Anderson, "Using race in college admissions protected by First Amendment, groups say," *The Washington Post*, August 1, 2022, https://www.washingtonpost.com/education/2022/08/01/supreme-court-college-admissions-race-first-amendment/ (last accessed May 10, 2025).

[52] Supreme Court of the United States, Students for Fair Admission, Inc. v. President and Fellows of Harvard College, No. 20–1199. Argued October 31, 2022—Decided June 29, 2023 (Together with No. 21–707, Students for Fair Admissions, Inc. v. University of North Carolina et al., on certiorari before judgment to the United States Court of Appeals for the Fourth Circuit) https://www.supremecourt.gov/opinions/22pdf/20-1199_hgdj.pdf (accessed May 10, 2025).

[53] Mark J. Perry, "New Chart Illustrates Graphically the Racial Preferences for Blacks, Hispanics Being Admitted to US Medical Schools," American Enterprise Institute, June 25, 2017, https://www.aei.org/carpe-diem/new-chart-illustrates-graphically-racial-preferences-for-blacks-and-hispanics-being-admitted-to-us-medical-schools/ (last accessed May 10, 2025).

[54] Eugene Robinson, "Ketanji Brown Jackson asks the right question about affirmative action," *The Washington Post*, October 31, 2022, https://www.washingtonpost.com/opinions/2022/10/31/ketanji-brown-jackson-legacies-affirmative-action/ (last accessed May 10, 2025).

[55] Roland G. Fryer, "Affirmative action in college admissions doesn't work—but it could," *The Washington Post*, October 30, 2022, https://www.washington post.com/opinions/2022/10/30/affirmative-action-supreme-court-college-admissions/ (last accessed May 10, 2025).

[56] Ibid.

[57] Chisom Michael, "Top 10 African migrant communities thriving financially in the US," *Business Day*, January 6, 2025, https://businessday.ng/news/article/top-10-african-migrant-communities-thriving-financially-in-the-us/ (last accessed May 17, 2025).

[58] Tunku Varadarajan, "The Long View of Higher Ed's Decline," *The Wall Street Journal*, May 31, 2024, https://www.wsj.com/opinion/the-long-view-of-higher-eds-decline-college-university-professor-conservative-harvard-96bb 22a5 (last accessed May 1, 2025).

[59] "Grade Inflation at Harvard: What Does It Mean for Academic Rigor?" *The Harvard Crimson*, November 8, 2024, https://www.crimsoneducation.org/us/blog/grade-inflation-at-harvard:/ (last accessed May 1, 2025).

[60] Varadarajan, "The Long View of Higher Ed's Decline."

[61] Rachel Poser, "He Wants to Save Classics from Whiteness. Can the Field Survive?" *The New York Times*, February 2, 2021, https://www.nytimes.com/2021/02/02/magazine/classics-greece-rome-whiteness.html (last accessed May 1, 2025).

[62] Simon Hankinson, "The Ideological Roots of the Open Borders Push: The BorderLine," The Daily Signal, May 2, 2024, https://www.dailysignal.com/2024/05/02/ideological-roots-open-borders-push-borderline/ (last accessed May 1, 2025).

[63] "Notable & Quotable: Tearing Down Princeton," *The Washington Post*, September 6, 2021

[64] Louis Galarowicz, "Indoctrinate" New Hires," *City Journal*, June 3, 2024, https://www.city-journal.org/article/indoctrinate-new-hires (last accessed May 1, 2025).

[65] Ibid.

[66] Colin Wright, "'Positionality Statements' Undermine Scientific Integrity," Reality's Last Stand, March 27, 2025, https://www.realityslaststand.com/p/positionality-statements-undermine (last accessed May 1, 2025).

[67] Jay P. Greene, "The Professor Racket: How Universities Could Reduce Poor Teaching and Shoddy Research," Heritage Foundation Backgrounder No. 3901, March 24, 2025, https://www.heritage.org/education/report/the-professor-racket-how-universities-could-reduce-poor-teaching-and-shoddy (last accessed May 1, 2025).

[68] Dimitrije Curcic, "Number of Academic Papers Published Per Year," WordsRated, June 1, 2023, https://wordsrated.com/number-of-academic-papers-published-per-year/ (last accessed March 14, 2025), cited in ibid.

[69] Lokman I. Meho, "The Rise and Rise of Citation Analysis," *Physics World*, Vol. 20, No. 1 (January 2007), https://www.researchgate.net/publication/28805884_The_rise_and_rise_of_citation_analysis (last accessed March 14, 2025), cited in Greene, "The Professor Racket."

[70] Greene, "The Professor Racket."

[71] Ibid.

[72] Christopher F. Rufo, "Plagiarism and Disparities," Christopherrufo.com, July 11, 2024, https://christopherrufo.com/p/plagiarism-and-disparities (last accessed May 1, 2025).

[73] *The Washington Free Beacon*, https://freebeacon.com/wp-content/uploads/2024/10/Jackson_complaint.pdf

[74] Aaron Sibarium, "'A Mockery of Education': Dean of Michigan State's Top-Ranked Ed School Is a Serial Plagiarist, Complaint Alleges," *The Washington Free Beacon*, October 8, 2024, https://freebeacon.com/campus/a-mockery-of-education-dean-of-michigan-states-top-ranked-ed-school-is-a-serial-plagiarist-complaint-alleges/ (last accessed May 3, 2025).

[75] Owen McCarthy, "MSU: Dean accused of plagiarism, targeted by DEI opponents, 'exonerated,'" *The State News*, January 23, 2025, https://state

news.com/article/2025/01/msu-dean-accused-of-plagiarism-targeted-by-dei-opponents-exonerated (last accessed May 3, 2025).

[76] Christopher F. Rufo, "Kamala Harris's Plagiarism Problem, Christopherrufo.com, October 14, 2024, https://christopherrufo.com/p/kamala-harriss-plagiarism-problem?utm_source=substack&utm_medium=email (last accessed May 3, 2025).

[77] Ibid.

[78] Jonathan Turley, "Is Kamala Harris a plagiarist?" *The Hill*, October 16, 2024, https://thehill.com/opinion/campaign/4935406-is-kamala-harris-a-plagiarizer/ (last accessed May 3, 2025).

[7979] Jack Izzo, "What We Know About Plagiarism Allegations Against Harris," Snopes.com, October 26, 2024, https://www.snopes.com/news/2024/10/26/harris-plagiarism-book/ (last accessed May 3, 2025).

[80] Phillip W. Magness and David Waugh, "The Hyperpoliticization of Higher Ed:Trends in Faculty Political Ideology, 1969–Present," *The Independent Review*, Vol. 27, No. 3 (Winter 2022/23), https://www.independent.org/publications/tir/article.asp?id=1782 (last accessed May 3, 2025).

[81] Ibid.

[82] Ibid.

[83] U.S. House of Representatives, Committee on Education and the Workforce, Hearing on "Holding Campus Leaders Accountable and Confronting Antisemitism," December 5, 2023, video, https://www.youtube.com/watch?v=3J0Nu9BN5Qk (last accessed May 17, 2025).

[84] Carol Swain, "Claudine Gay and My Scholarship," *The Wall Street Journal*, December 17, 2023, https://www.wsj.com/articles/claudine-gay-and-my-scholarship-plagiarism-elite-system-unearned-position-24e4a1b1 (last accessed January 17, 2024).

[85] Christopher F. Rufo, "'A White Male Would Probably Already Be Gone': Former Vanderbilt professor Carol Swain discusses the situation of Harvard president Claudine Gay," *City Journal*, December 11, 2023, https://www.city-journal.org/article/white-male-would-probably-already-be-gone (last accessed May 3, 2025).

[86] Harvard Corporation, "Statement from the Harvard Corporation: Our President," December 12, 2023, https://www.harvard.edu/2023/12/12/statement-from-the-harvard-corporation-our-president/ (last accessed May 3, 2025).

[87] "Has Claudine Gay Wrecked Harvard?" *The Spectator*, Americano Podcast, January 5, 2024, https://www.spectator.co.uk/podcasts/americano/ (last accessed May 11, 2025).

[88] Emily Crane, "Harvard won't condemn Claudine Gay because she's a 'high pedigree' minority, professor says," *New York Post*, December 18, 2023, https://nypost.com/2023/12/18/news/professor-says-harvard-wont-condemn-claudine-gay-because-shes-a-high-pedigree-minority/ (last accessed May 11, 2025).

[89] Harvard Kennedy School, Shorenstein Center, About us, "Diversity, Inclusion and Belonging," https://shorensteincenter.org/about-us/diversity-inclusion-belonging-shorenstein/ (last accessed May 6, 2025).

[90] "America Gets a Harvard Education," *The Wall Street Journal*, December 12, 2023, https://www.wsj.com/articles/harvard-claudine-gay-congress-testimony-antisemitism-plagiarism-496a685b (last accessed May 3, 2025).

[91] "Harvard Canceled Its Best Black Professor. Why?" Real Clear Investigations, March 13, 2022, https://www.realclearinvestigations.com/video/2022/03/13/harvard_canceled_its_best_black_professor_why_good_kid_productions_821461.html# (last accessed May 3, 2025).

[92] Foundation for Individual Rights and Expression, "2025 College Free Speech Rankings," https://www.thefire.org/research-learn/2025-college-free-speech-rankings (last accessed March 26, 2025).

[93] Andrew Sullivan, "The Day The Empress' Clothes Fell Off," The Weekly Dish, https://andrewsullivan.substack.com/p/the-day-the-empress-clothes-fell-ffa?r=p2aj0&utm_medium=ios&utm_campaign=post (last accessed May 7, 2025).

[94] Christopher F. Rufo and Ryan Thorpe, "Harvard Researcher: the University Is "Totally Corrupted," *City Journal*, May 20, 2025, https://www.city-journal.org/article/harvard-university-left-bias-trump-omar-sultan-haque (last accessed June 9, 2025).

[95] Abigail Anthony, "Princeton Faculty, Students Release Letters Supporting Arrested Pro-Palestinian Protesters," *National Review*, May 2, 2024, https://www.nationalreview.com/news/princeton-faculty-students-release-letters-supporting-arrested-pro-palestinian-protesters/ (last accessed March 26, 2025).

[96] Michael Stratford, "Education Department investigates Princeton for admitting 'systemic racism' on campus," *Politico*, September 17, 2020, https://www.politico.com/news/2020/09/17/education-department-investigates-princeton-for-systemic-racism-417454 (last accessed March 26, 2025).

[97] Christopher F. Rufo and Ryan Thorpe, "Princeton's War on Civil Rights," Christopherrufo.com, April 24, 2025, https://christopherrufo.com/p/princetons-war-on-civil-rights?publication_id=1248321&post_id=161973038&isFreemail=true&r=j8y2f&triedRedirect=true&utm_source=substack&utm_medium=email (last accessed March 26, 2025).

[98] Ibid.

[99] Joshua T. Katz, "Princeton Fed Me to the Cancel Culture Mob," *The Wall Street Journal*, May 24, 2022, https://www.wsj.com/opinion/joshua-katz-princeton-campus-cancel-culture-woke-mob-11653350161?st=s5ewfm122ogmcdr (last accessed May 3, 2025).

[100] Anemona Hartocollis, "Princeton Fires Tenured Professor in Campus Controversy," *The New York Times*, May 23, 2022, https://www.nytimes.com/2022/05/23/us/princeton-fires-joshua-katz.html

[101] Brian Caplan, "Let's Talk About Josh Katz," *Bet on It*, August 24, 2022, https://www.betonit.ai/p/reflections-on-katz-witch-trial

[102] Glenn Loury, "The Truth about Roland Fryer," The Glenn Show, March 13, 2022, https://glennloury.substack.com/p/the-truth-about-roland-fryer (last accessed May 3, 2025).

[103] The White House, "President Bush Addresses NAACP Annual Convention," Archive, July 20, 2006, https://georgewbush-whitehouse.archives.gov/news/releases/2006/07/20060720.html (last accessed May 3, 2025).

[104] Rob Montz, "Harvard Canceled Its Best Black Professor. Why?" Good Kid Productions, YouTube, https://www.youtube.com/watch?v=m8xWOlk3WIw (last accessed May 3, 2025).

[105] Loury, "The Truth about Roland Fryer."

[106] Sara Wilder, "Amid $14 million in budget cuts, UNH closes art museum, keeps DEI administrators," The College Fix, February 13, 2024, https://www.thecollegefix.com/amid-14-million-in-budget-cuts-unh-closes-art-museum-keeps-dei-administrators/ (last accessed May 3, 2025).

[107] John D. Sailer, "Will the University of Michigan Abolish DEI?" *City Journal*, November 22, 2024, https://www.city-journal.org/article/will-the-university-of-michigan-abolish-dei (last accessed May 3, 2025).

[108] Mark J. Perry, X, January 9, 2024, https://x.com/Mark_J_Perry/ status/174476 9560471900178 (last accessed May 3, 2025).

[109] Nicholas Confessore, "The University of Michigan Doubled Down on D.E.I. What Went Wrong?" *The New York Times*, October 16, 2024, https://www.nytimes.com/2024/10/16/magazine/dei-university-michigan.html (last accessed May 3, 2025).

[110] Ibid.

[111] Ibid.

[112] Ibid.

[113] Ibid.

[114] "UNC Takes on the University Echo Chamber," *The Wall Street Journal*, January 26, 2023, https://www.wsj.com/articles/university-of-north-carolina-school-of-civic-life-and-leadership-board-of-trustees-11674773696 (last accessed May 3, 2025).

[115] John Sailer, @JohnDSailer, X, January 18, 2023, https://x.com/JohnDSailer/status/1615735612182519809?s=20

[116] Anemona Hartocollis, "M.I.T. Will No Longer Require Diversity Statements for Hiring Faculty," *The New York Times*, May 6, 2024, https://www.nytimes.com/2024/05/06/us/mit-diversity-statements-faculty-hiring.html (last accessed May 3, 2025).

[117] Alan Blinder and Jennifer Schuessler, "Harvard's Largest Faculty Division Will No Longer Require Diversity Statements," *The New York Times*, June 3, 2024, https://www.nytimes.com/2024/06/03/us/harvard-diversity-statements.html (last accessed May 3, 2025).

[118] American Bar Association, "Consumer FAQs," https://www.americanbar.org/groups/professional_responsibility/resources/resources_for_the_public/consumer_faqs/ (accessed April 25, 2025).

119 John Sailer, "How One Medical Board Is Injecting DEI Into All Aspects of Medical Education," *The Washington Free Beacon*, July 30, 2022, https://freebeacon.com/campus/how-one-medical-board-is-injecting-dei-into-all-aspects-of-medical-education/ (last accessed May 4, 2025).

120 Aaron With, "Forcing Lawyers To Join Leftist Bar Associations Violates Basic First Amendment Freedoms," The Federalist, May 26, 2025, https://the federalist.com/2025/05/26/forcing-lawyers-to-join-leftist-bar-associations-violates-basic-first-amendment-freedoms/?utm_source=rss&utm_medium=rss&utm_campaign=forcing-lawyers-to-join-leftist-bar-associations-violates-basic-first-amendment-freedoms&utm_term=2025-05-27 (last accessed June 24, 2025).

121 Ibid.

122 Barton Swaim, "'Lawless' Review: The Rule of Radicals," *The Wall Street Journal*, March 10, 2025, https://www.wsj.com/us-news/education/lawless-review-the-rule-of-radicals-3993b35c?st=k7LHjX&reflink=article_email_share (last accessed May 4, 2025).

123 Ibid.

124 Ibid.

125 Movement Law Lab, About Movement Lawyering, "What is Movement Lawyering," https://www.movementlawlab.org/about/movement-lawyering (last accessed March 18, 2025).

126 Terry Schilling, "The Leftist American Medical Association Created A Federally-Funded Cash Cow That Fuels Their Woke Agenda," *The Federalist*, April 17, 2025, https://thefederalist.com/2025/04/17/how-the-amas-federally-funded-cash-cow-fuels-their-woke-agenda/?utm_source=rss&utm_medium=rss&utm_campaign=how-the-amas-federally-funded-cash-cow-fuels-their-woke-agenda&utm_term=2025-04-17 (last accessed May 4, 2025).

127 Robert Schmad, "Medical Schools Must Go Woke, Accreditor Declares," *The Washington Free Beacon*, July 29, 2022, https://freebeacon.com/campus/medical-schools-must-go-woke-accreditor-declares/ (last accessed May 4, 2025).

128 Ibid.

129 Ibid.

130 Sailer, "How One Medical Board Is Injecting DEI Into All Aspects of Medical Education."

131 Georgetown University, "Social Medicine & Health Equity Track," https://medstargme.net/smhe/ (last accessed March 26, 2025).

132 Sailer, "How One Medical Board Is Injecting DEI Into All Aspects of Medical Education."

133 Ibid.

134 Aaron Sibarium, "Report Reveals Just How Much the DEI Complex Has Infiltrated Medical Education," *The Washington Free Beacon*, November 21, 2022, https://freebeacon.com/campus/report-reveals-just-how-much-the-dei-complex-has-infiltrated-medical-education/ (last accessed May 4, 2025).

[135] Ibid.

[136] Ibid.

[137] Ibid.

[138] Lauren Weber, Caitlin Gilbert, and Taylor Lorenz, "Documents show how conservative doctors influenced abortion, trans rights," *The Washington Post*, June 15, 2023, https://www.washingtonpost.com/health/2023/06/15/abortion -transgender-christian-doctors/ (last accessed May 4, 2025).

[139] Sailer, "How One Medical Board Is Injecting DEI Into All Aspects of Medical Education."

[140] National Association of Independent Schools, "NAIS Vision, Mission, and Values," https://www.nais.org/about/vision-mission-values/ (last accessed March 27, 2025).

[141] National Association of Independent Schools, "2025 NAIS People of Color Conference," https://www.nais.org/pocc/ (last accessed March 27, 2025).

[142] National Association of Independent Schools, "NAIS Resource Guide: Inclusion and Belonging," https://www.nais.org/learn/resource-guides/inclusion-and-belonging/ (last accessed March 27, 2025)

[143] Hans von Spakovsky, "Despite Trump Order, Another Bureaucrat Stubbornly Clings to Power," The Daily Signal, March 25, 2025, https://www.daily signal.com/2025/03/25/the-beltway-circus-rolls-on-at-u-s-commission-on-civil-rights/ (last accessed May 4, 2025).

[144] Ibid.

[145] American Civil Liberties Union, "Fight for Immigrants' Rights," https://www.aclu.org/issues/immigrants-rights, (last accessed March 25, 2025).

[146] Von Spakovsky, "Despite Trump Order, Another Bureaucrat Stubbornly Clings to Power."

[147] Neetu Arnold, "DEI Corrupts Education Research," *City Journal*, November 25, 2024, https://www.city-journal.org/article/dei-corrupts-education-research (las accessed May 18, 2025).

[148] Ibid.

[149] Kristen Holmes, Kaitlan Collins, and John Towfighi, "Trump names Linda McMahon as his pick for Education," CNN, November 20, 2024, https://www.cnn.com/2024/11/19/politics/linda-mcmahon-education-secretary-trump/index.html (last accessed May 4, 2025).

[150] The White House, "Fact Sheet: President Donald J. Trump Empowers Parents, States, and Communities to Improve Education Outcomes," March 20, 2025, https://www.whitehouse.gov/fact-sheets/2025/03/fact-sheet-president-donald-j-trump-empowers-parents-states-and-communities-to-improve-education-outcomes/ (last accessed May 4, 2025).

[151] M. Anthony Mills, Tyranny Without A Tyrant, *National Review*, May 2025

[152] Christopher F. Rufo, "How DEI Corrupted the NIH," *City Journal*, October 24, 2024, https://www.city-journal.org/article/how-dei-corrupted-the-nih (last accessed May 4, 2025).

[153] Ibid.

154 Jessie Hellmann, "Trump cancels NIH grants on equity research," *Roll Call*, March 24, 2025, https://rollcall.com/2025/03/24/trump-cancels-nih-grants-on-equity-research/ (last accessed May 4, 2025).

155 Rufo, "How DEI Corrupted the NIH."

156 Ibid.

157 Ibid.

158 The Great Barrington Declaration, https://gbdeclaration.org/#read (last accessed March 26, 2025).

159 "How Fauci and Collins Shut Down Covid Debate," *The Wall Street Journal*, December 21, 2021, https://www.wsj.com/articles/fauci-collins-emails-great-barrington-declaration-covid-pandemic-lockdown-11640129116 (last accessed May 4, 2025).

160 Hellmann, "Trump cancels NIH grants on equity research."

161 Ibid.

162 Ibid.

163 Aislinn Murphy and Louis Casiano, "SpaceX Dragon capsule sticks splashdown landing as NASA astronauts return home after months stuck in space," Fox Business, March 18, 2025, https://www.foxbusiness.com/technology/spacex-dragon-capsule-sticks-splashdown-landing-nasa-astronauts-return-home-after-months-stuck-space (last accessed May 4, 2025).

164 Stacy Liberatore, "NASA staff beg Elon Musk to 'clean house' after agency spent millions of Americans' money on DEI agenda," *Daily Mail*, November 15, 2024, https://www.dailymail.co.uk/sciencetech/article-14079781/elon-musk-nasa-millions-americans-money-dei-agenda.html (last accessed May 4, 2025).

165 Monique Mulima, "NASA to Close DEI Branch as Part of Phased Workforce Reduction," Bloomberg, March 10, 2025, https://news.bloomberglaw.com/business-and-practice/nasa-to-close-dei-branch-as-part-of-phased-workforce-reduction (last accessed May 4, 2025).

166 NASA, Jet Propulsion Laboratory, "Neela Rajendra, Chief Team Excellence and Employee Success Officer," https://www.jpl.nasa.gov/who-we-are/executive-council/neela-rajendra-chief-team-excellence/ (last accessed April 4, 2025).

167 Aaron Sibarium, "NASA's Jet Propulsion Lab Laid Off 900 Workers Due to Budget Cuts—But Hasn't Fired Its Top DEI Officer," *The Washington Free Beacon*, April 1, 2025, https://freebeacon.com/campus/nasas-jet-propulsion-lab-laid-off-900-workers-due-to-budget-cuts-but-hasnt-fired-its-top-dei-officer/ (last accessed May 4, 2025).

168 The Daily Wire, post of unclassified NSA "P65 DEI Glossary," https://dw-wp-production.imgix.net/2023/11/NSA-DEI-GLOSSARY-WM-FINAL.pdf (last accessed May 7, 2025).

169 Spencer Lindquist, "Leaked NSA Doc Reveals Massive Woke Glossary Pushing Critical Race Theory, Gender Ideology At Intel Agency," *The Daily Wire*, November 15, 2023, https://www.dailywire.com/news/exclusive-

leaked-nsa-doc-reveals-massive-woke-glossary-pushing-critical-race-theory-gender-ideology-on-govt-employees (last accessed May 4, 2025).

170 Martin Matishak, "NSA says it is investigating potential misuse of chat platform," *The Record*, February 26, 2025, https://therecord.media/nsa-investigation-potential-misuse-chat-platform (last accessed May 4, 2025).

171 Judge Glock, "A Federal Agency Is Awarding Contracts Based on 'Discrimination Essays,'" *City Journal*, May 1, 2025, https://www.city-journal.org/article/small-business-administration-federal-contracts-race-discrimination-essays (last accessed June 23, 2025).

172 John Derbyshire, "Conquest's Laws," *National Review*, June 25, 2003, https://www.nationalreview.com/corner/conquests-laws-john-derbyshire/ (last accessed May 4, 2025).

173 Chuck Ross, "Dem Heavyweights, Including Laurene Powell Jobs, Bankroll 'Black Liberation' Activist Who Called Jewish Museum Shooting 'Morally Righteous,'" *Washington Free Beacon*, June 3, 2025, https://freebeacon.com/democrats/dem-heavyweights-including-laurene-powell-jobs-bankroll-black-liberation-activist-who-called-jewish-museum-shooting-morally-righteous/ (last accessed June 24, 2025).

174 Fred Lucas, "Arabella Network's Leftist 'Dark Money' Influence Expanding, Author Reveals," The Daily Signal, April 29, 2024, https://www.dailysignal.com/2024/04/29/arabella-networks-leftist-dark-money-influence-expanding-author-reveals/ (last accessed May 4, 2025).

175 Isabel Vincent, "$375B EPA slush fund handled by John Podesta gave billions to charities founded only months earlier," *New York Post*, March 5, 2025, https://nypost.com/2025/03/05/business/john-podesta-375m-epa-slush-fund-gave-billions-to-newly-formed-charities/?utm_campaign=nypost&utm_medium=social&utm_source=twitter (last accessed May 4, 2025).

176 Power Forward Communities, https://powerforwardcommunities.org/ (last accessed May 6, 2025)

177 Emma Colton, "Stacey Abrams slammed after defending $2 billion in Biden-era EPA funds to buy green energy appliances," Fox News, March 9, 2025, https://www.foxnews.com/politics/stacey-abrams-slammed-after-defending-2-billion-biden-era-epa-funds-buy-green-energy-appliances (last accessed May 4, 2025).

178 Kyle Morris, "Stacey Abrams gets a new job after election loss, joins environmental group trying to eliminate gas stoves," Fox News, March 14, 2023, https://www.foxnews.com/politics/stacey-abrams-getsnew-job-after-election-loss-joins-environmental-group-trying-eliminate-gas-stoves (last accessed May 4, 2025).

179 Ibid.

180 Colton, "Stacey Abrams slammed after defending $2 billion in Biden-era EPA funds to buy green energy appliances."

181 Press Release, "Power Forward Communities Receives $2 Billion to Affordably Decarbonize American Homes, Boost Local Economies," Power

Forward Communities, August 16, 2024, https://powerforwardcommunities. org/press-release (last accessed May 4, 2025).

[182] Zoë Richards, "Nonprofit founded by Stacey Abrams to pay record Georgia fine for violating state campaign laws," NBC News, January 15, 2025, https://www.nbcnews.com/politics/politics-news/nonprofit-founded-stacey-abrams-pay-record-georgia-fine-violating-stat-rcna187885 (last accessed May 4, 2025).

[183] Jeff Amy, "Stacey Abrams reaches millionaire status before 2nd campaign," AP News, April 5, 2022, https://apnews.com/article/2022-midterm-elections-biden-business-atlanta-georgia-c4e30b9bbabb586ba1f5f5ad8cc0301c (last accessed May 4, 2025).

[184] Mike Gonzalez, *BLM: The Making of a New Marxist Revolution* (New York: Encounter Books, 2021).

[185] Mike Gonzalez, "Reckoning With Black Lives Matter," Heritage Foundation *Commentary*, July 12, 2023, https://www.heritage.org/progressivism/commentary/reckoning-black-lives-matter (last accessed May 4, 2025).

[186] Ibid.

[187] Keith Griffith, "BLM leader is accused of pilfering $10M from the organization by local chapters," *Daily Mail*, September 23, 2022, https://www.dailymail.co.uk/news/article-11176931/Black-Lives-Matter-leader-accused-pilfering-10M-organization.html (last accessed May 4, 2025).

[188] Rich Lowry, "The Ferguson Fraud," *Politico*, November 25, 2014, https://www.politico.com/magazine/story/2014/11/ferguson-fraud-113178/ (last accessed May 4, 2025).

[189] NPR, "'Hands Up, Don't Shoot' Movement Built on False Rumors, Columnist Says," *All Things Considered*, March 17, 2015, https://www.npr.org/2015/03/17/393646640/hands-up-dont-shoot-movement-built-on-false-rumors-columnist-says (last accessed May 4, 2025).

[190] Julio Rosas, *Fiery But Mostly Peaceful: The 2020 Riots and the Gaslighting of America* (Nashville: DW Books, 2022), p. 162.

[191] Griffith, "BLM leader is accused of pilfering $10M from the organization by local chapters."

[192] "Black Lives Matter executive accused of 'syphoning' $10M from BLM donors, suit says," CBS News, September 4, 2022, https://www.cbsnews.com/sacramento/news/black-lives-matter-executive-accused-of-syphoning-10m-from-blm-donors-suit-says/ (last accessed May 4 2025).

[193] "Corporate America Promised to Hire a Lot More People of Color. It Actually Did," Bloomberg, September 23, 2023, https://www.bloomberg.com/graphics/2023-black-lives-matter-equal-opportunity-corporate-diversity/ (last accessed May 11, 2025).

[194] Nitasha Tiku, "Google's approach to historically Black schools helps explain why there are few Black engineers in Big Tech," *The Washington Post*, March 4, 2021, https://www.washingtonpost.com/technology/2021/03/04/google-hbcu-recruiting/ (last accessed May 11, 2025).

[195] AnnaMaria Andriotis and Lauren Weber, "Morgan Stanley Went Big on DEI, and No One Is Happy About It," *The Wall Street Journal*, March 17, 2025, https://www.wsj.com/finance/banking/morgan-stanley-corporate-dei-what-happened-4a61427c?st=TPERxi&reflink=article_email_share (last accessed May 11, 2025).

[196] Ibid.

[197] Ibid.

[198] Christopher F. Rufo, Ryan Thorpe, "Whistleblower: Lockheed Martin Awarded Bonuses Based on Race," *City Journal*, June 12, 2025, https://www.city-journal.org/article/lockheed-martin-civil-rights-law-bonuses-race-merit?utm_source=virtuous&utm_medium=email&utm_campaign=cjdaily (last accessed June 16, 2025).

Chapter 3

[1] Jennifer Richmond, "Hallie Quinn Brown," American Heroes Series, *Journal of Free Black Thought*, March 28, 2025, https://freeblackthought.substack.com/ (last accessed April 29, 2025).

[2] Melanie Kirkpatrick, "'The Girl in the Middle' Review: Conquest and Sacred Ground," *The Wall Street Journal*, April 21, 2025, https://www.wsj.com/arts-culture/books/the-girl-in-the-middle-review-conquest-and-sacred-ground-08c07946?st=pYZ5XZ&reflink=article_email_share (last accessed April 29, 2025).

[3] Lewis M. Andrews, "The trouble with the progressives' proposed wealth tax," *The Spectator,* February 13, 2024, https://thespectator.com/topic/trouble-progressives-proposed-wealth-tax-elizabeth-warren/ (last accessed Aril 29, 2025).

[4] "Yes, Real Socialism Has Been Tried—and It Has Failed Every Time," *Cornell Review*, February 17, 2022, https://www.thecornellreview.org/yes-real-socialism-has-been-tried-and-it-has-failed-every-time/ (last accessed April 29, 2025).

[5] New York Times Magazine, The 1619 Project, https://www.nytimes.com/interactive/2019/08/14/magazine/1619-america-slavery.html (accessed April 30, 2025).

[6] Nikole Hannah-Jones, "Our founding ideals of liberty and equality were false when they were written. Black Americans fought to make them true. Without this struggle, America would have no democracy at all," *The New York Times Magazine,* August 18, 2019.

[7] Phillip Magness, "The 1619 Project: A Critique," American Institute for Economic Research, 2020; Peter W. Wood, *1620: A Critical Response to the 1619 Project* (New York: Encounter Books, 2020); and Mary Graber, *Debunking the 1619 Project Exposing the Plan to Divide America* (Washington, DC: Regnery, 2021).

[8] Timoty Sandefur, "The Founders Were Flawed. The Nation Is Imperfect. The Constitution Is Still a 'Glorious Liberty Document,'" *Reason*, August 21,

2019, https://reason.com/2019/08/21/the-founders-were-flawed-the-nation-is-imperfect-the-constitution-is-still-a-glorious-liberty-document/ (last accessed April 29, 2025).

[9] Frederick Douglass, "What to the Slave is the Fourth of July?" Selected Speeches and Writings, Philip S. Foner, ed. (Chicago: Lawrence Hill, 1852), pp. 188–206.

[10] James Oakes, "What the 1619 Project Got Wrong," *Catalyst*, Vol. 5, No. 3 (2021), https://catalyst-journal.com/2021/12/what-the-1619-project-got-wrong (last accessed April 29, 2025).

[11] "Nikole Hannah-Jones Denied Tenure at University of North Carolina," *The New York Times*, July 15, 2022.

[12] Steven Mintz, "Historical Context: Facts about the Slave Trade and Slavery," History Resources, Gilder Lehrman Institute of American History, https://www.gilderlehrman.org/history-resources/teacher-resources/historical-context-facts-about-slave-trade-and-slavery (last accessed April 11, 2025).

[13] Joe Feagin, *How Blacks Built America* (New York: Routledge, 2015).

[14] National Museum of African American History and Culture, "The Value of Freedom," Chapter 1, https://www.searchablemuseum.com/a-nation-bound-by-slavery/ (last accessed April 11, 2025).

[15] Paul W. Rhode, "What fraction of antebellum US national product did the enslaved produce?" *Explorations in Economic History*, Vol. 91 (January 2024), https://www.sciencedirect.com/science/article/pii/S0014498323000463 (last accessed April 29, 2025).

[16] Ibid.

[17] Glenn Loury, "To Praise Cultural Appropriation, Not to Bury It," The Glenn Show, May 2, 2023, https://glennloury.substack.com/p/to-praise-cultural-appropriation (last accessed April 29, 2025).

[18] Census.gov, "About the Topic of Race," https://www.census.gov/topics/population/race/about.html (last accessed April 11, 2025).

[19] Ronan McGreevy, "Early Irish people were dark skinned with blue eyes—documentary," *The Irish Times*, April 19, 2021, https://www.irishtimes.com/news/ireland/irish-news/early-irish-people-were-dark-skinned-with-blue-eyes-documentary-1.4541124 (last accessed April 29, 2025), and Hannah Devlin, "First modern Britons had 'dark to black' skin, Cheddar Man DNA analysis reveals," *The Guardian*, February 7, 2018, https://www.theguardian.com/science/2018/feb/07/first-modern-britons-dark-black-skin-cheddar-man-dna-analysis-reveals (last accessed April 29, 2025).

[20] Wu-jing He et al., "A study of the greater male variability hypothesis in creative thinking in Mainland China: Male superiority exists," *Personality and Individual Differences*, Vol. 55, No. 8 (2013), pp. 882–886, https://www.sciencedirect.com/science/article/pii/S0191886913003036 (last accessed April 29, 2025).

[21] Ibid.

22 Phillip W. Magness, "Down the 1619 Project's Memory Hole," *Quillette*, September 19, 2020, https://quillette.com/2020/09/19/down-the-1619-projects-memory-hole/ (last accessed April 29, 2025).

23 Tyler Austin Harper, "Ibram X. Kendi's fall is a cautionary tale—so was his rise," *The Washington Post*, September 28, 2023, https://www.washingtonpost.com/books/2023/09/28/ibram-kendi-stamped-center-antiracist-research/ (last accessed April 29, 2025), and Keeanga-Yamahtta Taylor, "Ibram X. Kendi's Anti-Racism," *The New Yorker*, October 21, 2023, https://www.newyorker.com/news/our-columnists/ibram-x-kendis-anti-racism (last accessed April 29, 2025).

24 From George Orwell's novel *1984*.

25 Nile Gardiner, "Monuments Are Only the Start of Radical Left's War on Western Values," The Daily Signal, June 30, 2020, https://www.dailysignal.com/2020/06/30/fight-back-against-radical-left-they-want-to-destroy-much-more-than-monuments/ (last accessed April 29, 2025).

26 Aimee Minbiole, "Dartmouth Removes Baker Tower Weather Vane," Dartmouth College, June 25, 2020, https://home.dartmouth.edu/news/2020/06/dartmouth-removes-baker-tower-weather-vane (last accessed April 29, 2025).

27 Sara Smart, "A statue of Thomas Jefferson is removed from New York City Hall after 187 years," CNN, November 24, 2021, https://www.cnn.com/2021/11/24/us/thomas-jefferson-statue-removed/index.html (last accessed April 29, 2025).

28 Kelly Hayes, "Charlottesville takes down Lewis, Clark and Sacagawea statue after Confederate removals," Fox 10, July 12, 2021, https://www.fox10phoenix.com/news/charlottesville-takes-down-lewis-clark-and-sacagawea-statue-after-confederate-removals (last accessed April 29, 2025).

29 "145-year-old Civil War statue in Saratoga Springs demolished by vandals," NYup.com, July 17, 2020, https://www.newyorkupstate.com/saratoga-springs/2020/07/145-year-old-civil-war-statue-in-saratoga-springs-demolished-by-vandals.html (last accessed April 29, 2025).

30 "Statue of Virgin Mary Beheaded at Tennessee Parish," *National Catholic Register*, July 15, 2020, https://www.ncregister.com/news/statue-of-virgin-mary-beheaded-at-tennessee-parish (last accessed April 29, 2025).

31 Robbin Simmons and Gina Benitez, "Statue of Jesus Christ decapitated, knocked off pedestal outside SW Miami-Dade church," 7 News Miami, July 15, 2020, https://wsvn.com/news/local/statue-of-jesus-christ-decapitated-knocked-off-pedestal-outside-sw-miami-dade-church/ (last accessed April 29, 2025).

32 Ben Kesslen, "Jackson, Mississippi, votes to remove statue of President Andrew Jackson from City Hall," NBC News, July 8, 2020, https://www.nbcnews.com/news/us-news/jackson-mississippi-votes-remove-statue-president-andrew-jackson-city-hall-n1233138 (last accessed April 29, 2025).

33 Joseph Guzman, "Statue of Lincoln standing over freed slave in Boston has been removed," *The Hill*, December 29, 2020, https://thehill.com/changing-

america/respect/equality/532012-statue-of-lincoln-standing-over-freed-slave-in-boston-has/ (last accessed April 29, 2025).

[34] "Wisconsin crowd pulls down statue of abolitionist who died fighting slavery," Global News, June 24, 2020, https://globalnews.ca/news/7101452/madison-wisconsin-hans-christian-heg/ (last accessed April 29, 2025).

[35] Dana Sparks, "Activists topple pioneer statues on University of Oregon campus," The Register Guard, June 13, 2020, https://www.registerguard.com/story/news/2020/06/14/activists-topple-pioneer-statues-on-university-of-oregon-campus/42103065/ (last accessed April 29, 2025).

[36] Isabel Hughes, "Delaware law enforcement memorial in Dover axed, state flags left nearby 'soaked' in urine," Delaware News Journal, June 12, 2020, https://www.delawareonline.com/story/news/2020/06/12/delaware-law-enforcement-memorial-dover-axed-state-flags-left-nearby-soaked-urine/3174278001/ (last accessed April 29, 2025).

[37] Bill Chappell, "Columbus, Ohio, Takes Down Statue of Christopher Columbus," NPR, July 1, 2020, https://www.npr.org/sections/live-updates-protests-for-racial-justice/2020/07/01/885909530/columbus-ohio-takes-down-statue-of-christopher-columbus (last accessed April 29, 2025).

[38] Dominic Green, "Much Ado About 'Decolonizing' Shakespeare," The Wall Street Journal, March 25, 2025, https://www.wsj.com/arts-culture/theater/much-ado-about-decolonizing-shakespeare-93631ff2?st=odsqb4&reflink=article_email_share (last accessed April 29, 2025).

[39] Ibid.

[40] Ibid.

[41] Merriam-Webster Dictionary, "epistemic," https://www.merriam-webster.com/dictionary/epistemic (last accessed April 29, 2025).

[42] Jonathan Turley, "How 'silence is violence' threatens true free speech and public civility," The Hill, August 29, 2025, https://thehill.com/opinion/civil-rights/514251-how-silence-is-violence-threatens-true-free-speech-and-public-civility/ (last accessed April 29, 2025).

[43] Marina Watts, "In Smithsonian Race Guidelines, Rational Thinking and Hard Work Are White Values," Newsweek, May 25, 2021, https://www.newsweek.com/smithsonian-race-guidelines-rational-thinking-hard-work-are-white-values-1518333 (last accessed April 29, 2025).

[44] Chacour Koop, "Smithsonian museum apologizes for saying hard work, rational thought is 'white culture,'" Miami Herald, July 17, 2020, https://www.miamiherald.com/news/nation-world/national/article244309587.html (last accessed April 29, 2025).

[45] Michael O. Magbagbeola, "Black Masters; The Ownership of Slaves by Free People of Color in the Antebellum South 1780–1861," Master's thesis completed at University of Massachusetts-Boston, 2020, https://scholarworks.umb.edu/masters_theses/661(last accessed April 29, 2025), and Zachary M. Saddow, "Black Joining the Ranks of White: Black Slaveowning in 1800s South Carolina," Master's thesis completed at Winthrop University,

2023, https://digitalcommons.winthrop.edu/graduatetheses/153 (last accessed April 29, 2025).

[46] Stven Mintz, "Historical Context: Facts about the Slave Trade and Slavery," The Gilder Lehrman Institute of American History, 2025, https://www.gilder lehrman.org/history-resources/teacher-resources/historical-context-facts-about-slave-trade-and-slavery (last accessed April 29, 2025).

[47] Irwin Arieff, "If Africa Is So Rich, Why Is It So Poor?" PassBlue, May 18, 2015, https://www.passblue.com/2015/05/18/if-africa-is-so-rich-why-is-it-so-poor/ (last accessed April 29, 2025).

[48] Mike Gonzalez, "Defund the Smithsonian's Latino Museum—a woke indoctrination factory," *New York Post*, December 24, 2023, https://nypost.com/2023/12/24/opinion/why-the-national-museum-of-the-american-latino-should-be-defunded/ (last accessed April 29, 2025).

[49] Ibid.

[50] Ibid.

[51] Weiss, Elizabeth Weiss, "I spent a year in NYC's museums—and found them drowning in identity politics," *New York Post*, September 11, 2024, https://nypost.com/2024/09/11/opinion/my-year-in-nycs-museums-found-them-drowning-in-politics/ (last accessed April 29, 2025).

[52] Ibid.

[53] Ibid.

[54] Ibid.

[55] Ibid.

[56] Brenda Hafera, "Woke History at James Madison's Montpelier Backed by Southern Poverty Law Center," The Daily Signal, July 29, 2022, https://www.dailysignal.com/2022/07/29/the-splc-backs-woke-history-at-james-madisons-montpelier/ (last accessed April 29, 2025).

[57] Ibid.

[58] Ibid.

[59] Engaging Communities in the Interpretation of Slavery at Museums and Historic Sites, a Rubric of Best Practices, The National Summit on Teaching Slavery, October 19, 2018, https://montpelierdescendants.org/wp-content/uploads/2024/07/Interpreting-Slavery-10_19_18.pdf (last accessed April 29, 2025).

[60] Ibid.

[61] Eric, Gibson, "Woke Ideologues Are Taking Over American Art Museums," *The Wall Street Journal*, September 2, 2022.

[62] Michael Deacon, "The woke takeover of our museums is almost complete," *The Telegraph*, November 1, 2022.

[63] Lynn Brown, "Which US will tourists find when they visit?" BBC News, April 10, 2025, https://www.bbc.com/travel/article/20250409-which-version-of-the-us-will-visitors-find (last accessed April 29, 2025).

[64] Bill Barrow, "Critics see Trump attacks on the 'Black Smithsonian' as an effort to sanitize racism in US history," AP News, March 29, 2025, https://apnews.

com/article/trump-black-history-smithsonian-dei-687fd306dc9c6d7611300d 74fe49b8aa (last accessed April 29, 2025).

65 American Historical Association, "Historians Defend the Smithsonian," March 31, 2025, https://www.historians.org/news/historians-defend-the-smithsonian / (last accessed April 29, 2025).

66 Brown, "Which US will tourists find when they visit?"

Chapter 4

1 Marissa Ventrelli, "Colorado governor signs transgender bill into law," 9News, May 16, 2025, https://www.9news.com/article/news/local/local-politics/ colorado-governor-polis-signs-transgender-bill/73-f4cccd81-347c-4f90-9c6 5-1035a816dc73 (last accessed May 18, 2025).

2 Christopher F. Rufo, "A World in Miniature: Raising children in an era of ideological capture," ChrisRufo.com, March 17, 2024, https://christopher rufo.com/p/a-world-in-miniature (last accessed April 16, 2025).

3 Benedict Smith, "Parents asked if newborn babies identify as transgender," *The Telegraph*, March 17, 2025, https://www.telegraph.co.uk/us/news/2025/ 03/17/parents-asked-if-newborn-babies-identify-as-transgender/ (last accessed April 16, 2025).

4 "Rupert Grint joins JK Rowling transgender row," BBC, June 12, 2020, https://www.bbc.com/news/entertainment-arts-53023580 (last accessed April 16, 2025).

5 JKRowling.com, "J.K. Rowling Writes about Her Reasons for Speaking out on Sex and Gender Issues," June 10, 2020, https://www.jkrowling.com /opinions/j-k-rowling-writes-about-her-reasons-for-speaking-out-on-sex-and -gender-issues/ (last accessed April 16, 2025).

6 Abigail Shrier, *Irreversible Damage*, Regnery Books, Washington, DC, 2020.

7 Psychology Today, "New Book "Irreversible Damage" Is Full of Misinformation," Devon Frye, December 6, 2020, https://www.psychology today.com/us/blog/political-minds/202012/new-book-irreversible-damage- is-full-of-misinformation

8 Helen Joyce, *Trans: When Ideology Meets Reality* (London: Oneworld Publications, 2021), p. 72.

9 Ibid., p. 77.

10 Ibid., p. 33.

11 Deborah Soh, *The End of Gender* (New York: Simon and Schuster, 2020), p.144.

12 Society for Evidence-Based Gender Medicine, "Accurate transition regret and detransition rates are unknown," September 11, 2023, https://segm.org/regret -detransition-rate-unknown (last accessed April 16, 2025).

13 Charles Bowyer and Jerry Bowyer, "Target Hits Books," *National Review*, July 30, 2021, https://www.nationalreview.com/2021/07/target-hits-books/ (last accessed April 16, 2025).

14 Dr. Debra Soh, Bio, https://www.drdebrasoh.com/bio (accessed April 22, 2025).

---

[15] Shrier, *Irreversible Damage*, p. xxi.

[16] Soh, *The End of Gender*, p. 151.

[17] Shrier, *Irreversible Damage*, p. 26.

[18] Ibid., p. 155.

[19] Ibid., p. 27.

[20] Ibid., p. 32.

[21] Ibid., p. 37.

[22] Colin Wright, "Sex Is Not a Spectrum," *Reality's Last Stand*, February 1, 2021, https://www.realityslaststand.com/p/sex-is-not-a-spectrum (last accessed April 16, 2025).

[23] Joyce, *Trans*, p. 13.

[24] Dave Baxter, @justdaviddavid, Twitter, March 7, 2020, https://x.com/JustDavidDavid/status/1236436583366176771 (last accessed April 16, 2025).

[25] Ray Blanchard, @blanchardphd, Twitter, August 15, 2022, https://x.com/BlanchardPhD/status/1559171970696110081 (last accessed April 16, 2025).

[26] Carole Hooven, "A Person's Sex Is Not Assigned," *The New York Times*, April 3, 2024, https://www.nytimes.com/2024/04/03/opinion/sex-assigned-at-birth.html (last accessed April 16, 2025).

[27] Carole Hooven, "Why I Left Harvard," *The Free Press*, January 16, 2024, https://www.thefp.com/p/carole-hooven-why-i-left-harvard (last accessed April 16, 2025).

[28] Abigail Anthony, "Sex—at Birth?" *National Review*, April 5, 2024, https://www.nationalreview.com/corner/sex-at-birth/ (last accessed April 16, 2025).

[29] Hannah Sparks, "The biggest gender reveal fails ever: 11 parties gone terribly wrong," *New York Post*, May 17, 2021, https://nypost.com/article/gender-reveal-fails-parties-gone-wrong/ (last accessed April 16, 2025).

[30] Joyce, *Trans*, p. 7.

[31] Shrier, *Irreversible Damage*, p. xxi.

[32] Soh, *The End of Gender*, p. 141.

[33] Shrier, *Irreversible Damage*, p. 98.

[34] Ibid., p. 165.

[35] Ibid., p. 170.

[36] Jo Taylor et al., "Interventions to suppress puberty in adolescents experiencing gender dysphoria or incongruence: a systematic review," *Archives of Disease in Childhood*, Vol. 109, 2024, https://doi.org/10.1136/archdischild-2023-326669 (last accessed April 16, 2025).

[37] Jasmine Andersson and Andre Rhoden-Paul, "NHS to close Tavistock child gender identity clinic," BBC News, July 28, 2022, https://www.bbc.com/news/uk-62335665 (last accessed April 16, 2025).

[38] Joyce, *Trans*, p. 91.

[39] Transgender Trend, "Keira Bell: The High Court hands down a historic judgment to protect vulnerable children," December 1, 2020, https://www.transgendertrend.com/keira-bell-high-court-historic-judgment-protect-vulnerable-children/ (last accessed April 16, 2025).

[40] Andersson and Rhoden-Paul, "NHS to close Tavistock child gender identity clinic."

[41] Kathleen McDeavitt, "Paediatric gender medicine: Longitudinal studies have not consistently shown improvement in depression or suicidality," *Acta Paediatrica* (2024), 17309. https://doi.org/10.1111/apa.17309

[42] Joyce, *Trans*, p. 289.

[43] Michael Brendan Dougherty, "Anthony Fauci: I Am the Science," *National Review*, July 20, 2021, https://www.nationalreview.com/2021/11/anthony-fauci-i-am-the-science/ (last accessed April 16, 2025).

[44] GLAAD, "Tips for Allies of Transgender People," https://glaad.org/transgender/allies/ (last accessed March 22, 2025).

[45] John J. Straub et al., "Risk of Suicide and Self-Harm Following Gender-Affirmation Surgery," Cureus, April 2, 2024, https://pmc.ncbi.nlm.nih.gov/articles/PMC11063965/ (last accessed April 16, 2025).

[46] Cecilia Dhejne et al., "Long-term follow-up of transsexual persons undergoing sex reassignment surgery: cohort study in Sweden," *PLOS One*, February 22, 2011, https://journals.plos.org/plosone/article?id=10.1371/journal.pone.0016885 (last accessed April 16, 2025).

[47] Straub et al., "Risk of Suicide and Self-Harm Following Gender-Affirmation Surgery."

[48] Azadeh Mazaheri Meybodi, Ahmad Hajebi, and Atefeh Ghanbari Jolfaei, "Psychiatric Axis I Comorbidities among Patients with Gender Dysphoria," *Psychiatry Journal*, August 11, 2014, https://onlinelibrary.wiley.com/doi/10.1155/2014/971814 (last accessed April 16, 2025).

[49] Jess Thompson, "How Transgender Hormone Therapy Affects the Brain," Newsweek, March 28, 2023, https://www.newsweek.com/audrey-hale-hormones-transgender-shooting-nashville-1790804

[50] Reuters, "Fact Check: Planned Parenthood founder Margaret Sanger's 1939 quote on exterminating Black population taken out of context," May 9, 2022, https://www.reuters.com/article/fact-check/planned-parenthood-founder-margaret-sangers-1939-quote-on-exterminating-black-p-idUSL2N2X11YN/ (last accessed July 16, 2025).

[51] Planned Parenthood, "What should I teach my elementary school aged child about identity?" https://www.plannedparenthood.org/learn/parents/elementary-school/what-should-i-teach-my-elementary-school-aged-child-about-identi#:~:text=Be%20aware%20that%20puberty%20can,and%20other%20transgender%20medical%20care (last accessed April 16, 2025).

[52] Len Meyer, "Why are pronouns so important?" Planned Parenthood of Illinois, June 30, 2021, https://www.plannedparenthood.org/planned-parenthood-illinois/blog/why-are-pronouns-so-important-2#:~:text=There%20is%20scientific%20evidence%20to,%2C%20or%20being%20left%2Dhanded (last accessed April 16, 2025).

[53] Planned Parenthood of South and Central Florida, "Gender-Affirming Hormone Therapy," https://www.plannedparenthood.org/planned-parenthood -southwest-

central-florida/medical-services/transgender-hormone-services (last accessed April 16, 2025).

[54] Ryan Gilbey, "'I get misgendered all the time': Elliot Page on his return to acting on the big screen," *The Guardian*, August 16, 2024, https://www.theguardian.com/film/article/2024/aug/16/i-get-misgendered-all-the-time-i-dont-care-elliot-page-on-his-return-to-acting-on-the-big-screen (last accessed April 16, 2025).

[55] Gabriel Mac, "My Penis, Myself: I didn't need a penis to be a man. But I needed one to be me," *New York*, December 20, 2021, https://nymag.com/intelligencer/article/gabriel-mac-essay.html (last accessed April 16, 2025).

[56] Aaron L . Heston, et al., "Phalloplasty: techniques and outcomes," *Translational Andrology and Urology*, Vol. 8, No. 3 (June 2019), pp. 254–265, https://pmc.ncbi.nlm.nih.gov/articles/PMC6626313/ (last accessed April 19, 2025).

[57] Mac, "My Penis, Myself."

[58] Ibid.

[59] Do No Harm, "Detransitioner Bill of Rights," https://donoharmmedicine.org/bill-of-rights/?gad_source=1&gclid=EAIaIQobChMImrWhvP2djAMV82lHAR2QAyuYEAAYASAAEgJQp_D_BwE, (accessed March 22, 2025).

[60] Chloe Cole, "I'm a detransitioner—Congress must stop hospitals' abuse of kids like me," *New York Post*, March 11, 2025, https://nypost.com/2025/03/11/opinion/im-a-detransitioner-congress-must-protect-kids-like-me/ (last accessed April 19, 2025).

[61] United Kingdom High Court of Justice, Case No: CO/60/2020, Quincy Bell et al v. Tavistock and Portman NHS Foundation Trust, et al., https://www.judiciary.uk/wp-content/uploads/2020/12/Bell-v-Tavistock-Judgment.pdf (last accessed April 19, 2025).

[62] Ibid.

[63] Stella O'Malley and Keira Bell, "We Need to Complexify Our Understanding of Transition and Detransition," Genspect, March 12, 2024, https://genspect.org/we-need-to-complexify-our-understanding-of-transition-and-detransition/ (last accessed April 19, 2025).

[64] @jonnywsbell, X post, April 1, 2025, https://x.com/Jonnywsbell/status/1907002911407673580 (last accessed April 5, 2025).

Chapter 5

[1] Joyce, *Trans*, p. 19.

[2] Ibid., p. 20.

[3] Ibid., p. 22.

[4] MasterClass, "Queer Theory: Definition, History, and Impact—What is Queer Theory?" October 24, 2022, https://www.masterclass.com/articles/queer-theory#2EPCgTtACIsUKVkQBFoPr1 (last accessed April 19, 2025).

[5] Joyce, *Trans*, p. 139.

[6] Ibid., p. 39.

[7] Ibid., p. 49.

[8] Andrew Doyle, GB News, YouTube, March 26, 2023, https://www.youtube.com/watch?v=0QHmJL-a5tM (last accessed April 19, 2025).

[9] Joyce, *Trans*, p. 150.

[10] Ibid., p. 156.

[11] Charles Hymas, "One in 50 prisoners identifies as transgender amid concerns inmates are attempting to secure prison perks," *Daily Telegraph*, July 9, 2019, https://www.telegraph.co.uk/news/2019/07/09/one-50-prisoners-identify-transsexual-first-figures-show-amid/ (last accessed April 19, 2025).

[12] Sean Rayment, "More than 70 per cent of transgender prisoners are in for sex offences or violent crimes," *Daily Telegraph*, February 24, 2024, https://www.telegraph.co.uk/news/2024/02/24/government-figures-70-per-cent-of-transgender-prisoners-are/ (last accessed April 19, 2025).

[13] Joyce, *Trans*, p. 160.

[14] Kevin Klein, "Trudeau's prison policy endangers women and defies common sense," *The Winnipeg Sun*, December 28, 2024, https://winnipegsun.com/opinion/columnists/klein-trudeaus-prison-policy-endangers-women-and-defies-common-sense (last accessed April 19, 2025).

[15] Press Release: "Advocates Sue to Challenge Withholding of Gender-Affirming Care in Federal Prisons," American Civil Liberties Union, March 7, 2025, https://www.aclu.org/press-releases/advocates-sue-to-challenge-withholding-of-gender-affirming-care-in-federal-prisons (last accessed May 17, 2025).

[16] Katie Burkholder, "Department of Justice reverses support of trans Georgia prisoner," Rough Draft Atlanta, April 30, 2025, https://roughdraftatlanta.com/2025/04/30/doj-reverses-trans-prisoner-surgery/ (last accessed May 17, 2025).

[17] Amie Ichikawa and Erin Friday, "California Bill Highlights Epidemic of Male Rapists Transferring to Women's Prisons," *The Federalist*, April 29, 2025, https://thefederalist.com/2025/04/29/california-bill-highlights-epidemic-of-male-rapists-transferring-to-womens-prisons/?utm_source=rss&utm_medium=rss&utm_campaign=california-bill-highlights-epidemic-of-male-rapists-transferring-to-womens-prisons&utm_term=2025-04-29 (last accessed May 17, 2025).

[18] United States District Court, Eastern District of California, Fresno Division, *Chandler et al v. Macomber et al*, Case 1:21-cv-01657-JLT-HBK, https://static1.squarespace.com/static/5f232ea74d8342386a7ebc52/t/669bdcca2c96eb4538e77fe0/1721490645800/20240719_Doc_84_Amended_Complaint.pdf (last accessed May 17, 2025).

[19] "LA sex offender sentenced to 15 years for voluntary manslaughter," BakersfieldNow, December 7, 2023, https://bakersfieldnow.com/news/local/la-sex-offender-sentenced-to-15-years-for-voluntary-manslaughter-crime-court-kern-county-los-angeles (last accessed April 19, 2025).

[20] Ichikawa and Friday, "California Bill Highlights Epidemic of Male Rapists Transferring to Women's Prisons."

[21] Jill Lyman, "Transgender inmate from Evansville wins lawsuit to get surgery," 14News, September 24, 2025, https://www.14news.com/2024/09/26/transgender-inmate-evansville-wins-lawsuit-get-surgery/ (last accessed May 17, 2025).

[22] Luke Andrews, "Transgender inmate arrested for strangling 11-month-old daughter allowed to receive gender reassignment surgery," *Daily Mail*, March 29, 2025, https://www.dailymail.co.uk/health/article-14536051/Indiana-transwoman-strangled-daughter-gender-transition-surgery.html (last accessed May 17, 2025).

[23] Title IX of the Education Amendments of 1972.

[24] Sarah Parshall Perry, "Biden's Illegal Title IX Rule Is Set for Enforcement. The School Year Is Going to Be Complicated," The Daily Signal, July 31, 2024, https://www.dailysignal.com/2024/07/31/bidens-illegal-title-ix-rule-is-set-enforcement-school-year-is-going-to-be-complicated/ (last accessed April 19, 2025).

[25] Laura Meckler, "Biden Title IX rules set to protect trans students, survivors of abuse," *The Washington Post*, April 19, 2024, https://www.washingtonpost.com/education/2024/04/19/titleix-biden-transgender-sexual-assault/ (last accessed April 19, 2025).

[26] Collin Binkley, "Biden's new Title IX rules protect LGBTQ+ students, but avoid addressing transgender athletes," AP News, April 19, 2024, https://apnews.com/article/title-ix-sexual-assault-transgender-sports-d0fc0ab7515de02b8e4403d0481dc1e7 (last accessed April 19, 2025).

[27] CUPA-HR, "Title IX Rule Goes Into Effect in 24 States," August 1, 2024, https://www.cupahr.org/blog/title-ix-rule-goes-into-effect-in-24-states-2024-08-01/ (last accessed April 19, 2025).

[28] Meckler, "Biden Title IX rules set to protect trans students, survivors of abuse."

[29] Whittney Evans, "Federal judge strikes down Biden's Title IX rules protecting LGBTQ+ students," VPM News, January 13, 2025, https://www.vpm.org/news/2025-01-13/federal-judge-strikes-down-bidens-title-ix-rules-protecting-lgbtq-students (last accessed April 19, 2025).

[30] Lexi Lonas-Cochran, "Department of Education undoes Biden's Title IX rules on gender," *The Hill*, January 31, 2025, https://thehill.com/homenews/education/5118925-trump-biden-title-ix-education-gender-lgbtq/ (last accessed April 19, 2025).

[31] National Women's Law Center, "Summary of Changes to the Title IX Rules," *Fact Sheet*, June 2024, https://nwlc.org/wp-content/uploads/2024/06/Biden-Title-IX-Rule-Fact-Sheet-6.12.24-vF.pdf (last accessed April 19, 2025).

[32] Rebeka Zeljko, "Vague Title IX Rules At UC Davis Turn Free Speech Into Sexual 'Harassment,'" *The Federalist*, November 28, 2023, https://thefederalist.com/2023/11/28/vague-title-ix-rules-at-uc-davis-turn-free-speech-into-sexual-harassment/ (last accessed April 19, 2025).

[33] Ibid.

[34] Ibid.

[35] University of California, "Sexual Violence and Sexual Harassment," interim policy, August 29, 2024, p. 39, https://policy.ucop.edu/doc/4000385/SVSH (last accessed April 19, 2025).

[36] United Nations, High Commission for Human Rights, "A/79/325: Report of the Special Rapporteur on violence against women and girls, its causes and consequences - Violence against women and girls in sports," August 27, 2024, https://www.ohchr.org/en/documents/thematic-reports/a79325-report-special-rapporteur-violence-against-women-and-girls-its (last accessed April 16, 2025).

[37] Andrew Schroedter and Ben Bradley, "Transgender athletes in girls' sports: It rarely happens in Illinois," Central Illinois Proud, February 6, 2025, https://www.centralillinoisproud.com/news/national/transgender-athletes-in-girls-sports-it-rarely-happens-in-illinois/ (last accessed April 19, 2025).

[38] The Chistian Institute, "Two men compete for the women's pool final," April 11, 2025, https://www.christian.org.uk/news/two-biological-men-compete-for-the-womens-pool-final/ (last accessed April 12, 2025).

[39] John Oliver, "Trans Athletes: Last Week Tonight with John Oliver," HBO, April 7, 2025, https://www.youtube.com/watch?v=flSS1tjoxf0 (last accessed April 19, 2025).

[40] Sandra K. Hunter et al., "The Biological Basis of Sex Differences in Athletic Performance: Consensus Statement for the American College of Sports Medicine," *Medicine & Science in Sports & Exercise*, Vol. 55, No. 12 (December 2023), pp. 2328–2360, https://pubmed.ncbi.nlm.nih.gov/3777 2882/#:~:text=Thus%2C%20for%20athletic%20events%20and,the%20requ irements%20of%20the%20event (last accessed April 19, 2025).

[41] Ibid.

[42] Quillette podcast, December 27, 2018.

[43] Fatima Goss Graves, "The Importance of Protecting Female Athletics and Title IX," National Women's Law Center, testimony before House Committee on Oversight and Accountability, Subcommittee on Health Care and Financial Services, December 5, 2023, https://oversight.house.gov/wp-content/uploads /2023/12/2023.12.05_Written-Testimony-FGG.pdf (last accessed April 19, 2025).

[44] Title IX of the Education Amendments of 1972.

[45] Graves, "The Importance of Protecting Female Athletics and Title IX," Ibid.

[46] Ibid.

[47] Ibid.

[48] Ibid.

[49] Ibid.

[50] Ibid.

[51] Rachel McKinnon, "I Won a World Championship. Some People Aren't Happy," *The New York Times*, December 5, 2019, https://www.nytimes.com /2019/12/05/opinion/i-won-a-world-championship-some-people-arent-happy .html (last accessed April 16, 2025).

[52] Melissa Koenig, "Transgender cyclists once again take gold and silver at major female competition: 'Outrageous,'" *New York Post*, December 5, 2023, https://nypost.com/2023/12/05/news/transgender-cyclists-take-gold-and-silver-at-womens-race/?utm_campaign=iphone_nyp&utm_source=com. microsoft.Office.Outlook.compose-shareextension (last accessed April 19, 2025).

[53] S. Shahi, "'Mediocre male bodies taking podium places from female athletes'—Martina Navratilova blasts transgender athletes' Cyclocross win in women's category," Sportskeeda, December 6, 2023, https://www.sports keeda.com/tennis/news-mediocre-male-bodies-taking-podium-places-female-athletes-martina-navratilova-blasts-transgender-athletes-victory-women-s-category (last accessed April 19, 2025).

[54] Roger Gonzalez, "FC Dallas under-15 boys squad beat the U.S. Women's National Team in a scrimmage," CBS Sports, April 4, 2017, https://www.cbssports.com/soccer/news/a-dallas-fc-under-15-boys-squad-beat-the-u-s-womens-national-team-in-a-scrimmage/ (last accessed April 19, 2025).

[55] Katie Jerkovich, "Girls' Soccer Team Refuses to Play Team with Biological Male, Following Similar Move by University," *The Daily Wire*, October 2, 2024, https://www.dailywire.com/news/girls-soccer-team-refuses-to-play-team-with-biological-male-following-similar-move-by-university (last accessed April 21, 2025).

[56] Tom Joyce, "New Hampshire Transgender Track Athlete Wins State Championship Meet," *New Boston Post*, February 12, 2025, https://newbostonpost.com/2024/02/12/new-hampshire-transgender-track-athlete-wins-state-championship-meet/ (last accessed May 17, 2025).

[57] Alan Blinder, "Lia Thomas Wins an N.C.A.A. Swimming Title," *The New York Times*, March 17, 2022, https://www.nytimes.com/2022/03/17/sports/lia-thomas-swimmer-wins.html (last accessed April 19, 2025).

[58] Valeri Guevarra, Derek Wong, and Sean McKeown, "Here's what to know about former Penn swimmer Lia Thomas," *The Daily Pennsylvanian*, March 10, 2025, https://www.thedp.com/article/2025/03/penn-lia-thomas-timeline-transgender-athlete (last accessed April 19, 2025).

[59] Swimming World Staff, "Riley Gaines: 'I Left There With No Trophy' After Tie With Lia Thomas; Kentucky Standout Disappointed With NCAA," *Swimming World*, March 24, 2025, https://www.swimmingworldmagazine.com/news/riley-gaines-i-left-there-with-no-trophy-after-tie-with-lia-thomas-kentucky-standout-disappointed-with-ncaa/ (last accessed April 19, 2025).

[60] Guevarra, Wong, and McKeown, "Here's what to know about former Penn swimmer Lia Thomas."

[61] Madeline Leesman, "Another Lia Thomas? A Transgender Swimmer Crushed the Competition at a Championship Event," Town Hall, May 3, 2025, https://townhall.com/tipsheet/madelineleesman/2025/05/03/transgender-swimmer-n2656440 (last accessed May 17, 2025).

[62] "How to...beat both Williams sisters in one afternoon," *The Observer*, September 2, 2001, https://www.theguardian.com/observer/osm/story/0, 543962,00.html (last accessed April 19, 2025).

[63] Boys vs Women, "Male High School Athletes vs Female Olympians," https://boysvswomen.com/#/ (last accessed December 10, 2024).

[64] Boys vs Women, "Male High School Athletes vs Female Olympians," https://boysvswomen.com/#/ (last accessed March 21, 2025).

[65] Minna Svärd, "My Stolen NCAA Championship," *The Wall Street Journal*, March 17, 2025, https://www.wsj.com/opinion/my-stolen-ncaa-championship-transgender-athletes-womens-sports-7464db0a?st=eMCFTe&reflink=article_email_share (last accessed April 19, 2025).

[66] Ibid.

[67] Chelsea Mitchell, "I Was the Fastest Girl in Connecticut. But Transgender Athletes Made It an Unfair Fight," Alliance Defending Freedom, May 26, 2021, revised June 6, 2024, https://adflegal.org/article/i-was-fastest-girl-connecticut-transgender-athletes-made-it-unfair-fight/ (last accessed April 21, 2025).

[68] Rikki Schlott, "Fastest girl in Connecticut' Chelsea Mitchell suing state after losing to trans athletes," *New York Post*, May 31, 2023, https://nypost.com/2023/05/31/runner-chelsea-mitchell-who-lost-to-trans-athletes-this-is-about-fairness/ (last accessed April 21, 2025).

[69] Haley Strack, "California School Board Bashes State Policy Allowing Male Participation in Female Sports: 'Absolute Travesty,'" *National Review*, March 27, 2025, https://www.nationalreview.com/news/california-school-board-bashes-state-policy-allowing-male-participation-in-female-sports-absolute-travesty/ (last accessed April 21, 2025).

[70] Daniel Matthews, "Fresh trans sports feud breaks out in Oregon as controversial athlete wins 400m race by nearly 10 seconds," *Daily Mail*, March 21, 2025, https://www.dailymail.co.uk/sport/othersports/article-14523127/Trans-sports-feud-Oregon-ada-gallagher-track.html (last accessed April 19, 2025).

[71] Sally Jenkins, "In transgender fight, volleyball 'saviors' miss the point of sports," *The Washington Post*, November 28, 2024, https://www.washingtonpost.com/sports/2024/11/27/save-womens-sports-transgender-athletes/ (last accessed April 19, 2025).

[72] Ibid.

[73] Jenkins, "In transgender fight, volleyball 'saviors' miss the point of sports."

[74] "Bill Maher *Eviscerates* Neil deGrasse Tyson on Transgender Athletes Controversy," *The Hill*, YouTube, November 28, 2024, https://www.youtube.com/watch?v=BgJpa8MGKs4 (last accessed April 19, 2025).

[75] Jack Turban, "Trans Girls Belong on Girls' Sports Teams," *Scientific American*, March 16, 2021, https://www.scientificamerican.com/article /trans-girls-belong-on-girls-sports-teams/ (last accessed April 19, 2025).

[76] Daniel García-Martínez et al., "Morphological and functional implications of sexual dimorphism in the human skeletal thorax," *American Journal of*

Physical Anthropology, Vol. 161, No. 3 (November 2016), pp. 467 and 477, https://pubmed.ncbi.nlm.nih.gov/27444750/ (last accessed April 21, 2025).

[77] Turban, "Trans Girls Belong on Girls' Sports Teams."

[78] John J. Straub et al., "Risk of Suicide and Self-Harm Following Gender-Affirmation Surgery," *Cureus*, Vol. 16, No. 4 (April 2024;), p .e57472, https://pmc.ncbi.nlm.nih.gov/articles/PMC11063965/ (last accessed April 21, 2025).

[79] U.S. Department of Education, "Fact Sheet: U.S. Department of Education's Proposed Change to its Title IX Regulations on Students' Eligibility for Athletic Teams," April 6, 2023, https://www.ed.gov/sites/ed/files/about/offices/list/ocr/docs/t9-ath-nprm-factsheet.pdf (last accessed April 21, 2025).

[80] Marc Raimondi, "Transgender fighter Alana McLaughlin submits Celine Provost in MMA debut," ESPN, September 11, 2021, https://www.espn.com/mma/story/_/id/32186035/transgender-fighter-alana-mclaughlin-submits-celine-provost-mma-debut (last accessed April 21, 2025).

[81] Bhavesh Purohit, "When transgender fighter Fallon Fox broke her opponent's skull in MMA fight," Sportskeeda, September 30, 2021, https://www.sportskeeda.com/mma/news-when-transgender-fighter-fallon-fox-broke-opponent-s-skull-mma-fight (last accessed April 21, 2025).

[82] Chris Nesi, "Volleyball player hurt by trans opponent—and honored by Trump—calls out Democrats for 'failing women,'" *New York Post*, March 5, 2025, https://nypost.com/2025/03/05/us-news/volleyball-star-hurt-by-trans-opponent-say-dems-are-failing-women/ (last accessed April 21, 2025).

[83] Becky Sullivan and Fatima Al-Kassab, "Algerian boxer Imane Khelif wins Olympic gold in face of political controversy," NPR, August 9, 2024, https://www.npr.org/2024/08/09/g-s1-16308/imane-khelif-algeria-boxer-olympic (last accessed April 21, 2025).

[84] "Lin follows Khelif by winning gold amid controversy," BBC News, August 10, 2024, https://www.bbc.com/sport/olympics/articles/c1w7q075pw0o#:~:text=An%20emotional%20Lin%20Yu%2Dting,Khelif%20became%20the%20welterweight%20champion (last accessed April 21, 2025).

[85] Sullivan and Al-Kassab, "Algerian boxer Imane Khelif wins Olympic gold in face of political controversy."

[86] Chicago Cyclocross Cup, "Frequently Asked Questions," https://chicrosscup.com/races/rules-faqs/ (last accessed December 5, 2023).

[87] Tate Miller, "Nearly 80 percent of Americans don't want men playing in women's sports," The Center Square, February 1, 2025, https://www.thecentersquare.com/national/article_b6537968-dff2-11ef-b274-9fbf7250bf7f.html (last accessed April 21, 2025).

[88] United Nations, "Global ban needed on bogus 'conversion therapy,' argues UN rights expert," UN News, June 21, 2020, https://news.un.org/en/story/2020/06/1066652 (last accessed April 21, 2025).

[89] Press release, "Foxx Introduces the Parental Right to Protect Act," U.S. House of Representatives, Committee on Education and the Workforce, December

14, 2022, https://edworkforce.house.gov/news/documentsingle.aspx?
DocumentID=408723 (last accessed April 21, 2025).

[90] Grace Melton, "How UN Undermines Parental Rights by Pushing Gender Ideology," The Daily Signal, November 17, 2023, https://www.dailysignal.com/2023/11/17/how-un-undermines-parental-rights-by-pushing-gender-ideology/ (last accessed April 21, 2025).

[91] "I want to apologise to Khelif–Italian boxer Carini," BBC Sport, August 2, 2024, https://www.bbc.com/sport/olympics/articles/c2j3jg51rg4o (last accessed April 21, 2025).

[92] Melissa Koenig, "Martial arts competition changes rules after female fighters pull out over safety fears after facing trans grapplers," New York Post, October 31, 2023, https://nypost.com/2023/10/31/news/naga-martial-arts-org-changes-rules-on-trans-fighters/ (last accessed May 17, 2025).

[93] Scott Thompson, "Female pool player forfeits final due to facing trans woman opponent: reports," Daily Mail, November 14, 2023, https://www.foxnews.com/sports/female-pool-player-forfeits-final-facing-trans-woman-opponent (last accessed April 21, 2025).

[94] Dan Sales, "The pool matriarch who snubbed her transgender opponent because she 'refuses to be silenced,'" Daily Mail, November 15, 2023, https://www.dailymail.co.uk/news/article-12751603/lynne-pinches-pool-matriarch-snubbed-transgender-opponent-family-elite-players-cried-trans-competitor-rules-change.html (last accessed April 21, 2025).

[95] Clair McFarland, "Fourth Team Joins UW Volleyball In Refusing To Play Squad With Trans Player," Cowboy State Daily, October 3, 2024, https://cowboystatedaily.com/2024/10/03/fourth-team-joins-uw-volleyball-in-refusing-to-play-squad-with-trans-player/ (last accessed April 21, 2025).

[96] Jennifer Sey, X post, April 3, 2025, https://x.com/JenniferSey/status/1907810688178991593 (last accessed April 21, 2025).

[97] Oliver Salt, "What transgender fencer told protesting female rival before watching her get kicked out," Daily Mail, April 3, 2025, https://www.dailymail.co.uk/sport/othersports/article-14568057/transgender-fencer-redmond-sulivan-stephanie-turner-disqualified.html (last accessed April 21, 2025).

[98] Professional Disc Gold Association, Natalie Ryan, https://www.pdga.com/player/114560 (last accessed April 5, 2025).

[99] Mairead Elordi, "'Most Likely Ended My Career': Disc Golfer Who Protested Trans Competitor Says She Has No Regrets," Daily Wire, April 4, 2025, https://www.dailywire.com/news/most-likely-ended-my-career-disc-golfer-who-protests-trans-competitor-says-she-has-no-regrets (last accessed April 21, 2025).

[100] Soh, The End of Gender, p.141

[101] Andrew Sullivan, "Will Big Trans Be Held to Account?" The Weekly Dish, Substack, April 12, 2024, https://andrewsullivan.substack.com/p/will-big-trans-be-held-to-account-3ad?utm_campaign=email-half-post&r=j8y2f&utm_source=substack&utm_medium=email (last accessed April 21, 2025).

[102] Ibid.

[103] Christina Buttons, "The Tragedy of Yarden Silveira," *City Journal*, March 12, 2025, https://www.city-journal.org/article/yarden-silveira-death-transgender -surgery-complications?utm_source=virtuous&utm_medium=email&utm_ campaign=cjdaily&vcrmeid=WCwziXyodkewpoAPiHvSew&vcrmiid=T-Fi_6SrbEu6UHLU4O3tBA (last accessed May 17, 2025).

[104] Ibid.

[105] Ibid.

[106] Hilary Cass, "Independent review of gender identity services for children and young people," *The Cass Review*, Final report, 2024, https://cass.independent -review.uk/home/publications/final-report/ (last accessed April 21, 2025).

[107] Sullivan, "Will Big Trans Be Held to Account"?

[108] Helen Joyce, Interview with Peter Boghossian, YouTube.com, July, 3, 2023, https://www.youtube.com/watch?v=ZG9_lcln7FU&t=0s (last accessed May 17, 2025).

[109] Martin Cleaver, @MCleaver, X, November 18, 2023, https://x.com/Mcleaver /status/1725843318804766873?s=20 (last accessed May 17, 2025).

[110] Society for Evidence-Based Gender Medicine, https://segm.org/ (last accessed March 22, 2025).

[111] Presidential Actions, "Defending Women from Gender Ideology Extremism and Restoring Biological Truth to the Federal Government," The White House, January 20, 2025.

[112] Nathaniel Blake, "Detrans Awareness Day Heralds a Reckoning for Transgender 'Medicine' Fraudsters," *The Federalist*, March 14, 2025, https://thefederalist.com/2025/03/14/detrans-awareness-day-heralds-a-reckoning-for-transgender-medicine-fraudsters/ (last accessed April 21, 2025).

[113] Dave Yost, "Ohio Stands for Children and against Gender Activists," *National Review*, April 4, 2024, https://www.nationalreview.com/2024/04/ohio-stands-for-children-and-against-gender-activists/(last accessed April 21, 2025).

Chapter 6

[1] Adam Ellwanger, "'Social Justice' and the Right," *The American Mind*, September 10, 2024, https://americanmind.org/salvo/social-justice-and-the-right/ (last accessed May 11, 2025).

[2] Ozlem Sensoy and Robin DiAngelo, *Is Everyone Really Equal? An Introduction to Key Concepts in Social Justice Education*, first edition (New York: Teacher's College Press, 2012), p. xviii.

3. Robin DiAngelo, *White Fragility* (Boston: Beacon Press, 2018).

[4] Ellwanger, "'Social Justice' and the Right."

[5] Martin Luther King Jr., Speech at the Lincoln Memorial in Washington, DC, August 28, 1963.

[6] Wilfred Reilly, *Hate Crime Hoax* (Washington, DC: Regnery Publishing, 2019).

[7] John T. Bennett, "Gun violence, white supremacy and the economy: What Black voters want Democrats to fix," *Roll Call*, May 19, 2023, https://rollcall.com/2023/05/19/gun-violence-white-supremacy-and-the-economy-what-black-voters-want-democrats-to-fix/ (last accessed May 11, 2025).

[8] Andrew Sullivan, "America's New Religions," The Intelligencer, December 7, 2018, https://nymag.com/intelligencer/2018/12/andrew-sullivan-americas-new-religions.html (last accessed May 11, 2025).

[9] Helen Pluckrose and James Lindsay, *Cynical Theories: How Activist Scholarship Made Everything About Race, Gender, and Identity—and Why This Harms Everybody* (Durham, NC: Pitchstone Publishing, 2020).

[10] Ibid., p. 53.

[11] Ibid., p. 35.

[12] Ibid., p. 111.

13. Ibram X. Kendi, *How to Be an Antiracist* (New York: Random House, 2019).

14. Richard Delgado and Jean Stefancic, *Critical Race Theory: An Introduction* (New York: New York University Press, 2012).

[15] Marina Watts, "In Smithsonian Race Guidelines, Rational Thinking and Hard Work Are White Values," *Newsweek*, July 17, 2020, https://www.newsweek.com/smithsonian-race-guidelines-rational-thinking-hard-work-are-white-values-1518333 (last accessed May 11, 2025).

[16] Anthony Bernardi, "Why Waking Up Early Is Rooted in White Supremacy," Medium, March 18, 2023, https://medium.com/@anthonybernardi/why-waking-up-early-is-rooted-in-white-supremacy-f487b04376f1 (last accessed May 11, 2025).

[17] Sowell, "Social Justice Fallacies," p. 23.

[18] Karissa Provenza, "Operating within Systems of Oppression," *Hastings Race and Poverty Law Journal*, Vol. 18, No. 2 (Summer 2021), https://repository.uclawsf.edu/cgi/viewcontent.cgi?article=1169&context=hastings_race_poverty_law_journal (last accessed May 11, 2025).

[19] Rita Panahi, @RitaPanahi, X, May 8, 2025, https://x.com/RitaPanahi/status/1920335119023222845 (last accessed May 12, 2025).

[20] William Elder, "The Aborigines of Nova Scotia," The North American Review, Vol. 112, No. 230 (Jan., 1871), pp. 1-30 (30 pages), https://www.jstor.org/stable/25109587 (last accessed May 12, 2025).

[21] Heather MacDonald, "Disparate Impact Thinking Is Destroying Our Civilization," *Imprimis*, February 2024, Vol. 53, No. 2 (February 2024), https://imprimis.hillsdale.edu/disparate-impact-thinking-is-destroying-our-civilization/

[22] American College Testing, "ACT Test Day, Everything you need to know for the day of the test," https://www.act.org/content/act/en/products-and-services/the-act/test-day.html (last accessed April 5, 2025).

[23] *The Journal of Blacks in Higher Education*, "Black Scores on the ACT College Entrance Examination Are in Freefall," October 23, 2023, https://jbhe.com/2023/10/black-scores-on-the-act-college-entrance-examination-are-in-freefall/ (last accessed May 11, 2025).

[24] Mac Donald, "Disparate Impact Thinking Is Destroying Our Civilization."

[25] Ibid.

[26] Ibid.

[27] S. Mac Healey and Angelina J. Parker, "Harvard Launches New Intro Math Course to Address Pandemic Learning Loss," *The Harvard Crimson*, September 3, 2024, https://www.thecrimson.com/article/2024/9/3/new-math-intro-course/ (last accessed May 11, 2025).

[28] Mac Donald, "Disparate Impact Thinking Is Destroying Our Civilization."

[29] Ibid.

[30] Institute for Free Speech, "Johnson v. Watkin," Case Status, June 5, 2023, https://www.ifs.org/cases/johnson-v-watkin/ (last accessed May 12, 2025).

[31] Taylor Penley, "California college professor says 'completely fabricated' claims of racism may cost him his job," Fox News, January 17, 2023, https://www.foxnews.com/media/professor-sues-california-college-villainizing -conservative-speech-culled-disruptive-animal (last accessed May 11, 2025).

[32] Sara Weissman, "Conservative Professor Settles With Community College District for $2.4M," Inside Higher Ed, July 31, 2024, https://www.inside highered.com/news/quick-takes/2024/07/31/conservative-professor-promised -24m-lawsuit-settlement, (last accessed May 12, 2025).

[33] Kristina Watrobski, "Prof sues California college trustee who compared opponents of diversity efforts to 'livestock' that need 'the slaughterhouse,'" ABC15 News, June 26, 2023, https://wpde.com/news/nation-world/prof-sues-california-college-trustee-who-compared-opponents-of-diversity-efforts-to-livestock-that-need-the-slaughterhouse-bakersfield-kern-community-college-district-daymon-johnson-john-corkins-institute-for-free-speech (last accessed May 12, 2025).

[34] Micah Zenko, "The Foreign-Policy Blob Is Structurally Racist," *Foreign Policy*, July 10, 2020. https://foreignpolicy.com/2020/07/10/foreign-policy-is-structurally-racist/ (last accessed May 12, 2025).

[35] Ibid.

[36] Simon Hankinson, "'Woke' Public Diplomacy Undermines the State Department's Core Mission and Weakens U.S. Foreign Policy," Heritage Foundation *Backgrounder* No. 3738, December 12, 2022, https://www.heritage.org/global-politics/report/woke-public-diplomacy-undermines-the-state-departments-core-mission-and (last accessed May 11, 2025).

[37] Brad McDowell, "DEI Got Me Sacked From My Nursing Job," *The Wall Street Journal*, March 15, 2024.

[38] Ibid.

[39] Naomi Schaefer Riley, "Doctors are embracing identity politics – and harming babies," The Spectator, April 26, 2025, https://thespectator.com/topic/doctors-embracing-identity-politics-harming-babies/

[40] Abigail Anthony, "Major Infant-Mortality Study Was Edited to Preserve Racial 'Perspective,'" *National Review*,

April 2, 2025, https://www.nationalreview.com/2025/04/major-infant-mortality-study-was-edited-to-preserve-racial-perspective/ (last accessed May 11, 2025).

[41] Brad N. Greenwood et al., "Physician–patient racial concordance and disparities in birthing mortality for newborns," *Proceedings of the National Academy of Sciences*, July 16, 2020, https://www.pnas.org/doi/10.1073/pnas.1913405117 (last accessed May 11, 2025).

[42] John Murawski, "Why did it take four years to debunk the black baby study?" Unherd, September 18, 2024, https://unherd.com/newsroom/why-did-it-take-four-years-to-debunk-the-blac-baby-study/ (last accessed May 11, 2025).

[43] Anthony, "Major Infant-Mortality Study Was Edited to Preserve Racial 'Perspective.'"

[44] Emily Kopp, "EXCLUSIVE: Researchers Axed Data Point Undermining 'Narrative' That White Doctors Are Biased Against Black Babies," *The Daily Caller*, March 31, 2025, https://dailycaller.com/2025/03/31/exclusive-researchers-axed-data-point-undermining-narrative-that-white-doctors-are-biased-against-black-babies/ (last accessed May 11, 2025).

[45] Ibid.

[46] Anthony, "Major Infant-Mortality Study Was Edited to Preserve Racial 'Perspective.'"

[47] Lauren Underwood, "The 100 Most Influential People of 2024: Rachel Hardeman," *Time*, April 17, 2024, https://time.com/6964631/rachel-hardeman/ (last accessed May 11, 2025).

[48] Kopp, "EXCLUSIVE: Researchers Axed Data Point Undermining 'Narrative' That White Doctors Are Biased Against Black Babies.'"

[49] Elliot Hughes and Zoë Jackson, "University of Minnesota's Rachel Hardeman steps down as plagiarism accusations are made public," *The Minnesota Star Tribune*, April 15, 2025, https://www.startribune.com/university-of-minnesotas-rachel-hardeman-steps-down-as-plagiarism-accusations-are-made-public/601331138 (last accessed May 11, 2025).

[50] Brigette A. Davis, "I've been quiet about Rachel Hardeman's plagiarism for far too long," LinkedIn, April 10, 2025, https://www.linkedin.com/pulse/ive-been-quiet-rachel-hardemans-plagiarism-far-too-davis-phd-mph-u0lvc/ (last accessed May 11, 2025).

[51] Center for Disease Control, "About Mpox," January 31, 2025, https://www.cdc.gov/mpox/about/index.html#:~:text=Mpox%20(formerly%20known%20as%20monkeypox,rash%2C%20along%20with%20other%20symptoms (;ast accessed March 16, 2025).

[52] Fenit Nirappil, "CDC: Consider fewer sexual partners to avoid monkeypox," *The Washington Post*, August 5, 2022, https://www.washingtonpost.com/health/2022/08/05/monkeypox-sex-cdc-guidance/ (last accessed May 11, 2025).

[53] Ibid.

[54] Hannah Natanson, "Virginia is changing the way it teaches history, social studies. Here's how," *The Washington Post*, November 16, 2022,

https://www.washingtonpost.com/education/2022/11/16/virginia-school-history-standards-youngkin/ (last accessed May 11, 2025).

[55] Ibid.

[56] The Nation's Report Card, "U.S. History: Achievement-Level Results," https://www.nationsreportcard.gov/ushistory/results/achievement/ (last accessed April 22, 2024).

[57] Elizabeth Troutman, "Minnesota School District Pours Millions Into 'Woke' Math as Student Scores Plummet," *The Washington Free Beacon*, August 3, 2022, https://freebeacon.com/campus/minnesota-school-district-pours-millions-into-woke-math-as-student-scores-plummet/ (last accessed May 11, 2025).

[58] The Nation's Report Card, "2024 Mathematics State Snapshot Report," 2024, https://nces.ed.gov/nationsreportcard/subject/publications/stt2024/pdf/2024 219MN4.pdf (last accessed March 27, 2025).

[59] University of Illinois Urbana-Champaign, College of Education, "Rochelle Gutierrez, Biography," https://education.illinois.edu/faculty/rochelle-gutierrez (last accessed May 11, 2025).

[60] Alexa Schwerha, "Math Education Discriminates Against Queer, Trans Students, Prof Argues," *The Daily Caller*, January 20, 2023, https://dailycaller.com/2023/01/20/professor-math-white-cisheteropatriarchal-space-conference/ (last accessed May 11, 2025).

[61] Kim Dacey, "Just 7% of students proficient in math in Baltimore City, according to test results," WBALTV, April 27, 2023, https://www.wbaltv.com/article/students-proficient-math-baltimore-city/43733243# (last accessed May 11, 2025).

[62] Gerry Canavan, "The racist literary origins of Indiana Jones," *The Washington Post*, June 28, 2023, https://www.washingtonpost.com/books/2023/06/28/indiana-jones-racism-books/ (last accessed May 11, 2025).

[63] Meena Venkataramanan, "This scholar is pulling back the curtain on race in Shakespeare," *The Washington Post*, August 23, 2023, https://www.washingtonpost.com/books/2023/08/23/farah-karim-cooper-great-white-bard/ (last accessed May 11, 2025).

[64] Ibid.

[65] Nathan Biller, "Famed Shakespeare's Globe theatre hosts 'Anti-Racist Shakespeare,'" The College Fix, February 21, 2023, https://www.thecollegefix.com/famed-shakespeares-globe-theatre-hosts-anti-racist-shakespeare / (last accessed May 11, 2025).

[66] Mike LaChance, "Scholars Obtain $500K Grant to Deconstruct Whiteness in Physics," The College Fix, Jue 12, 2022, https://legalinsurrection.com/2022/06/scholars-obtain-500k-grant-to-decontruct-whiteness-in-physics/ (last accessed May 11, 2025).

[67] Aaron Sibarium, "'Disqualifying': Member of Top DOE Physics Panel Said 'White Empiricism' Undermines Theory of Relativity, Accused Israel of Genocide," *The Washington Free Beacon*, March 17, 2025, https://freebeacon.com/campus/disqualifying-member-of-top-doe-physics-panel-said-

white-empiricism-undermines-theory-of-relativity-accused-israel-of-genocide / (last accessed May 11, 2025).

[68] Chanda Prescod-Weinstein, "Making Black Women Scientists under White Empiricism: The Racialization of Epistemology in Physics, *Signs*, Vol. 45, No. 2 (Winter 2020), https://www.journals.uchicago.edu/doi/full/10.1086 /704991 (last accessed May 11, 2025).

[69] Chanda Prescod-Weinstein, "Our job is to protect student curiosity," August 20, 2024, https://news.chanda.science/archive/our-job-is-to-protect-student-curiosity/

[70] Michael Powell, "M.I.T.'s Choice of Lecturer Ignited Criticism. So Did Its Decision to Cancel," *The New York Times*, October 20, 2021, https://www.ny times.com/2021/10/20/us/dorian-abbot-mit.html (last accessed May 11, 2025).

[71] Michael de Adder, "Two Americas," *The Washington Post*, January 28, 2023, https://www.washingtonpost.com/opinions/2023/01/28/two-americas/ (last accessed May 11, 2025).

[72] "Jussie Smollett: Timeline of a hoax, jail time and an overturned conviction," BBC News, November 21, 2024, https://www.bbc.com/news/newsbeat-47317701 (last accessed May 11, 2025).

[73] David Chang, "Pa. woman put noose on desk, accused someone else of placing it, police say," NBC News Philadelphia, March 24, 2025, https://www.nbcphiladelphia.com/news/local/pa-woman-put-noose-on-desk-accused-someone-else-of-placing-it-police-say/4142658/ (last accessed May 11, 2025).

[74] Reilly, *Hate Crime Hoax*, p. xvii.

[75] Ibid., p. xvii.

[76] The Rabbit Hole, X, December 9, 2024, https://x.com/TheRabbit Hole84/status/1866174521625235729 (last accessed May 11, 2025).

[77] Reilly, *Hate Crime Hoax*, p. xvii.

[78] Mac Donald, "Disparate Impact Thinking Is Destroying Our Civilization."

[79] Reilly, *Hate Crime Hoax*, p. xvi.

[80] Mac Donald, "Disparate Impact Thinking Is Destroying Our Civilization."

[81] Van Jones, CNN, January 27, 2023, https://www.cnn.com/2023/01/27/ opinions/tyre-nichols-memphis-police-department-jones (last updated June 26, 2025)

[82] CNN Editorial Research, "Trayvon Martin Shooting Fast Facts," CNN, February 5, 2025, https://www.cnn.com/2013/06/05/us/trayvon-martin-shooting fast facts (last accessed May 12, 2025).

[83] Cheryl Corley, "Whether History Or Hype, 'Hands Up, Don't Shoot' Endures," August 8, 2015, NPR, https://www.npr.org/2015/08/08/430411141/whether-history-or-hype-hands-up-dont-shoot-endures, (last accessed May 11, 2025).

[84] Ben Johnson, "Exclusive: What The Media Didn't Tell You About Breonna Taylor's Shooting," The Daily Wire, March 22, 2022, https://www.dailywire.com/news/exclusive-what-the-media-didnt-tell-you-about-breonna-taylors-shooting, (last accessed May 12, 2025).

[85] María Luisa Paúl, "NAACP issues travel advisory, calling Florida 'hostile' to Black Americans," *The Washington Post,* May 22, 2023, https://www.washingtonpost.com/nation/2023/05/22/naacp-travel-advisory-florida-desantis/ (last accessed May 11, 2025).

[86] Ibid.

[87] NBC 6, "Rap legend Luther 'Uncle Luke' Campbell to have Miami street named after him," NBC6, March 5, 2025, https://www.nbcmiami.com/news/local/rap-legend-luther-uncle-luke-campbell-to-have-miami-street-named-after-him/3558922/ (last accessed May 11, 2025).

[88] Dave McIntyr, "Wine vocabulary is Eurocentric. It's time to change that," *The Washington Post,* March 2, 2023, https://www.washingtonpost.com/food/2023/03/02/wine-vocabulary-exclusionary/ (last accessed May 11, 2025).

[89] Brandon D. Dull, Leoandra Onnie Rogers, Jade Ross, "Learning (Not) to Know: Examining How White Ignorance Manifests and Functions in White Adolescents' Racial Identity Narratives," Child Development, January 23, 2025, https://doi.org/10.1111/cdev.14215 (last accessed June 24, 2025).

[90] James L. Nuzzo, "Woke Academics Are Rigging Their Research Methods To Support Their Ideology," Reality's Last Stand, June 23, 2025, https://www.realityslaststand.com/ (last accessed June 24, 2025)

[91] Linda Martin Alcoff, quoted in Brandon Dull, et al, Ibid.

[92] Neil Young, "Ambulance Blues," *On the Beach,* Reprise Records, 1974

[93] Samantha Chery, "Black English is being misidentified as Gen Z lingo, speakers say," *The Washington Post,* August 17, 2022, https://www.washingtonpost.com/nation/2022/08/17/black-english-misidentified-internet-slang/ (last accessed May 11, 2025).

[94] Ariel Zilber, "Whoops! CRT advocate Ibram X. Kendi is mocked for deleting tweet about how white college applicants are LYING about their race to get accepted 'because it undermined his argument about privilege,'" The Daily Mail, October 31, 2021, https://www.dailymail.co.uk/news/article-10150967/Ibram-X-Kendi-deletes-tweet-white-college-applicants-LIE-black.html (last accessed May 11, 2025).

[95] Amber Payne, "Rachel Dolezal on Why She Can't Just Be a White Ally," NBC News, March 28, 2017, https://www.nbcnews.com/news/nbcblk/rachel-dolezal-why-she-can-t-just-be-white-ally-n738911 (last accessed May 11, 2025).

[96] Andrew Kerr, "Fake Muslim Activist Scored Invite to Obama White House and Rubbed Shoulders with 'Squad' Members," *The Washington Free Beacon,* February 22, 2023, https://freebeacon.com/democrats/fake-muslim-activist-scored-invite-to-obama-white-house-and-rubbed-shoulders-with-squad-members/ (last accessed May 11, 2025).

[97] Addie Morfoot, "Inside the Doc World Controversy Pitting Ken Burns Against His Peers," *The Atlantic,* September 16, 2022, https://variety.com/2022/film/features/doc-world-controversy-ken-burns-against-his-peers-1235363481/ (last accessed May 11, 2025).

[98] We See You, White American Theater, "Principles for Building Anti-Racist Theatre Systems," https://www.weseeyouwat.com/ (last accessed May 12, 2025).

[99] Michael Paulson, "Theater Artists of Color Enumerate Demands for Change," *The New York Times*, July 10, 2020, https://www.nytimes.com/2020/07/10/theater/we-see-you-theater-demands.html#:~:text=A%2029%2Dpage%20document%20released,backstage%2C%20on%20Broadway%20and%20beyond.&text=Rename%20half%20of%20all%20Broadway,limits%20for%20theater%20industry%20leaders (last accessed May 11, 2025).

[100] Mark Landler, "Outcry over Britain's racist past moved into the boardrooms," *The New York Times*, June 19, 2020, https://www.nytimes.com/2020/06/18/world/europe/uk-slavery-trade-lloyds-greene-king.html (last accessed May 11, 2025).

[101] Frank Ricci, "The harm that DEI has done to public safety cannot be overstated," *The Spectator*, March 2, 2025, https://thespectator.com/topic/harm-dei-done-public-safety-overstated/ (last accessed May 11, 2025).

[102] Press Release, "Justice Department Sues South Bend, Indiana, for Discriminating Against Black and Female Police Officer Applicants," U.S. Department of Justice, October 11, 2024, https://www.justice.gov/opa/pr/justice-department-sues-south-bend-indiana-discriminating-against-black-and-female-police?utm_source=substack&utm_medium=email (last accessed May 11, 2025).

[103] *United States v. City of South Bend, Indiana*, USDC IN/ND case 3:24-cv-00830, filed October 11, 2024, https://www.justice.gov/crt/media/1373236/dl?utm_source=substack&utm_medium=email (last accessed May 11, 2025).

[104] Nellie Bowles, "TGIF: Super Heavy Booster," *The Free Press*, October 18, 2024, https://www.thefp.com/p/tgif-super-heavy-booster?utm_campaign=email-post&r=j8y2f&utm_source=substack&utm_medium=email (last accessed May 11, 2025).

[105] Press Release, "Justice Department Secures Agreement with Maryland Department of State Police to Resolve Allegations of Race and Gender Discrimination in State Trooper Hiring Process," U.S. Deparatment of Justice, October 2, 2024, https://www.justice.gov/opa/pr/justice-department-secures-agreement-maryland-department-state-police-resolve-allegations (last accessed May 11, 2025).

[106] Press Release, "Justice Department Secures Agreement with Durham, North Carolina, to End Discriminatory Hiring Practices in City's Fire Department," U.S. Department of Justice, October 8, 2024, https://www.justice.gov/opa/pr/justice-department-secures-agreement-durham-north-carolina-end-discriminatory-hiring (last accessed May 11, 2025).

[107] U.S. Department of Justice, Civil Rights Division, "Fact Sheet: Combating Hiring Discrimination by Police & Fire Departments," https://www.justice.gov/crt/fact-sheet-combating-hiring-discrimination-police-fire-departments (last accessed October 21, 2024).

[108] John R. Lott, Jr., "Biden Made Communities Less Safe By Forcing DEI On Police And Fire Departments," The Federalist, June 04, 2025, https://thefederalist.com/2025/06/04/biden-made-communities-less-safe-by-forcing-dei-on-police-and-fire-departments/?utm_source=rss&utm_medium=rss&utm_campaign=biden-made-communities-less-safe-by-forcing-dei-on-police-and-fire-departments&utm_term=2025-06-04, (last accessed June 23, 2025).

[109] Ibid.

[110] Jena McGregor, Intel Diversity Report Shorts No Pay Gap Between Its Male, Female Workers, *The Washington Post*, February 3, 2016, https://www.washingtonpost.com/news/on-leadership/wp/2016/02/03/intel-says-there-is-no-pay-gap-between-men-and-women-at-the-chipmaker/ (last accessed May 13, 2025).

[111] Pave Data Lab, "The Gender Pay Gap: Normalized vs Adjusted," September 30, 2024, https://www.pave.com/blog-posts/gender-pay-gap-normalized-vs-adjusted (last accessed May 11, 2025).

[112] Phil Gramm and John Early, "The 'Gender Pay Gap' Is a Myth That Won't Go Away," *The Wall Street Journal*, March 8, 2024, https://www.wsj.com/opinion/the-gender-pay-gap-is-a-myth-that-wont-go-away-1f0e3841 (last accessed May 11, 2025).

[113] Melissa Koenig, "Los Angeles Fire Department's diversity chief blames fire victims in shocking viral video defending DEI," *Daily Mail*, January 12, 2025, https://www.dailymail.co.uk/news/article-14276655/Los-Angeles-Fire-Department-Kristine-Larson-diversity-fire-victims.html (last accessed May 11, 2025).

[114] Ricci, "The harm that DEI has done to public safety cannot be overstated."

[115] Ken Dilanian, "Trump upends DOJ's Civil Rights Division, sparking 'bloodbath' in senior ranks," NBC News, April 23, 2025, https://www.nbcnews.com/politics/justice-department/trump-upends-dojs-civil-rights-division-sparking-bloodbath-senior-rank-rcna202622 (last accessed May 11, 2025).

[116] Press Release, "Justice Department Corrects Past Administration's Manipulation of Legal System that Sought to Force States to Provide Surgery to Transgender Inmates," U.S. Department of Justice, April 25, 2025, https://www.justice.gov/opa/pr/justice-department-corrects-past-administrations-manipulation-legal-system-sought-force (last accessed May 11, 2025).

[117] Logan Dubil, "Students call out university for its 'power and privilege' workshop," Campus Reform, August 3, 2022, https://www.campusreform.org/article?id=19901 (last accessed May 11, 2025).

[118] Pamela Paresky and Lee Jussim, "A reckoning with DEI pedagogy," *The Spectator*, December 18, 2024, https://thespectator.com/topic/reckoning-dei-pedagogy-study/ (last accessed May 11, 2025).

[119] David Zimmerman, "Boston University Plans to Close Antiracist Center as Ibram X. Kendi Departs for Howard," *National Review*, January 31, 2025,

https://www.nationalreview.com/news/boston-university-plans-to-close-antiracist-center-as-ibram-x-kendi-departs-for-howard/ (last accessed May 11, 2025).

[120] Amanda Kijera, "We are not your weapons, we are women," Race Talk, Kirwan Institute for the Study of Race and Ethnicity, 2010, https://archive.ph/IvEDJ#selection-755.0-755.492 (last accessed March 26, 2025).

[121] Ibid.

[122] Tim Johns, "Friends of murdered Oakland baker call for alternatives to prison for alleged teen killer," ABC News, June 24, 2023, https://abc7news.com/oakland-robbery-angle-cakes-jennifer-angel-ishmael-burch-charged/134204 41/ (last accessed May 11, 2025).

[123] Ibid.

[124] Roland Fryer, "The Economics of DEI and Merit," *The Wall Street Journal*, March 6, 2025, https://www.wsj.com/opinion/the-economics-of-dei-and-merit-hiring-productivity-1fc094d2 (last accessed May 11, 2025).

[125] Ibid.

Chapter 7

[1] Kerry Picket, "Only 3.4% of U.S. journalists are Republicans: Survey," *The Washington Times*, December 30, 2023, https://www.washingtontimes.com/news/2023/dec/30/only-34-us-journalists-are-republicans-survey/ (last accessed April 12, 2025).

[2] Curt Mills, "Journalists Donate Far More To Clinton," USNews, October 18, 2016, https://www.usnews.com/news/national-news/articles/2016-10-18/hillary-clinton-gets-more-donations-from-the-media-than-donald-trump-study-says

[3] Shannon Thaler, "Google News' bias skewed even further left in 2023—63% from liberal media sources, only 6% from the right: analysis," *New York Post*, February 23, 2024, https://nypost.com/2024/02/23/business/google-news-bias-skewed-even-further-left-in-2023-63-from-liberal-media-sources-only-6-from-the-right-analysis/?utm_campaign=iphone_nyp&utm_source=mail_app (accessed April 12, 2025).

[4] Leif Le Mahieu, "FCC to Make Broadcasters Publicly Post Race and Gender 'Scorecard' of All Employees," *The Daily Wire*, February 23, 2024, https://www.dailywire.com/news/fcc-to-make-broadcasters-publicly-post-race-and-gender-scorecard-of-all-employees (last accessed April 12, 2025).

[5] Nellie Bowles, "TGIF: Every Sperm Is Sacred," *The Free Press*, February 23, 2024, https://www.thefp.com/p/nellie-bowles-tgif-every-sperm-is-sacred (last accessed April 12, 2025).

[6] Lindsay Penney, "The Divided State of Google," X, February 24, 2024, https://x.com/TexasLindsay_/status/1761455150206423289?s=20 (last accessed February 26, 2024).

[7] Ibid.

[8] Andrew Chung and John Kruzel, "US Supreme Court leans toward allowing youth transgender care ban," Reuters, December 4, 2024, https://www.reuters.com/world/us/us-supreme-court-set-hear-major-transgender-rights-case-2024-12-04/?utm_source=Sailthru&utm_medium=Newsletter&utm_campaign=Daily-Briefing&utm_term=120424&lctg=64e4ee22405c84e68a050a7f (last accessed April 12, 2025).

[9] Shia Kapos, "Republicans say Biden is a 'liar' after he pardons Hunter, his son," *Politico*, December 1, 2024, https://www.politico.com/news/2024/12/01/republicans-pounce-on-biden-pardoning-his-son-hunter-00192091 (last accessed April 12, 2025).

[10] Selina Wang, Anne Flaherty, and Luke Barr, "Trump falsely claims Biden used FEMA funds for migrants—something Trump did himself," ABC News, October 7, 2024, https://abcnews.go.com/Politics/trump-falsely-claims-biden-fema-funds-migrants-trump/story?id=114577647 (last accessed April 12, 2025).

[11] Simon Hankinson, "DOGE discovers the Biden-Mayorkas illegal migration funding machine," Fox News February 13, 2025, https://www.foxnews.com/opinion/doge-discovers-biden-mayorkas-illegal-migration-funding-machine (last accessed April 12, 2025).

[12] FEMA, Fiscal Year 2024 Awards, https://www.fema.gov/grants/preparedness/shelter-services-program/fy24-awards, (accessed April 15, 2025).

[13] Jack Birle, "Karine Jean-Pierre gives mixed answer on FEMA funds for illegal immigrants," *Washington Examiner*, October 7, 2024, https://www.washingtonexaminer.com/news/white-house/3179679/karine-jean-pierre-mixed-answer-fema-funds-illegal-immigrants/ (last accessed April 12, 2025).

[14] The White House, "Press Briefing by Press Secretary Karine Jean-Pierre, September 15, 2022," https://bidenwhitehouse.archives.gov/briefing-room/press-briefings/2022/09/15/press-briefing-by-press-secretary-karine-jean-pierre-september-15-2022/ (last accessed April 12, 2025).

[15] Kevin Dalton, "ABC News: President Trump is lying about FEMA allocating funds to illegal immigrants," X, October 8, 2024, https://x.com/TheKevinDalton/status/1843724295824126076 (last accessed April 12, 2025).

[16] Timur Kuran, "If you're worried about 'misinformation,' this video editing should infuriate you…" October 8, 2024, https://x.com/timurkuran/status/1844012170813796682?utm_source=substack&utm_medium=email (last accessed April 12, 2025).

[17] Michael P. Hill, "CBS agrees to release transcript, video of Harris interview to FCC, public," NewscastStudio, February 5, 2025, https://www.newscaststudio.com/2025/02/05/cbs-news-trump-60-minutes-lawsuit-release/ (accessed April 13, 2025).

[18] Ibid.

[19] David Bauder, "When is an interview too tough? CBS News grappling with question after Dokoupil interview," AP News, October 10, 2024, https://apnews.com/article/cbs-news-dokoupil-israel-coates-interview-tone-01035b94b1a824c1589555def1a52c6b (last accessed April 12, 2025).

20 Ibid.

21 Ibid.

22 Paul Farhi and Elahe Izadi, "NPR is losing some of its Black and Latino hosts. Colleagues see a larger crisis," *The Washington Post*, January 5, 2022, https://www.washingtonpost.com/lifestyle/media/audie-cornish-npr-all-things-considered/2022/01/05/48e2d306-6d86-11ec-aaa8-35d1865a6977_story.html (last accessed April 12, 2025).

23 See the Reddit thread "Anyone else play Matt's NPR game?" https://www.reddit.com/r/WeTheFifth/comments/1b1kjxf/anybody_else_play_matts_npr_game/ (last accessed April 12, 2025). Also see David Zimmer, "National Public Radio exposed from the inside," American Experiment, April 10, 2024, https://www.americanexperiment.org/national-public-radio-exposed-from-the-inside/ (last accessed April 12, 2025).

24 Farhi and Izadi, "NPR is losing some of its Black and Latino hosts."

25 Paul du Quenoy, "NPR's Demise Long Overdue," Newsmax, February 8, 2024, https://www.newsmax.com/paulduquenoy/maher-nielsen-totenberg/2024/02/08/id/1152823/ (last accessed April 12, 2025).

26 Uri Berliner, "I've Been at NPR for 25 Years. Here's How We Lost America's Trust," *The Free Press*, April 9, 2024, https://www.thefp.com/p/npr-editor-how-npr-lost-americas-trust (last accessed April 12, 2025).

27 Kevin Mims, "Bad News—a Review," *Quillette*, October, 25, 2021, https://quillette.com/2021/10/25/bad-news-a-review/ (last accessed April 12, 2025).

28 Ibid.

29 Glenn Kessler, "No, Biden didn't take FEMA relief money to use on migrants — but Trump did," *The Washington Post*, October 4, 2024, https://www.washingtonpost.com/politics/2024/10/04/no-biden-didnt-take-fema-relief-money-use-migrants-trump-did/ (last accessed June 26, 2025).

30 *The Washington Post*, "People: Anne Branigin, Washington, D.C., Reporter, Style," https://www.washingtonpost.com/people/anne-branigin/ (last accessed April 12, 2025).

31 Mary Chastain, "Medical Journal The Lancet Abandons Science, Tells Authors to Use 'Sex Assigned at Birth,'" *Legal Insurrection*, June 2, 2024, https://legalinsurrection.com/2024/06/medical-journal-the-lancet-abandons-science-tells-authors-to-use-sex-assigned-at-birth/ (last accessed April 12, 2025).

32 *The Lancet*, "Information for Authors," June 2024, https://legalinsurrection.com/wp-content/uploads/2024/05/The-Lancet-Author-Guidelines.pdf (last accessed April 12, 2025).

33 Ibid.

34 Yaron Steinbuch, "Leading British medical journal ripped for calling women 'bodies with vaginas,'" *New York Post*, September 28, 2021, https://nypost.com/2021/09/28/the-lancet-ripped-for-calling-women-bodies-with-vaginas/ (last accessed April 12, 2025).

[35]   Sarah Naffa, "The Morning Wire," AP News, March 11, 2025, https://link.apnews.com/view/63933bc5a681d4d3690b81d5m2o3k.c2i5/b3f b249a (last accessed April 12, 2025).

[36] Sarah Ellison, "Trump's triumph threatens an already battered democracy, experts say," *The Washington Post*, November 6, 2024, https://www. washingtonpost.com/politics/2024/11/06/trump-victory-threatens-democracy / (last accessed April 12, 2025).

[37] Glenn Kessler, "Trump's 'crazy,' false ad claiming 'massive layoffs' among autoworkers," *The Washington Post*, October 22, 2024, https://www. washingtonpost.com/politics/2024/10/22/trumps-crazy-false-ad-claiming-massive-layoffs-among-auto-workers/ (last accessed April 12, 2025).

[38] Allysia Finley, "Press Bias Bolsters Trump, Again," *The Wall Street Journal*, October 27, 2024, https://www.wsj.com/opinion/press-bias-bolsters-trump-again-unhinged-attacks-helped-him-2016-they-might-again-ecfb3f37?st=DqvFMM&reflink=article_email_share (last accessed April 12, 2025).

[39] Chris Mueller, "Post misleads on funds for internet access, EV charging stations," *USA Today*, October 18, 2024, https://www.usatoday.com/story/news/factcheck/2024/10/18/internet-access-ev-charging-funds-fact-check/7 5686407007/ (last accessed April 12, 2025).

[40] Nathan Gonzalez, "Trump's second administration set to be filled with losers," *Roll Call*, November 25, 2024, https://rollcall.com/2024/11/25/donald-trump-administration-losers-elections/ (last accessed April 12, 2025).

[41] CNN headline, screenshot taken by author.

[42] Nectar Gan, "Hersh Goldberg-Polin: The 'happy-go-lucky' Israeli-American who became a symbol of Israel's enduring hostage heartbreak, CNN, September 1, 2024, https://www.cnn.com/2024/09/01/middleeast/israel-gaza-hostage-polin-goldberg-profile-intl-hnk/index.html (last accessed April 12, 2025).

[43] Online front page of the New York Times, October 28, 2024

[44] Online front page of the *New York Times*, November 2, 2024.

[45] David A. Graham, "Trump Suggests Training Guns on Liz Cheney's Face," *The Atlantic*, November 1, 2024, https://www.theatlantic.com/politics /archive/2024/11/trump-liz-cheney-war/680485/ (last accessed April 12, 2025).

[46] Kat Rosenfeld, "I don't support Donald Trump but I also don't support journalists lying to their audiences…" X, November 1, 2024, https://x.com/ katrosenfield/status/1852321956420362286 (last accessed April 12, 2025).

[47] *The Washington Post*, "Former president Donald Trump appeared to suggest on Thursday that…" X, November 1, 2024, https://x.com/washingtonpost/ status/1852343355536986598 (last accessed April 12, 2025).

[48] David Bauder, "Washington Post columnist quits after her opinion piece criticizing owner Jeff Bezos is rejected," AP News, March 10, 2025, https://apnews.com/article/washington-post-resignation-marcus-bezos-8d6ce32b27f5c965fc972d73d0f95aac (last accessed April 12, 2025).

[49] Jennifer Rubin, "Republicans (rightly) panic. Good luck finding a viable alternative," *The Washington Post*, October 1, 2023, https://www.washington post.com/opinions/2023/10/01/trump-gop-alternative/ (last accessed April 12, 2025).

[50] Ibid.

[51] Jennifer Rubin, "A wasteland: Political coverage ignores the threat to democracy," *The Washington Post*, November 12, 2023, https://www. washingtonpost.com/opinions/2023/11/12/political-coverage-broken/ (last accessed April 12, 2025).

[52] "Biden appears to read teleprompter instructions out loud in latest gaffe," Fox News, April 24, 2024, https://www.washingtonpost.com/opinions/ 2024/04/23/trump-losing-courtroom-campaign-bragg-trial/ (last accessed April 12, 2025).

[53] Rex Huppke, "Crime in America is down, rudely interfering with GOP narrative that it's out of control," *USA Today*, December 20, 2023, https://www.usatoday.com/story/opinion/columnist/2023/12/20/crime-murde r-violence-down-biden-fox-news/71974355007/ (last accessed April 12, 2025).

[54] Nellie Bowles, "TGIF: Super Heavy Booster," *The Free Press*, October 18, 2024, https://www.thefp.com/p/tgif-super-heavy-booster?utm_campaign= email-post&r=j8y2f&utm_source=substack&utm_medium=email (last accessed April 12, 2025).

[55] Thomas Gray, "Ode on a Distant Prospect of Eton College," Poetry Foundation, undated, https://www.poetryfoundation.org/poems/44301/ode-on-a-distant-prospect-of-eton-college (last accessed April 12, 2025).

Chapter 8

[1] Gideon Rachman, "Kissinger never wanted to dial Europe," *Financial Times*, July 22, 2009, https://www.ft.com/content/c4c1e0cd-f34a-3b49-985f-e708b247eb55 (last accessed May 7 , 2025).

[2] United States Constitution, 14th Amendment, Section 1, https://constitution.congress.gov/constitution/ (last accessed May 7, 2025).

[3] Amy Swearer and Hans A. von Spakovsky, "9 Things to Know About Birthright Citizenship," Heritage Foundation Commentary, October 31, 2018, https://www.heritage.org/immigration/commentary/9-things-know-about-birthright-citizenship (last accessed July 10, 2024).

[4] Ibid.

[5] Samuel Estreicher and Rudra Reddy, "Revisiting the Scope of Birthright Citizenship," *The Wall Street Journal*, March 27, 2025, https://www.wsj.com/opinion/revisiting-the-scope-of-birthright-citizenship-trump-illegal-alien-01f4ef2c?st=goejpR&reflink=article_email_share (last accessed May 7 , 2025).

[6] Emma Waters and Simon Hankinson, "The New Face of Birth Tourism: Chinese Nationals, American Surrogates, and Birthright Citizenship," Heritage

Foundation *Issue Brief* No. 5357, July 15, 2024, https://www.heritage.org/china/report/the-new-face-birth-tourism-chinese-nationals-american-surrogates-and-birthright (last accessed May 7, 2025).

[7] U.S. Senate, Minority Staff Report, "Birth Tourism in the United States, December 20, 2022, https://www.hsgac.senate.gov/wp-content/uploads/imo/media/doc/2022.12.20-%20Final_Birth%20Tourism%20Report.pdf

[8] Ibid.

[9] Ibid.

[10] Emma Waters, "California's New Handmaid's Tale," *The American Mind*, November 28, 2022, https://americanmind.org/salvo/california-new-handmaids-tale/ (last accessed July 10, 2024).

[11] "America's Rent-a-Womb Industry Lures an Alarming Number of Chinese Nationals," *The Federalist*, December 14, 2023, https://thefederalist.com/2023/12/14/americas-rent-a-womb-industry-lures-an-alarming-number-of-chinese-nationals/ (last accessed July 10, 2024).

[12] Waters and Hankinson, "The New Face of Birth Tourism: Chinese Nationals, American Surrogates, and Birthright Citizenship," Ibid.

[13] American Society for Reproductive Medicine, "Chinese Special Interest Group (CHSIG)," https://www.asrm.org/membership/asrm-member-groups/special-interest-groups/chinese-special-interest-group-chsig/ (last accessed July 10, 2024).

[14] Teny Sahakian, "Chinese 'Rent-a-Womb' Industry Using American Surrogates Is a National Security Threat: Heritage Researcher," Fox News, April 22, 2023, https://www.foxnews.com/us/chinese-rent-womb-industry-using-american-surrogates-national-security-threat-heritage-researcher (last accessed July 10, 2024).

[15] "Thailand plans to legalise surrogacy for foreign couples," Reuters March 1, 2024, https://www.reuters.com/world/asia-pacific/thailand-plans-legalise-surrogacy-foreign-couples-2024-03-01/ (last accessed May 7, 2025).

[16] Simon Hankinson, "Foreign Surrogacy: Should We Allow Outsourcing of Labor?" *The Brunswick News*, April 6, 2023, https://thebrunswicknews.com/news/business/commentary-foreign-surrogacy-should-we-allow-outsourcing-of-labor/article_f4a3aaa9-10e7-57f0-b89b-b21e085ea880.html (last accessed May 7, 2025).

[17] "Termination of the Migrant Protection Protocols," Memorandum from Alejandro Mayorkas to Tae Johnson et al., October 29, 2021, https://www.dhs.gov/sites/default/files/2022-01/21_1029_mpp-termination-memo.pdf (last accessed October 3, 2023).

[18] "Agreement Between the United States of America and Guatemala," July 26, 2019, Treaties and Other International Acts Series, 19-1115.

[19] TRAC Immigration, "Immigration Court Asylum Backlog, https://trac.syr.edu/phptools/immigration/asylumbl/ (last accessed November 18, 2024).

[20] Elizabeth Jacobs, "Affirmative Asylum Backlog Exceeds One Million for the First Time," Center for Immigration Studies, July 26, 2024, https://cis.org/Jacobs/Affirmative-Asylum-Backlog-Exceeds-One-Million-First-Time (last accessed May 7, 2025).

[21] Julia Ainsley and Abigail Williams, "U.S. to set up processing centers for migrants in Central and South America," NBC News, April 27, 2023, https://www.nbcnews.com/politics/immigration/biden-us-processing-centers-migrants-guatemala-colombia-rcna81751 (last accessed October 4, 2023).

[22] "Termination of the Migrant Protection Protocols," Memorandum from Alejandro Mayorkas to Tae Johnson et al.,

[23] U.S. Customs and Border Protection, "Nationwide Encounters," https://www.cbp.gov/newsroom/stats/nationwide-encounters (last accessed May 7, 2025).

[24] The White House, "ICYMI: Illegal Border Crossings Hit New Record Low in March," April 1, 2025, https://www.whitehouse.gov/articles/2025/04/icymi-illegal-border-crossings-hit-new-record-low-in-march/#:~:text=It's%20called%20the%20%E2%80%9CTrump%20Effect,decrease%20from%202022%20(211%2C181) (last accessed May 7, 2025).

[25] Bill Melugin and Greg Wehner, "Daily average of known gotaways at southern border plummets, down 93% from Biden administration highs," Fox News, February 11, 2025, https://www.foxnews.com/us/daily-average-known-gotaways-southern-border-plummets-from-biden-administration-highs (last accessed May 7, 2025).

[26] "Fact-checking the Trump White House's claims about illegal immigration dropping sharply,' PBS News, February 22, 2025, https://www.pbs.org/newshour/politics/fact-checking-the-trump-white-houses-claims-about-illegal-immigration-dropping-sharply (last accessed May 7, 2025).

[27] Andrew R. Arthur, "Judge Orders Return of Alien Removed to El Salvador in 'Administrative Error,'" Center for Immigration Studies, April 4, 2025, https://cis.org/Arthur/Judge-Orders-Return-Alien-Removed-El-Salvador-Administrative-Error (last accessed May 7, 2025).

[28] Centro de Confinamiento del Terrorismo, in Tecoluca, El Salvador. Built in late 2022.

[29] Gram Slattery, Simon Lewis, and Jeff Mason, "El Salvador's Bukele says he will not return man the US mistakenly deported," Reuters, April 15, 2025, https://www.reuters.com/world/us/trump-meet-with-el-salvadors-president-amid-questions-over-deportations-2025-04-14/ (last accessed May 7, 2025).

[30] Mikenzie Frost, "DHS: Abrego Garcia driving convicted human smuggler's vehicle during TN traffic stop," Fox45 News, April 23, 2025, updated April 24, 2025, https://foxbaltimore.com/news/local/dhs-abrego-garcia-driving-convicted-human-smugglers-vehicle-during-tn-traffic-stop (last accessed May 7, 2025).

[31] Patrisse Cullors, "Abolition And Reparations: Histories of Resistance, Transformative Justice, and Accountability," *Harvard Law Review*, Vol. 132,

No. 6, April 2019, https://harvardlawreview.org/print/vol-132/abolition-and-reparations-histories-of-resistance-transformative-justice-and-accountability/#footnote-1 (last accessed May 7, 2025).

[32] Ibid.

[33] Nicole Silverio, "'Just Not True': Marco Rubio Calls Out 'Misleading' Reports About Recent Deportations of Three US Citizen Children," *The Daily Caller*, April 27, 2025, https://dailycaller.com/2025/04/27/marco-rubio-misleading-reports-deportations-us-citizen-children/ (last accessed May 7, 2025).

[34] Bill Melugin, @BillMelugin, X, March 31, 2025, https://x.com/BillMelugin_/status/1906858129465454862 (last accessed May 7, 2025).

[35] Henrik Schildt, "I Saw How Georgetown's Prestigious School of Foreign Service Coddles Violent Anti-Semites—Who Are Plotting to Transform US Policy From Within," *Washington Free Beacon*, November 19, 2024, https://freebeacon.com/campus/i-saw-how-georgetowns-prestigious-school-of-foreign-service-coddles-violent-anti-semites-who-are-plotting-to-transform -us-policy-from-within/

[36] Collin Anderson, "'Death to Jews': Inside the Home of 2 SJP Leaders at George Mason University, Police Find Guns, Ammo, and Terrorist Flags," Washington Free Beacon, December 9, 2024, https://freebeacon.com/campus/death-to-jews-inside-the-home-of-2-sjp-leaders-at-george-mason-university-police-find-guns-ammo-and-terrorist-flags/

[37] Louis Casiano and Bill Melugin, "State Department revokes first visa of foreign student linked to 'Hamas-supporting disruptions,'" Fox News, March 6, 2025, https://www.foxnews.com/politics/state-department-revokes-first-visa-foreign-student-linked-hamas-supporting-disruptions (last accessed May 7, 2025).

[38] Eitan Fischberger, @Efischberger, X, March 10, 2025, https://x.com/EFischberger/status/1898953594763673789 (last accessed May 7, 2025).

[39] Jason Bedrick and Simon Hankinson, "US Can Deport Green Card Holders Who Support Terrorism," The Daily Signal, March 11, 2025, https://www.dailysignal.com/2025/03/11/yes-we-can-deport-terrorism-supporting-green-card-holders/ (last accessed May 7, 2025).

[40] Chloe Atkins and Matt Lavietes, "Marco Rubio memo cites Mahmoud Khalil's beliefs in justifying his deportation," NBC News, April 10, 2025, https://www.nbcnews.com/news/us-news/mahmoud-khalil-deported-serious-foreign-policy-consequences-rubio-memo-rcna200612 (last accessed May 7, 2025).

[41] The Heritage Foundation, "Election Fraud Map: A Sampling of Proven Instances of Election Fraud," https://electionfraud.heritage.org/ (last accessed April 28, 2025).

[42] Brianna Lyman, "21 Million Voters Can't Provide Proof of Citizenship—Making the SAVE Act Even More Necessary," *The Federalist*, March 27, 2025, https://thefederalist.com/2025/03/27/21-million-voters-cant-provide-proof-of-citizenship-making-the-save-act-even-more-necessary/?utm_

source=rss&utm_medium=rss&utm_campaign=21-million-voters-cant-provide-proof-of-citizenship-making-the-save-act-even-more-necessary&utm_term=2025-03-28 (last accessed May 7, 2025).

[43] Kevin Morris and Cora Henry, "Millions of Americans Don't Have Documents Proving Their Citizenship Readily Available," Brennan Center for Justice, June 11, 2024, https://www.brennancenter.org/our-work/analysis-opinion/millions-americans-dont-have-documents-proving-their-citizenship-readily (last accessed May 7, 2025).

[44] Ballotpedia, "Voter identification laws by state," https://ballotpedia.org/Voter_identification_laws_by_state, (last accessed June 23, 2025).

[45] The Heritage Foundation, "Election Integrity Scorecard: Assessing the Status of State Laws Needed for Election Fairness and Security," https://www.heritage.org/electionscorecard/ (last accessed March 28, 2025).

[46] Christina A. Cassidy, "GOP pushes ahead with citizenship voting bill. Some state election officials say it's problematic," AP News, March 2, 2025, https://apnews.com/article/congress-elections-citizenship-voter-id-republicans-17c6e7877b7ba63a08b68a771c92da92 (last accessed May 7, 2025).

[47] U.S. Citizenship and Immigration Services, "About SAVE," https://www.uscis.gov/save/about-save/about-save (last accessed March 24, 2025).

[48] Michael Casey, "New Hampshire town elections offer a preview of citizenship voting rules being considered nationwide," AP News, March 22, 2025, https://apnews.com/article/save-act-voting-proof-citizenship-new-hampshire-5105986c3fc354d3d61ec3480b49c788?user_email=2aab676cd9dbd628c74bc2a654ca80becd6259495d56c843274a940110d0e9b5&utm_medium=Morning_Wire&utm_source=Sailthru_AP&utm_campaign=Morning%20Wire_24%20Mar_2025&utm_term=Morning%20Wire%20Subscribers (last accessed May 7, 2025).

[49] Ibid.

[50] State of New Hampshire, "How to Register to Vote," https://www.sos.nh.gov/elections/frequently-asked-questions/how-register-vote (last accessed March 24, 2025).

[51] Holly Ramer, "New Hampshire governor signs voter proof-of-citizenship to take effect after November elections," AP News, September 12, 2024, https://apnews.com/article/new-hampshire-voter-registration-citizenship-4009cda6ce88bccc0c8bd447ffd27974 (last accessed May 7, 2025).

[52] Arya Sundaram, "New York has more than 600K 'undocumented' immigrants, data shows. Who are they?" Gothamist, December 2, 2024, https://gothamist.com/news/new-york-has-more-than-600k-undocumented-immigrants-data-shows-who-are-they (last accessed May 7, 2025).

[53] Carl Campanile, Craig McCarthy, and Matt Troutman, "NYC's law allowing noncitizens to vote is dead as state's highest court shuts it down," *New York Post*, March 20, 2025, https://nypost.com/2025/03/20/us-news/nyc-law-allowing-noncitizens-to-vote-struck-down-by-ny-court-of-appeals/?utm_campaign=iphone_nyp&utm_source=com.microsoft.Office.Outlook.compose-shareextension (last accessed May 7, 2025).

[54] Ibid.

[55] Floyd Buford, "Washington State Bill Paves The Way For More Non-Citizen Voting, Critics Say," *The Daily Caller*, April 24, 2025, https://dailycaller.com/2025/04/24/washington-state-bill-paves-the-way-for-more-non-citizen-voting-critics-say/ (last accessed May 7, 2025).

[56] Ibid.

[57] M.D. Kittle, "WI Voters Overwhelmingly Approve Voter ID Amendment To State Constitution," The Federalist, April 01, 2025, https://thefederalist.com/2025/04/01/wi-voters-overwhelmingly-approve-voter-id-amendment-to-state-constitution/ (last accessed June 23, 2025).

[58] Ibid.

[59] David Martin Davies, "Texas Matters: Why Abbott wants Plyler v. Doe overturned," NPR, May 16, 2022, https://www.tpr.org/podcast/texas-matters/2022-05-16/texas-matters-why-abbott-wants-plyler-v-doe-overturned (last accessed May 18, 2025).

[60] Hayden Dublois and Addison Scherler, "How Congress can kick illegal immigrants off Medicaid—and save us billions," *New York Post*, March 30, 2025, https://nypost.com/2025/03/30/opinion/how-congress-can-kick-illegal-immigrants-off-medicaid-and-save-us-billions/?utm_campaign=iphone_nyp&utm_source=mail_app (last accessed May 7, 2025).

[61] Victor Davis Hanson, "California and Its Collapsing Blue-State Democrat Model," American Greatness, March 24, 2025, https://amgreatness.com/2025/03/24/california-and-its-collapsing-blue-state-democrat-model/ (last accessed May 7, 2025).

[62] Ibid.

[63] Deane Waldman, "Red States Are Paying for California's Illegal Aliens' Health Care," *The Federalist*, March 24, 2025, https://thefederalist.com/2025/03/24/red-states-are-paying-for-californias-illegal-aliens-health-care/?utm_source=rss&utm_medium=rss&utm_campaign=red-states-are-paying-for-californias-illegal-aliens-health-care&utm_term=2025-03-24 (last accessed May 7, 2025).

[64] Shelby Hawkins, "Pritzker Cutting Health Care Program for Noncitizens as Report Reveals Costs Far Exceeded Estimates," WTTW News, February 28, 2025, https://news.wttw.com/2025/02/27/pritzker-cutting-health-care-program-noncitizens-report-reveals-costs-far-exceeded (last accessed May 7, 2025).

[65] Taryn Luna, "Cost of undocumented healthcare in California is billions over estimates, pressuring Democrats to consider cuts," *Los Angeles Times*, March 13, 2025, https://www.latimes.com/california/story/2025-03-13/3b-above-estimates-democrats-in-california-face-pressure-to-cut-medi-cal-for-undocumented-immigrants#:~:text=The%20cost%20estimate%20to%20provide,an%20increase%20from%20earlier%20projections (last accessed May 7, 2025).

[66] Press Release, "Florida Releases Updated Hospital Patient Immigration Status Dashboard

Highlighting the Cost of Uncompensated Care for Illegal Immigrants," State of Florida, Agency for Health Communication, March 7, 2025, https://ahca.myflorida.com/content/download/26215/file/3.7.25_Hospital_Patient_Immigration_Status.pdf (last accessed May 7, 2025).

[6767] Stephanie Bennett, "Yuma hospital spent $26M last year treating migrant patients: 'They have no ability to pay,'" Fox 10 Phoenix, March 3, 2023, https://www.fox10phoenix.com/news/yuma-hospital-spent-26m-last-year-treating-migrant-patients-they-have-no-ability-to-pay (last accessed May 7, 2025).

[68] Brandon Waltens, "Illegal Aliens Cost Texas Hospitals $121.8 Million in Just One Month," Texas Scorecard, April 25, 2025, https://texasscorecard.com/state/illegal-aliens-cost-texas-hospitals-121-8-million-in-just-one-month/ (last accessed May 7, 2025).

[69] Steven A. Camarota, "America Is a Country, Not a Labor Market," *National Review*, December 22, 2023, https://www.nationalreview.com/2024/03/america-is-a-country-not-a-labor-market/ (last accessed May 7, 2025).

[70] Ibid.

[71] Dylan Sharkey, "Chicago spending on migrants reaches nearly $300M as evictions begin," Illinois Policy, March 18, 2024, https://www.illinoispolicy.org/chicago-spending-on-migrants-reaches-nearly-300m-as-evictions-begin/ (last accessed May 7, 2025).

[72] Ryan Mills, "Migrants Cost Denver Area Up to $340 Million to Shelter, Educate, New Report Finds," *National Review*, June 12, 2024, https://www.nationalreview.com/news/migrants-cost-denver-area-up-to-340-million-to-shelter-educate-new-report-finds/?bypass_key=dngxMzhXdU1wQURBNkIxc2l1c1VCdz09OjpNRWN5YUdS2RWSndaVXBqYjBsRE9XeFJWazFxWnowOQ%3D%3D?utm_source%3Demail&utm_medium=breaking&utm_campaign=newstrack&utm_term=35688474&utm_source=Sailthru (last accessed May 7, 2025).

[73] NYC.gov, "Updating the Costs of NYC's Asylum Seeker Crisis," https://www.nyc.gov/content/getstuffdone/pages/asylum-seeker-update (last accessed April 28, 2025).

[7474] Simon Hankinson, "The BorderLine: Cities, States Can't Continue to Shoulder Costs of Biden's Deliberate Border Crisis," The Daily Signal, October 26, 2023, https://www.dailysignal.com/2023/10/26/borderline-could-unicorns-be-solution-nycs-illegal-immigrant-problem/ (last accessed May 7, 2025).

[75] Wendy Wei and Oscar B. Castillo, "At a NYC Reticketing Site, Some Migrants Are Choosing Chicago," *South Side Weekly*, November 17, 2023, https://southsideweekly.com/at-a-nyc-reticketing-site-some-asylum-seekers-and-migrants-are-choosing-chicago/ (last accessed May 7, 2025).

[76] Simon Hankinson, "What I Saw on My Visit to Springfield, Ohio: The BorderLine," The Daily Signal, October 11, 2024, https://www.dailysignal.com/2024/10/11/what-saw-springfield-ohio-challenges-residents-face-haitian-immigration-surge-borderline/ (last accessed May 7, 2025).

[7777] National Immigration Forum, "Fact Sheet: Immigrants and Public Benefits," August 21, 2018, https://immigrationforum.org/article/fact-sheet-immigrants-and-public-benefits/ (last accessed May 7, 2025).

[78] John Hulsman, *The Last Best Hope: A History of American Realism* (London: Whitefox Publishing, 2024).

Chapter 9

[1] John Miltimore, "Black Lives Matter's Goal to 'Disrupt' the Nuclear Family Fits a Marxist Aim That Goes Back a Century and a Half," Foundation for Economic Freedom, September 24, 2020, https://fee.org/articles/black-lives-matter-s-goal-to-disrupt-the-nuclear-family-fits-a-marxist-aim-that-goes-back-a-century-and-a-half/ (last accessed May 9, 2025).

[2] Mike Gonzalez, "Marxism Underpins Black Lives Matter Agenda," September 8, 2021, Heritage Foundation *Commentary*, https://www.heritage.org/progressivism/commentary/marxism-underpins-black-lives-matter-agenda (last accessed May 9, 2025).

[3] Rob Henderson, "How the luxury beliefs of an educated elite erode society," *The Times*, February 23, 2024, https://www.thetimes.com/uk/article/how-the-luxury-beliefs-of-an-educated-elite-erode-society-0mx8fd2nl?region=global (last accessed May 9, 2025).

[4] Black Lives Matter at School, "13 Guiding Principles," https://www.blacklivesmatteratschool.com/13-guiding-principles.html (last accessed May 9, 2025).

[5] Brad Wilcox, Wendy Wang, and Alysse ElHage, "Life Without Father': Less College, Less Work, and More Prison for Young Men Growing Up Without Their Biological Father," Institute for Family Studies, June 17, 2022, https://ifstudies.org/blog/life-without-father-less-college-less-work-and-more-prison-for-young-men-growing-up-without-their-biological-father (last accessed May 9, 2025).

[6] Hindi for "Northern Province."

[7] "Children in Single-Parent Families by Race and Ethnicity in the United States," Annie E. Casey Foundation, 2022, https://datacenter.aecf.org/data/tables/107-children-in-single-parent-families-by-race-and-ethnicity#detailed/1/any/false/1095,2048,1729,37,871,870,573,869,36,868/8223,4040,4039,2638,2597,4758,1353/432,431 (last accessed May 9, 2025).

[8] Christina Rosen, "From a Broken Home to a Broken Institution," *The Washington Free Beacon*, February 25, 2024, https://freebeacon.com/culture/from-broken-home-to-broken-institution/ (last accessed May 9, 2025).

[9] Facing History & Ourselves, "Spying on Family and Friends," updated August 2, 2026, https://www.facinghistory.org/resource-library/spying-family-friends#citation-information-1135 (last accessed April 15, 2025).

[10] Professor Richard J. Evans, "Coercion and Consent in Nazi Germany," Raleigh Lecture on History, 2006, https://www.thebritishacademy.ac.uk/documents/770/09-evans.pdf (last accessed May 9, 2025).

[11] "Traitors in the family: Stalin's informers," *Daily Mail*, September 22, 2007, https://www.dailymail.co.uk/columnists/article-483230/Traitors-family-Stalins-informers.html (last accessed May 17, 2025).

[12] Yukong, Zhao, "America Has Yet to See The Worst Consequences of Wokeness," *The Daily Caller*, January 20, 2023, https://dailycaller.com/2023/01/20/cultural-revolution-china-wokeness-critical-race-theory-black-lives-matter/ (last accessed May 9, 2025).

[13] Saloni Dattani et al., "Life Expectancy," Our World in Data, https://ourworldindata.org/life-expectancy (last accessed May 9, 2025).

[14] Holodomor Museum, "Holodomor History," https://holodomormuseum.org.ua/en/the-history-of-the-holodomor/ (last accessed May 9, 2025).

[15] Xi Van Fleet, *Mao's America: A Survivor's Warning* (New York: Center Street Books, 2023).

[16] Ibid., p. 35.

[17] Jonathan Butcher, *Splintered: Critical Race Theory and the Progressive War on Truth* (New York: Bombardier Books, 2022), p. 106.

[18] Robert Maranto, "What the 'Grievance Studies affair' says about academia's social justice warriors," *The Hill*, April 20, 2020, https://thehill.com/opinion/education/490366-what-the-grievance-studies-affair-says-about-academias-social-justice/ (last accessed May 9, 2025).

[19] Van Fleet, *Mao's America*, p. 99.

[20] Herman Edward Harms, "A History of the Concept of In Loco Parentis in American Education," dissertation at the University of Florida, 1970, https://ufdcimages.uflib.ufl.edu/AA/00/06/04/88/00001/AA00060488_00001.pdf (last accessed May 9, 2025).

[21] Sarah Parshall Perry and Thomas Jipping, "Public School Gender Policies That Exclude Parents Are Unconstitutional," Heritage Foundation *Legal Memorandum* No. 355, June 12, 2024, https://www.heritage.org/gender/report/public-school-gender-policies-exclude-parents-are-unconstitutional (last accessed May 9, 2025).

[22] Stephen Sawchuk, "Are Teachers Obliged to Tell Parents Their Child Might Be Trans? Courts May Soon Decide," *Education Week*, April 28, 2022, https://www.edweek.org/policy-politics/are-teachers-obliged-to-tell-parents-their-child-might-be-trans-courts-may-soon-decide/2022/04 (last accessed May 9, 2025).

[23] LegiScan, California Assembly Bill 1955, Chapter 95, https://legiscan.com/CA/text/AB1955/id/3014589 (last accessed May 9, 2025).

[24] "California bans school rules requiring parents notification of child's pronoun change," NPR, July 16, 2024, https://www.npr.org/2024/07/16/nx-s1-5041437/california-bans-school-rules-requiring-parents-notification-of-childs-pronoun-change#:~:text=California%20bans%20school%20rules%20requiring%20parents%20notification%20of%20child's%20pronoun%20change&text=SACRAMENTO%2C%20Calif.,Gavin%20Newsom (last accessed May 9, 2025).

25 Tyler O'Neil, "'Empire of Gender Secrecy Policies Is Going to Crumble' After Trump Education Probe in California, Lawyer Says," The Daily Signal, March 28, 2025, https://www.dailysignal.com/2025/03/28/trump-doe-move-makes-harder-californias-department-education-weasel-parental-notification-lawsuit-attorney-says/ (last accessed May 9, 2025).

26 Press Release, "U.S. Department of Education Launches Investigation into California Department of Education for Alleged FERPA Violations," U.S. Department of Education, March 27, 2025, https://www.ed.gov/about/news/press-release/us-department-of-education-launches-investigation-california-department-of-education-alleged-ferpa-violations (last accessed May 9, 2025).

27 O'Neill, "'Empire of Gender Secrecy Policies Is Going to Crumble' After Trump Education Probe in California, Lawyer Says."

28 Ibid.

29 Taylor Penley, "Colorado's 'totalitarian' transgenderism bill sparks concerns from parents," Fox News, April 22, 2025, https://www.foxnews.com/media/colorados-totalitarian-transgenderism-bill-sparks-concerns-from-parents (last accessed May 10, 2025).

30 Colorado General Assembly, HB25-1312, "Legal Protections for Transgender Individuals," Session: 2025 Regular Session, https://leg.colorado.gov/bills/hb25-1312 (last accessed May 10, 2025).

31 Erin Friday and Erin Lee, "Colorado's Totalitarian Transgenderism Bill," *The Wall Street Journal*, April 17, 2025, https://www.wsj.com/opinion/colorados-totalitarian-transgenderism-bill-parental-rights-freedom-e841acd2?st=zgPkE7&reflink=article_email_share (last accessed May 10, 2025).

32 Breccan F. Thies, "Exclusive: Colorado Father Fights To Keep Government From Sterilizing His 14-Year-Old Son," The Federalist, April 03, 2025, https://thefederalist.com/2025/04/03/exclusive-colorado-father-fights-to-keep-government-from-sterilizing-his-14-year-old-son/ (last accessed June 23, 2025).

33 Emilie Kao, "Pelosi's Equality Act Could Lead to More Parents Losing Custody of Kids Who Want 'Gender Transition,'" Heritage Foundation *Commentary*, January 15, 2019, https://www.heritage.org/marriage-and-family/commentary/pelosis-equality-act-could-lead-more-parents-losing-custody-kids-who (last accessed May 10, 2025).

34 Sara Boboltz, "A Brief History of Drag Queen Story Hour," *Huffington Post*, May 25, 2023, https://www.huffpost.com/entry/brief-history-of-drag-queen-story-hour_n_64077824e4b0e0a15960a4a0 (last accessed May 10, 2025).

35 Drag Queen Story Hour, "Storytelling around the world," https://www.dragstoryhour.org/chaptermap (last accessed May 11, 2025)

36 Ethan Weinstein, "In Chester, a library's hesitation to host Drag Queen Story Hour sparks controversy," VT Digger, May 19, 2022, https://vtdigger.org/2022/05/19/in-chester-a-librarys-hesitation-to-host-drag-queen-story-hour-sparks-controversy/ (last accessed May 10, 2025).

[37] Maggie Baska, "Man jailed in France for protesting drag queen story time event," Pink News, October 18, 2023, https://www.thepinknews.com/2023 /10/18/france-protest-drag-story-time-event-lgbtq/ (last accessed May 10, 2025).

[38] Casey Harper, "Biden Rule Takes Lunch Money from Schools That Reject Progressive Gender, Sexuality Agenda," The Center Square, December 4, 2023, https://foreigndesknews.com/us/biden-rule-takes-lunch-money-from-schools-that-reject-progressive-gender-sexuality-agenda/ (last accessed May 10, 2025).

[39] Theresa Vargas, "D.C. could offer free meals to all students. Every city should," The Washington Post, January 28, 2023, https://www.washington post.com/dc-md-va/2023/01/28/free-school-lunch-dc-nation/ (last accessed May 10, 2025).

[40] James Fishback, "The Truth About Banned Books," The Free Press, January 17, 2024, https://www.thefp.com/p/the-truth-about-banned-books (last accessed May 10, 2025).

[41] "The Illinois Assault on Home-Schoolers," The Wall Street Journal, March 21, 2025, https://www.wsj.com/opinion/illinois-homeschool-act-democrats-education-public-schools-6065d5ab?st=GskBGE&reflink=article_email_ share (last accessed May 10, 2025).

[42] Billie-Jo Grant et al., "A Case Study of K–12 School Employee Sexual Misconduct: Lessons Learned from Title IX Policy Implementation," Office of Justice Programs, September 15, 2017, https://www.ojp.gov/pdffiles 1/nij/grants/252484.pdf (last accessed May 10, 2025).

[43] Selim Algar, "At least 6 female teachers arrested for sexual misconduct with students over two days across US," New York Post, April 14, 2023, https: //nypost.com/2023/04/14/6-female-teachers-arrested-for-sex-misconduct-with-students/ (last accessed May 10, 2025).

[44] "The Illinois Assault on Home-Schoolers," The Wall Street Journal.

[45] The Nation's Report Card, "2024 Reading State Snapshot Report," https://nces.ed.gov/nationsreportcard/subject/publications/stt2024/pdf/2024 220IL8.pdf (last accessed April 15, 2025).

[46] Taal Hasak-Lowy, "Many Chicago Public Schools students struggle with illiteracy. The consequences are devastating," Chicago Sun Times, April 16, 2024, https://chicago.suntimes.com/other-views/2024/04/15/reading-literacy -low-income-chicago-students-illiteracy-high-dosage-tutoring-taal-hasak-lowy -op-ed (last accessed May 10, 2025).

[47] National Center for Education Statistics, "A higher percentage of K–12 students are receiving academic instruction at home," September 17, 2024, https://nces.ed.gov/whatsnew/press_releases/9_17_2024.asp (last accessed May 10, 2025).

[48] "Ohio's School Choice Success Story Voucher recipients saw substantially improved academic outcomes," The Wall Street Journal, April 22, 2025, https://www.wsj.com/opinion/edchoice-ohio-voucher-study-urban-institute-

school-choice-4a480720?st=BpxzLk&reflink=article_email_share (last accessed May 10, 2025).

[49] The Editorial Board, "Indiana's Big School Voucher Breakthrough," *The Wall Street Journal*, May 11, 2025, https://www.wsj.com/opinion/indiana-school-choice-vouchers-eligibility-charter-schools-mike-braun-todd-huston-1605ed 1a?st=U3Z2Lj&reflink=article_email_share (last accessed May 13, 2025).

[50] Ibid.

[51] Heather Mac Donald, "Funding for Failure," *City Journal*, December 27, 2023, https://www.city-journal.org/article/los-angeles-schools-are-funding-for-failure (last accessed May 10, 2025).

[52] Ibid.

[53] Ibid.

[54] "State of D.C. Schools, Challenges to pandemic recovery in a new normal," D.C. Policy Center, March 8, 2024, https://www.dcpolicycenter.org/wp-content/uploads/2024/02/State-of-D.C.-Schools.pdf (last accessed May 10, 2025).

[55] Ibid.

[56] Shayanne Gal and Aylin Woodward, "How coronavirus symptoms compare with those of the flu, allergies, and the common cold," *Business Insider*, April 29, 2020, https://www.businessinsider.com/coronavirus-symptoms-compared -to-flu-common-cold-and-allergies-2020-3 (last accessed May 10, 2025).

[57] For an excellent summary of the state's abuse of powers during the Covid pandemic, see Mark Chenoweth "'15 Days to Slow the Spread': How Bad Bureaucratic Decisions Made Covid-19 Worse," New Civil Liberties Alliance, March 2025, https://nclalegal.org/how-bad-bureaucratic-decisions-made-covid-19-worse/ (last accessed May 10, 2025).

[58] John P. A. Ioannidis, Francesco Zonta, and Michael Levitt, "Variability in excess deaths across countries with different vulnerability during 2020–2023," PNAS, November 29, 2023, https://www.pnas.org/doi/epub/10.1073 /pnas.2309557120 (last accessed May 10, 2025).

[59] "Sweden's excess death rate during the pandemic was the lowest in Europe," Cato Institute, April 15, 2024, https://www.cato.org/insights/swedens-excess-death-rate-was-lowest-in-europe (last accessed May 10, 2025).

[60] Cynthia Littleton, "How the Coronavirus Crisis Turned Governor Andrew Cuomo Into a TV Sensation," *Variety*, May 28, 2020, https://variety.com/20 20/tv/news/andrew-cuomo-new-york-governor-coronavirus-donald-trump-1203548123/ (last accessed May 10, 2025).

[61] Hannah Fry, "Paddle boarder chased by boat, arrested in Malibu after flouting coronavirus closures," *Los Angeles Times*, April 3, 2020, https://www. latimes.com/california/story/2020-04-03/paddle-boarder-arrested-in-malibu-after-flouting-coronavirus-closures (last accessed May 10, 2025).

[62] The Heritage Foundation, "COVID Hypocrisy: Policymakers Breaking Their Own Rules," updated February 24, 2022, https://datavisualizations.heritage .org/public-health/covid-hypocrisy-policymakers-breaking-their-own-rules/ (last accessed May 17, 2025).

63 Rakgadi Grace Malapela, Gloria Thupayagale-Tshweneagae, and William M. Baratedi, "Use of home remedies for the treatment and prevention of coronavirus disease: An integrative review," *Health Science Reports*, December 12, 2022, https://doi.org/10.1002/hsr2.900 (last accessed May 10, 2025).

64 Liv Finne, "New study reveals the long-term harm to children of COVID-era school closures," Washington Policy Center, June 27, 2023, https://www.washingtonpolicy.org/publications/detail/new-study-reveals-the-long-term-harm-to-children-of-covid-era-school-closures (last accessed May 10, 2025).

65 Tina Nguyen, "Conservatives charge liberals with social-distancing hypocrisy," *Politico*, June 6, 2020, https://www.politico.com/news/2020/06/06/conservatives-charge-liberals-with-social-distancing-hypocrisy-304435 (last accessed May 10, 2025).

66 Holmes Lybrand, "Fact check: Four times Walensky's comments were out of step with CDC guidance," CNN, May 21, 2021, https://www.cnn.com/2021/05/21/politics/walensky-comments-cdc-guidance-fact-check/index.html (last accessed May 10, 2025).

67 Constitution of the United States, Tenth Amendment, https://constitution.congress.gov/constitution/amendment-10/ (last accessed May 10, 2025).

68 Florida Parental Rights in Education Act, 2022, CS/CS/HB 1557.

69 The 2024 Florida Statutes, Title XLIX, Chapter 1014: "Parents' Bill of Rights," http://www.leg.state.fl.us/statutes/index.cfm?App_mode=Display_Statute&URL=1000-1099/1014/1014.html (last accessed May 10, 2025).

Chapter 10

1 Dan Lamothe, "An Army trailblazer set her sights on a new target," *The Washington Post*, May 8, 2021, https://www.washingtonpost.com/national-security/2021/05/11/women-trailblazers-army-set-their-sights-new-target-what-gender-equality-means/ (last accessed May 10, 2025).

2 Kristen M. Griest, "With Equal Opportunity Comes Equal Responsibility: Lowering Fitness Standards to Accommodate Women Will Hurt the Army—and Women," Modern War Institute, West Point, February 25, 2021, https://mwi.westpoint.edu/with-equal-opportunity-comes-equal-responsibility-lowering-fitness-standards-to-accommodate-women-will-hurt-the-army-and-women/ (last accessed May 10, 2025).

3 Elaine Donnelly, "Military Finds Physical Reality Shatters DEI-Fueled Theories About The Sexes," *The Federalist*, April 22, 2025, https://thefederalist.com/2025/04/22/military-finds-physical-reality-shatters-dei-fueled-theories-about-the-sexes/?utm_source=rss&utm_medium=rss&utm_campaign=military-finds-physical-reality-shatters-dei-fueled-theories-about-the-sexes&utm_term=2025-04-22 (last accessed May 10, 2025).

4 Samantha Nerove, "Hegseth Is Right To Hold Military Men And Women To The Same Fitness Standards," The Federalist, April 02, 2025,

https://thefederalist.com/2025/04/02/hegseth-is-right-to-hold-military-men-and-women-to-the-same-fitness-standards/

[5] Ibid

[6] Marshall Cohen, "Fox News to pay $12 million to former producer who accused the network of rampant sexism," CNN, June 30, 2023, https://www.cnn.com/2023/06/30/media/fox-news-abby-grossberg-settlement/index.html?utm_source=substack&utm_medium=email (last accessed May 10, 2025).

[7] "Jury awards $25.6 million to white Starbucks manager fired after the arrests of 2 Black men," AP News, June 14, 2023, https://apnews.com/article/starbucks-racism-philadelphia-manager-lawsuit-bfa9cd9a897dff402f8547f167455d10 (last accessed May 10, 2025).

[8] Joe Concha, "CNN ridiculed for 'Fiery But Mostly Peaceful' caption with video of burning building in Kenosha," *The Hill*, August 27, 2020, https://thehill.com/homenews/media/513902-cnn-ridiculed-for-fiery-but-mostly-peaceful-caption-with-video-of-burning/ (last accessed May 10, 2025).

[9] Mairead Elordi, "New York City to Pay $13.7 Million to George Floyd Protesters for Mass Arrests," *The Daily Wire*, July 20, 2023, https://www.dailywire.com/news/new-york-city-to-pay-13-7-million-to-george-floyd-rioters-for-mass-arrests (last accessed May 10, 2025).

[10] Vivian Ho, "Los Angeles County plans historic $4 billion payout for sex abuse claims," *The Wall Street Journal*, April 5, 2025, https://www.washingtonpost.com/nation/2025/04/05/los-angeles-county-4billion-sex-abuse-settlement/ (last accessed May 10, 2025).

[11] Ibid.

[12] New York State, Governor Hochul Signs Adult Survivors Act, May 24, 2022, https://www.governor.ny.gov/news/governor-hochul-signs-adult-survivors-act (last accessed May 10, 2025).

[13] Adam Reiss and Dareh Gregorian, "Trump found liable for sexually abusing and defaming E. Jean Carroll in civil trial and is ordered to pay $5 million," NBC News, May 9, 2023, https://www.nbcnews.com/politics/donald-trump/jury-reaches-verdict-e-jean-carroll-rape-defamation-case-trump-rcna82778 (last accessed May 10, 2025).

[14] Ximena Bustillo, "Jury orders Trump to pay $83 million for defaming columnist E. Jean Carroll," NPR, January 26, 2024, https://www.npr.org/2024/01/26/1226626397/trump-defamation-trial (last accessed May 10, 2025).

[15] Barry Latzer, "What Role Does Culture Play in Crime Rates?" The Wall Street Journal May 9, 2025, https://www.wsj.com/opinion/what-role-does-culture-play-in-crime-rates-riley-economics-cc9c07ec?st=7BhjG9&reflink=article_email_share (last accessed May 14, 2025).

[16] Hannah E. Meyers, "Albany to crime victims: Drop dead," *New York Post*, March 17, 2025, https://nypost.com/2025/03/17/opinion/albany-to-crime-victims-drop-dead/?utm_campaign=iphone_nyp&utm_source=com.microsoft.Office.Outlook.compose-shareextension (last accessed May 10, 2025).

[17] Ibid.

[18] Joe Tabor, "There is no longer cash bail in Illinois. What happens now?" Illinois Policy Institute, September 18, 2023, https://www.illinoispolicy.org/ there-is-no-longer-cash-bail-in-illinois-what-happens-now/ (last accessed May 10, 2025).

[19] Katrina Pross, "Minnesota should end cash bail, reform pretrial detention practices, report says," *Sahan Journal*, February 14, 2025, https://sahan journal.com/public-safety/minnesota-cash-bail-system-pretrial-release/ (last accessed May 10, 2025).

[20] Madison Colombo, "Minneapolis-St. Paul restaurant shutting down over crime, owner blames officials for 'out of control' violence," *New York Post*, May 3, 2025, https://nypost.com/2025/05/03/us-news/minneapolis-st-paul-restaurant-shuts-down-over-crime-owner-blames-officials-violence/ (last accessed May 10, 2025).

[21] "New York rolls back bail reforms that gave judges more discretion," Heard on *All Things Considered*, May 4, 2023, https://www.npr.org/2023/05 /04/1174083658/new-york-rolls-back-bail-reforms-that-gave-judges-more-discretion (last accessed May 10, 2025).

[22] Jim Quinn, "Bail fail: Study shows that repeat crime INCREASED in New York because of justice 'reforms,'" *New York Post*, March 3, 2024, https://nypost.com/2024/03/03/opinion/bail-fail-study-shows-that-repeat-crime-increased-in-new-york-because-of-justice-reforms/ (last accessed May 10, 2025).

[23] Rafael A. Mangual, *Criminal (In)Justice: What the Push for Decarceration and Depolicing Gets Wrong and Who it Hurts the Most* (Nashville, TN: Center Street Books, 2022), p. 50.

[24] Susannah Luthi, "Millionaire Wives Pour $1 Million Into Criminal Justice Reform as Californians Sour on Soft-on-Crime Policies," *The Washington Free Beacon*, February 1, 2025, https://freebeacon.com/california/millionaire -wives-pour-1-million-into-criminal-justice-reform-as-californians-sour-on-soft-on-crime-policies/ (last accessed May 10, 2025).

[25] Ibid.

[26] Rafael A. Mangual, "Oakland's 'Doom Loop': A conversation with Seneca Scott on the Bay Area city's interlinked public safety and budget crises," *City Journal*, May 5, 2024, https://www.city-journal.org/article/oaklands-doom-loop (last accessed May 10, 2025).

[27] Maanvi Singh, "Oakland mayor and county's district attorney ousted in historic recall," *The Guardian*, November 12, 2024, https://www.theguardian.com /us-news/2024/nov/12/oakland-mayor-sheng-thao (last accessed May 10, 2025).

[28] MyProp47.org, "About Proposition 47," https://myprop47.org/about/ (last accessed April 16, 2025).

[2929] Carlos E. Castañeda, "Target to close 3 Bay Area stores because of retail theft; 6 other stores closing in New York, Portland, Seattle," CBS News, September 26, 2023, https://www.cbsnews.com/sanfrancisco/news/target-stores-closing-retail-theft-san-francisco-oakland-pittsburg-new-york-portland-seattle/ (last accessed May 10, 2025).

[30] Nic White, "Chicago's progressive mayor Brandon Johnson claims REPARATIONS will help tackle 'the cycle of violence' amid a 17 per cent surge in crime," *Daily Mail*, December 28, 2023, https://www.dailymail.co.uk/news/article-12906999/Chicagos-progressive-mayor-Brandon-Johnson-claims-REPARATIONS-help-tackle-cycle-violence-amid-17-cent-surge-crime.html (last accessed May 10, 2025).

[31] "'What Is a Justice-Involved Individual?': Tom Cotton Grills Top Prison Official About Semantics," Senate Judiciary Committee Hearing, September 13, 2023, video, https://www.youtube.com/watch?v=wP-Z7MwVdj4 (last accessed May 10, 2025).

[32] Philip Bump, "How hate crime has—and hasn't —changed over the past decade," *The Washington Post*, October 18, 2023, https://www.washingtonpost.com/politics/2023/10/18/hate-crimes-us/ (last accessed May 10, 2025).

[33] Larry Celona et al., "Deranged man pushes Asian woman to death at Times Square subway station," *New York Post*, January 15, 2022, https://nypost.com/2022/01/15/woman-pushed-to-her-death-at-times-square-subway-station/ (last accessed May 10, 2025).

[34] "Woman dies from being pushed into San Francisco-area commuter train," AP News, July 2, 2024, https://apnews.com/article/homeless-push-passenger-death-subway-d2fdf51c5851409b57480d0776684024 (last accessed May 10, 2025).

[35] "D.C.'s crime bill could make the city more dangerous," *The Washington Post*, January 15, 2023, https://www.washingtonpost.com/opinions/2023/01/15/dc-crime-bill-dangerous/ (last accessed May 10, 2025).

[36] Susan Davis, "Congress overturns D.C. crime bill with President Biden's help," NPR, March 8, 2023, https://www.npr.org/2023/03/08/1161902691/d-c-crime-bill-biden-overturn (last accessed May 10, 2025).

[37] Erinn Broadus and Trevor Schakohl, "Crime Has Risen Under the Watch of Soros-Backed Prosecutors in Six Major Cities," *The Daily Caller*, February 12, 2023, https://dailycaller.com/2023/02/12/soros-prosecutors-cities-crime/ (last accessed May 10, 2025).

[38] Sandag.org, "43 Years of Crime in the San Diego Region: 1980 Through 2022," May 2023, https://www.sandag.org/data-and-research/criminal-justice-and-public-safety/-/media/D225A333057B4A7691D48F74C69A49CA.ashx (last accessed May 10, 2025).

[39] Charles Stimson and Zack Smith, "George Soros's Prosecutors Wage War on Law and Order," The Heritage Foundation, June 22, 2023, https://www.heritage.org/crime-and-justice/commentary/george-soross-prosecutors-wage-war-law-and-order (last accessed May 11, 2025).

[40] House of Representatives, Commonwealth of Pennsylvania, Select Committee on Restoring Law and Order, "Second Interim Report," October 24, 2022, https://www.pahousegop.com/Display/SiteFiles/1/2022/Select%20Committ

ee%20on%20Restoring%20Law%20and%20Order%202ndInterim%20Rep
ort%20102422.pdf (last accessed May 10, 2025).

[41] The Editorial Board, "A Labor Strike Over Shoplifting," The Wall Street
Journal, November 27, 2023, https://www.wsj.com/opinion/macys-strike-
shoplifting-ufcw-liisa-luick-c0f89ec6 (last accessed May 13, 2025).

[42] Olivia Land, "Fury as Minneapolis' 'woke' DA Mary Moriarty allows accused
rapists and killers to stay free—too much even for Soros-backed AG," New
York Post, October 3, 2023, https://nypost.com/2023/10/03/minneapolis-
woke-da-draws-criticism-from-families-soros-ally/ (last accessed May 10,
2025).

[43] Ibid.

[44] Patrick Reilly, "Minnesota state employee who allegedly caused over $20K in
damages to Teslas is let off by woke DA—as cops slam deal," New York Post,
April 22, 2025, https://nypost.com/2025/04/22/us-news/tim-walz-employee-
who-allegedly-caused-over-20k-in-damages-to-teslas-let-off-by-woke-
minnesota-da/ (last accessed May 10, 2025).

[45] Andrew R. Arthur, "Brother of Suspect in Laken Riley Killing Is a Case Study
of Biden Non-Enforcement," Center for Immigration Studies, March 11,
2024, https://cis.org/Arthur/Brother-Suspect-Laken-Riley-Killing-Case-Study
-Biden-NonEnforcement (last accessed May 10, 2025).

[46] Nicole Chavez, "Laken Riley's killer sentenced to life in prison after heart-
wrenching pleas from her family," CNN, November 20, 2024, https://www.
cnn.com/2024/11/20/us/jose-ibarra-laken-riley-murder-trial/index.html (last
accessed May 11, 2025).

[47] Michael Shellenberger, @shellenberger, X, November 17, 2021,
https://x.com/shellenberger/status/1461033851925372932 (last accessed
May 10, 2025).

[48] Megan Palin, "Addicts in drug-ravaged Philadelphia reveal gruesome risks to
get high: 'You could paralyze somebody,'" New York Post, January 1, 2024,
https://nypost.com/2024/01/01/news/drug-hitters-help-addicts-inject-tranq-
in-philadelphia/?utm_campaign=iphone_nyp&utm_source=com.microsoft.
Office.Outlook.compose-shareextension (last accessed May 10, 2025).

[49] Ibid.

[50] Colbert I. King, "Is D.C. juvenile justice a revolving door? We need to know,"
The Washington Post, February 24, 2023, https://www.washingtonpost.com/
opinions/2023/02/24/dc-youth-crime-data-needed/ (last accessed May 10,
2025).

[51] Washington DC, Department of Youth Rehabilitation Services, "Current
Funding Opportunities, Notice of Funding Availability - Credible Messenger
Initiative," https://dyrs.dc.gov/page/current-funding-opportunities?utm_
source=newsletter&utm_medium=email&utm_campaign=newsletter_axiosl
ocal_dc&stream=top (last accessed April 21, 2025).

[52] Evan Gorelick, "Faculty report reveals average Yale College GPA, grade
distributions by subject," Yale Daily News, November 30, 2023,
https://yaledailynews.com/blog/2023/11/30/faculty-report-reveals-average-

yale-college-gpa-grade-distributions-by-subject/ (last accessed May 10, 2025).

[53] Jessica E. Vascellaro, "Faculty Tries To Combat Grade Inflation," The Harvard Crimson, June 6, 2002, https://www.thecrimson.com/article/2002/6/6/faculty-tries-to-combat-grade-inflation/ (last accessed May 11, 2025).

[54] S. Avi-Yonah and Delano R. Franklin, "Over the Past Decade, Harvard Seniors Faced Rising GPA Cutoffs for Latin Honors," The Harvard Crimson, April 30, 2019, https://www.thecrimson.com/article/2019/4/30/rising-GPA-cutoffs-honors/ (last accessed May 11, 2025).

[55] Brandon Poulter, "Over 90% of Gender Studies Majors at Ivy League University Received A's," *The Daily Caller*, December 1, 2023, https://dailycaller.com/2023/12/01/over-90-of-gender-studies-majors-at-ivy-league-university-received-as/ (last accessed May 10, 2025).

[56] Sara Randazzo, "To Increase Equity, School Districts Eliminate Honors Classes," *The Wall Street Journal*, February 17, 2023, https://www.wsj.com/us-news/education/to-increase-equity-school-districts-eliminate-honors-classes-d5985dee (last accessed May 13, 2025).

[57] Jessica Resuta, "Survey finds college graduates struggle with basic civic literacy," The College Fix, October 10, 2019, https://www.goacta.org/news-item/survey-finds-college-graduates-struggle-with-basic-civic-literacy/ (last accessed May 10, 2025).

[58] "The Study of American History in Our Universities," Center for American Institutions, Arizona State University, https://cai.asu.edu/americanhistory (last accessed May 10, 2025).

[59] John Sailer, "The DEI Rollback," *The Free Press*, January 16, 2024, https://www.thefp.com/p/john-sailer-the-dei-rollback (last accessed January 18, 2024).

[60] Jonathan Butcher, "Moral Corruption at Community Colleges: DEI Harms Students Everywhere," Heritage Foundation *Backgrounder* No. 3798, November 13, 2023, https://www.heritage.org/education/report/moral-corruption-community-colleges-dei-harms-students-everywhere (last accessed May 10, 2025).).

[61] Anti-Defamation League, "Students for Justice in Palestine (SJP)," Backgrounder, updated August 9, 2024, https://www.adl.org/resources/backgrounder/students-justice-palestine-sjp (last accessed May, 2025).

[62] Hannah E. Meyers, "How Racial Entitlement Leads to Anti-Semitism," *Commentary*, February 2024, https://www.commentary.org/articles/hannah-meyers/racial-entitlement-leads-to-anti-semitism/ (last accessed January 18, 2024).

[63] Aaron Sibarium, "The Yale Law School Dean Who Presided Over the 'Trap House' Scandal Is Now Under Consideration to Be the University's Next President," *The Washington Free Beacon*, January 18, 2024, https://freebeacon.com/campus/the-yale-law-school-dean-who-presided-over-the-trap-house-scandal-is-now-under-consideration-to-be-the-universitys-next-president/ (last accessed January 18, 2024)

[64] U.S. Department of Education, Office for Civil Rights, "Know Your Rights: Title VI and Religion," https://www2.ed.gov/about/offices/list/ocr/docs/know-rights-201701-religious-disc.pdf (last accessed January 17, 2024).

[65] Adam Kredo, "American University Hit With Federal Complaint Over 'Rampant and Pervasive Anti-Semitism," The *Washington Free Beacon*, January 17, 2024, https://freebeacon.com/campus/american-university-hit-with-federal-complaint-over-rampant-and-pervasive-anti-semitism/ (last accessed January 17, 2024).

[66] Jonathan Stempel, "Harvard is sued by Jewish students over 'rampant' antisemitism on campus," Reuters, January 11, 2024, https://www.reuters.com/legal/harvard-sued-by-jewish-students-over-antisemitism-campus-2024-01-11/ (last accessed January 17, 2024).

[67] Liz Navratil, "U.S. Department of Education investigates University of Minnesota after antisemitism complaint," *Star Tribune*, January 17, 2024, https://www.startribune.com/university-minnesota-antisemitism-department-education-discrimination-shared-ancestry-investigation/600336303/ (last accessed January 17, 2024).

[68] Hurabie Meko, "U.S. Investigates Colleges for Antisemitism and Islamophobia Complaints," *The New York Times*, November 17, 2023, https://www.nytimes.com/2023/11/17/nyregion/universities-antisemitic-anti-muslim-investigation.html (last accessed January 17, 2024).

[69] House Committee on Education and Workforce, "Holding Campus Leaders Accountable and Confronting Antisemitism, House Committee on Education and the Workforce, full hearing, December 5, 2023, https://edworkforce.house.gov/calendar/eventsingle.aspx?EventID=409777 (last accessed May 10, 2025).

[70] Allan P. Sindler, "The University of California V. Bakke: The Court's Three Decisions," American Enterprise Institute, September 1, 1978, https://www.aei.org/articles/the-university-of-california-v-bakke-the-courts-three-decisions/ (last accessed January 18, 2024).

[71] After Ibram X. Kendi, see above.

[72] "Has Claudine Gay Wrecked Harvard?" *The Spectator*, Americano Podcast, January 5, 2024, https://www.spectator.co.uk/podcasts/americano/ (last accessed May 11, 2025).

[73] Supreme Court of the United States, No. 20–1199, decided June 29, 2023, https://www.supremecourt.gov/opinions/22pdf/20-1199_hgdj.pdf (last accessed May 10, 2025).

[74] John Paul Wright et al., "Prior problem behavior accounts for the racial gap in school suspensions," *Journal of Criminal Justice*, Vol. 42, No. 3, 2014, pp. 257–266, https://doi.org/10.1016/j.jcrimjus.2014.01.001 (last accessed May 10, 2025).

[75] John Christenson, How the Left's 'Equity' Obsession Enabled a Virginia School Shooting," The Daily Wire, February 2, 2023, https://freebeacon.com/campus/how-the-lefts-equity-obsession-enabled-a-virginia-school-shooting/ (last accessed May 13, 2025).

[76] Alec Schemmel, "Portland Public Schools Must Now Consider Race, Gender Identity When Disciplining Students," *The Washington Free Beacon*, December 2, 2023, https://freebeacon.com/campus/portland-public-schools-must-now-consider-race-gender-identity-when-disciplining-students/ (last accessed May 10, 2025).

[77] Ibid.

[78] Harold Hutchinson, "Blue City School Asks Governor to Send in National Guard to Tame Student Violence, Drug Use," *The Daily Caller*, February 19, 2024, https://dailycaller.com/2024/02/19/blue-city-school-asks-governor-to-send-in-national-guard-to-tame-student-violence-drug-use/ (last accessed May 10, 2025).

[79] Elaine Gunthorpe, "Another University Removes SAT/ACT Requirement," Campus Reform, July 15, 2022, https://www.campusreform.org/article?id=19840 (last accessed May 7, 2024).

[80] Karen Sloan, "End of the LSAT? Law School Entry Test Is on the Chopping Block Again," Reuters, May 6, 2022, https://www.reuters.com/legal/legalindustry/end-lsat-law-school-entry-test-is-chopping-block-again-2022-05-06/ (last accessed May 7, 2024); Hugh Mighty, "Eliminating Bias from Medical School Admissions," AAMC Viewpoints, March 24, 2022, https://www.aamc.org/news-insights/eliminating-bias-medical-school-admissions (last accessed May 7, 2024); and Anthony Wong, "School of Medicine Makes the MCAT Optional Amid COVID-19 Testing Disruptions," *The Stanford Daily*, July 15, 2020, https://stanforddaily.com/2020/07/15/school-of-medicine-makes-mcat-optional-amid-covid-19-testing-disruptions/ (last accessed May 7, 2024).

[81] Press Release, "Yale Announces New Test-Flexible Admissions Policy," Yale University, February 22, 2024, https://news.yale.edu/2024/02/22/yale-announces-new-test-flexible-admissions-policy (last accessed May 7, 2024).

[82] Monica Velez, "Dartmouth First Ivy League to Bring Back SAT, ACT Requirement," EdSource, February 8, 2024, https://edsource.org/updates/dartmouth-first-ivy-league-to-bring-back-sat-act-requirement#:~:text=Dartmouth%20College%20will%20require%20applicants,to%20bring%20back%20the%20requirement (last accessed March 5, 2024).

[83] David Holmes, "The Character Moment in College Admission," Inside Higher Ed, August 24, 2020, https://www.insidehighered.com/admissions/views/2020/08/24/character-important-part-college-admissions-opinion (last accessed May 7, 2024).

[84] "Harvard Canceled Its Best Black Professor. Why?" Good Kid Productions, March 13, 2022, https://www.realclearinvestigations.com/video/2022/03/13/harvard_canceled_its_best_black_professor_why_good_kid_productions_821461.html# (last accessed May 10, 2025).

[85] Bari Weiss, "Economist Roland Fryer on Adversity, Race and Refusing to Conform," Honestly Podcast, February 13, 2024, https://www.thefp.com/listen/honestly.

[86] Ibid.

[87] Thomas Sowell, *Social Justice Fallacies* (New York: Basic Books, 2023), p. 25.

[88] Nicole Ault, "An Alabama School Runs on Faith, Family and Fatherhood," *The Wall Street Journal*, June 7, 2024, https://www.wsj.com/opinion/an-alabama-school-runs-on-faith-family-and-fatherhood-2eddb119 (last accessed May 10, 2025).

[89] Michaela Community School, "#MichaelaResults," School, https://michaela.education/ (last accessed May 9, 2025).

[90] Kate Manne, "Doctors have fatphobia, too—which does serious harm to patients," *The Washington Post*, January 31, 2024, https://www.washingtonpost.com/opinions/2024/01/31/kate-manne-fatphobia-health-care-discrimination / (last accessed May 10, 2025).

[91] Eilis O'Neill, "Some doctors are ditching the scale, saying focusing on weight drives misdiagnoses," NPR, December 2, 2024, https://www.npr.org/sections/health-shots/2023/12/02/1216455346/doctors-weight-loss-neutral-inclusive-misdiagnoses (last accessed May 10, 2025).

[92] Ibid.

[93] Alexander Riley, "NPR Hypes Doctors Who Downplay Obesity Risks to Spare Patients' Feelings," *The Federalist*, January 3, 2024, https://thefederalist.com/2024/01/03/npr-hypes-doctors-who-downplay-obesity-risks-to-spare-patients-feelings/?utm_source=rss&utm_medium=rss&utm_campaign=npr-hypes-doctors-who-downplay-obesity-risks-to-spare-patients-feelings&utm_term=2024-01-03 (last accessed May 10, 2025).

[94] Ariana Eunjung Cha, "What you need to know about the new childhood obesity guidelines," *The Washington Post*, January 20, 2023, https://www.washingtonpost.com/health/2023/01/20/childhood-obesity-treatment-guidelines/ (last accessed May 10, 2025).

[95] Ibid.

[96] Leana Wen, "The Checkup With Dr. Wen: The new guidelines for childhood obesity are crucial," *The Washington Post*, January 26, 2023, https://www.washingtonpost.com/opinions/2023/01/26/childhood-obesity-guidelines-crucial/ (last accessed May 10, 2025).

[97] Ibid.

[98] Ibid.

[99] Kristine Parks, "Seattle hosts 'biggest fat celebration of the year' to generate 'fat joy' and promote 'fat liberation,'" Fox News, January 7, 2024, https://www.foxnews.com/media/seattle-hosts-biggest-fat-celebration-year-generate-fat-joy-promote-fat-liberation (last accessed May 10, 2025).

[100] Ibid.

[101] Sophie van Brugen, "Your Fat Friend: Documentary examines the way fat people are seen on screen," BBC News, February 8, 2024, https://www.bbc.com/news/entertainment-arts-68227820 (last accessed May 10, 2025).

[102] Jacob Passy, "At Theme Parks, You Must Be This Tall—and This Thin—to Ride," *The Wall Street Journal*, January 28, 2023, https://www.wsj.com/articles/universal-studios-mario-kart-too-big-11674855513 (last accessed May 10, 2025).

[103] Tristan Justice, "Body Positivity Book *Plus-Size in Paris* Is Really a Myth About Health," *The Federalist*, July 13, 2023, https://thefederalist.com/2023/07/13/body-positivity-book-plus-size-in-paris-is-really-a-myth-about-health/?utm_source=rss&utm_medium=rss&utm_campaign=body-positivity-book-plus-size-in-paris-is-really-a-myth-about-health&utm_term=2023-07-13 (last accessed May 10, 2025).

[104] Ibid.

[105] Brendan McDonald, "'Fat Fashion' course coming to New School next semester," Campus Reform, November 28, 2024, https://www.campusreform.org/article/fat-fashion-course-coming-new-school-next-semester/26911 (last accessed May 10, 2025).

[106] Leslie Eastman, "As Recruiting Numbers Shrink, U.S .Air Force Expands Body Fat Ranges in New Requirements," *Legal Insurrection*, April 6, 2023, https://legalinsurrection.com/2023/04/as-recruiting-numbers-shrink-u-s-air-force-expands-body-fat-ranges-in-new-requirements/ (last accessed May 10, 2025).

[107] Fred Lucas, "2 FBI Agents Who Knelt at BLM Rally Gained Promotions," The Daily Signal, April 17, 2023, https://www.dailysignal.com/2023/04/17/exclusive-2-fbi-agents-who-knelt-at-blm-rally-gained-promotions/ (last accessed May 10, 2025).

[108] Kyle Seraphin, @kyleseraphin, March 28, 2023, X, https://x.com/KyleSeraphin/status/1640755662174175232 (last accessed May 10, 2025).

[109] Northwestern University, "Policy on Discrimination, Harassment, and Sexual Misconduct," August 12, 2024, https://www.northwestern.edu/civil-rights-office/policies-procedures/policies/policy-on-discrimination-harassment-and -sexual-misconduct.pdf (last accessed May 10, 2025).

[110] Patrick McDonald, "Northwestern University bans fat jokes," Campus Reform, September 13, 2024, https://www.campusreform.org/article/northwestern-university-bans-fat-jokes-/26348 (last accessed May 10, 2025).

[111] Ray A. Smith, "The Hidden Career Cost of Being Overweight," *The Wall Street Journal*, July 24, 2023, https://www.wsj.com/articles/the-hidden-career-cost-of-being-overweight-68f4b8e7 (last accessed May 10, 2025).

[112] Anumita Kaur, "Size discrimination may limit job prospects. New York City may ban it," *The Washington Post*, March 22, 2023, https://www.washingtonpost.com/politics/2023/03/22/weight-discrimination-ban/ (last accessed May 10, 2025).

[113] Smith, "The Hidden Career Cost of Being Overweight."

Chapter 11

[1] The Heritage Foundation, "Parental Rights Initiative," https://www.heritage.org/parental-rights-initiative (last accessed June 23, 2025).

[2] Heather Mac Donald, "Trump Takes His Biggest Step Yet Toward Restoring Meritocracy," *City Journal*, April 24, 2025, https://www.city-journal.org/

article/trump-restoring-meritocracy-executive-order-disparate-impact-theory - civil-rights (last accessed May 10, 2025).

[3] Ibid.

[4] Richard Vedder, "Ohio Senate Bill 1 Takes the Lead Against Woke Schools," *The Wall Street Journal*, March 27, 2025, https://www.wsj.com/opinion/ohio-senate-bill-1-takes-the-lead-against-woke-schools-4e75c166?st=FZQuRN& reflink=article_email_share (last accessed May 10, 2025).

[5] Leif Le Mahieu, "Major Medical Org Changes Tune On DEI After Trump Executive Order," *The Daily Wire*, May 12, 2025, https://www.dailywire.com /news/major-medical-org-changes-tune-on-dei-after-trump-executive-order (last accessed May 13, 2025).

[6] T. Keung Hui, "NC student gets $20,000 and apology for suspension after 'illegal aliens' comment," The News and Observer, June 6, 2025, https://www.newsobserver.com/news/local/education/article308029370.htm l (last accessed June 24, 2025).

[7] Hollie, Silverman, "High Schooler Suspended for Saying 'Illegal Alien' in Class Wins $20,000," Newsweek, June 4, 2025, https://www.newsweek.com /high-schooler-suspended-saying-illegal-alien-wins-lawsuit-2080993 (last accessed June 24, 2025).

[8] Matt Lamb, "U. Oregon to pay $191,000 after blocking conservative professor on Twitter," The College Fix, June 18, 2025, https://www.thecollegefix.com /u-oregon-to-pay-193000-after-blocking-conservative-professor-on-twitter/ (last accessed June 24, 2025).

[9] Families Organizing for Racial Justice at Newton North High School (FORJ NNHS), "Tools to Help Combat Racism," https://www.forjnnhs.org/ resources/tools-to-help-combat-racism (last accessed June 24, 2025).

[10] Fiona Hamilton, "Porton Down scientist forced out over gender beliefs wins legal battle," *The Sunday Times*, March 21, 2025, https://www.thetimes. com/uk/society/article/scientist-forced-out-over-gender-beliefs-wins-two-year-legal-battle-g3pz0w25h?mc_cid=6d6b3ae867&mc_eid=d27d0a7dba (last accessed May 10, 2025).

[11] Nicola Woolcock, "Sussex University fined record £585,000 for free speech failures," *The Sunday Times*, March 26, 2025, https://www.thetimes.com/uk/ society/article/university-fined-record-585000-for-failing-to-protect-free-speech-0zj6mcjbj?mc_cid=d112d18fec&mc_eid=d27d0a7dba&region= global (last accessed May 10, 2025).

[12] Jennifer Kabbany, "U. Louisville pays almost $1.6M to settle case with professor who criticized trans ideology," The College Fix, April 22, 2025, https://www.thecollegefix.com/u-louisville-pays-almost-1-6m-to-settle-case -with-professor-who-criticized-trans-ideology/ (last accessed May 10, 2025).

[13] Joseph Figliolia, "How Medical Groups Twist the Truth About Gender Medicine," *City Journal*, May 16, 2025, https://www.city-journal.org/article /hhs-gender-dysphoria-report-american-academy-of-pediatrics (last accessed June 9, 2025).

[14] U.S. Department of Health and Human Services, "Treatment for Pediatric Gender Dysphoria, Review of Evidence and Best Practices," Foreword & Executive Summary, May 1, 2025, https://opa.hhs.gov/sites/default/files/2025-05/gender-dysphoria-report-exec-summary.pdf (last accessed May 1, 2025).

[15] Rikki Schlott, "Detransitioner suing American Academy of Pediatrics: 'I don't want this to happen to other young girls,'" *New York Post*. December 13, 2023, https://nypost.com/2023/12/13/news/detransitioner-suing-american-academy-of-pediatrics/ (last accessed June 23, 2025).

[16] Colin Wright, "These Scientists Are Attacking Biology," *City Journal*, June 11, 2025, https://www.city-journal.org/article/uk-supreme-court-biological-sex-gender-open-letter?utm_source=Twitter&utm_medium=Organic_Social (last accessed June 16, 2025).

[17] Ibid

[18] Supreme Court of the United States, United States v. Skrmetti, No. 23–477. Argued December 4, 2024—Decided June 18, 2025,

[19] Rikki Schlott, "rack, soccer, basketball and more: The trans athlete scandals that rocked high school sports this year, from NY to California," *New York Post*, June 3, 2025, https://nypost.com/2025/06/03/us-news/trans-athlete-scandals-that-rocked-high-school-sports-this-year/?utm_campaign=iphone_nyp&utm_source=com.microsoft.Office.Outlook.compose-shareextension (last accessed June 23, 2025).

[20] Nancy Armour, "Simone Biles shows her greatness again in standing up for transgender community," USA Today, June 6, 2025, https://www.usatoday.com/story/sports/columnist/nancy-armour/2025/06/06/simone-biles-stands-up/84080176007/ (last accessed June 17, 2025).

[21] Ibid.

[22] Woolcock, "Sussex University fined record £585,000 for free speech failures."

[23] Anya Fielding, "NHS nurse punished for calling transgender paedophile 'Mr,'" *The Telegraph*, March 23, 2025, https://www.telegraph.co.uk/news/2025/03/23/nhs-nurse-punished-for-calling-transgender-paedophile-mr/?mc_cid=d112d18fec&mc_eid=d27d0a7dba (last accessed May 10, 2025).

[24] Jerry A. Coyne, "Losing My Nonreligion," *The Wall Street Journal*, March 30, 2025, https://www.wsj.com/opinion/losing-my-nonreligion-transgender-ideology-essay-resign-b7e6d745?st=ariLMt&reflink=article_email_share (last accessed May 10, 2025).

[25] Spencer Lindquist, "The Group Behind the MCAT Said It Was Ditching DEI. Insiders Say It Lied," *The Daily Wire*, April 27, 2025, https://www.dailywire.com/news/the-group-behind-the-mcat-said-it-was-ditching-dei-insiders-say-that-was-a-lie (last accessed May 10, 2025).

[26] Breccan F. Thies, "Three Rogue Judges Block Trump Admin Efforts to Eradicate Discriminatory DEI from Schools," *The Federalist*, April 25, 2025, https://thefederalist.com/2025/04/25/three-rogue-judges-block-trump-admin-efforts-to-eradicate-discriminatory-dei-from-schools/?utm_source=rss&utm_medium=rss&utm_campaign=three-rogue-judges-block-trump-admin-

efforts-to-eradicate-discriminatory-dei-from-schools&utm_term=2025-04-
26 (last accessed May 10, 2025).

www.ingramcontent.com/pod-product-compliance
Lightning Source LLC
Chambersburg PA
CBHW060416100426
42812CB00037B/3489/J